EDUCATIONAL RESEARCH IN EUROPE
EERA YEARBOOK 2000

Christopher W. Day & Dolf van Veen
(Eds.)

Educational Research in Europe
Yearbook 2000

Garant

Christopher W. Day & Dolf van Veen (Eds.)
Educational Research in Europe. EERA Yearbook 2000
Leuven – Apeldoorn
Garant
2000

347 p. – 24 cm
D/2000/5779/93
ISBN 90-441-1061-6

Layout: Jos Dohmen
Cover design: Danni Elskens

Garant
Tiensesteenweg 83, 3010 Louvain (Belgium)
Koninginnelaan 96, 7315 EB Apeldoorn (The Netherlands)
uitgeverij@garant.be

Foreword

It is a pleasure for me to introduce the first Yearbook of the European Educational Research Association. This Yearbook is based on a selection of texts presented at the EERA annual meeting in 1999, which took place in Lahti, Finland. Its appearance represents another sign of the continuing strength of the EERA and its development as a significant force in Europe. The Yearbook represents in three ways the ideas and practices of EERA.

First, in the Yearbook, educational researchers from different parts of Europe present their research to each other. This is important for EERA, which was founded in 1994 by a group of national associations of educational researchers, in order to improve co-operation and collaboration among educational researchers, research organisations and research institutes in Europe. This was considered as especially important in a changing Europe where international organisations are becoming more and more important as actors in the education arena and as sponsors of educational research. It is important to underline that several of the texts are produced by researchers outside of Little Europe framed by the current European Union borders. It is the ambition of EERA to include researchers from all parts of Europe and to help support their national associations.

Second, the Yearbook deals with a range of themes, reflecting a variety of national and professional interests, with teachers, students, intercultural issues, vocational training and lifelong learning represented as well as different theoretical and methodological approaches in educational research. This is another basic feature of the EERA, since we consider that it is of vital concern to be pluralistic. This is necessary as educational phenomena, in all its complexities, demands research on different aspects or levels of education. We feel that this complexity demands an association able to facilitate the interaction and collaboration of researchers with different perspectives and research traditions.

Such a pluralistic approach demands organisation, however. EERA strives to improve its internal communications through its website and newsletter, the European Educational Researcher, and outwardly, with the European Commission. In the EERA, our strategy is to emphasise the work of the interest networks. The networks are academic groupings which organise their own programmes within the annual conference. In EERA we at present have 22 networks focusing on, for example, Inclusive Education, Teacher Education, ICT in Education and Training, Social Justice, History of Education, Comparative Education. The essays in this Yearbook have been selected by the network convenors and the editors from the seminars and symposia in Lahti.

And third, the work in EERA is based on the engaged and idealistic work of educational researchers and their initiatives. On the EERA executive committee the former president Peter Döbrich strongly supported the idea of a Yearbook and helped its birth. Thanks to the efforts of the educational researchers whose essays were selected for this Yearbook we can learn about, and learn from, a variety of substantive and methodological approaches to European educational research. And last, but not least, through the editing work of Christopher Day and Dolf van Veen, the idea of a European Educational Research Yearbook has successfully materialised for the first time. Thanks to their engagement and expertise this book was made a reality.

The EERA Yearbook is part of the development of a European conversation about educational research and about the uses of educational knowledge and ideas. This conversation is important as it strengthens professional expertise and engagement across Europe at a time when the national arena is not the only significant context in which educational policy is being created. As national systems move closer together so must the critical engagement of educational researchers, allowing the emergence of a deeper level of dialogue and collaboration.

It is my hope that this first Yearbook will be followed by a number of editions presenting European educational research at its best.

Sverker Lindblad
EERA President
Uppsala, June 2000

Contents

Introduction

Christopher W. Day & Dolf van Veen (Editors)

This collection of selected papers from the 1999 Conference is another landmark in the development of the European Educational Research Association, and is the first of an initial series of three annual Yearbooks designed to provide illustrations of the work of members of many of the research networks which form the core of the association's ongoing research work. The papers have been selected in co-operation with these networks, against a number of criteria relating to quality, country and gender. None have been published elsewhere previously.

Although as editors we have identified a coherence among the papers and so have grouped them under different section headings, there is considerable overlap. What is interesting is both the homogeneity and the diversity. There is a homogeneity in that the majority of research reported is of relatively small scale projects with limited funding; and that all the papers are concerned with *educational change*, both through critiques of the efficiency, effectiveness and implementation of current policies and practices and through the design and application of innovative projects designed for improvement. Also, whilst cultures of different countries differ, there remains in the research reported here a core, cross cultural set of democratic values which are concerned with social justice, equity and constant quest for the betterment of citizens of all ages through high quality teaching supported by intelligent policy, whether such policy be concerned with children and young people's education at school, vocational education and training or lifelong learning.

The diversity of the research reported here – which constitutes a small fraction of the educational research throughout Europe and beyond – is illustrated by the many different content foci. All the papers present snapshots of reality and while governments and other national and international agencies continue to limit longitudinal research and direct funding to short term design and evaluation studies directly linked to policy, rather than providing a balance based upon jointly developed projects which encapsulate short, medium and long term understandings of need in relation to educational improvements, this is likely to remain the case in all countries. What shines through, however, is the commitment to and care for the quality education of all students, teachers, teacher educators and the determination to further our understandings of what it means to be a good professional.

'*Hope is a Factor in Teachers' Thinking and Classroom Practice*', Vivienne Collinson, Maureen Killeavy and Joan Stephenson is a fitting opening paper to this first selection of papers from the EERA Conference. The authors report upon a small scale qualitative collaborative study between their respective universities of Michigan, Dublin and De Montfort involving interviews with twelve exemplary teachers. Whilst hope is recognised as a powerful and important resource in teachers' professional lives, there is as yet little research on the concept. This cross cultural study identifies three 'principles' of hope: hope as other centred (in which teachers moral purposes for the betterment of students are paramount); hope as having high expectations and goals for self and others (in which teachers define performance individually and in relation to broad rather than narrow learning goals); and hope as perseverance and persistence (in which teachers continue to support and challenge themselves and students no matter what the obstacles).

The second paper, '*Regular Classroom Teachers' Perceptions of Inclusion: Implications for Teacher Preparation Programs in Spain*', by Cristina Cardona from the University of Alicante, Spain, provides a somewhat different perspective, centring upon pre and in-service teachers' beliefs about their students. Using a survey approach with 82 teachers enrolled on a graduate program, the author found that whilst most teachers believed that students with disabilities had a right to be taught alongside other students, only a minority believed that the regular classroom was a better environment than a special education classroom. In the author's view this attitude is the product of inadequate opportunities through teacher education and continuing professional development programmes for teachers to be provided with appropriate training experiences.

These two papers provide illustrations of the dilemmas faced by many teachers in Europe and beyond. On the one hand, their professionalism is demonstrated in their aspirations for themselves and their students, their intentions to educate each to their highest potential. On the other hand, these ideals – so important to be cherished over the whole careers of teachers – are often set within the reality of the consequences of ill thought through and poorly supported reform efforts – inadequate or inappropriate training and further education possibilities – and their own limitations to change.

The next clutch of five papers focus upon teachers' responses to reform in four different countries. The first '*Early Childhood Educators in England and Finland: An Exploratory Study*', reports the initial findings of qualitative research carried out with thirty seven teachers in England and Finland where early years education is high on the reform agenda. The reforms in England are centrally prescribed and directed, whilst those in Finland demand the full participation of municipalities (local government) in curriculum formation. It is clear that whilst both sets of teachers placed importance upon personal and professional experiences, the English teachers were far more negative about the reform processes than those from Finland. The former cited feelings of isolation and increased bureaucracy, whereas the latter expressed a more 'hopeful' collegial attitude stemming from participa-

tion. The next three focus upon the use of ICT in enhancing teaching and learning in classrooms.

The first, '*ICT to optimise didactic management in early education*', by Ton Mooij of
the University of Nijmegen, the Netherlands, describes the impact of information and communications technology software designed to assist kindergarten
teachers in their management of diversity in the classroom. Programmes were
designed and tested, for example, which enabled diagnosis of progress and differentiation of learning processes. In the world of the twenty first century, such
innovations, if successful, will serve to increase teachers' ability to attend to the
individual learning and achievement of all pupils and classrooms will become
'learning' rather than 'teaching' environments.

A second example of research into the effects of ICT, this time in Finnish
classrooms, is provided by Pirjo Linnakylä, Marja Kankaanranta and Maarit Arvaja
in a paper entitled, '*Collaboration and authenticity in technologically enriched and virtual
learning contexts*'. The authors, from the University of Jyväskylä, take a constructivist
stance on learning in presenting an action research project designed to strengthen
collaboration between diverse educational environments and cultures by means
of digital portfolios, published on the web, on the development of pupil and
teacher expertise and the assessment of teaching and learning.

Whilst the paper is long on theory and short on evaluation of practice, it does,
nevertheless, provide another indication of the active increase in the use of technology in classrooms, as does the third '*The Effect of Using a Graphics Tool on the
Collaborative Learning of Java Programming with a Videoconferencing System: A Pilot Study*',
by Bernhard Ertl, Lai-Chong Law and Heinz Mandl from the University of Munich, Germany. This paper investigates how the use of 'whiteboard' (a tool supporting freehand drawing) can influence the extent of conceptual changes of
student programmers in solving Java programming problems, in the context of
videoconferencing. The authors found that the use of graphics can enhance the
learning of Java programming but that this depends upon the level of programming expertise of the individuals; the pattern of communication; and the demands of the task.

These three papers collectively confirm both the complexity of the change
processes and the inability of information and communications technology itself
to promote change where it is not used in harmony with teachers who are confident and able to apply their own discretionary judgement to the teaching and
learning situations which it serves to support and with students who are able to
work collegially on tasks which relate to their learning preferences and achievement goals.

The final paper in this section is from England. In '*Change for the Better? The
impact of Baseline Assessment on Reception Class Teaching*', Jane Stout, Peter Tymms
and Linda Thompson from the University of Durham, report the results of a

three year national survey of the impact of baseline assessment upon teachers of pupils in their first year at school. This formalisation of the Early Years Curriculum is one of a series of controversial policy reforms in England and Wales through which the government is seeking to raise standards in education by extending central control of curriculum content and a range of measurable pupil achievement outputs (rather than the more complex learning outcomes). As with reforms in other phases of schooling, problems of inadequate training were identified. Alongside these, were changes in attitudes of Reception Class teachers. Of particular concern – and this relates back to the first paper on 'Hope' in this section – is the reported decrease in enjoyment in their work, a sense of being devalued and a growing tendency for them to advise others against entering the teaching profession.

This small selection of European research suggests that despite culture specific differences and differences in policy contexts, there are a number of cross cultural factors which are common to teaching. It also provides three important messages for policy makers and other leaders in education. First, good teaching is characterized by a persistence of hopefulness combined with high levels of subject knowledge, knowledge of student learning and classroom expertise; second, not all teachers remain hopeful, and this is at least in part a consequence of negative policy contexts; and third, because all teachers are currently caught up in a number of imposed innovations not of their own making, it is vital that they are provided with adequate and appropriate long term training and education.

The focus of the four papers in *Part 2* is on *Teacher Education*. The first is by Jacqueline Beckers and Germaine Simons from the University of Liege, Belgium. '*Establishing a Research/Training Partnership to Facilitate the Professional Integration of Novice Teachers and Help Them Become 'Reflective Practitioners*' recognizes the need to prepare teachers for a world in which change is a permanent feature. Basing their work upon the 'reality shock' faced by teachers in their first year of teaching and the importance of self efficacy, the two researchers report on a series of problems centred cross school workshops with five novice teachers, using peer observation and feedback in order to assist them in the development of their teaching. This action research in service programme, though time consuming, provides a good example of the ways in which teachers whose training has not equipped them for the realities of life in school may be supported in their early years of teaching.

In '*ICT in Finnish Teacher Education Evaluation with Special Reference to Active Learning and Democracy*', Hannele Niemi from the University of Helsinki, Finland, reports on an evaluation of the impact and potential impact of ICT on teacher education students and how it might promote or constrain the development of democracy. The research is based upon survey data from 581 student teachers and teacher educators in five higher education institutions. These were supplemented with qualitative case study data drawn from seven 'innovative' practices of ICT in different areas of teacher education. The results, like those of studies in other countries, show that whilst attitudinal resistance to the importance of ICT has been overcome, its use in classrooms remains limited to word processing and email. Given the amount of investment of governments worldwide, and the importance of school settings as places which can promote ICT, this research sounds a warning to the unwarranted optimism of those who believe that ICT will promote speedy change in teaching and learning, and a reminder that change is a complex process which needs time and sustained support.

'*Teachers' Discourses in Social Learning*' by Maria Martinez and Narcissus Sauleda from the University of Alicante, Spain provides perhaps part of the answer to problems of change identified in the previous two papers. Their research is based upon twenty four biographical narratives of nursery teachers which show the importance of attending to teachers' expressed needs for support from colleagues for their own personal and professional development; and it points to the significance of adult learning cultures in schools as a means of supporting or constraining socially distributed processes of learning. Like Beckers and Simon's paper, a significant number of teachers found that pre-service education had been of little significance, and the extracts from the testimonies of these teachers indicate clearly the benefits gained from sustained peer support in practice cultures.

The final paper in this section returns us to the world of information and communications technology and describes an attempt to harness one aspect of this to the promotion of reflection within a teacher education programme in Norway. In '*Using E-mail to Promote Reflection in Teacher Education*', Torlaug Hoel and Sigrun Gudmundsdottir report the processes and effects of one to one email interactions between students on teaching practice and their tutors at the university campus. The theoretical stage model which is used (ALACT) was developed in the Netherlands and Vygotsky's zone of proximal development provides the conceptual basis for the research. The authors present a framework for action which may be used by all teacher educators and the case study of one student teacher provides a living testament of the value of the model. As with the other papers in this section, the findings demonstrate the paramount need to ensure that teacher and student teacher isolation is countered by regular, structured, needs focused opportunities for written and spoken interchange.

Part 3 of this book focuses on *intercultural issues*. In '*Ethnography of Education in the Waldensian Valleys (Italy): Analysis of the relationship between a religious minority identity, its cultural history and current educational experiences*', Francesca Gobbo from the University of Padua presents the results of her fieldwork in the Waldensian valleys west of Turin. The findings indicate, among other things, that high school provides the students, age 18-19, with an identity as students rather than as Waldensian, while the minority identity is transmitted and acquired in out-of-school contexts, both religious and secular ones. Furthermore, the educational experience is described as relevant to the students identity as Italian citizens, but not to higher education future choices. On the bases of these findings Gobbo questions the current descriptions of Italian "multiculturalism", showing that education and schooling have still a major role to play in the process of maintaining and broadening both the students' minority identity and their identity as Italian citizens. In 'The Multicultural Issue in Portuguese Schools: Seeking justice or another morality', the sociologists Jose Manuel Resende and Maria Manuel Vieira, describe the social issue of multiculturality in mass school contexts, that only gained visibility in the social sciences in Portugal during the last decade, in terms of the arguments involved and the models of justification that they reveal.

The final paper of this section moves away from multicultural issues in compulsory education and schooling. In 'The Role of Western Universities in the Development of the New Generation of Researchers in Education in Lithuania', Palmira Juceviciene from the Kaunas University of Technology in Lithuania describes the current problematic situation of doctoral studies in Lithuanian Higher Education and suggest ways of improving this situation. The last part of this paper discusses why it may be beneficial for European universities to consolidate their efforts in assisting Lithuanian universities in educating doctoral students and points to the ways this can be done.

Part 4 focuses on values in education and consists of four papers. The first paper of this section, 'Participative Education: An incomplete project of modernity', by Joe Harkin from the Oxford Brooks University, England, advocates the concept of critical modernity, in contradistinction to that of postmodernity, as a foundation for educational practice, drawing on the work of Habermas, Giddens and Rorty. It has become increasingly clear that schools must become dramatically more successful with a wide range of learners if many more citizens are to acquire the necessary skills they need to participate in a knowledge-based society. Reformed practice, as well as new policy, is critical to this objective. In 'Lifelong learning strategy calls for equity in Education', Reijo Laukkanen of the Permanent Delegation of Finland to the OECD, analysing OECD education ministerial meetings in the last two decades, concludes that in this context both building access to education and improving the quality of teaching are persistent recommendations in the OECD-documents, justified too by a commitment to values of equity and equality. Moreover, for further economic development education is key to establishing an increased participation of citizens as productive members of their societies.

The third paper in this section 'Ethical dilemmas in mixed ability grouping', by Zdenko Kodelja from the Educational Research Institute in Ljubljana, Slovenia reminds us, if reminders are needed, of the differences between educational and pedagogical sciences. Conflicting research evidence concerning a pervasive problem in practice, namely the question whether to group students according to ability or not, presents ethical dilemmas. The author addresses the emerging dilemmas using Kant's work on the categorial imperative.

   The final paper in this section, by Luis Vila, Spain focuses on the changes in the match between education and employment during the 1977-1997 period. In 'Educational Expansion and Labour Market Changes in Spain: Integration and Polarisation' he argues that the educational expansion has reduced the gender gap both in labour force and employment participation and that higher education is clearly the best investment for young people and women in obtaining status equity through better jobs and positions. The public sector appears also to be a key factor in the labour market integration. However, there is evidence of increasing polarisation of the labour market in terms of job-opportunities.

Part 5 of this book focuses upon the often silent voices in school and classroom focused research – those of the pupils whose perspectives are so vital to all those interested in understanding teaching and learning in schools and who wish to improve standards in both. Anders Garpelin, from Uppsala University in Sweden, reports a case study of students who have come together from different school backgrounds to meet in the first year of the lower secondary school. This paper, 'They can be fawning if they please, I won't interfere: Transitions in School Life as Critical Incidents for Young People' uses interview data from sixty two 12-13 year old students in two classes in two schools who have different policies. One is to separate students from different primary schools on entry, the other to allow choice. The results suggest that there has been a more negative effect upon individual students in the former system in terms of attitudes to school. Taking account of existing peer group relationships would seem, from this research, to be an important factor in promoting harmony in the classroom and motivation to learn.

   In the second of the two papers, Marilyn Osborn and Clare Panel from the University of Bristol, England examine pupil perspectives of schooling, teaching and learning in schools in England, France and Denmark. 'Life in School: Constants and Contexts in Pupil Experience of Schooling and Learning in Three European Countries' presents the results of questionnaire returns from 1800 pupils and individual and group interviews with a smaller sample in which the authors found a 'striking unanimity' about the definitions of 'interesting' lessons and 'good' teachers. Less similar were students' attitudes to gender and social inequality, and teacher-pupil relationships. Students from Denmark were more enthusiastic about school than those in England and those in France did not feel they were getting the guidance needed to improve. Such differences reflected the relative emphasis of the curriculum, social relationships and national values.

Part 6 focuses upon *vocational education and lifelong learning*. It is strange to us that as the concept of lifelong learning has been popularised and politicized over the last decade, it has come to be associated more with adult learning and work than with school centred teaching and learning – despite the unanimous agreement that it is in schools where attitudes towards, skills, and habits of lifelong learning might first be inculcated and encouraged. There is a sense, then, that lifelong learning has been highjacked by business (in order to produce a flexible workforce, able to be adaptive to new competitive circumstances) and further education concerned to offer 'second chance' continuing education. Personal fulfilment and social understanding as essential parts of lifelong learning seem to be of less importance than the acquisition of 'core', 'transferable', 'measurable' skills.

In *'Modelling Lifelong Learning: Costs and benefits compared'*, Marko Leeuwen and Bernard van Praag from the Foundation for Economic Research, the University of Amsterdam, present an economic model for vocational lifelong learning and apply it to the Netherlands. Taking account of economic, training and different types of employee factors, they present two policy scenarios. They conclude that the costs and benefits can be quite different and that further case study research will be needed. In *'The Contribution of "inclusion" to active citizenship: Examples of effective practice within the French VET system'*, M'hamed Dif, of the University of Strasbourg, France, provides a reminder of the importance of attending to the transition of school to work, focusing upon the inclusion of 'non-qualified' and thus disadvantaged young people (16-25 years old). The first part of the paper provides a conceptual framework for inclusion in the French vocational education and training system (VET). This is based upon the promotion of the individual's ability to participate effectively in larger and multidimensional social production processes. The second part provides two examples of effective practice. Dif concludes that the effectiveness of anti-exclusion measures is highly dependent upon the way in which citizenship is conceived and applied in practice, the fragmented nature of the VET system itself, the differential status between VET and the dominant forms of 'normal' education, and the social and economic selectivity of the more prestigious institutions.

These dilemmas of prestige and selectivity affect all countries where market driven competitive economics dominates issues of social inclusion. In businesses which demand commitment, investments in lifelong learning and increasing searches for higher qualifications by their workforce it is becoming more difficult to provide the means for those who – often for reasons of family, sub-culture and education have a history of disadvantage – to enter and prosper. It is perhaps fitting that this selection of research papers should have begun with a statement of the need for hope by teachers who work sometimes in seemingly hopeless social situations and end with a view of the flaws in the system itself. Certainly, whilst one of the functions of educational research is to increase understandings of individual and systemic problems in schools and other educational settings in European countries, another is to influence those responsible for policy and policy implementation. We hope that this book will provide stimulation for both.

Part 1
Teachers and Teaching

Hope as a Factor in Teachers' Thinking and Classroom Practice

Vivienne Collinson, Maureen Killeavy & H. Joan Stephenson

Universally recognised as a powerful and important resource in people's lives, hope is a central theme in mythology and religions, prose and poetry. However, hope has largely been neglected in educational research despite its recognition as an important factor among competent caregivers. This cross-cultural study illustrates three principles of hope: hope is other-centred, hope sets high expectations and goals for self and others, and hope perseveres, even in the face of obstacles. The study indicates how the thinking of twelve second-level teachers appears to be permeated by hope and how their hope seems to rely on several beliefs. They share the strong belief that all students can succeed in some way and that they as teachers have a unique contribution to make to their students. Their beliefs appear to help the teachers bring out the best in students, work to achieve high expectations for themselves and their students, and persist in reaching all students. The participants' self-reported thinking and practices about these three principles of hope cut across gender, race, age, nationality, and school contexts.

Hope profoundly affects human beings' thinking, emotions, and achievements (Bloch, 1959/1986). The ancient Greek myth of Zeus's gift of hope to Pandora and the story of Viktor Frankl's (1963) struggle to make each day meaningful amid the utter hopelessness of a Nazi concentration camp are only two of countless stories that indicate human beings' recognition of the motivational power of hope. It is generally perceived as a positive force in Western countries although non-western thinkers have remarked that one facet of hope, which is mere desire, can seem to be 'self-centred, covetous, and open to all manner of wishful thinking and self-deception' (Godfrey, 1987, p.xi).

Hope is such a complex concept that there is currently no full theory of hope. Part of the difficulty with a comprehensive theory is that hope with good intentions can range from trivial hope or wishful thinking (e.g., 'I hope our team wins!') to 'deep aimed' hope. This chapter is informed by Godfrey's (1987) outline of a general theory of hope, specifically deep aimed hope. Deep aimed hope or 'ultimate hope' has a social aim and a 'core of trust' (p.3). Its focus is on 'hope when there is obstacle, when the one who hopes cares a great deal, and when a great deal is at stake' (p.14). Such hope is particularly applicable to caring professions like teaching because 'what is wanted directly [...is] the flourishing existence of the other' (p.158). Godfrey refers to this relationship as non-covetous love or altruism. He argues that hope, like other emotions, can be learned; that is, it can be 'shaped by factors of experience, education, authority, satisfaction or disappointment [...and] by reality-testing, contributions from parents, peers, and the appeal of social allegiances' (p.23) (also see Bloch, 1959/1986 and Goleman, 1995).

Universally recognised as a powerful and important resource in people's lives, hope is a central theme in mythology and religions, prose and poetry. 'But as a topic for study, hope has largely been left to psychologists and theologians. For the most part philosophers treat hope *en passant*' (Godfrey, 1987, p.xi). Hope is also neglected in educational research. Although hope can be taught and learned (Bloch, 1959/1986; Godfrey, 1987; Goleman, 1995), and although Cuban (1995) argues that 'to teach is to be full of hope' (p.xi), it is rarely a topic in the literature on teaching. Empirical studies of hope in teaching are even more rare. Hope 'seems to be a disposition which lies outside of the technological rationality of modern culture' (Elbaz, 1992, p.426). Hope also appears to lie outside the disillusionment of the post-modern era. Nevertheless,

> [...] competence studies show that top performers in the human services – everything from health care and counselling to teaching – express hope for those they seek to help. [...] In jobs like these, where stress is high and frustrations common [...] hope is crucial (Goleman, 1998, p.128).

This paper indicates that whereas researchers have largely ignored hope in teaching, the thinking and classroom practices of a sample of second-level exemplary teachers in England, Ireland, and the United States are permeated by hope. Their hope is supported by the belief that all children can be successful and contribute in some way. The first part of the paper provides a brief background of the cross-cultural study from which illustrations are drawn. The second section clarifies three principles of hope that cut across both the general literature and the educational literature on hope: hope is other-centred, hope sets high expectations and goals for self and others, and hope perseveres, even in the face of obstacles. The three principles of hope are illustrated with examples from the sample of exemplary teachers in the three countries.

Background of the Cross-Cultural Study

This section briefly describes the qualitative study from which examples are drawn to illustrate the remainder of the paper. The study was undertaken to determine exemplary teachers' understanding of the role and development of an ethic of care in good teaching. Exemplary teachers are defined as those whose professional accomplishments and results can serve as a model for peers. Hope emerged as a major theme in the teachers' perceptions of caring and good teaching.

The sample of practising teachers (N=12) in second-level schools in England, Ireland, and the United States was determined by reputational method (Hunter,

1953). Teachers in England (n=4) and Ireland (n=4) were identified by peers, principals, local inspectors or educational advisors, university faculty whose students had been interns in their classes, or a combination of these. In the United States (n=4), participants were identified by groups of peers such as staff developers and subject specialists who frequently visit schools and work with teachers in their particular region. The seven female teachers and five male teachers had 15 to 33 years of classroom experience at the time of data collection. Their subject areas included English, mathematics and technology, the sciences, humanities, history, French, and Spanish.

The ten White and two Black teachers teach in rural, suburban, and urban schools. One of the urban schools is quite new and is considered state-of-the-art, but several of the schools have difficulties that are particularly challenging for teachers. The pleasant surface of one English school hides social and economic problems. One American rural school is very poor and has difficulty retaining principals. At the time of the study, a committee was searching for the fifth principal in four years. Another American school had made national news twice in three months as one of the worst schools. This huge inner city school with about 3000 high school students is located in a desperately poor, drug- and crime-ridden government housing project with a mostly Black population. School attendance is sporadic and the teacher in this study is teaching the third generation of welfare recipients. When a local research study sought students who lived with their married, biological parents, this school found one boy who qualified. He was murdered before the study was completed.

The teacher participants filled out a pre-interview survey, then engaged in a two to three hour individual interview. A semi-structured interview guide provided flexibility for differences among participants, cultural contexts, and researcher styles. The interview guide reflected a synthesis of research and empirical studies (see Collinson, 1994, 1996) and was designed to elicit responses to seven broad research questions: Over the course of their careers, what have the secondary school teachers come to believe is 'good teaching'? How do they structure the physical, intellectual, and social culture in their classrooms to improve student learning and get to know students? How do they get to know students outside the classroom? How do they know when they are/are not reaching students? How, if at all, do they use their knowledge of students to inform their teaching? How do students know that these teachers care about them as individuals and learners? How do the teachers think they acquired their interpersonal skills and a disposition to care?

Interviews were audio-taped and transcribed. When necessary, clarification was sought through follow-up telephone conversations. Content analysis provided a basis for comparative examination. First, each researcher reviewed her individual interview transcripts and coded the data into categories related to the seven research questions (e.g., teachers' perceptions of good teaching). Those categories were expanded as patterns or sub-themes emerged (e.g., how teachers try to establish safe classroom environments). The researchers then pooled data from each theme and, working together instead of individually, re-analysed the coded data to identify cross-cultural themes (e.g., hope). During the final stage, teacher quotes were selected with a view to being representative of the aggregated data and reflecting as much balance as possible among the participants and the three countries.

Three Principles of Hope

Three principles cut across both the general literature and the educational literature on hope: hope is other-centred, hope sets high expectations and goals for self and others, and hope perseveres, even in the face of obstacles. The following section elaborates these three principles of hope and illustrates them with the exemplary teachers' thinking and practices.

Hope as Other-Centred

Hope that is other-centred 'involves beliefs about the possibility and the worth of what is hoped for' (Godfrey, 1987, p.29). When ultimate hope is used for good purposes, it seeks 'the flourishing existence of the other' and can motivate humans to benefit others (p.158). The exemplary teachers in this study hold strong beliefs that teaching 'is important work' (Irish sample), that learning 'is lifelong and not just towards exams' (Irish sample), that 'each person has a contribution to make' (US sample), and that 'given the right circumstances, everyone can succeed' (UK sample). They look for strengths in students and for 'a way of helping each student as an individual, to take them from where they are at as a starting point, and progress from there' (Irish sample).

In the classroom, the teachers focus on 'the possibility and worth of what is hoped for': helping all students to learn and experience success. 'All children, and particularly the children with special needs that I work with, are entitled to a high quality education service' (Irish sample). One way of seeking the 'flourishing existence' of students is 'by expecting well of them and, on the whole, by the value you put on their work and caring about what they do, you know, how they're learning' (UK sample). Although teachers' hope usually focuses on classroom learning, it may also extend beyond the classroom. One teacher sent some science students to work on the farm of a successful landowner to get them out of the inner city for the summer. His hope was 'to educate kids who will make things happen,' and he wanted to expose them to a different way of living where they could enjoy working and experience immediate success (US sample).

Godfrey (1987) argued that fundamentally, hope is an 'attitude taken with respect to the future' (p.176). Teaching, by nature, involves goals directed toward the future and national goals of education typically recognise that today's students are the nation's hope for the future. 'If you look at [the] State's goal for education, [...] it's creating a system where students become healthy and productive citizens of the twenty-first century. [...] We definitely try to do that' (US sample). Teachers may influence their students for a short time in the present, but they can only hope that what students learn from teachers will also contribute to their development in the future.

Perhaps because they teach adolescents, the teachers consistently commented on their efforts to help students develop socially. They understand how important relationships are to students' present and future growth.

> If [teachers] are consistent all the way through [school], then [students] have got a very, very good chance of achieving and [...] going out [into the world] with much, much better social skills (UK sample).
>
> Occasionally, students recognise their teachers' efforts to help them. 'More often than not, [it's] little notes on the end of the final exam at the end of the year or whatever, which is really nice. [...] Sometimes [it's] years later' (US sample).

Hope as High Expectations and Goals

Learning has always been the desired goal of education. 'The primary aim of education is the training of the powers of intelligence and will—that the object to be attained is a certain quality of character. [...A teacher] applies the science of education to help another to the full realisation of his personality' (Dewey, 1895/1964, p.197). Dewey understood education as lifelong learning, of which formal schooling is only one of many sources. He thus considered 'an educated person [to be] the person who has the power to go on and get more education' (Dewey, 1934/1964, p.4).

The teachers in this study do not just focus on academic performance, but on learning in its broadest sense. They also distinguish between teaching for immediate learning (the explicit curriculum) and developing a disposition toward learning for life. Like Dewey, they envision learning as the fullest possible development of human beings:

> I think [one] of the things we must get from education is the idea that it is lifelong and not just towards exams, but that learning is a disposition in life that [students] should acquire. If we don't continue to learn academically, socially, and every other way, and achieve that kind of flexibility and potential for growth as a human being, education has failed (Irish sample).

The goal of hope is as straightforward as Dewey's primary aim of education: 'What is wanted directly [...is] the flourishing existence of the other' (Godfrey,

1987, p.158). For the exemplary teachers, the goal of bringing out the best in students, whatever their best may be, is a prerequisite for learning: 'In the class-room, beyond everything else, I work with changing the child's attitude [...] bringing the best out' (US sample) and 'giving them the belief that if they do their best they have been successful' (Irish sample).

Over and over again in different ways, the teachers emphasised that their goal is to bring out the best in their students:

> I think you should expect the best. You should expect very high standards. And I think that if you know your children well, you know exactly what they are capable of and you will know when they are achieving their best, or when they are shirking, or when you can gently push, or when you can give a bigger push and say, 'That just isn't good enough' (UK sample).

However, they worry about the possibility of pushing students too hard even when knowing them well:

> I work hard and they know I value hard work and expect it from them. Of course this only means that they do their best. They know I love for them to do well and they often say they don't want to let me down. I have to be careful about this; one can push too hard (Irish sample).

Another worry for teachers occurs when deep aimed hope is confused with trivial hope (Godfrey, 1987). In other words, hope 'is not to be confused with wishful thinking and unfounded expectations' (Mayeroff, 1971, p.32). One teacher is aware of both the power of dreams and the allure of wishful materialistic thinking among his teenage students. He tries to convey his belief that living well on wel-fare represents wishful thinking while education represents hope:

> ' I'm not teaching anybody who has a welfare mentality. [...] I don't believe in welfare. [I tell them,] 'If you have a Mercedes mind, you're going to drive a Mercedes if it stays in your mind. That's what I'm teaching for and I want you to aspire for. [...] The reason you're sitting in this classroom for ten months with me learning all this information is to be able to not wish for things, not to dream about it and say, "Oh God, I wish I had this or that" [...] but go around town and you have them.' [...] This is what I'm teaching for (US sample).

On the other hand, teachers also occasionally have students with unfounded or unrealistic expectations, sometimes from their parents:

> I work in a fairly academic school so the impetus would be towards academic achievement anyway. To personalise – this is the problem – and to give [students] the freedom within that to fulfil their own potential and not to feel that they have to reach unreachable goals. It is a problem. I remember those who wanted to go into medicine and I knew that they were not going to make it (Irish sample).

Teachers in this study have clear and high expectations that they try to articulate to their students through word and deed. Expectation studies (e.g., Pedersen and Faucher, 1978; Rosenthal and Jacobson, 1968), as well as theoretical research on the self-fulfilling prophecy (Merton, 1948), indicate that when teachers expect high performance from students, they increase the likelihood of high student performance. Students 'achieve highly when their teachers emphasise academic goals, make them explicit, and have high expectations for their students' (Ramsay and Oliver, 1995, p.334-335).

The exemplary teachers in this study focus on learning and bringing out the best in their students, but appear to expand the ideas in the literature in at least two ways. First, they hold the same high expectations for themselves as for their students, and they support their expectations with action. Second, they encourage reciprocal expectations by students.

High expectations for self and others

'High expectations [...] means a respect for excellence. [...Teachers] cannot hope to have that kind of impact unless they themselves have a high level of morale' (Gardner, 1990, pp.197-198). In this study, wanting their students to do their best means that the teachers want to do their best as well (also see Noddings, 1994). One teacher said, '[I] model from the first day [...] the positive reinforcement that I expect to hear from them [...] that you encourage others and you compliment others' (US sample). Another reiterated the idea: 'I try to teach by example, and if [students] see that I get their work back in the same amount of time I expect them to get it to me, that's important and students make that comment' (US sample).

For these teachers, holding high expectations applies to themselves as well as to the students. For example, one teacher has her students do a little questionnaire each Friday. The first two questions help the students learn to assess their weekly work and determine what they need to do to improve, but the third question asks them what they think the teacher can do to help them learn better. The teacher finds the students' suggestions reasonable, and they help her improve her teaching.

The same teacher does not fault students when they do not reach her expectations. Instead, she asks herself what she can do to help them:

One of the things that I have the kids do in the Science classes are big projects and each year the projects get better because I get better at giving directions. [...] The kids do a really nice job with their projects, with their presentations [but] their write-up is not the calibre that I want them to be when they actually write up their project and stuff. And I don't think it's a matter of the kids getting tired and not doing their work. I think it's still that I haven't done a good enough job in giving them an example of what it's supposed to look like. And although I gave them some examples [of strong and weak writing], I don't think we spent enough time doing it (US sample).

Whether their expectations deal with academic learning or social development, the teachers hold themselves to the same high standards they want to see from their students. As one said, 'I expect a climate of respect for one another [and] I will show them the same respect that I expect in return' (US sample). Another teacher elaborated this idea:

> So if you respect people, and you're consistent in doing that, and you model that consistency and respectfulness most of the time – I don't think anybody can do it all of the time – then the students rise to the occasion and they meet those expectations (US sample).

Respect is a reasonable but high expectation for all students. Another reasonable expectation is that all students are capable of giving their best effort. 'I believe in showing I have the same expectations of everyone – not necessarily of standard – but effort [...] and it's the same for everybody' (UK sample). This expectation of students' best efforts requires deep knowledge of students as well as good judgement by teachers.

> I have got to be careful that I can expect a certain amount from them, but that I cannot be tyrannical in the amount of work and study I can demand from them. I can enable them to do things but I cannot be over-demanding (Irish sample).

Only occasionally do teachers find out whether they strayed from the fine line that separates challenging students to their limit from being over-demanding. One teacher met a former student at a wedding ten years after he had completed high school. The teacher recalled that the young man had wanted to be a sports coach and was surprised to hear him say, 'I'm just ready to start my student teaching. I decided to be a teacher.' When she asked him why, he replied, 'You were the only teacher who really held me to it and who really cared about what happened and made me do it' (US sample).

High expectations for students are not sufficient. They require active assistance and support, thus demanding high expectations of teachers as well. Expectations accompanied by action is a hallmark of hope: Hope is 'knowing the steps needed to get to a goal and having the energy to pursue those steps' (Goleman, 1998, p.128). Refining and articulating goals is the first step. Making goals explicit and expecting much from students seems to help teachers narrow their goals to the most important ones and focus more clearly on helping students achieve those specific goals (Collinson, 1999). One science teacher, who had helped write the state science curriculum, commented somewhat tongue-in-cheek on her

[…] attitude of not particularly caring whether or not I get through the curriculum if I can teach the kids how to ask questions, how to look up the questions, and how to ask more questions based upon what they have [found]. And those are the three basic tenets of my classroom because that's really what I'm interested in. There is no way that I can teach them everything they need to know, particularly in science where it's changing every moment. […] It just means that my focus is very much on those three issues (US sample).

Once goals are clearly defined, the teachers in this study reported that they actively attempt to engage students so that participation is easier for them:

I don't accept 'I don't know.' I want them to try. […] I want them to be engaged. I mean it's ideal if they're engaged 100% of the time but we know that that doesn't happen. But I attempt to keep them engaged in some way. […] I like to keep them guessing about what's going to be happening and I like to vary the activities a lot (US sample).

The teachers recognise that some students require more time and energy than others. One teacher dedicates one day a week for 'school after school' to help students who need more time. Many referred particularly to their students with learning problems:

I really find that I have to do a lot of tutoring outside of class. And I think that says they're doing what they need to do in class [but they need extra help]. And if there's make-up work that needs to be done because of illness, then sometimes it's after school (US sample).

Reciprocal expectations

When the literature encourages and applauds high expectations, the expectations are often unidirectional – teachers are urged to have high expectations of students. The sample of exemplary teachers differs from the literature in that some articulated a belief in reciprocal expectations – students should articulate high expectations for their teachers too:

I think the students should be able to have from their teachers a sense of their own worth. I think the expectation of the student would [be that teachers] feed back to them positively and give them constructive advice and support on whatever learning tasks they are engaged on (Irish sample).

Several teachers make a point of asking what their students' expectations are for them. For example, one teacher said, '[On the first day], I try to be very clear about what my expectations are and I try to help the students be clear about what their expectations are of me' (US sample). Another teacher explained what she does on the first day of Spanish classes to uncover students' expectations:

I ask the questions: What do you expect to get from this class? What do you expect to be able to do when you leave this room? I want to see how realistic their goals are. If they say that they're going to speak fluent Spanish after [level one], I need to do some work in that area on them so that they aren't just demoralised when they leave the classroom. [I ask them,] How do you want me to evaluate you? And what do you think are qualities of a good teacher? I want to know what they think (US sample).

The teachers commented that students like knowing what to expect. Reciprocally, the teachers like to find out what they can expect as each student's best effort:

I'm certainly much, much firmer at the beginning of a year, but once I've established [the expectations] then [...] I find that you don't have to remind them very often. [...] It's a team effort then. It is a two-way thing because they know how far they can go with you, and you know exactly what they are capable of (UK sample).

This study also suggests that the teachers understand the reciprocal nature of school and societal expectations on students. That is, students' expectations and capacities may be influenced within the classroom, but they are also related to external factors, such as socio-economic status and expectations within their specific community. Anyon's (1981) work indicated that in one study, teachers had given up hope of teaching disadvantaged children. A teacher in that study said, 'You can't teach these kids anything' and the principal told a teacher, 'If they learn to add and subtract, that's a bonus' (p.7). However, in a study of eight exemplary urban teachers, Brookhart and Rusnak (1993) found that although the teachers were understanding of students' problems, 'personal and social problems had little influence on how these teachers conducted or graded a class. Each teacher expressed very high expectations for each student and would not be influenced by factors outside the classroom' (p.26).

Gardner (1990) warned of the danger of viewing 'teacher expectations as [an] inexpensive means of compensating for profound social disadvantage as a factor in performance' (p.210). However, the operative word seems to be 'performance.' The exemplary teachers in this study share a similar attitude to the teachers in the Brookhart and Rusnak (1993) study. They do not limit themselves to viewing academic scores as a barometer of learning. Rather, performance seems to mean best effort and is defined individually: '[For students with difficulties] I would demand work from them. I would try to simplify it but I would expect it to be done' (Irish sample). Although the teachers in this study recognise the impact of social factors on performance, they continue to hold high expectations of what students can manage: doing their best under the circumstances. The teachers' expectation that students will do their best does not waver although their approaches may vary depending on students' individual circumstances:

I try not to let knowledge of their background influence my expectations of them, but at the same time, if I know someone comes from a background that is not, let us say, so conducive to learning, then I'll take that into account when I'm planning work and support for them. It will change my approach to the child's learning, but not to expectations of their achievement. I believe, given the right circumstances, everyone can succeed (UK sample).

Hope and Persistence

The teachers' belief that 'everyone can succeed' (UK sample) represents hope. Hope 'is in love with success rather than failure' (Bloch, 1959/1986, p.3). In addition to hope being in love with success, 'hope, as an expression of a present alive with possibilities, rallies energies and activates our powers' (Mayeroff, 1971, p.33). This kind of hope persists even 'when a great deal is at stake' and obstacles impede success (Godfrey, 1987, p.14; also see Hogan, 1997). For the teachers, '[Success] is essential. Every student can do something well, so let them shine and be a star no matter how many "learning difficulties" they have in the major areas' (Irish sample). The teachers work at 'setting tasks that are, above all, achievable by all [students] – to allow them the experience of success in a new, and maybe intimidating environment' (Irish sample). One teacher found a simple strategy that helps foster student success:

> A strategy that I use a lot is getting children to talk about what they have done [...] sometimes in groups, sometimes it might be individually [...] What did you do and how did you do that? How did you tackle that? [...] Giving them a chance to explain what they have done gives them a sense of worth, a sense of importance, a sense of success (UK sample).

The teachers do not appear to consciously recognise that they are teaching hope. However, they seem to believe that helping students be successful is a prerequisite for teaching them:

> I want every child to think that they're valued, that they're loved, and to know that I'm convinced that they're good at something, because I think that finding one thing that a person's good at enables them to develop the things that they're not so good at. But you know, if you feel a total failure, then there is no reason to be motivated, is there? (UK sample).

Feeling a failure is particularly typical of students whose academic successes are limited and whose other strengths have not been valued:

> With my remedial class, for example, they are always saying things like 'We are not very good at this.' And I try to show them by helping them to succeed, that they are just as good – "intelligent" if you like – but for various reasons they don't find it easy to be academic, but that they can succeed. It will just take them a little longer (UK sample).

Teaching students who are academically disadvantaged demands persistence. 'There has to be patience to work with that kid again and again and again' (US sample) (also see Hansen, 1995). Another aspect of patient persistence recognises that students may need to have material presented in different ways. One teacher creates a safe environment where her students feel comfortable telling her when they did not understand:

> I won't have to pull it out of them. They'll just say, 'I just don't get it.' And that's when I, if I cannot spontaneously think of a different way of teaching it – because obviously it has to be a different way of teaching it if you haven't gotten them the first time – I'll ask the kids, 'Can any of you explain this better than I am?' And often they can (US sample).

Persistence is also necessary for students who are not particularly likeable. 'A central responsibility built into teaching [is] that one should not give up on students one may dislike or find disappointing, but rather should persist in seeking ways to reach them' (Hansen, 1995, p.37; also see Collinson, 1996). No teacher can humanly be expected to like all students, but teachers can be expected to persist with all students. This does not always happen. In one school, a teacher said of his colleagues, 'Many of them saw ways to give me kids that have behaviour problems. They were recommending children to come to me and that would calm them down' (US sample).

Two of the teachers mentioned that they have received phone calls from former students in jail. Somehow, the students must have believed that the teachers had not given up on them:

> I now receive three or four [...] phone calls [a year ...] from kids [former students] that have killed people and got into serious trouble. [...It happens] over and over again. And when they get out of prison, they come right back to the school and tell the kids – it's just like, 'I'm coming to tell you what I've gone through. I wish I had listened.' And they write letters back to the classroom. [...] And I've gone to trial, I mean many times. [...One former student served time for drugs and] returned back. [...I] got him a job downtown [and he's] doing very well. And I told him, 'I'm not here to be [judgmental]. I don't believe in drugs' [...] He looks at it one way and we look at it differently. This is what he's surrounded with. This is how people make their living. This is part of a culture of doing things that way (US sample).

This teacher clearly lives what Goleman (1998) observed: hope is a motivating force that allows competent performers to 'persist in seeking goals despite obstacles and setbacks, operate from hope of success rather than fear of failure, [and] see setbacks as due to manageable circumstance rather than a personal flaw' (p.122). In the classroom, none of the teachers sees mistakes as failures. Instead, they view mistakes as an important way to learn:

I certainly try to make the children realise that things are a challenge, that they can do it. [...] I really believe that we learn from mistakes. We learn from doing things and not getting them right the first time. [...] There is no point in children very, very much thinking things are right or wrong and feeling success or failure on that basis (UK sample).

I talk about the two steps forwards, one step backwards – that all learning is two steps forwards, one step backwards. That's the way babies learn to walk. They get up and they fall down. You've got to make mistakes. Unless you make mistakes, you'll never do the learning – and never to worry about making mistakes. I sometimes enjoy it when I ask a child a question and they say, 'Oh, Miss, I think I'll have another step backwards.' I can find that funny and I say, 'That's okay' (Irish sample).

Another teacher tries to teach students that apparent failures are manageable with help:

You get discipline problems from kids who are unable to achieve, who have low self-esteem or whatever. They have to be dealt with in an individual way so that if somebody can't write, you face it squarely and say, 'Look, you have a problem and I can help you. Let's see what we can do about this' or 'You and I can do something about this' (Irish sample).

The message the teachers send is a message of hope and a message that persistence works: 'I can't think of a time when I've given up on something. And I try to model that to them – that you just keep chipping away at it until you find a way to be successful' (US sample). Despite the complexities, frustrations, and setbacks, these teachers manage to remain hopeful. The teacher in the inner city faces daily what might appear to be especially insurmountable setbacks. Nevertheless, he is the one who said forcefully, 'There is hope, absolutely!' When asked how he sustains hope, he replied:

By looking at individual children. [...] Oh, there are so many brilliant, beautiful children. These kids, many of them are so nice. [...] And then I look at the kids [in the school] and say, 'If I was growing up over there [in the projects], which one would I be?' (US sample).

Conclusion

Throughout history, writers have universally recognised the power and importance of hope in human beings' thinking, emotions, and achievements. But despite its potential for motivating individuals to help others and its importance among competent caregivers, the development of both an awareness of the importance of hope and its use in dealing with students has not become a part of the explicit curriculum in teacher education.

This study indicates how the thinking of 12 teachers appears to be permeated by hope and how their hope seems to rely on several beliefs. For example, they view learning in the broadest sense and consider learning to be a lifelong process of development, both for themselves and for their students. They see students as individuals and believe that 'each person has a contribution to make' in the world. Moreover, they share the strong belief that all students can succeed in some way and that they as teachers have a unique contribution to make to their students. These beliefs appear to be important in allowing the teachers to be other-centred, to set high expectations and goals for themselves and their students, and to persist in reaching students. The participants' self-reported thinking and practices about these three principles of hope cut across gender, race, age, nationality, and school contexts.

The teachers' thinking about high expectations is particularly intriguing. Even in an era of increasing emphasis on academic performance, these teachers consider learning to be much more than test scores. They define success in terms of doing one's best and are conscious of the uniqueness of each individual in this regard. Their two principal expectations for all students, regardless of personal or socio-economic circumstances, are doing one's best and showing respect for others. These teachers do not appear to be aware of teaching 'hope' to students but they purposefully teach some of the principles of hope. For example, one teacher explained that he is 'giving [students] the belief that if they do their best, they have been successful' (Irish sample). Although the teachers willingly alter their approaches to teaching individuals, they do not alter their expectations. They are not naïve or sentimental about students or their influence on students, but they are prepared to expend energy and provide assistance to support their high expectations. Further, these teachers appear to believe in reciprocal or two-way expectations. They hold the same high expectations for themselves as for their students: doing their personal best and respecting others. Indeed, some also ask students to articulate their expectations for the teacher.

Given that in the literature, hope is an identified aspect of an ethic of care and is evident in competent performers in the caring professions, we should expect to find an attitude of hope prevalent among teachers, although perhaps at various levels of development. Moreover, if hope in teaching is as powerful as our study suggests, its principles, development, and impact on students merit much closer attention and research. This study is exploratory and comparatively small, but the findings indicate that hope is a very important, albeit complex, attitudinal disposition for teachers. The results of this study also begin to clarify the amorphous concept of hope as it relates to teaching. Identification of some of the principles of hope, some of the underlying beliefs, and some of the ways in which hope manifests itself in teachers' thinking and practices can assist researchers in designing specific questions to further examine hope in teaching.

References

Anyon, J. (1981) Social class and school knowledge. *Curriculum Inquiry,* 11 (1), 3-42.

Bloch, E. (1986) *The principle of hope* (N. Plaice, S. Plaice, P. Knight, Trans.). Oxford: Basil Blackwell. (Original work published 1959)

Brookhart, S.M. and Rusnak, T.G. (1993) A pedagogy of enrichment, not poverty: Successful lessons of exemplary urban teachers. *Journal of Teacher Education,* 44(1), 17-26.

Collinson, V. (1994) *Teachers as learners: Exemplary teachers' perceptions of personal and professional renewal.* San Francisco: Austin and Winfield.

Collinson, V. (1996) *Reaching students: Teachers' ways of knowing.* Thousand Oaks, CA: Corwin Press.

Collinson, V. (1999, April) *Improving college teaching: Learning from exemplary secondary school teachers.* Paper presented at the annual meeting of the American Educational Research Association, Montreal, Canada.

Cuban, L. (1995) Foreword. In D.T. Hansen, *The call to teach* (pp. ix-xi). New York: Teachers College Press.

Dewey, J. (1964) What psychology can do for the teacher. In R.D. Archambault (Ed.), *John Dewey on education* (pp.195-211). New York: The Modern Library. (Original work published 1895)

Dewey, J. (1964) The need for a philosophy of education. In R.D. Archambault (Ed.), *John Dewey on education* (pp.3-14). New York: The Modern Library. (Original work published 1934)

Elbaz, F. (1992) Hope, attentiveness, and caring for difference: The moral voice in teaching. *Teaching & Teacher Education,* 8(5/6), 421-432.

Frankl, V.E. (1963) *Man's search for meaning: An introduction to logotherapy.* New York: Washington Square Press.

Gardner, J.W. (1990) *On leadership.* New York: The Free Press.

Godfrey, J.J. (1987) *A philosophy of human hope.* Dordrecht, The Netherlands: Martinus Nijhoff.

Goleman, D. (1995) *Emotional intelligence.* New York: Bantam Books.

Goleman, D. (1998) *Working with emotional intelligence.* New York: Bantam Books.

Hansen, D.T. (1995) *The call to teach.* New York: Teachers College Press.

Hogan, P. (1997) Forlorn hopes and great expectations: Teaching as a way of life in an age of uncertainty. *Irish Educational Studies,* 16, 1-18.

Hunter, F. (1953) *Community power structure.* Chapel Hill, NC: University of North Carolina Press.

Mayeroff, M. (1971) *On caring.* New York: Harper Collins.

Merton, R. K. (1948) Self-fulfilling prophecy. *Antioch Review,* 8(2), 193-210.

Noddings, N. (1994) Foreword. In L.G. Beck, *Reclaiming educational administration as a caring profession* (pp.ix-x). New York: Teachers College Press.

Pedersen, E. and Faucher, T.A. (1978) A new perspective on the effects of first-grade teachers on children's subsequent adult status. *Harvard Educational Review,* 48(1), 1-31.

Ramsay, P. and Oliver, D. (1995) Capacities and behaviour of quality classroom teachers. *School Effectiveness and School Improvement,* 6(4), 332-366.

Rosenthal, R. and Jacobson, L. (1968) *Pygmalion in the classroom: Teacher expectations and pupil's intellectual development.* New York: Holt, Rinehart, and Winston.

Regular Classroom Teachers' Perceptions of Inclusion: Implications for Teacher Preparation Programmes in Spain

Cristina M. Cardona

This study examined and compared regular classroom teachers' perceptions of inclusion in Spain. The 'Inclusion Attitudes and Beliefs' survey instrument was administered to a sample of 115 preservice and inservice teachers enrolled in a postgraduate program. The instrument included 30 statements to which respondents reacted on a five-point scale ranging from strongly agree to strongly disagree. Results indicated that regular classroom teachers do not have positive attitudes toward inclusion. Their perceptions divided into two major areas: (1) recognition of inclusion as a basic right with beneficial effects for students, particularly, on the social domain, and (2) reluctance in accepting new responsibility in educating diverse students because of additional work load, lack of skills, and scarcity of resources necessary to teach students with special needs. The study suggests two waves of reform. One in the way teachers think about inclusion, and the other in the way they teach. Future studies should assess the impact of new university teacher training programs and special education courses which offer better methodologies and adequate opportunities to alter teachers' beliefs and attitudes toward inclusion.

The movement toward inclusion is currently an irreversible trend in education. The educational policies of all developed countries support inclusion because it is considered a principle of social justice and a basic human right. As a developed country, Spain, twenty years after the approval of the LISMI (*Ley de Integración Social de las Personas con Minusvalías*), clearly advocates for the inclusion of all children into general education classrooms and schools, with appropriate assistance (LISMI, 1982; LOGSE, 1990; Real Decreto 696/1995).

Inclusion describes the process of integrating students with disabilities into general education classes in order to address the requirement of 'least restrictive environment' (Scruggs, & Mastropieri, 1996), which means that the majority of students with disabilities should be educated in regular classrooms and schools. It becomes apparent that many of this movement's basic assumptions can be easily acknowledged, however, there has been an enormous misunderstanding in supposing that regular classroom teachers would automatically assume new responsibilities and, consequently, would face new challenges.

In general, regular classroom teachers have not reacted favourably to the new demands. If, as many authors have concluded, inclusion's success or failure depends in large part upon the teachers' attitudes (Parish, Nunn, & Hattrop, 1982) and current research has shown that when educators are prepared for inclusive classrooms, attitudes toward inclusion change (Cardona, 2000; Dickens-Smith, 1995), then it is imperative to explore and understand what actual teachers' perceptions and/or school conditions may inhibit the possibility of effective inclusion and, concurrently, plan for better teacher training programs.

Most of the available information about teacher' beliefs and attitudes toward inclusion comes from the United States (Bender, Vail, & Scott, 1995; Center, & Ward, 1987; Minke, Bear, Deemer, Griffin, 1996; Scruggs, & Mastropieri, 1996; Yanito, Quintero, Killoran, & Striefel, 1987). This research supports the warning of critics that regular classroom teachers are likely to resist the placement of children with disabilities into the regular classroom based on the following perceptions: lack of skills (Semmel, Abernathy, Butera, & Lesar, 1991), low competence or self-efficacy (Soodak, & Podell, 1993), unfeasibility of instructional adaptations (Schumm, & Vaughn, 1991; Scott, Vitale, & Masten, 1998), or lack of supports and collaboration (Wolery, Werts, Caldwell, Snyder, & Lissowski, 1995).

In such a context, very little is known about teachers' beliefs and perceptions relative to inclusion in Spain. In addition, a major criticism of the inclusion movement in this country is that it has been imposed by law, rather than after a process of consultation and, consequently, without taking into account teachers' reactions. Furthermore, inquiry into regular classroom teachers' beliefs and attitudes toward inclusion in Spain reveals (Aguilera *et al.*, 1990; Balbás, 1998; Cardona, 1996; García, & Alonso, 1985) not only a scarcity of research but also a need to systematically explore and understand teacher initial resistance. If as we know, beliefs influence how teachers think, teach, react to change, and learn to teach, before we continue implementing inclusive programs we need to explore the interplay of such variables on teacher thinking.

Nothing has been done in Spain to determine whether or not regular classroom teachers' beliefs of inclusion differ according to experience with schooling and instruction. Preservice and inservice teachers may think differentially about inclusion, may differ in the appreciation of its benefits and concerns, or even may perceive different training needs. And this knowledge could be of great interest for planning teachers training programs and courses. Therefore, two questions guided this study:

1. What do regular classroom teachers in Spain believe about inclusion?
2. Do Spanish teachers' beliefs (benefits and concerns of inclusion) differ as a function of school experience?

We hypothesised that regular classroom teachers would perceive inclusion as a basic right of students, and as a learning strategy that can be beneficial for almost all students, but also that they would express resistance to accept new demands and responsibilities. Skills, support assistance, need of training, and availability of resources would be critical variables of greatest concern for them. We did expect that preservice and inservice regular classroom teachers would differ significantly in their judgements.

Method

Participants

The participants were 115 certified regular education teachers enrolled in a post-graduate teacher university program and registered in a required special education course. The total number of respondents completing the survey was 82 (71%). Teachers included in the study came from urban, suburban, and rural areas around the province of Alicante, Spain, and were ethnically homogeneous. The sample was 78% female and 22% male. Ages ranged from 21 to 59 years (average = 30.84, $SD = 9.79$). All of the sample possessed a Bachelor degree and 5% of these held a Master degree as well. Eighty-four percent of these regular education teachers had taken no course work in special education, while 16% were in possession of a special education credential. Half of the sample consisted of preservice teachers and the remaining half of inservice teachers. Percentages for other subject characteristics in inservice teachers are presented in Table 1.

Survey Instrument and Procedure

A modified version of the 'Inclusion Attitudes and Beliefs' (Ellis, 1995) survey instrument was selected and adapted for use in the study. Fifteen items comprised the Benefits Scale and the remaining fifteen items the Concerns Scale. Item number 14 (*Inclusion is a basic right of students*) and 15 (*Teachers should be prepared to teach all students*) of the Benefits Scale were totally new. The instrument was administered to two classes (one preservice and one inservice) of general education teachers enrolled in a postgraduate teacher university program before beginning a special education course included in that program. The Pre Benefits and Pre Concerns Scales exhibited fair internal consistency reliability (above .85).

The survey consisted of 30 questions. Each question assessed a teacher's belief about the benefits/concerns of inclusion and was rated on a Likert scale ranging from 1 (*strongly disagree*) to 5 (*strongly agree*). The items were totalled to generate a composite score for each Subscale and for the Total Scale (60 + B - C). A composite score for the Total Scale between 0-40 was indicative of negative perceptions of inclusion; between 41-80, neutral perceptions; and over 80, positive perceptions. Similarly, by Subscales, a score below 40 indicated low appreciation of benefits/concerns of inclusion; between 41-80, average appreciation; and over 80, high benefits/concerns of inclusion. The instrument also included a section with 3 open-ended questions to add additional comments relative to inclusion.

Table 1 – Additional Demographic Data on Inservice Teachers

Variable	N	%
Years of Teaching Experience		
0-3	6/41	14.6
4-8	6/41	14.6
9-15	13/41	31.8
+ 15	16/41	39.0
Grade Level Taught		
Kindergarten	11/41	26.8
Elementary	19/41	46.4
Secondary	11/41	26.8

Results

What Do Regular Classroom Teachers in Spain Believe About Inclusion?
The results are reported in Table 2 and Table 3 for benefits and concerns, respectively. In reviewing statements associated with benefits, a minority (12%) of the respondents had the opinion that special education should provide education for disabled (and nondisabled) only in the regular classrooms. This response indicates that 71% of regular education teachers prefer sending students with special needs to resource-room and special education classrooms, rather than having special education teachers deliver services in the regular classroom. Sixty-two percent of the respondents felt that students with disabilities placed in inclusive classrooms would benefit socially. Only 20 percent of the respondents thought that children with disabilities do not learn enough meaningful information in special education. Sixty percent of the respondents agreed that teachers need technical expertise to ensure that children with disabilities are successfully learning. According to 88% of the respondents, students with disabilities would have a better chance of success if strategies developed by special education were commonly used in the regular classroom. Eighteen percent of the respondents indicated that only expert teachers should teach in inclusive classrooms. In reviewing statements associated with student performance, 32% of the respondents stated that special students performed better on average in regular classrooms, and 40% had the opposite opinion. Finally, 87% of the respondents felt that inclusion is a basic right of students and that teachers should be prepared to teach *all* students in the regular classroom.

Overall, most of the regular education teachers agreed that inclusion is a right of students and a primary responsibility for teachers, and that some degree of

Table 2 – Survey of Regular Classroom Teachers' Beliefs on Inclusion Subscale of Benefits

	Disagree			Agree	
1. Special educators should provide education for disabled (and nondisabled) only in regular classrooms	20%	51%	17%	11%	1%
2. The more time students spend in the general education program, the less socially isolated they are	1%	12%	24%	33%	29%
3. Children with disabilities do not learn enough meaningful information in special education	13%	37%	30%	14%	6%
4. In an inclusion classroom teacher needs technical expertise to teach children with disabilities	2%	16%	22%	37%	23%
5. Social education with non disabled peers is the appropriate education for students with disabilities	6%	23%	33%	26%	13%
6. Special education historically has served as general education's 'dumping ground' for 'unteachables'	0%	5%	34%	38%	23%
7. Special education placements are inherently unequal	0%	16%	59%	18%	7%
8. Students with disabilities would have a better chance to success in regular education classes if more of the strategies developed by special education were commonly used	2%	5%	5%	37%	51%
9. It is very important for children to have the opportunity to learn and grow within communities that represent the kind of world they will live in when they finish school	1%	2%	15%	30%	52%
10. Inclusion places the emphasis on improving instruction rather than classifying and placing students	1%	12%	22%	39%	26%
11. The problem of maintaining the 'continuum of placements' is that it keeps politicians from making far-reaching changes they need to make	5%	24%	48%	16%	7%
12. Only experts teachers with years of experience should teach in inclusive classrooms	17%	43%	22%	17%	1%
13. Special students generally perform better on average in regular classrooms	7%	33%	28%	25%	7%
14. Inclusion is a basic right of students	0%	2%	11%	30%	57%
15. Teachers should be prepared to teach all students	0%	2%	11%	26%	61%

inclusion could provide benefits (academic and social) to the student with disabilities. However, only a minority of teachers agreed that the regular classroom was the best environment for students with special needs when compared with special education (items 1 and 3).

Regular classroom teachers were also asked about concerns regarding inclusion (see Table 3). One of the main concerns for 46 percent of the respondents was that the elimination of special education placement would deprive many students of an appropriate education. More specifically, respondents believed (89 percent) that children with disabilities do not receive sufficiently intensive instruction in regular classrooms because teachers cannot attend to their needs, and that consequently maintaining a continuum of placements is a sensible solution for 83 percent of the respondents. Directly related to these statements were the opinions of those respondents who maintain that nothing is currently being done to make the regular classroom an inclusive environment (75% of the respondents), or that the resource room represents a good chance to work one-to-one (87% in agreement). However, in regards to the question of whether or not mainstreaming/inclusion is ineffective, only 14% of teachers agreed. Overall, a significant percentage of teachers agreed that students with disabilities could create special classroom problems for them. This is the reason why regular classroom teachers in the Autonomous Community of Valencia expressed their agreement in maintaining diverse placement options.

Total Scale and Subscales composite scores for the whole group of teachers and by subgroups (preservice and inservice teachers) are reported in Table 4. Considering that the mid point in the scales is 60, and that the composite score

Table 4: Whole Group and Subgroups Regular Classroom Teachers' Beliefs Toward Inclusion

Group/Subgroups	N	M	SD	Range
Whole Group				
Benefits	82	52.11	6.48	38-66
Concerns	82	40.79	6.31	30-58
Total Scale	82	70.77	9.73	42-88
Preservice Teachers				
Benefits	41	50.73	5.48	38-62
Concerns	41	39.71	5.83	30-51
Total Scale	41	70.85	1.37	51-87
Inservice Teachers				
Benefits	41	53.49	7.16	39-66
Concerns	41	41.88	6.65	30-58
Total Scale	41	70.68	10.74	42-88

Table 3 – Survey of Regular Classroom Teachers' Beliefs on Inclusion – Subscale of Concerns

	Disagree				Agree
1. Inclusion is an untested model advocated by persons with a liberal agenda.	42%	42%	8%	5%	3%
2. Eliminating special education placements will deprive many disabled students an appropriate education.	17%	37%	24%	15%	7%
3. Abolishing separate placements will force mainstream teachers to deal with children they heretofore had avoided.	0%	7%	33%	45%	15%
4. The special education teacher is basically treated like an aid in the regular classroom.	16%	51%	22%	10%	1%
5. Normal children cannot possibly learn as much in inclusion classrooms where the teacher is constantly having to deal with learning and behavior problems.	27%	45%	11%	15%	2%
6. Students who are pulled out for special instruction actually receive less direct instruction than their non-disabled peers.	20%	61%	10%	19%	0%
7. Too often children with disabilities do not receive sufficiently intensive instruction in the regular classroom because teachers can not attend to their needs like they like to do.	0%	11%	48%	33%	8%
8. We must maintain the alternative of moving kids to other places when that appears necessary in the judgment of teachers and parents.	11%	28%	42%	9%	10%
9. Trying to force every body into the inclusion mold promises to be just as coercive as trying to force everybody into the mode of special class.	7%	9%	26%	12%	6%
10. A continuum of placement options is sensible.	0%	18%	60%	15%	7%
11. Children are dumped into classrooms in the name of inclusion, when in fact nothing is in place to make that an inclusive environment.	1%	4%	34%	27%	14%
12. We need different types of instruction for different kids.	5%	42%	22%	24%	7%
13. It is not fair to the rest of class when the teacher has to spend inordinate amounts of time and energy dealing with the behaviors of a couple of 'included kids'.	22%	32%	24%	18%	4%
14. The resource rooms give the resource teacher a chance to work one on one and to experiment with authentic ways of teaching.	0%	13%	26%	33%	28%
15. Mainstreaming is ineffective.	32%	54%	8%	6%	0%

for the Total Scale (whole group) had a mean of 70.77 (SD = 9.73), we can more appropriately talk of *acceptance* than of positive beliefs and perceptions of inclusion. By subgroups, mean scores for Total Scale were 70.85 and 70.68 for preservice and inservice teachers, respectively.

These results indicate that regular classroom teachers in Spain have neutral perceptions of inclusion. They do not perceive either high benefits (mean of 52.11, SD = 6.48) nor important concerns (mean of 40.79, SD = 6.31). According to the results of the survey, regular classroom teachers have some reservations about inclusion. They clearly prefer the current popular practice of providing assistance to students with special needs in resource-room or special education classrooms.

Do Regular Education Teachers' Beliefs Differ as a Function of School Experience?
A series of t tests for independent samples were used to identify possible statistically significant differences in teacher perception as a function of experience with school and instruction. Total Scale composite scores reflected no significant differences between preservice and inservice regular classroom teachers (t = .08, p = .94). By Subscales, data reveal that preservice and inservice teachers in Spain did not differ significantly in their judgements of benefits (t = -1.96, p = .05), and concerns (t = -1.57, p = .12) of inclusion; however, further examination of results indicated the following trend: Inservice teachers perceived more benefits (53.49 *vs* 50.73) and also more concerns (41.88 *vs* 39.71) than preservice teachers, but these differences were not statistically significant.

Discussion and Educational Implications

The purpose of the study was to explore, analyse, and compare preservice and inservice regular classroom teachers perceptions of inclusion. Although at the beginning of the inclusion movement, regular education teachers did not react favourably to the demands of inclusion, our expectation, after a couple of decades, was that their perceptions might have changed. Therefore, we anticipated that regular classroom teachers would recognise inclusion as beneficial for almost all students, and would have assumed their primary responsibilities in educating students with disabilities or those who are gifted. In other words, we expected that teachers would value the innovative experience as positive and their work would reflect compromise and responsibility to teach diverse students. Additionally, we thought that inservice teachers, those who had had experience with schooling, would perceive more benefits than concerns when compared with preservice teachers.

The analyses conducted on the survey revealed some informative results. Twenty year after the publication of the LISMI, regular classroom teachers in Spain remain reluctant to embrace inclusion. Only 12% of the respondents believe that special education should provide for disabled (and non disabled) *only* in the regular classroom. Or what is the same, 71% of Spanish regular classroom teachers prefer sending students with special needs to resource-room classrooms. These responses are congruent with the main concern expressed by regular classroom teachers (89 percent agreed that children with disabilities do not receive sufficiently intensive instruction in regular classrooms because teachers cannot attend to their needs due to lack of skills, time, or resources.)

These results are surprisingly similar to those obtained in other studies (Minke *et al.*, 1996; Scruggs, & Mastropieri, 1996; Semmel *et al.*, 1991) and confirm the trend identified in previous research: the *teacher resistance to accept full inclusion.* As Kauffman, Gerber, and Semmel (1988) have argued, 'resistance among regular education teachers does not reflect their dislike of children with disabilities or necessarily their lack of competencies' (p. 8). Rather, it expresses a clearheaded calculation of costs/benefits for *all* children. This statement perfectly applies to regular classroom teachers in Spain who, as we have seen before, support inclusion principles but still cling to resource and special education classrooms as a means of sharing and/or reducing their responsibilities.

In sum, the findings of this study are divided into two major areas: (1) acceptance of the principles of inclusion and recognition of its positive effects on the students' academic and social domains, and (2) strong reservations in taking on new responsibilities because of work load issues, lack of skills necessary to teach diverse students, and fear of eliminating the resource and self-contained special education placements.

We think that the findings of this study reveal a lack of teacher compromise as a consequence of broken promises. When the Experimental Plan of Integration was introduced in Spain during the eighties, all Spanish Autonomous Communities and School Districts began to facilitate additional personnel and material resources to experimental schools. The central idea was to generalize inclusion after this experimental period to all elementary and secondary schools. Ten years later, the situation remains the same. The nineties did not bring the necessary help and, although the Spanish educational administration invested time and money to train teachers and to expand supports, what was done was not enough.

In conclusion, this study suggests two waves of reform. One, in the way regular education teachers in Spain think about inclusion and, the other, in the way they teach. In order to change teacher attitudes, continuous teacher education training courses must provide regular classroom teachers with opportunities and experiences to become personally involved in inclusive situations. To improve the way teachers teach, a reshaping of university teacher preparation programs and special education courses must occur. Future studies should assess the impact of these new university programs and/or special education courses which offer better methodologies and adequate opportunities to alter teachers' beliefs and attitudes toward inclusion.

References

Aguilera *et al.* (1990). *Evaluación del programa de integración escolar de alumnos con deficiencias.* Madrid: Centro de Publicaciones del Ministerio de Educación y Ciencia.

Balbás, M. J. (1998). Un instrumento para evaluar las necesidades formativas de los profesores ante la integración. *Revista de Educación Especial, 20,* 41-59.

Bender, W. N., Vail, C. O., & Scott, K. (1995). Teachers' attitudes to increased mainstreaming: Implementing effective instruction for students with learning disabilities. *Journal of Learning Disabilities, 28,* 87-94.

Cardona, M. C. (1996). *Educación en la diversidad: evaluación y perspectivas.* Alicante: Generalitat Valenciana-Instituto de Cultura Juan-Gil Albert.

Cardona, M. C. (2000). *Changing Spanish teachers' beliefs toward inclusion through reshaping university special education courses.* Paper prepared to be presented at the European Conference on Educational Research. Edinburgh, UK.

Center, Y., & Ward, J. (1987). Teachers' attitudes towards the integration of disabled children in regular schools. *The Exceptional Child, 31*(1), 41-56.

Dickens-Smith, M. (1995). *The effect of inclusion training on teacher attitude toward inclusion.* Chicago Public Schools, Chicago, IL. (ERIC Document Reproduction Service No. ED 381 486).

Ellis, E. S. (1995). *Ellis Draft (03/15/95) of the Inclusion Attitudes and Beliefs survey.* Unpublished manuscript.

García, J. N., & Alonso, J. C. (1985). Actitudes de los maestros hacia la integración escolar de niños con necesidades especiales. *Infancia y Aprendizaje, 30,* 51-68.

Kauffman, J. M., Gerber, M. M., & Semmel, M. I. (1988). Arguable assumptions underlying the Regular Education Initiative. *Journal of Learning Disabilities, 21,* 6-11.

LISMI (1982). Ley 13/1982, de 7 de abril, de Integración Social de los Minusválidos. *BOÈ,* 30/04/82.

LOGSE (1990). Ley 1/1990, de 3 de octubre, de Ordenación General del Sistema Educativo. *BOE,* 04/10/90.

Minke, K. M., Bear, G. G., Deemer, S. A., & Griffin, S. M. (1996). Teachers' experiences with inclusive classrooms: Implications for special education reform. *The Journal of Special Education, 30*(2), 152-186.

Parish, R. S., Nunn, G. P., & Hattrop, D. (1982). An attempt to reduce negative attitudes of future teachers toward exceptional children. *College Student Journal, 16*(3), 254-257.

Real Decreto 696/1995, de 28 de abril, de la educación de los alumnos con necesidades educativas especiales. *BOE,* 02/06/95.

Scott, B. J., Vitale, M. R., & Masten, W. G. (1998). Implementing instructional adaptations for students with disabilities in inclusive classrooms. A literature review. *Remedial and Special Education, 19*(2), 106-119.

Scruggs, T. E., & Mastropieri, M. A. (1996). Teacher perceptions of mainstreaming/inclusion, 1958-1995: A research synthesis. *Exceptional Children, 63*(1), 59-74.

Soodak, L. C., & Podell, D. M. (1993). Teacher efficacy and student problem as a factors in special education referral. *The Journal of Special Education, 27*(1), 66-81.

Schumm, J. S., & Vaughn, S. (1991). Making adaptations for mainstreamed students: General classroom teachers' perspectives. *Remedial and Special Education, 12,* 18-25.

Semmel, M. I., Abernathy, T. V., Butera, G, & Lesar, S. (1991). Teacher perceptions of Regular Education Initiative. *Exceptional Children, 58,* 9-24.

Wolery, M., Werts, M. G., Caldwell, N. K., Snyder, E. D., & Lisowski, L. (1995). Experienced teachers' perceptions of resources and supports for inclusion. *Education and Training in Mental Retardation and Developmental Disabilities, March,* 15-26.

Yanito, T., Quintero, M. C., Killoran, J. C., & Striefel, S. (1987). *Teacher attitudes toward mainstreaming: A literature review.* Logan, UT: Utah State University. Developmental Center for Handicapped Persons. (ERIC Document Reproduction No. ED 290 290).

Early Childhood Educators in England and Finland: An Exploratory Study

ANNE CHOWNE

This article presents the preliminary findings from an exploratory study carried out by the author and a colleague, Viv Moriarty, in the early part of 1999. The principle objective was to explore the responses of Early Years teachers to current curriculum change in England and Finland. It is hoped that the exploratory study will initiate a discussion of the issues raised in this paper and lead to further research. Other aspects of the research were reported at the conference of the British Educational Research Association held at the University of Sussex in September 1999.

The overall purpose of this research is to understand better what Early Years teachers consider to be the aims of pre-school education of children, and to give voice to the concerns and opinions of Early Years teachers. By discussing the curriculum development in both countries opportunities will arise for dialogue between the two groups of teachers. The first and fourth of the following five research questions will be discussed:

- What do Early Years teachers consider are the aims for the year before compulsory schooling?
- What place does professional development have in shaping the views of Early Years teachers in Finland and England?
- What are the different responses of Early Years educators in England and Finland to their respective curriculum policies?
- How are these responses related to local contexts, national contexts and trans-national contexts?
- How do Early Years teachers in Finland and England view the role of parents in the early years of education?

Our interest in Early Years teachers derives from our own experiences as teachers of young children in England and as teacher educators at the Institute of Education, University of London. These experiences have led us to analyse the processes of policy formation. Additionally, we have an interest in the conceptions of professionality that Early Years teachers have. 'Professionality' is used here to define understandings, knowledge, skills and procedures that are applied by early years educators in their work with young children (Hoyle 1975) and is used in preference to the term 'professionalism'.

We chose the national contexts of England and Finland because reforms in Early Years education are currently an issue in both countries. Early years education is high on the agenda for the two governments, with an emphasis being put on 'diversity, innovation, flexibility and choice in education provision' (National Board of Education 1998), and the stated priority being to prepare children for compulsory schooling.

However, despite some similarities, there are also significant differences in the way decisions about the curriculum to be followed in the early years are made in England and in Finland. In Finland the pre-school curriculum Framework outlines general objectives and subject fields to be addressed in early years settings with an emphasis on the need for preparation for school. It is the task of local government, known as municipalities, to contextualise these general objectives. Further, each early years setting, or group of settings within a particular locality, must devise their own curriculum.

Published in the same year in England, the United Kingdom government's Desirable Outcomes for Children's Learning (SCAA 1996) were devised by the Schools Curriculum and Assessment Authority (a quasi-government agency). These Desirable Learning Outcomes (hereafter referred to as DLOs) describe areas of learning, which were designed to enable children to progress smoothly onto the National Curriculum when they are five years old. These are to be revised, along with the National Curriculum, in the year 2000, by the Qualifications and Curriculum Authority. Consultation about the new so-called Early Learning Goals began during the time when the field work for this study was being carried out (QCA 1999).

Although early years settings in England are being encouraged to devise their own documents outlining how they plan to enable children to achieve these Desirable Learning Outcomes, there has been no place for local government to be involved with curriculum formation. This means that in Finland the curriculum is potentially much more responsive to the needs of each community and is more likely to share the values of the families it supports.

Theoretical and Epistemological background
This study is based on the principle that knowledge is a socially constructed phenomenon and that individuals actively construct their own meanings based on their existing perceptions and understandings, in transaction with their social environment and through the use of language. It is also recognised that construction of meaning is effected by existing structures and constrained by them. These structures are broad and are concerned with issues of power and control.
Whilst it was considered important to understand the constraints within which Early Years teachers are operating, it was also the premise for this project that there is a role for human agency within social situations and that action is predicated on how particular events are perceived, in relation to a person's self-identity.

As there is a restriction to the amount of time I can give to discussing the theories of teacher thinking, action and belief today, I will focus on a model suggested by Nisbett and Ross (Wittrock 1980). This concerns the constraints that settings impose on planning, decision making and interaction in the classroom, and the ways that conflict between what *teachers* see as the aims of education, with that of curriculum makers, may lead to feelings of disempowerment. Many English teachers feel isolated because of problems experienced by what Fullan and Stiegelbauer (1991) call 'classroom press'. This distracts teacher focus, exhausts them and limits sustained reflection. There are many reasons why this happens, one of which is new and changing curriculum implementation.

Several examples of research show the empowering effects of professional development (Burgess-Macey and Rose 1997; Connelly et al 1997). By engaging in professional development programmes, not only does self-image and professional confidence rise (Biott and Nias 1992), but also existing knowledge and beliefs change (Borko and Putnam 1995). This is especially true when the dilemmas experienced are shared with other teachers (Freeman 1991). The writings that mention the importance of collaboration emphasise that reflection alone is not sufficient for development; there has to be a mix of confrontation and support so that the issues which arise out of daily practice can be analysed and re-thought. Keiny (1994), in a study on MA education students in Israel, describes a seminar programme in which groups discussed problems. By observing each other and then engaging in discourse they were able to represent and reflect on what had happened and hence reformulate theories of teaching and learning. It is Richardson's assertion (1997) that it is an essential feature of constructivist teacher education programmes that they closely involve the participants themselves in their own learning, so that they can examine and challenge their own understandings and assumptions about their work. For Richardson, the outcome will be empowerment of the teachers involved.

Sample

The sample for the study consisted of 19 Early Years educators from Finland and 18 Early Years educators from England. These educators are working with six year old children in the pre-school sector in Finland and with four year old children in the education sector in England; the year before formal schooling begins in each country. It was deemed important that sampling procedures served the purpose of developing theory and allowed for the elaboration of categories during the analysis. We chose research participants who would be able to articulate their responses to the Early Years curriculum and we invited them to come forward from schools in England that already had some contact with the researchers. Similarly, in Finland, colleagues from the University of Helsinki helped to select participants who were willing to be an active part of the research. It was the decision of the researchers to take this approach so that a type of discourse could be sampled (Epstein and Johnson 1998). It should be clearly acknowledged at this point that the Finnish teachers expressed themselves in a language that was not their native tongue, and this may have inhibited both the articulation of their opinions and their confidence to answer the research questions.

Methodology

It was decided to use a semi-structured interview as a data collection method. For this study it was also important that the method of collecting data served the purpose of allowing the research questions to be answered and also to affirm the importance of the interviewee (Seidman 1991). Both the interviewee and the interviewer, in this conception of the process, are actively engaged in co-constructing meanings and uncovering understandings. Through language, the individual is provided with a way of structuring experiences within a social context. What is being asserted here is that humans monitor what they do in a reflexive way and that this is expressed to other individuals through the medium of language

The data for the main study were collected between March and June 1999 in England and Finland. The interview schedule was designed to allow early years educators to express their understandings of Early Years practice, especially related to children in the year before they begin school and to think about from where these understandings may have originated. Additionally, educators were invited to express their opinion of national policy and their view of the origins of their beliefs.

Data handling

Interview conversations from the tapes were transcribed and imported into the computer analysis programme NU*DIST. Initial coding categories were devised, based on the questions asked and then further subdivided where the interview data clustered around different themes. This led to further coding and it was the task of analysis to attempt to find relationships and emerging themes from the data.

Findings

This section discusses analysis of the data related to two questions: 'What do Early Years teachers consider the aims to be for the year before compulsory schooling?' and 'What place does professional development have in shaping the views of Early Years teachers in Finland and England?' The speech extracts chosen to illustrate the points are representative of the sample responses.

English teachers: answering the question 'What do you think is important for young children to be doing in the year before they start school?', said the following things:

'To work on basic skills.'
'A bit of everything that's on the Desirable Learning Outcomes.'

'The time before they start school should just be time for being a small child really.'

'It's a continuum, from pre-school through early years provision.'

'Just open them up to try and – so that they're ready to take on board a new perspective.'

The probes that followed were: 'Why do you think these are important' or 'What are the aims and objectives of these things you have described?'. These are some of the answers:

'I don't think that formal sitting and writing or whatever is appropriate.'

'Because they learn and they will enjoy their environment – they'll enjoy their time here much better.'

'I think it comes out of a basic philosophy that I think has been supported by my observations I've made about how children learn best.'

'Once they get into the National Curriculum there's never any time for that sort of thing.'

'They're too young to do the Year 1 stuff when they're 4 and 5 and they desperately need Reception just to settle in.'

The main themes from this analysis for English teachers are:
- a general aim for this period of education is to help children adjust to separation from home and to become inculcated into the institutional setting of school
- this is a time for children to get used to being one of many, to mix with their peers, to meet new adults that they can trust, and to experience a different routine to the day
- the skills and habits of concentration, communicating and listening are encouraged during this period, as well as the attitudes and dispositions that will be needed later in school life
- it is imperative that these young people are helped to become independent learners, to make decisions for themselves and to be confident in all that they do.

Finnish teachers when asked the same question, 'What do you think is important for young children to be doing in the year before they start school?' responded thus:

'They learn playing, it moves them easily to work with that group. It's good to find if they have some difficulty with learning in some way and we can find them and so we can start to help them.'

'I think when they start to read and write the child must be interested in letters and sentences, reading books.'

'We do more of the same things, we are now in the mixed group from 3 to 6 years. For the older ones it's good to be an example.'

'I think it's important for them to be in a group where there are other six year old kids.

So they know how to be together in a larger group and how they can communicate and that's important.'
'I think they should learn the common rules so that they can do things together not only by themselves or with an adult.'

In answer to *the two probe questions*, Finnish teachers said:

'Because we are people.'
'If you don't know any letters before you go to school I think that would be giving you some problems.'
'That prepares them to the school of course.'
'Maybe those things you can't do at school anymore.'
'Because if some child has some problems learning these things then we can find them out early enough before school because it is more difficult to repair them at school.'

The main themes from this analysis for Finnish teachers are:
- there is a different understanding expressed regarding the professional role of Early Years teachers
- the achievement of higher status seems to have been facilitated by their involvement in curriculum formulation
- relationships with parents and the work early years educators do with the families in the locality has a different emphasis than that in England
- the absence of statements about dilemmas in practice suggests that Finnish teachers have greater control over issues of power in their practice

Influences on teachers

In the sample of teachers we investigated in England, there was a majority who were already involved in studying at Masters level, and of the Finnish sample there was a significant percentage who were studying at a higher university level. When asked what had influenced their views of the aims of Early Years Education, teachers in England said that reading and going on courses had had an impact. The Early Years teachers in Finland tended to say that talking, observing and working with colleagues had affected their views most. In the present study, evidence suggests that higher education with a more theoretical basis had an important influence on both English and Finnish teachers work with young children. This may be related to their understandings of pedagogy. There were differences in the ways English and Finnish teachers related a course or other influence on their professionality.

Finnish Early Years teachers were positive about the arrangements for curriculum planning. Although they received no training for the process, they felt it had been a positive experience and were pleased with the outcomes. Each day care centre had written its own curriculum, using guidelines from the municipality, and in consultation with other day care centres in the locality. The teachers valued the opportunity to meet with other professionals and consider important issues about early years education. The Finnish teachers expressed a more collegial attitude to their work than English teachers did.

English Early Years teachers expressed feelings of isolation and being devalued by colleagues. They were negative about the increase in paperwork they felt had been engendered by planning for the Desirable Learning Outcomes (SCAA 1996). Recent research in England by Blatchford (Moriarty et al 1999) found that 76% of teachers of four-year-olds felt that external pressures of change or new initiatives caused the most stress in their professional lives.

Similarities

Both teachers working in England and Finland said that personal and professional experiences had been important:

> 'Having my own children. Working with young children and seeing how difficult it is for them to move into that very structured, formal setting' (England).
> 'And my parents so they have put me to think and they have decided they have wanted to make me and my sisters very independent and so that we manage in our lives so they pushed us in the way that we know that they trust us and we had many different kinds of opportunities to manage. So this is perhaps the main thing' (Finland).

Differences

English teachers: Teachers in England either gained an initial degree that gave them teacher status or qualified as post-graduates. The following illustrate the variety of views that have been coded under 'Professional education'. The two response types that English teachers fell into were, the reinforcement of ways of working or thinking, or the links with concepts previously not understood and the influence of the clarification of them on approaches to teaching:

> 'My PGCE [Post Graduate Certificate of Education] set me off on a platform of understanding ... I think I teach the way I do because of my experiences.'
> 'The diploma I am doing at the moment has cleared up a lot of thoughts.'
> 'I can keep doing it this way.'
> 'I picked up a lot, you think, "Gosh!" when you've read something or you've been thinking something... Or you hear somebody say something you've been thinking – yeah, that's it.'
> 'This feels right – these professional academic women are saying exactly what I'd felt for years.'
> 'The MA provided understandings about philosophical questions.'

Two interviewees mentioned particular models or experts in terms of the skills of knowledge acquired. This is mirrored in the conclusions drawn by Pennell and Firestone (1996) who wrote of teacher evaluation of successful programmes in terms of how useful they were in practical terms or in the teaching strategies and resources they had acquired for use in the classroom.

> 'What I took from the High/Scope was the taking responsibility – it's not enough just to go on them [courses], you have to reflect on it, what is useful, what would I use again in this context.'
>
> 'Professor Katz speaking at a conference – putting into words things that I felt and I believed in but had never been able to express.'

Finnish teachers: Teachers in Finland gained teacher status through a two or three year college or university degree for kindergarten or pre-school education. Of the teachers in Finland, the 'influence' responses fell into Initial training, courses and studies or research and fields of study which have affected the ways they understand early years education. The following show some examples of answers:

> 'The latest fifteen weeks I studied in university – put me to think about theories and things … I have to know okay this is humanism and this is constructivism'.
>
> 'It has changed…. this Early Years education is now at the University, so there is coming in the future researches and it is always developing points of view you are having in this field or area… With my drama studies .. we learn more than when we are just reading books… I think knowing is doing.'
>
> 'We have to do more teaching theory... we have to go deeper and I am very interested how and what and do we have other methods to do and very open eyes to going – open minds.'
>
> 'I liked very much that 15 week course. That has influenced me very much.'

Significant numbers of Early Years teachers said that their colleagues had influenced their views about early years education:

> 'It is also my colleagues, bad or good, because we are working in a team and if you have different kinds of views, different opinions so I have mostly quite different compared to many others because I want to develop everything…. It is developing all the time yourself and I think it is good to work in a team, whatever kind of team it is.'

Conclusions and ways forward

It is Elbaz's view (Russell and Munby 1982) that teachers construct their work in terms of 'frames', which are all value-laden. She suggests the following as the most significant of these frames:

- preconceptions about teaching, learning and children
- their professional and contextual constraints
- their overall commitment to their profession

In this study it is intended to look at how teachers articulate these dimensions in their professional life. Ashton et al state that teachers prioritise educational aims into 'individualistic' and 'societal' terms (Pollard et al 1994). The first promotes the differentiated curriculum, whereas the second is concerned with basic knowl-

edge, skills and understanding. As in all educational settings there are many things for teachers to consider. Early Years teachers have to study and apply:
- knowledge and understanding of children's linguistic, cognitive, social, emotional and physical development
- curriculum theory, development and evaluation
- highly developed observation, interaction and communication skills
- professional ethics and child advocacy (Siraj-Blatchford 1993)

It has not been possible to examine the professional histories of either the Finnish or English Early Years teachers in enough detail to draw conclusions about the different influences of degree type, work setting, cultural context or the professional development programmes that individuals have followed. However the following are the intended outcomes for further research:
- Develop an understanding of the way Early Years teachers make meaning of educational policy and mediate it in practice
- Consider the implications of reforms to the curriculum for children in the year prior to compulsory schooling in England and Finland
- Develop understandings about early years educators' conceptions of professionality
- Give opportunities for Early Years teachers to be reflexive about their own practice and articulate their understandings
- Develop opportunities for Early Years teachers to engage in a dialogue with other early years professionals in their own and another country.
- Foster professional partnerships between early years educators in Finland and England for further in-service work
- Raise new research questions, which might include:
  - How are the aims and objectives for early years education conceptualised by:
  a) Parents
  b) Early Years educators
  c) Managers of early years settings
  d) Officials in municipalities and local education authorities
  e) Policy makers?
  - How do these different bodies conceptualise the professionality of Early Years teachers?
  - How are these conceptualisations related and what has influenced them?
  - How can reflexivity be advocated in Early Years teachers' practice?

As the Foundation Stage is introduced next September in England, similar transitions are occurring in Finland. In England the QCA is publishing curriculum guidance, whilst in Finland regional groups of Early Years teachers are networking together to consider this crucial period of Early Childhood. We will be observing these different approaches with great interest.

References

Biott, C. and Nias, J. (eds), (1992), 'Working and learning together for change'. *DevelopingTeachers and Teaching Series*. Buckingham: Open University Press.

Borko, H. and Putnam, R.T. (1995), 'Expanding a teacher's knowledge base: a cognitive psychological perspective on professional development'. In Guskey, T.R. and Huberman, M. (eds), *Professional Development in Education: New Paradigms and Practices*. London: Teachers College Press.

Burgess-Macey, C. and Rose, J. (1997), 'Breaking through the barrier: professional development action research and the early years.' *Educational Action Research*, 5 (1), pp 55-70.

Connelly, M.F., Clandinin, J.D. and He, M.F. (1997), 'Teachers' personal practical knowledge on the professional knowledge landscape.' *Teaching and Teacher Education*. Vol 13, No 7, pp 665-674.

Elbaz F. (1982). In Russell, T. and Munby, H. (1992), *Teachers and Teaching: from classroom to reflection*. London: Falmer Press.

Epstein, D. and Johnson, R. (1998), *Schooling Sexualities*. Bucks: Open University Press.

Freeman, D. (1991), 'To make the tacit explicit: teacher education emerging discourse and conceptions of teaching.' *Teaching and Teacher Education 7*, pp 439-454.

Fullan, M.G. and Stiegelbauer, S. (1991), *The New Meaning of Educational Change*. London: Cassell.

Hoyle, E. (1975), 'Professionality, professionalism and control in teaching.' In Houghton, V., McHugh, R., and Morgan, C. (eds), *Management in Education 1*. London: Sage.

Keiny, S. (1994). Constructivism and teachers' professional development. *Teacher and Teacher Education 10* (2), 157-167.

Moriarty, V., Edmonds, S., Blatchford, P., and Martin, C., (1999), *Teaching young children: perceived satisfaction and stress*. Forthcoming publication.

National Board of Education (1998), *Curricular Development*. Website: www.edu.fi/e/oph/kehitt.html

Nias, J. (1987), *Seeing Anew: Teachers' Theories of Action*. Deakin: Deakin University Press.

Pennell, J.R. and Firestone, W.A. (1996), 'Changing Classroom Practice through Teacher Networks: Matching programme features with teacher characteristics and circumstances.' In *Teachers College Record*, Vol 98, No 1, Fall 1996. Columbia University, USA.

Pollard, A., Broadfoot, P., Croll, P., Osborn, M. and Abbott, D. (1994), *Changing English Primary Schools? The Impact of the Education Reform Act at Key Stage One*. London: Cassell.

Qualifications and Curriculum Authority (1999), *Review of Desirable Learning Outcomes,* Consultation Report, SMSR. Website: www.smsr.co.uk

Richardson, V. (1997), 'Constructivist teaching and teacher education: theory and practice'. In Richardson, V. (ed), *Constructivist Teacher Education: Building a World of New Understandings*. London: Falmer Press.

School Curriculum and Assessment Authority (1996), *Desirable Learning Outcomes for Childrens' Learning (DLO)*, London: HMSO.

Seidman, I. E. (1991), *Interviewing as Qualitative Research*. New York: Teachers College Press.

Siraj-Blatchford, I. (1993), 'Educational Research and Reform: some implications for the professional identity of early years teachers'. *British Journal of Educational Studies*, 41, (4), pp. 393-408.

Smyth, W.J. (1987), *A Rationale for Teachers' Critical Pedagogy: a handbook*. Geelong: Deakin University Press.

Wittrock, M. C. (ed) (1986), *Handbook of Research on Teacher Thinking*. New York: MacMillan, pp 257-292.

ICT to Optimise Didactic Management in Early Education

Ton Mooij

In early education children differ in a lot of respects. These differences may harm the development of 'deviating' pupils and increase didactic management problems of kindergarten teachers. It was therefore decided to develop software to try to help teachers and pupils. A first theoretical question concerns the didactic and management characteristics which should become part of this software. A second empirical question asks whether first experiences with a first prototype of the relevant software reveal the desired improvement in educational practice. The answer to the theoretical question is based upon research into innovation and improvement in early education. The information to answer the second question is given by qualitative research with a prototype of the software in two kindergarten classes. The conclusion is that the prototype already functions as a powerful tool to improve early education for both teachers and pupils, in particular for pupils at risk.

Information and Communication Technology (ICT) can play an important role in optimising education (Mooij, 1999a). For example, ICT may support a pupil's learning processes by accounting for initial competence or learning style, help the teacher in planning each pupil's learning progress and results, present clear didactic pictures of individual or small group progress, assist teacher and school staff in organising individual and social teaching processes, and generate evaluation indicators for policy decisions within and outside school (see also Pedersen, 1998).

However, compared to elementary and secondary education, ICT is hardly used in early education. Yet the differences between children in early education, and the corresponding management problems of a kindergarten teacher with a class of 25 or more children aged between four and seven, may be very large. In particular pupils whose development is different from most other pupils, are clearly at risk from the beginning in kindergarten onwards (Mooij, 1999b, 1999c). It therefore is worthwhile to develop software to try to help teachers and pupils in early education.

Two research questions need to be answered to present a clearer picture of the possibilities and effects of doing so. A first theoretical question concerns the relevance of specific courseware and didactic management characteristics in the improvement processes (see also Kynigos, 1998). What optimising didactic and management aspects and qualities of the instructional system should become part of software designed to support both teachers and pupils in early education? The second empirical question concentrates on implementation experiences and developmental effects of integrating a first software prototype into early educational practice. How is a first prototype implemented in early education and what are the first effects of introducing this potential ICT-support to teachers, pupils, and the school?

In this contribution I will successively answer both research questions. The answers will be oriented towards the designing and the first empirical results of software meant to optimise early education. This prototype has been developed in successive versions in classes in Dutch early education, that is for the kindergarten and for the first year of the elementary school for pupils aged four to about seven.

Theory

Pedagogical and didactic principles
At the beginning of kindergarten, differences in development between children may be large and a huge problem for the teacher already (Jewett, Tertell, King-Taylor, Parker, Tertell, & Orr, 1998). A mismatch between a child's actual or potential characteristics on the one hand, and the actual educational or didactic and instructional characteristics in kindergarten on the other, may create behavioural, emotional, social, and cognitive problems for a pupil (Walker, Kavanagh, Stiller, Golly, Severson, & Feil, 1998). At this early stage already, social and cognitive or other problems of marginal pupils in particular can become rather excessive. The social and pedagogical abilities of teachers to cope with such 'deviating' or 'difficult' pupils vary greatly. Some teachers or teams are managing quite nicely from social, pedagogical, and cognitive points of view (see also Kirschner, 1997), whereas other teachers or teams cannot get to grips with such pupils.

Given the actual differences between pupils, kindergarten teachers tend to have too few different sorts of play and learning materials (Mooij, 1999b, 1999c). Moreover, they usually cannot manage specific kinds of activities for certain pupils because the required materials are either not present or not ordered by significance or degree of difficulty. Also, teachers have too much to do with the other pupils or the whole group simultaneously, which also is a matter of management (cf. Skinner, Bryant, Coffman, & Campbell, 1998). It seems to be necessary to tackle the root of the didactic 'mismatch' problem between educational system offerings on the one hand, and pupil requirements on the other. This is necessary to prevent disruptive behaviour in class and more serious behavioural, social, cognitive, and motivational problems later on.

Moreover, from pedagogical and educational points of view, environmental circumstances should be designed as optimally as possible for every child. On a child's entrance of early education both the content and structure of education, and its interactions with and effects on characteristics of the pupil, should support the pupil's development. At the beginning of early education, parents and teachers should therefore inform each other as accurately and simply as possible about relevant entry behaviour of a child (see the procedures investigated by Mooij and Smeets (1997) and Walker et al. (1998)). Relevant behaviour and differences in developmental functioning of the pupils can then be used as basics to part of the play and didactic learning characteristics in class (Pellegrini & Boyd, 1993). The variation between developmental levels of the play and didactic characteristics should correspond to the diversity in entrance behaviour or characteristics between the pupils, which is a main principle in the pedagogy and psychology of 'pupil-based education' (Mooij, 1999a).

In pupil-based education, both free play and so-called 'instructional lines' can support the stimulation and integration of a child. An instructional line denotes a hierarchical arrangement of educational concepts and sub-concepts corresponding with specific play or curricular and instructional materials. For example, sensory motor development for 4 - 6 year-olds generally starts with global movement with the whole body, followed by movement with the arms and hands, and then by paying attention to writing conditions e.g., direction in moving, training of regularity in movement with hands and fingers, and motor exercises evolving into preliminary writing.

Furthermore, quality indicators need to be integrated in the instructional lines to diagnose and evaluate educational processes and their outcomes on every pupil, from the beginning in kindergarten onwards. Therefore, adequate screening and logging of beginning characteristics is also required. Continuous monitoring, quality control and improvement are very important, in particular for pupils at risk from a very early age. The role of ICT in optimising early education then becomes essential with respect to the educational system on the one hand, and concerning the support of each pupil's development on the other.

Educational system support by ICT
While free play remains a pedagogical necessity in early education, ICT can support curricular and didactic management processes in the following ways (cf. also Linnakylä, 1999; Schofield, 1997):
 — *curriculum structuring in instructional lines* of the most important play and developmental or learning activities and materials, and their functional or instructional and didactic characteristics or activities;
 — *integration of diagnostic and progress indicators* by specific play and developmental or learning activities or materials in the instructional lines. The goal is to screen or check each pupil's initial competence level, to measure and evaluate progress in both individual and group or age normed ways, and to relate progress scores or outcomes as indicators to specific support activi-

ties or lines for one or more conspicuous pupils or pupils at risk, if appropriate;
- *regular planning and logging* of developmental or learning activities and materials to be carried out by a pupil, a small group of pupils, a class of pupils,
or more pupils;
- *specific planning and logging* of developmental or learning activities and materials, if necessary supplied by external specialists, to support one or more
conspicuous pupils or pupils at risk, from the beginning of early education;
- *continuous monitoring and evaluation* of each pupil's development and achievement in the different instructional lines, which can be grouped also to the
level of a class, comparable classes, or the whole school.

Pupil development support by ICT
From the pupil point of view, from the beginning in early education each pupil
could be helped by software in the following aspects:
- *competence-based playing and working,* alone or in small groups, can be carried
out on more adequate levels of competence, individually or socially, with
didactically more fitting learning styles, more independently and more continuously, in didactically more controlled ways;
- *positive development and learning processes* and effects can be stimulated and
motivated by competence-based development or learning processes and
effects on e.g., social, motor, and cognitive behaviour;
- *more self-responsibility* becomes possible for an individual pupil or for a small
group of pupils helping each other. Choosing and planning of personal
activities is better realised, within the limits planned and set by the teacher;
- *better distribution of teacher time:* a pupil who can function more in accordance
with the software saves teacher time. This means that the teacher can spend
relatively more time to the pupil or pupils who most need her or his pedagogical or didactic attention.

Method

Use-oriented design
A software program was designed according to the above didactic system and
pupil development characteristics (see Mooij, 1998). Different versions of the
computer program were developed in educational practice, in co-operation with
teachers (cf. Kensing, Simonsen, & Bødker, 1998). Teachers were involved to
secure validity of both improvement and implementation processes. From the
beginning, they were to act as change-agents and as users. Recent methodology

supports a strategy in which users, for example teachers and school staff, co-operate with researchers and other specialists during an exploratory period (cf. Cronbach, 1983; Linnakylä, 1999). Wilson (1999) expects that 'use-oriented' strategies '(...) increase the likelihood of successful implementation because they take the end use into account at the beginning design stages' (p. 13). This strategy results in two desired outcomes. First, it becomes clear which characteristics seem essential to optimise early education and, second, information is generated about how this improvement could be stimulated by developing, introducing, or using ICT facilities, i.e. computers.

This method of use-oriented design in practice closely parallels the strategy of Clark and Estes (1999). These authors speak about the necessary development of authentic educational technologies by collaboration between for example, practitioners, technologists, scientists, craftspeople, and artists. They illustrate a developmental cycle of a science-based technology beginning with descriptive and empirical research, followed by constructing generic technology, then by contextualising the technology which intends to stimulate real-world problems with this technology, which, in turn, generates other or new issues or questions for descriptive research, et cetera.

Didactic system procedures

The usual planning system in the kindergartens consisted of a differently coloured board on the wall. Each colour referred to a day of the week. Small groups of pupils, corresponding with certain table groups, were indicated by different logos and colours. Activities to be done by a small group were assigned by placing the tags of these pupils on a logo representing a certain kind of activity, on a certain day of the week. The computer program was designed to improve this didactic management system. Teachers can interact with the software to put in and order didactic materials and to assign different activities to pupils. Pupils can interact to get information about these assignments. Usually they can choose out of different activities, which are carried out as before without computer. More specifically, version 1.4 of the software can be described according to the didactic system and pupil management features described above.

Curriculum structuring in instructional lines. Instructional lines in the prototype are made up of different learning contents e.g., motor behaviour, social-emotional development, projects, language, (preliminary) arithmetic, (preliminary) reading, and (preliminary) writing. Each instructional line is characterised by a specific logo, a specific colour, and the corresponding text. Activities or tasks within each line are visually represented by a photograph of the object as present in class because four-year-olds must also be able to work with the program. The activities can be ordered by difficulty level. To stimulate pupils adequately, variations of the same lines refer to different developmental levels e.g., of pupils developing in a more or less normal or regular way, of pupils who need remedial activities, or of pupils who are advanced on the topic of the line. Depending on their rate of development or progress, pupils can change a line. A screen shot of the activities or tasks within a remedial variant, a regular or normal variant, and a fast variant within a motor line at the lowest level 1, is given in Figure 1.

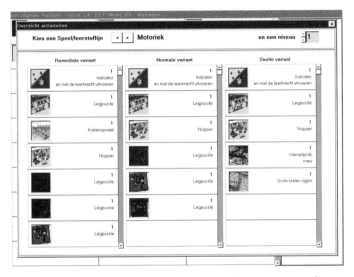

Figure 1 – Three didactic variants and materials within a sensory motor line

Integration of diagnostic and progress indicators. Within a line, specific activities can be assigned whether or not they belong to a remedial variant, a normal variant, or a fast variant. Moreover, an activity can be tagged with an indicator meaning that the pupil has to go to the teacher in order to go on. For example, this indicator may mean that a pupil's initial level of language has to be screened, as a basis to further support and placements. Also, a standardised diagnostic or achievement test can be included, in particular for measurement with a conspicuous pupil or a pupil at risk.

A pupil's progress is checked regularly by integrating diagnostic and normalised or standardised achievement tests, or parts of tests, in the instructional lines. The scores on these tests can be used as quality indicators of a pupil's school career which, checking for his or her entrance levels, express the rate of progress over the course of time. In these quality indicators the school's degree of support of the pupil's development may become visible. Construction of such progress measurements must of course occur on a sound methodological basis of reliability and validity (cf. Wegerif, Mercer, & Dawes, 1998).

Regular planning and logging. The teacher can change or extend the play or structured activities within a line, to improve the educational processes or to check their desired effects for one or more pupils. As illustrated in Figure 1, the teacher can also get detailed overviews or summaries of the lines included. Furthermore, the teacher can registrate pupils and teachers by integrating photographs of the pupils and the teachers involved in the relevant classes. Another facility is the automatic logging of activities done by each of the pupils working according to the software. Also, registration of each pupil's beginning characteristics is carried out conform to a statistically controlled procedure based on quantitative longitudinal research with 966 four-year-olds (Mooij & Smeets, 1997). An overview of the beginning characteristics of every pupil can be produced.

Specific planning and logging. Specific developmental or learning activities and materials, if necessary supplied by specialists, can be included in a certain instructional line to support, for example, only one conspicuous pupil or pupil at risk. This is relevant for a pupil who, compared to classmates, is developing much slower, or faster, on developmental areas of one or more of the instructional lines. A screen shot is shown in Figure 2.

Figure 2 – Assigning didactic specifics to a pupil

Figure 2 shows that a teacher can successively select a child (see the first program line with the photograph of the pupil), select a kind of instructional line (2), the actual difficulty level of this line (3), the variant of the line for the pupil (remedial, regular, fast, or some specific material: see 4), and finish by saving the changes made (5). The next time this boy accesses the computer software, his choices to play or work are determined by the teacher's planning and didactic decisions. The pupil's choices and consequent activities are thus regulated by the didactic management system. It should be noted that the pupil is not working on the computer to complete activities, though teachers can decide to include this possibility as one of the alternative instructional lines.

Continuous monitoring and evaluation. Each pupil's development and achievement in all relevant instructional lines can be monitored and printed. This means that the software assists the teacher in administrating and systemising the general and specific didactic information for the whole group of pupils. This information could be aggregated to the level of a class, comparable classes, or the school. The program thus functions as a planning, logging, monitoring, and evaluation system, to support the didactic and educational management for the teacher and the school as such. On the other hand, each pupil is helped by the software in the following ways.

Pupil management procedures
Competence-based playing and working. Kindergarten or elementary school activities can be carried out on different and adequate levels of competence, with fitting learning styles. This happens because the teacher assigns an instructional line, or specific line contents or tasks, in advance to every pupil separately, or to a small group of two or more pupils. As seen above, different kinds of colours and icons are used to make the software understandable for, and usable by, four-year-olds and older children.

Positive development and learning processes. Given the more adequate play and learning situations, it can be expected that motivation and next development or learning processes and effects are stimulated by using the software (cf. Mooij, 1999b, 1999c).

More self-responsibility. A pupil chooses, within the limits given before by the teacher, the lines or activities to work with. This is possible for an individual pupil or a small group of pupils helping each other, or collaborating with each other. A screen shot of the pupil's self-management is given in Figure 3.

After touching one's photograph with the cursor, a pupil is shown a screen as in Figure 3. The screen shows the photograph and the name of the pupil (to the top right hand corner). To the top left hand corner, the object or material the pupil is actually working with is being presented. The three pictures at the bottom of Figure 3 each illustrate one possibility: the pupil is ready and wants to stop his task (to the left), the pupil wants to select a new activity (in the middle), and the pupil has made a wrong choice and goes back one decision (to the right).

Better distribution of teacher time. The more pupils learn to use the software by themselves, or can be assisted in doing this by e.g., the help of parents or other pupils, the more the teacher can spend her or his time on the pupil or pupils who

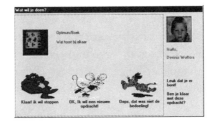

Figure 3 – Choice screen for the pupil's management

most need this pedagogical or didactic attention. Also, the more adequate the learning possibilities and learning styles do become in class.

Results

Development and implementation process

Implementation of the software was carried out in close co-operation with the teachers and school leadership. First, attention was focused on the potential and factual improvement of early educational practice as it was in kindergarten and elementary school.

Second, teachers first developed versions of instructional lines for specific pupils deviating from the other pupils (cf. Mooij, 1999b, 1999c).

Third, instructional lines were developed according to the information above. Ordering of didactic materials into instructional lines and supplying these materials with symbols (logo, colour, points) to make them understandable for young children, were very illuminating for the teachers from a didactic system point of view. The innovative work on didactic management required active commitment and professional co-operation between the teachers. They learned much from these activities.

Fourth, different versions of the software were successively developed and used in two classrooms to check their functioning in educational practice. In relation to this, the teachers had to get used to the idea that the software could support the regular planning as carried out by the handicraft information on the wall. In the same vein, the children were introduced to the possibilities of planning and working with the two systems.

First effects

The first experiences with the software can be used to clarify the assumed effects of the ICT-supported developmental processes in early education. First, stimulated by the use of the screening of pupils' beginning characteristics and the subsequent need to integrate the levels of initial competence into adequate instructional lines, the teachers discovered that their playing and learning activities and materials needed acute extension. In other terms, the variation between pupils in the beginning was much higher than was accounted for in the available activities and materials. A consequence was that a great deal of the school budgets in 1999 was spent on new playing and learning materials.

Second, teachers discovered didactically relevant relationships between the playing and learning activities of the pupils and the materials in school. According to the teachers, this enabled them to use the materials much better than before in promoting the functioning of the pupils.

Third, another consequence was that a teacher took much more time than before to instruct pupils who needed this instruction. This problem was reduced partly by including parents to assist in instructing pupils. More teacher assistance is needed, however. So this software accentuation of the usually assumed functions in kindergarten soon clarifies that there is far too much work for only one teacher in a class with 25 to 30 or more pupils. This is the most serious problem at the time. Fourth, some of the pupils of four, five, or six years old learned how to get along with the program very soon. They can assist other pupils too, if necessary.

Fifth, the pupils' self-management in these classroom activities was clearly stimulated, which enlarged the teacher's possibility to devote more time to the pupils who need this assistance most. Sixth, according to the teachers, in particular the pupils at risk could be helped by introducing this ICT-support. However, the teachers really need more assistance, or much fewer pupils in class, to get along with the time problem caused by this attention to pupils at risk.

Discussion

A pedagogical approach to improve early education with the aid of ICT was developed and tried out in educational practice. With respect to the usual play activities the pupils remain relatively free, but structured activities ordered into instructional lines are used to offer specific didactic contents and developmental support for each specific pupil, if desired. This 'pupil-based education' can be expressed in, for example, integration of information about the beginning level of the pupils, the progress in the course of time, and the kind of evaluation. This information is to be regulated by the teacher. Important indicators can be integrated also in the software by the teachers. For example, to regulate pupils' learning processes by using diagnostic or achievement tests, with respect to assignment or logging facilities, in the teacher's administration and monitoring, and in the school's overall administration and monitoring.

Usually, ICT is implemented in daily educational practice as it is (cf. Smeets, Mooij, Bamps, Bartolomé, Lowyck, Redmond, & Steffens, 1999). In the actual developmental research, however, early education is optimised before supporting it with ICT. The software prototype therefore contributes to essential didactic and curricular changes in optimising education for all pupils, in particular for pupils at risk. The main positive points of using this didactic management software can be summarised as follows.

First, the beginning characteristics of each pupil are discussed systematically by parents and teacher. If present, or assumed to be present, problems or risk characteristics can get systematic and preventive pedagogical attention, if necessary by inclusion of specialists outside school (Byrne, 1998; Mangione & Speth,

1998). This means that the factual co-operation between parents and kindergarten can increase considerably in comparison with present daily practice, at least in the Netherlands.

Second, next to the usual free play and whole group sessions, with respect to the most important developmental and learning areas each pupil can be given preventive, systematic, and continuous support on his or her own didactic levels of competency. This is already necessary in early education (see also Bennathan & Boxall, 1996; Byrne, 1998; Cooper & Ideus, 1996, 1998; Walker et al., 1998).

Third, the software allows a growth in the independence and self-responsibility of the pupils, which is also possible because the pupils themselves can assist each other in communicating with the computer. This advantage will increase when the pupils get older.

Fourth, immediate and controlled specific support is available for the pupils who need this.

Fifth, a more or less automatic, efficient, and general logging and monitoring of pupil and class or school results becomes available, which is not dependent on one teacher or a small group of teachers.

Sixth, more flexible organisation of developmental and learning processes becomes easy to realise, including more individual support and screening or testing. This, however, requires systematic innovation support in the developing kindergartens and schools. It seems that a lot of observation is done in kindergartens, but didactic or system consequences to provide adequate help to pupils are relatively rare.

Seventh, extending the software to higher classes in elementary or secondary education can be done without any problem.

Eighth, realisation of this software approach means factual operationalisation of e.g., giving equal opportunities to pupils from ethnic minorities, introducing quality standards in education, or increasing safety at school.

Ninth, in the long run, the frontiers between kindergarten and elementary education can disappear and be changed into continuous, progressive, developmental paths.

Tenth, because of its flexibility, the software seems to be basic to the further development of optimal education including ICT. Moreover, the software prototype acts like a supportive planning and didactic management change system for teacher, pupils, the school, and the parents alike. Therefore it is necessary to continue the developmental work using this kind of software in early education.

References

Bennathan, M., & Boxall, M. (1996). *Effective intervention in primary schools. Nurture groups.* London: David Fulton.

Byrne, B. (1998). *The foundation of literacy. The child's acquisition of the alphabetic principle.* Hove, United Kingdom: Psychology Press.

Clark, R. E., & Estes, F. (1999). The development of authentic educational technologies. *Educational Technology, 39*(2), 5-16.

Cooper, P., & Ideus, K. (Eds.) (1996). *Attention Deficit Hyperactivity Disorder. Educational, medical and cultural issues.* Charlton Court, United Kingdom: The Association of Workers for Children with Emotional and Behavioural Difficulties.

Cooper, P., & Ideus, K. (1998). *Attention Deficit / Hyperactivity Disorder. A practical guide for teachers.* London: David Fulton.

Cronbach, L. J. (1983). *Designing evaluations of educational and social programs.* San Francisco, CA: Jossey-Bass.

Jewett, J., Tertell, L., King-Taylor, M., Parker, D., Tertell, L., & Orr, M. (1998). Four early childhood teachers reflect on helping children with special needs make the transition to kindergarten. *The Elementary School Journal, 98*(4), 329-338.

Kensing, F., Simonsen, J., & Bødker, K. (1998). MUST: A method for participatory design. *Human-Computer Interaction, 13,* 167-198.

Kirschner, G. (1997). *Die Kinder stark machen. Aggressionsabbau durch Persönlichkeitsaufbau [Empowering children. Reduction of aggression by promotion of personality].* Lichtenau, Germany: AOL-Verlag.

Kynigos, C. (1998). *Perspectives in analysing classroom interaction data on collaborative computer-based mathematical projects.* Paper presented on the 'European Conference on Educational Research' (ECER), Ljubljana, Slovenia, 17-20 September 1998. Athens, Greece: University of Athens, Computer Technology Institute.

Linnakylä, P. (1999). *Collaboration and authenticity in technologically enriched and virtual learning environments.* Paper presented on the 'European Conference on Educational Research' (ECER), Lahti, Finland, 22-25 September 1999. Jyväskylä, Finland: University of Jyväskylä, Institute for Educational Research.

Mangione, P. K., & Speth, T. (1998). The transition to elementary school: A framework for creating early childhood continuity through home, school, and community partnerships. *The Elementary School Journal, 98*(4), 381-397.

Mooij, T. (1998). *Digitaal plan- en registratiesysteem (versie 1.4) [Digital planning and logging system (version 1.4)].* Nijmegen, the Netherlands: University of Nijmegen, ITS.

Mooij, T. (1999a). *Guidelines to Pedagogical Use of ICT in Education.* Paper presented on the eighth conference of the 'European Association for Research on Learning and Instruction' (EARLI). Göteborg, Sweden, 25-29 August 1999. Nijmegen, the Netherlands: University of Nijmegen, ITS.

Mooij, T. (1999b). Integrating gifted children into kindergarten by improving educational processes. *Gifted Child Quarterly, 43*(2), 63-74.

Mooij, T. (1999c). Preventing antisocial behaviour of young children at risk. *Risk Management: An International Journal, 1*(2), 49-61.

Mooij, T., & Smeets, E. (1997). *Beginkenmerken van leerlingen in de basisschool [Entry characteristics of pupils in kindergarten].* Nijmegen, the Netherlands: University of Nijmegen, ITS.

Pedersen, J. (1998). *Information Technology in the schools. A research survey.* Linköping, Sweden: Linköping University, Department of Education and Psychology, 1998. (http://www.skolver ket.se/cgi-bin/inframe.pl?c/it/cbcl.html).

Pellegrini, A. D., & Boyd, B. (1993). The role of play in early childhood development and education: issues in definition and function. In B. Spodek (Ed.), *Handbook of research on the education of young children* (pp. 105-121). New York: MacMillan.

Schofield, J. (1997). *Computers and classroom culture.* Cambridge: Cambridge University Press.

Skinner, D., Bryant, D., Coffman, J., & Campbell, F. (1998). Creating risk and promise children's and teachers' coconstructions in the cultural world of kindergarten. *The Elementary School Journal, 98*(4), 297-310.

Smeets, E., Mooij, T., Bamps, H., Bartolomé, A., Lowyck, J., Redmond, D., & Steffens, K. (1999). *The impact of Information and Communication Technology on the Teacher.* Nijmegen / Brussel: University of Nijmegen, Institute for Applied Social sciences / European Community, DG XXII.

Walker, H. M., Kavanagh, K., Stiller, B., Golly, A., Severson, H. H., & Feil, E. G. (1998). First step to success: An early intervention approach for preventing school antisocial behavior. *Journal of Emotional and Behavioral Disorders, 6*(2), 66-80.

Wegerif, R., Mercer, N., & Dawes, L. (1998). Software design to support discussion in the primary curriculum. *Journal of Computer Assisted Learning, 14,* 199-211.

Wilson, B. G. (1999). Adoption of learning technologies: Toward new frameworks for understanding the link between design and use. *Educational Technology, 39*(1), 12-16.

Change for the Better? The Impact of Baseline Assessment on Reception Class Teaching

Jane Stout, Peter Tymms & Linda Thompson

This paper reports a three-year longitudinal national survey of teachers of pupils in their first year at school (Reception teachers) in England. The project was designed to record changes in Reception teachers' priorities, practices and perception of their roles, in the light of the introduction and implementation of baseline assessment (BLA). Data were collected from questionnaires designed to discover the practices, views and opinions of 460 Reception teachers from three random samples covering 379 schools over the period 1997-99. The survey found considerable stability across the years but also revealed some interesting changes. Amongst these were: a tendency amongst teachers to think that pupils should be assessed for the first time at older ages; a lessening of the consensus that starting school at 4 is a good idea; a slight shift towards the view that teachers should 'nurture not teach' 4-year-olds and a decreasing tendency for teachers to recommend teaching as a profession to a close friend. The findings are discussed in relation to the momentous changes in the English education system and questions are raised about the nature and pace of change that Reception class teachers have experienced in recent years.

Pre-school education in the UK

In England the current debate in Early Years education centres around three issues: the school starting age, the curriculum and assessment arrangements. Recent political policy promoting parents' right to greater choice in the education of their children have impacted on Early Years education with many parents opting for formal education for their children soon after their fourth birthday. This practice differs from that of many other countries in Europe and where a clearer distinction is made between pre-school education (nursery or kindergarten) and formal schooling. It is also the case that formal schooling begins later at 5, 6 or even 7 years. In September 1998 schools in England were required by the 1997 Education Act to implement a baseline assessment. This has fuelled debate over whether present Reception class arrangements in England are serving the interests of the children.

Arrangements for the formal introduction of baseline assessment (BLA) into Reception classes in England are set out in the Education Act of 1997. The initiative, introduced by the Conservative party was implemented by the Labour Party when elected in May 1997. They declared that they 'want this to be the first form of assessment introduced on the basis of partnership with teachers, and not confrontation with them' (Lindsay and Desforges, 1998: 5). A unified national scheme was rejected with 91 schemes[1] (including Professional Monitoring Systems that had been running before BLA became statutory) accredited through the Qualifications and Curriculum Authority (QCA). Piloting of accredited schemes took place in schools from September 1997 and following evaluation and amendments, BLA became compulsory for mainstream Reception classes in September 1998.

Recent changes in the early years provision
The detailed curriculum and assessment arrangements of the 1988 Educational Reform Act have only recently made an impact on Reception classes. 'There is a certain inevitable logic about the fact that if there is a Key Stage assessment at 7 years, could or should there be one at entry to school?' (Wolfendale, 1993: 17). *Desirable Outcomes for Children's Learning on Entering Compulsory Education* (SCAA 1996a) specified a pre-school curriculum covering six themes: personal and social development, language and literacy, mathematics, knowledge and understanding of the world, physical development and creative development, leading to the National Curriculum Key Stage 1 (KS1). The links between *Desirable Outcomes* and KS1 of the National Curriculum are made clear in the White Paper *Excellence in Schools* (July 1997): 'The "outcomes" provide national standards for early years education ... and are designed to provide a robust first step towards the National Curriculum and we shall re-examine them at the same time as we review the National Curriculum' (quoted in Lindsay and Desforges, 1998: 4). Accredited BLAs have to ensure they cover the first three of the *Desirable Outcomes* themes.

Moves to formalise the Early Years curriculum coincided with the piloting and brief introduction of Nursery Vouchers in 1997. This initiative sought to extend nursery provision and increase parental choice. Schools were paid an incentive of £1,100 per pupil to admit four-year-olds to reception classes. The subsequent effect on play groups, nurseries and similar pre-school providers was dramatic and promoted widespread debate on a number of related issues, including: the aims and nature of pre-school provision; the most suitable age for starting formal education; and what constitutes an appropriate curriculum to cater for four-year-olds.

In a more radical move government asked advisors, as part of the curriculum review, to consider whether formal schooling should be delayed in line with practices elsewhere in Europe and whether ages 3-6 should be treated as a distinct phase in itself 'Key stage zero'? (Anning, 1995). *Desirable Outcomes* may be modified under the curriculum review, since many Early Years specialists feel they are over prescriptive and allow insufficient scope for play-based activities. More imminent changes include government plans for a fixed infant class size of no more than 30 pupils by September 2001. Commentators suggest that this could lead to an increase in mixed-age groups in Reception and other infant classes (Hackett and Pyke, 1998). The introduction of the Literacy hour from September 1998, and the Numeracy hour from September 1999, whilst 'optional' have increased the pace of change in Reception classes necessitating modification of existing curriculum plans.

The role of Baseline assessment

The roles and functions of BLAs are as diverse as the range of BLAs in existence. Wolfendale (1993) documents the use of baseline assessment from the 1970s when they were used to identify special needs. Most infant teachers have used a range of initial baseline assessment procedures (of varying degrees of sophistication), for formative, summative and lately evaluative assessments. Blatchford and Cline (1992: 249/250) summarise the purposes of BLA as:

- A basis for measuring future progress
- Getting a picture of the new intake
- Getting a profile of the new entrant
- Identifying children who may have difficulties in school

Wolfendale (1993:13) adds, 'an attempt to measure and estimate pre-school experience'. It is clear from these sources that BLA schemes serve a number of purposes although their uses are not always stated or transparent. The regulations governing BLAs in England are explicit about two purposes stating:

- BLAs should help the teacher in the classroom i.e. a formative role in helping to plan the curriculum.
- They should act as a basis for progress up to the end of KS1 (value-added).

BLAs can also serve in an evaluative role 'to provide information serving public accountability of schools and teachers for their successes and failures' (Lindsay and Desforges, 1998: 5). While this may never happen, there is a belief within government that parents should have attainment results and a measure of value-added by which to monitor the effectiveness of schooling. This would not be possible at KS1 without a form of baseline on entry to school. The current baseline assessment schemes include ones using informal teacher observations to well established Professional Monitoring Systems such as the Performance Indicators in Primary Schools (PIPS project) based at the Curriculum, Evaluation and Management Centre, University of Durham (Tymms 1999), which involves a series of tasks administered to individual children either using a booklet or CD ROM format. Time will tell whether all of the BLA schemes currently on offer can meet the two QCA aims referred to earlier.

'Many of the schemes are well meaning but lack a research base: what they think up to test may or may not predict later success or failure. I fear that in a few years' time, when some of these schemes are linked to KS1, we will find they have been poor indicators and the whole thing will be discredited. A lot of them will fall by the wayside,' (Tymms quoted in Parkin, *TES 11/9/98*).

A national project: monitoring the impact of BLA on reception class teachers' priorities and practice
The aim of the study is to record the impact of a new education policy on those implementing it, namely, the Reception class teachers. The project was carried out in three phases. Table 1 presents an overview of the three stages in this longitudinal project.

Phase of project	Timing	Reporting
Phase 1 *'Starting Points: A National survey of Reception Class Teachers' Priorities and Practice'*	June/July 1997 (prior to BLA piloting)	January 1998 ICSEI, Manchester
Phase 2 *'Plus ca Change'*	June/July 1998 (GEST funding for BLA piloting)[2]	The Third Warwick International Early Years Conference April 1999
Phase 3 *'Change for the Better? The impact of BLA on Reception class teaching'*	June/July 1999 (BLA now compulsory for all Reception classes)	This paper

Table 1 – An overview of the longitudinal study into the impact of BLA

Methodology
A national random sample of 300 schools was selected from the DfEE database in each year. Questionnaires were sent to the headteacher of each school with a request to pass them on to the Reception teacher(s). Estimates were made of the numbers of Reception class teachers before posting and schools were told that additional copies would be sent on request. Details of the responses are recorded below:

Phase of project	Number of responses	Number of schools	Response rate by school
Phase 1	177	137	46%
Phase 2	148	126	42%
Phase 3	135	116	39%

Table 2: Numbers of teachers and schools involved in the project

The vast majority of questions in each annual survey remained the same in each phase of the project; however feedback from respondents in Phase 1 prompted sections of the questionnaire to be modified for Phases 2 and 3.

The paper covering the findings from Phase 2 of the project examined relation-ships between variables[3]. It's title, 'Plus ca Change', indicates that despite many new initiatives impinging on the work of Reception teachers, there was a large degree of stability in the views and practices expressed. This paper focuses pri-marily on changes over time (1997-1999), making some reference to inter-rela-tionships that may be followed up in subsequent research.

Results of the survey

Composition of class: (1) Areas of stability
Reception classes varied in size from 3 to 44 pupils. On average, class sizes were close to 25 pupils across the three-year period. The composition of Reception classes showed little change over that time. The numbers of September starters remained similar averaging 20 children per year, as did the smaller numbers be-ginning school in January (mean 8) and at Easter (6). There was a small fall, from 24% to 21% in the number of mixed-year classes between 1998-9. Of the 28 mixed classes, 6 included pupils of Reception age, Year 1 and Year 2.

Mean numbers of bilingual staff, children for whom English is an additional lan-guage and children with a statement of Special Educational Needs also showed little variation over time. As in previous years there was a range of individual school circumstances, some teachers reporting up to 30 children in the class for whom English is an additional language and up to 15 children in another school were being considered for a statement of Special Educational Needs.

Composition of class (2) Areas of change
The number of teachers reporting that children started Reception class on a part-time basis had fallen from 67% in Phase 2 (1998) to 55% in Phase 3 (1999). This was a significant change ($p<.05$, ANOVA). The reasons for the change are not clear. Teachers could stagger the Reception starters over a few days and might prefer to adjust them to the new daily routine as quickly as possible. It might suggest that teachers feel that children can cope with starting full-time straight away, or it could be linked to the need to assess children formally within the first six weeks using a baseline assessment.

Adult:pupil ratios show a significant change over time ($p<.05$, ANOVA). The numbers of pupils per adult fell from a mean of 12.7 in 1997 to 11.9 in 1998, but rose to 13.7 by 1999. In practice, the range varied enormously from a minimum value of 1, for Reception children in a mixed-year class with several assistants to a maximum value of 33. The adult:pupil ratio is of necessity quite a crude meas-ure since the time spent by assistants varies considerably, as does their expertise, training and suitability for the task. Respondents in earlier phases pointed to the management role that has to be assumed by Reception teachers managing several assistants if effective use is to be made of their services. A third difference noted was that Phase 1 teachers reported that their schools had been inspected more recently that in the subsequent surveys. On average, inspections had taken place 19.7 months previously (1999).

Background of Reception teachers who responded
Teachers in all three phases were remarkably similar and no significant changes were found in their career profiles over the three surveys. They had been teaching for about 15 years on average, with 7 years experience of Reception class teaching. A full range of experience was represented in each phase, ranging from staff with over 35 years service, to newly qualified teachers. 37% said that they had been specifically trained to teach four-year-olds in 1999; a low figure given the numbers of these children in Reception classes who may well start on a full-time basis in September. The modal response in all years was that they were Infant-trained, followed by Junior-trained (up to 11 year-olds). In Phase 3 (1999) all teachers had received some in-service training relevant to their work in Reception classes. As in previous years the amount varied, some staff reported 15 sessions, with the mean number at 4.2 in the last year.

Baseline assessment (1) Impact of legislation
In 1997 some Reception teachers were not using any form of BLA. These were in the minority: 9% from Phase 1 and 17% in Phase 2. The remaining either used their own 'in-house' system or a purchased scheme. In Phase 2 (1998) 65% of respondents were in schools piloting some of the accredited schemes on offer. By Phase 3 (1999) it was statutory for all schools to use one of the 91 accredited schemes.

Baseline assessment (2) Areas of stability
In Phase 2 85% said they would be using the same baseline assessment the following year. This response had risen to 97% by 1999 and schools were clearly getting settled into one scheme. 'Plus ca Change' (Stout and Tymms, 1998) recorded that many teachers had chosen schemes for pragmatic, not necessarily educational reasons, some with a degree of coercion from their LEA.

Baseline assessment (3) Areas of change
There has been some change in who actually carries out the BLAs. Although there was not a statistically significant difference in the number of responses, a change is apparent. In Phase 1 (1997) 72% of all assessments were carried out by the reception class teacher. By Phase 2 (1998) this had dropped to 59%. This change is perhaps understandable during a pilot year given the unfamiliarity of

the procedures and the time-consuming nature of the task. Yet it removes a focus in the assessment procedure, since teachers not actually carrying out the assessment are deprived of contact with individual children and the opportunity to get to know them well. This appears to undermine some of the stated aims of baseline assessment referred to earlier. In 1999, 81% of teachers assessed all the children, yet still nearly 1 in 10 did not assess any of the children in their class. Someone else presumably carried out the task. There was a very significant change ($p<.0005$, ANOVA) in the number who reported being trained to carry out baseline procedures: 28% in 1997, 64% in 1998 and 76% in 1999. Almost a quarter were not trained. Other changes include the number of respondents reporting that feedback was sent to parents. This has changed significantly ($p<.0005$, one-way ANOVA) from 50% in Phase 2 (1998) to 82% in Phase 3 (1999). This is surprising given that feedback to parents was compulsory for the 1998-1999 assessments.

Links and records from pre-school
The number of feeder institutions remained similar in 1998 and 1999, as were the views concerning the quality of records received from them. In 1999 35% of records were reported to be either non-existent or poor, with a further 25% ranked 'OK'. *Desirable Outcomes* provides a linking curriculum between pre-school and formal schooling, so it is perhaps surprising that the findings suggest that records could be more informative.

Planning the curriculum
In Phase 2 a question was introduced to determine how much use was made of *Desirable Outcomes* and Key Stage 1 documentation when planning the curriculum. There were no significant changes in practice. In Phase 3 (1999) 77% used *Desirable Outcomes* either 'a lot' or 'entirely'. This represents a fall of 4% from the previous year. Key Stage 1 documentation was used 'a lot' by 54% and 'entirely' by 10%. Planning for Reception needs to be flexible and depends on the composition of the class, although responses for the two sets of documentation were inversely related as in Phase 2 ($r = -.28**$[4]) i.e. teachers tended to rely more on either one or the other.

Suggested age of first assessment
The answer to this question had shown a significant change over the three-year period ($p<.016$, one-way ANOVA). These results are shown in Diagram 1[5]. It is clear that the suggested age of first assessment is steadily rising towards 5 years. That is to say that an increasing number of Reception teachers now feel that the youngest Reception children are too young for baseline assessment. The possible explanations for this trend will be discussed later.

Views of assessment and teaching in the Reception year

Reception teachers were asked to indicate the extent to which they agreed with seven statements. The statements are reproduced below together with the means response from 1998 in parentheses. The five point scale ranged from 1 (Strongly disagree) to 5 (Strongly agree).

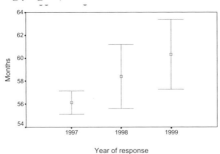

Year of response

Diagram 1 – Suggested age of first assessment

– Pupils aged 4 are too young to start school. (2.7)
– Reception classes provide an excellent learning environment for young children. (4.0)
– We need to assess pupils formally soon after they start school. (3.7)
– The job of teachers is to nurture – not teach – children aged 4. (2.8)
– There should be a national curriculum for the reception year. (2.8)
– In Reception we must adopt an holistic approach and develop the whole child. (4.6)
– Teachers should observe their pupils carefully in Reception so that they can build on their stage of development. (4.7)

Five individual statements were found to show significant shifts of opinion over the three-year period. More respondents now feel that 4 years is too young for school (p<.001, NOVA). Diagram 2 displays how the mean response has shifted.

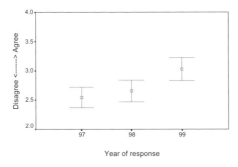

Year of response

Diagram 2 – Pupils aged 4 are too young fo school

Fewer teachers now feel there should be formal assessment so soon after school entry (p<.05, ANOVA) Diagram 3.

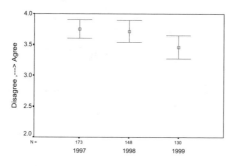

Diagram 3 – Need formal assessment soon after entry

More teachers now feel that their role is to nurture rather than teach (p<.01, ANOVA, Diagram 4).

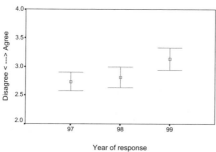

Diagram 4 – Nurture – not teach – children aged 4

Diagram 5 presents the same data in a different form. The dichotomy of views now becomes more apparent (very few selected the 'not sure' option). This distribution was not seen in the responses to other statements

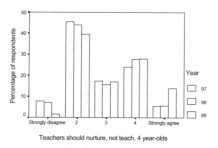

Diagram 5 – Nurture or teach four-year-olds?

Finally, a National Curriculum for Reception was seen more favourably (p<.05, ANOVA). Diagram 6.

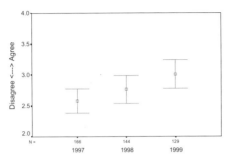

Diagram 6 – National Currriculum for Reception

Teachers' perceptions of an appropriate curriculum
In this section teachers were asked to rank order the importance they attached to seven aspects of the curriculum: teaching rhyme, letter recognition, listening to children talk, teaching number concepts, constructive play, physical activity and encouraging memory skills. In all three phases the vast majority of Reception teachers saw them all as important and no statistically significant changes in opinions over time were found. Nevertheless between 1997 and 1999 the views regarding letter recognition and teaching number concepts diminished in strength from 'Strongly agree' to 'Agree'. A further important shift of perception was seen from the increase in respondents who recorded 'Strong agreement' for responses about the importance of play.

Knowledge of Reception pupils
In this section of the questionnaire five statements were combined into a 'Knowledge scale'. The scale was internally consistent (alpha = .74) and is well represented by the two statements (mean scores from 1998 in parentheses):
   – I know the strengths and weaknesses of my pupils very well. (4.5)
   – I have successfully monitored the progress made by the pupils throughout the year. (4.1)
In all three years the teachers were very confident about their knowledge of the children: mean 3.91 on a scale of 1-5. None of the 5 components showed statistically significant variations over time, although there was evidence of stronger agreement over knowing the class well enough to plan the curriculum and being more confident about identifying children with Special Educational Needs. Over three-quarters of respondents felt that they had successfully monitored the progress made by pupils, but they felt less confident about whether they had been able to meet all children's individual learning needs over the year.

Aims during the Reception year

The respondents were asked to rank order 6 'main aims in reception'. They all involved encouraging or teaching pupils something. The rank order of the six aims remained constant in each year of the project as shown in Diagram 7.

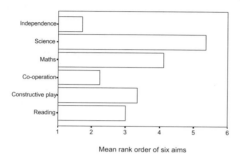

Mean rank order of six aims

Diagram 7 – Mean rank of aims across 3 phases

Social skills (independence and co-operation) were consistently rated highly but a cross-tabulation reveals that the percentage of respondents putting independence first has changed over time, from about 65% in 1997 to 54% in 1999. This was statistically significant (p<.009). Table 3 records the percentage of respondents putting Maths and Reading in their top three ranks.

	Phase 1 (1997)	Phase 2 (1998)	Phase 3 (1999)
Maths ranked 1-3 (%)	20.6	25.7	25.3
English ranked 1-3 (%)	57.5	57.7	52.6

Table 3 – Ranking of English and maths

Maths seems to figure more highly amongst these aims over time, whilst the opposite has happened to English.

Opinions about baseline assessment

Six pairs of contrasting semantic differentials were used and the respondents' answers were given a score from one to ten. Following the reversal of appropriate items an internally consistent ten-point scale (alpha = .89) was created. The items, together with mean responses from 1998 are shown in table 4.

Analysis of Variance indicated that five of the pairs had shown a significant change in response over time, as had the overall scale. On a ten-point scale[6] ranging from negative to positive the results for each year are recorded in table 5.

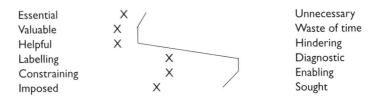

Essential	X	Unnecessary
Valuable	X	Waste of time
Helpful	X	Hindering
Labelling	X	Diagnostic
Constraining	X	Enabling
Imposed	X	Sought

Table 4 – Attitudes to baseline assessment

	Mean value for assessment on entry scale
Phase 1 (1997)	6.9
Phase 2 (1998)	6.6
Phase 3 (1999)	6.1

Table 5: Changes in attitudes to BLA

It should be emphasised that in each year Reception teachers had a positive attitude towards assessing children on entry to school. However, it is also apparent
that there has been a drift over time to viewing the process in a less positive light.
Statistically the change in the scale over time was very significant (p<.0005
ANOVA). This trend was not expected. In new educational initiatives, practitioners' initial hostility or resistance may be modified in the light of experience. Putting
a new idea into practice may convince the sceptical that it is a worthwhile enterprise and their views may moderate over time. This does not yet seem to be the
case for baseline assessment. It may be that teachers grew more negative after
BLA become imposed. Some Reception teachers who welcomed the process and
the information gleaned, still felt pressured by the LEA over the choice of scheme.
It may also be that teachers' views about baseline assessment vary from scheme
to scheme, but there were not sufficient data to allow for that analysis.

Perceptions of work: remaining positive
Ten pairs of semantic differentials formed a strong 'stress' scale (alpha = .81).
Examples of three of the items with mean responses are shown below:

Relaxing	X	Stressful
Motivating	X	Depressing
In the right job	X	Desperate to leave

Table 6 – Examples of stress items

The overall mean value of 3.8 on the 'stress' scale (1 (low) – 10 (high)) pointed to positive attitudes about work despite all the recent changes affecting Early Years. There was little evidence of change over time and only one of the ten items showed a significant change (p<.04, one-way ANOVA). This was that 'enjoyment' had waned slightly. Just one of the factors comprising the scale had a value over 5 on the ten-point scale. This was for the pair of adjectives 'relaxing-stressful' that had a value close to 7.

In summary it can be reported that Reception teachers are positive about their work; generally feeling motivated; supported by colleagues and Head teachers; and feel that they are in the right job. Equally clear is that they find it stressful.

Positive perceptions by colleagues and parents
This section was introduced in Phase 2 (1998) and there were no differences a year later with Phase 3 teachers. Colleagues held Reception teachers in admiration, feeling they had a hard and difficult job to do. Parents were generally thought to be trusting, appreciative and relaxed and were not perceived as interfering.

Recruitment crisis ahead?
One question asked whether the Reception teachers would advise a close friend to take up teaching. This produced a mixture of responses in all three phases. In each year, the mean response was to the negative side of 'Not sure' on a five-point scale. Analysis of Variance shows that this has become more negative over time (Diagram 8) and that this is a significant change (p<.02).

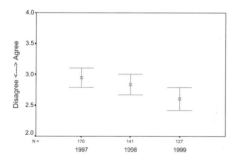

Diagram 8 – Advise a close friend to take up teaching

This trend coincides with a period of rapid change and adjustment for Reception teachers, with more uncertainty ahead. In every phase advising a close friend to take up teaching was negatively associated with stress (r = -.54) as shown on the scattergraph, Diagram 9.

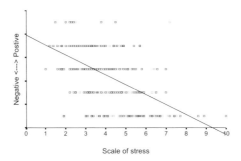

Diagram 9 – Advising a close friend to be a teacher & Stress

Summary of findings and discussion

The project has covered the practices, views and opinions of 460 Reception teachers from three random samples covering 379 geographically diverse schools over a three-year period. The schools range from small rural schools where children enter mixed-year Reception classes, to large urban schools with a number of parallel Reception classes. Some schools have sophisticated, yet varied arrangements as part of Early Years Units. Grouping arrangements for classes range from those that split the September intake by age, to schools where the cohort is divided using other criteria. Despite this, the composition of classes with Reception-aged children has remained relatively stable over the 3 years of the project. Class sizes averaged close to 25 children, but there is wide variation. Larger numbers of children start school in September, but there are areas of the country that continue with admissions at January and/or Easter. The numbers of bilingual assistants, working with children for whom English is an additional language and children being considered for a Statement of Special Needs, showed no variation over the project.

There were a number of statistically significant changes in Reception class composition over the three years.

- The numbers of children starting part-time had fallen in Phase 3.
- The adult/pupil ratios rose i.e. there were fewer adults per pupil.
- Children increasingly started full-time schooling in September.

The Reception teachers have a variety of professional training and preparation. Teaching experience ranged from the newly qualified to those approaching retirement. On average staff have 7 years' service in Reception. Whilst the modal response was that they were trained for infant teaching, a high proportion received no specific training for teaching four-year-olds. An encouraging sign was that the amount of training relevant to their work as Reception teachers continued to rise.

By Phase 3, the final stage of the project, all respondents reported receiving some in-service training.

We can report that the statutory requirement of baseline assessment has of course made an impact. A minority of schools used no form of baseline assessment in Phases 1 and 2, but by Phase 3, all schools were using one of the 91 accredited schemes. A large proportion of teachers in Phases 2 and 3 piloted baseline schemes. In Phase 3 97% declared that they would be using the same baseline assessment in September 1999. The number of teachers assessing all the children in the class themselves has risen in Phase 3, after a fall in the year when piloting took place (Phase 2).

There remain two areas of concern. One is the sizeable proportion of teachers who reported that they have received no training for conducting baseline assessment. The second is that it seems that the statutory requirement to inform parents of the results of baseline assessment is still not being followed by about a fifth of respondents in 1999.

The scale covering knowledge of Reception pupils is positive in all three phases. Over 75% of teachers feel they had successfully monitored the progress made by pupils. There was, in 1999, stronger agreement that the teachers knew the class well enough to plan the curriculum and more were confident about identifying children with Special Needs. This could be due to the benefits of statutory baseline assessment.

The *Desirable Outcomes* documentation is used extensively for planning, as was the KS1 material. However, there had been little change in the importance placed on teaching specific aspects of the curriculum or to the rank order of the educational aims in Reception classes.

It has already been noted that there were many areas of stability, but in many ways it is the changes in the attitudes and views of Reception class teachers that are of greatest interest. The main changes were:

- The suggested age of first assessment had risen over the three successive phases to a mean of 60.3 months. This is particularly relevant given that children of 48 months (4 years old) are being tested using a baseline assessment during the first few weeks in Reception class.
- Despite the last point the clear majority of Reception teachers thought that there was a "need for formal assessment soon after entry". However, the proportion expressing this view decreased in 1999.
- Views about assessment on entry were positive but became less positive. This seems puzzling at first sight since the surveys indicated that more than 90% were using some form of baseline assessment prior to its statutory requirement.
- Over the three years there was an increase in those who felt Reception teachers should 'nurture not teach' but they were still in the minority.

– Although a clear majority of respondents felt that Reception classes provided excellent learning environments for young children an increased proportion of respondents (35%) in Phase 3 were either unsure or felt otherwise.
– Amidst the current debate on their role, Reception teachers remain very
  positive about their work. The 'enjoyment' factor in teaching decreased
  only slightly over time, whilst the stressful element of the work was emphasised in all three phases. In the short term, Reception teachers seem to
  be taking new initiatives in their stride. However, fewer are recommending
  the profession with enthusiasm to their friends. This should be a matter for
  policy-makers since it impacts on the profession in the longer-term.

England has been the professional test-bed for a series of innovations, many of
which have involved the education of 4-year-olds. Ofsted inspection, literacy and
numeracy initiatives, statutory BLA, *Desirable Outcomes* and the Nursery Voucher
scheme have all had a direct impact on Reception classes, their teachers and the
children educated there. Accompanying these changes and perhaps being caused
by some of them has been a tendency for more and more children to start school
in September, when they are just 4 years old. There has also been extensive discussion in the press, television, journals and government about the arrangements
and education provision for children in their early years.

   Given these momentous events it would be unwise to single out individual
issues as being the cause of the changing views of Reception class teachers. However, it would seem probable that the decreased enjoyment and the negative advice that they would give to prospective teachers are likely to have their roots in a
combination of changes. The burden carried by Reception teachers as part of
their professional responsibility is enormous and they additionally find themselves subject to threatening Ofsted inspections as well as political talk of failing
teachers and failing schools. They can also read their work with four-year-olds in
schools being attacked by early years 'specialists', whilst simultaneously being pres-
surised by others to tackle numeracy and literacy. Little wonder, then, that they
feel chastened.

   But why should they be less positive about BLA when it has been part of
Reception class practice for so long? Perhaps its imposition has shifted attitudes.
Perhaps the nature of some of the schemes caused a reaction. Perhaps the wider
uses of baseline data had been of concern. Perhaps the reality of compulsory
baseline assessment has not matched the vision. Perhaps the national debate in
England about Early Years education has had an impact. Again it is not possible
to identify a single cause, but the formal requirement to carry out BLA has certainly increased the workload of teachers using some schemes. It also puts data
into the hands of those who can use it to bring pressure to bear on teachers.

There is a move towards payment by results. A baseline assessment could conceivably form part of a general scheme to do just that. Perhaps it is these factors that have dented the very positive view of baseline assessment held by Reception teachers.

Finally, there is the general shift of views towards nurturing and play and away from reading, assessment and school for 4-year-olds. This shift must not be overstated but the general drift is clear and the best guess is that it has come about as a result of the national debate. Amongst the many contributions the TV program 'Panorama' might well have had an important influence with its very aggressive condemnation of four-year-olds starting school.

When this three-year study was started it was felt that it would be useful to track teachers views over a period of time when an assessment was being made compulsory. It was hoped that we would be able to say something firm at the end of the study about the impact of statutory testing itself. In the event there have been so many concurrent changes on the national scene that any pure interpretation has not been possible. Nevertheless, an interesting picture has emerged. The most worrying of all the findings is the growing tendency for teachers not to advise others to become teachers. The educational system is dependent on a steady stream of high quality professionals being recruited to the system and anything that detracts from that is problematic.

The introduction of compulsory assessment was associated with a very positive perception of the assessment that has gradually shifted towards the negative during the years of its changing status. BLA has started to move away from its enviable position as an enthusiastically embraced professional feature of the Reception class.

Acknowledgements

All three phases of this project have been supported by Durham University Research and Initiatives Committee to whom we express our thanks. We should also like to thank all the busy Reception class teachers who provided us with these data. Thanks are also due to Professor Sheila Wolfendale who provided invaluable advice throughout the project.

References

Anning, A. (1995) *The Key Stage Zero Curriculum. A response to the SCAA draft proposals on pre-school education* Association of Teachers and Lecturers: London.

Blatchford, P. and Cline, T. (1992) Baseline assessment for school entrants. *Research Papers in Education.* Volume 7, number 3.

Hackett, G. and Pyke, P. (1998) In trouble over class sizes in *The Times Educational Supplement* 3/4/1998.

Lindsay, G. and Desforges, M. (1998) *Baseline Assessment. Practice, Problems and Possibilities*. David Fulton, London.

Parkin, J. (1998) Credibility on the line in *The Times Educational Supplement* 11/9/1998 pp.14-15.

Thompson, L. Stout, J. and Tymms, P. (1998) *Starting Points: A National Survey of Reception Class Teachers' Priorities and Practice*. Paper presented at the 11th International Congress for School Effectiveness and Improvement, Manchester. January 1998.

Stout, J., Tymms, P. and Thompson, L. (1998) *Reception class teachers: their aims, views and stories*. Paper presented at the European Conference on Educational Research, Ljubljana, Slovenia. September 1998.

Stout, J. and Tymms, P. (1999) *Plus ca Change?* A National Survey of Reception Class Teachers' Priorities and Practice. Paper presented at the 3rd Warwick International Early Years Conference. April 1999.

Tymms, P. (1999) *Baseline Assessment and Monitoring in Primary Schools* London: David Fulton Publishers.

Williams, E. (1998) 'All for one and one for all' in *The Times Educational Supplement* 'Primary' 27/11/1998 pp. 8-10.

Wolfendale, S. (1993) *Baseline Assessment: a review of current practice, issues and strategies for effective implementation*. An OMEP (UK) Report. Trentham books.

Notes

[1] The 91 schemes fall into three categories:
1. Open BLA schemes (will accept any school which wishes to use its scheme)
2. Semi-restricted schemes (which do not do the data collection and analysis for schools outside the area)
3. Restricted/closed schemes (only for schools within certain LEAs) (QCA, March 1998).

[2] Grants for Education Support and Training (GEST) money provided £8.5 million for the financial year 1997-8 to support the introduction of BLA (Lindsay and Desforges, 1998: 11).

[3] 'Plus ca Change?' (Stout and Tymms, 1999). Paper presented at The Third Warwick International Early Years Conference, April 1999.

[4] ** $p < .001$

[5] In this and other similar diagrams the mean response is shown together with the 95% Confidence Intervals

[6] The scores had been aligned from all items so that higher numbers corresponded to more positive attitudes towards baseline assessment.

Collaboration and Authenticity in Technologically Enriched and Virtual Learning Contexts

Pirjo Linnakylä, Marja Kankaanranta & Maarit Arvaja

The article discusses the theoretical views and empirical findings of the research project CATO (Collaboration and authenticity in technologically enriched and virtual learning contexts) which promotes integration of information technology in open, authentic and collaborative learning contexts to enhance the quality of learning and teaching through understanding changing instructional ecology and relations between individuals, artefacts and social groups. The study has a strong educational and computer science orientation. It assumes that learning is enriched by information technology; it is responsive to changes in the knowledge production in the society; it is based on a constructivist view of learning, mediated by collaboration, and anchored in authentic activities and technology-supported or virtual learning environments.

Society of knowledge and learning

The development of information and communication technology has changed the nature of knowledge, work and learning. Knowledge and learning have become the key factors both with regard to the quality of life of individuals and to the productivity and competitiveness of society at large. While knowledge and information are now increasingly attributed with the aspects of networking, interaction and multimedia, these aspects have also made information more accessible and diverse as well as enhanced its unrestricted flow and versatile use. Growing demands on knowledge and competencies have challenged the educational researchers to study learning and particularly open learning environments to understand changing relations between individuals, artefacts and various social groups.

Knowledge is no longer regarded as something scientifically proven and bound to certain academic disciplines, or as universal and hierarchical, but as contextual serving various needs and users. In information networks like Internet, data, knowledge and argumentation are transferred side by side. No technological applications can recognise the value of the pieces of information; that is left to the user to decide. Searching, selecting, refining and applying appropriate information in a critical fashion must be learnt and studied in earnest. This sets growing demands on knowledge, skills and competencies while learning must be extended to personal consideration of the reliability, truthfulness and value of information. The information found in networks can be valid and scientifically tested, but it may be mere trading, advertising, commerce or even outright cheating. The open nature and unrestricted flood of information tend to bring us faced with issues of ethics and morals. The openness of information networks - in good and in evil, in right and wrong, in truth and untruth - make it necessary for every user to select and validate the knowledge and experiences for their own part (Queau 1995). What sort of information are we entitled to distribute and produce, by what means and in what intention? Meaningful entities can be constructed only through human mind and shared understanding, and thus facilitate problem solving in everyday life.

Increased information, in itself, does not make things easier to control; rather it tends to result in increased uncertainty, which can be taken under control only through promptly facing, analysing and solving the problems arisen. Solving of complex, ill-defined problems is indeed becoming a key factor for managing the changes (Eteläpelto 1998). Ill-definable problems are to be encountered by both formal and informal, theoretical and practical tacit knowledge, which have to be picked up from various disciplines, practices and borderlines, and which are often facilitated by technological tools and guided by individual or joint goals and dreams. The users then boldly select, combine and utilise these elements, in order to solve problems and reach beyond the boundaries of traditional competencies (Stehr 1994).

Information technology and networks, in particular, open up new channels for broadening the range of opportunities for individuals' active participation and collaboration as well. They also promote new ways of communication, while offering flexible channels for informing and interacting both at work and in schools. As work and studying is becoming more independent of time and place, new ways of collaboration and related supporting information systems are being developed. New means of competition are founded on the mastery of modern technologies, innovative competence, and above all, on swift and extensive learning. The notions of lifelong learning and breaking the limits of one's own capacity have become essential strategies in life politics both for individuals and for communities.

Along with information and communication technology, the nature of expertise and its development has changed drastically. The concept of expertise, which used to be based narrowly on highly specified skills and knowledge, has now become broader, involving various disciplines and fields of knowledge and emphasising co-operation and social skills. It is now seen as a process of solving real-life problems. In this process, expertise is shared as widely as possible among the community of users, employing information networks and other channels and the forms of written texts and multimedia. Expertise does not reside in the expert systems of information networks but rather in their user communities, who contribute to the construction of knowledge and skills, and at best, work for common goals and benefit, sharing their own expertise wisely and sincerely (Lehtinen & Palonen 1997). The concept of expertise also includes broad-based management of the processes and contexts of operation as well as understanding of the demands of various interest groups and the functions of co-operation. The essential elements in this context include continuous learning, breaking own limits, as well as knowing the needs and goals of the various constituencies (Eteläpelto 1998).

Growing demands in learning and teaching

'Imagine schools in which students work on extended projects, discuss complex problems, and generally think their way through a demanding curriculum aimed at the kinds of knowledge and skills they will need as citizens and workers of the future.' (Simmons & Resnick 1993.)

Schools and their opening learning environments can be seen as expert organisations of learning (Bereiter & Scardamalia 1993). At its best, studying and learning involves authentic, i.e. topical and relevant, problems and their solving, which derive from the learners' own questions and interests. Problem solving calls for searching and interpretation of various and diverse information within the framework of collaboration. Studying is most efficient when taking place through inquiry and collaborative projects (Littleton & Häkkinen 1998; Häkkinen et al. 1998). Shared knowledge and enriching interaction in the community of learners play a key role in instruction. In open learning environments various information networks may serve as sources of information or as spaces for discussion, enhancing interaction and facilitating team work and co-operation both within a school as well as regionally, nationally, or even internationally (Järvelä & Häkkinen 1998; Linnakylä & Kankaanranta 1999). Learning is no longer tied with the time and place but virtual environments can be constructed in the networks to simulate real-life communities with various social relations and authentic problems.

The learning environments of information networks necessitate widening the concept of learning. The cognitive view is rendered narrow, as shared construction of knowledge is strongly mediated through social and affective processes (Häkkinen & Järvelä 1998; Häkkinen & Arvaja 1998). Learning is associated with experiencing, where the emotions, social relationships, and fascination of collaborative action play a significant role. Visualised information and the possibilities of virtual environments and worlds give students the opportunity to learn through exploration and experiment, placing them in contexts, in groups and situations that provide settings otherwise impossible to examine (Doyle & Hayes-Roth 1998). Exploring expedition through the human body may create a sense of exhilaration, which could be defined as an optimal experience (Csikszentmihalyi 1990).

The utilisation of information networks and virtual learning environments is not unproblematic, because the traditional learning practices tend to transfer to the new environments, as well. The short history of using information networks in instruction is connected with much of unsubstantiated confidence in the possibilities of technology in terms of reforming the mechanisms of learning. For example, many experiments with distance teaching have in the first place lead to quite traditional, teacher-directed methods (Sinko & Lehtinen 1999). In the long run, video lectures with their formally 'talking heads' have not been able to sustain the motivation of learners. This is true despite the fact that distance instruction would have an important function of their own, for instance, with regard to arranging education in outlying districts or in the teaching of more infrequent foreign languages.

On the other hand, open learning environments have been criticised also for the lack of guidance and for fruitless wandering in the name of spontaneous exploration and joy of discovery (Lehtinen 1997). Although large-scale meta-analyses have proven technology-assisted learning more effective than the traditional classroom teaching (Khaili & Shashaani 1994), learning has often remained superficial, disconnected and varied in quality (e.g. Admiraal et al. 1998). Learning at a deeper level is often impeded by the fact that many of the tools used in distance teaching are not 'cognitive tools'. Instead, they tend to yield most benefit to those students whose thinking and learning skills are already highly developed. While virtual environments have become more common, it is important to consider what kind of pedagogical, social and supportive practices would best enhance extensive and meaningful interaction and knowledge construction (Häkkinen 1999; Häkkinen et al. 1997; Järvelä & Häkkinen 1998). Collaborative learning in open learning environments presents a challenge also for the research of potentials and obstacles with regard to group dynamics, motivation and guidance.

Innovative methodology needs support besides from pedagogical research also from informed and enthusiastic teachers who master both the methodology and the underlying theoretical thinking (Sinko & Lehtinen 1998) and have the courage for open dialogue and for crossing the traditional limits of our school and education culture. Educators are challenged to transform schools into places where students encounter knowledge and build skills by engaging in authentic, problem-based inquiry. Learning in complex, challenging and authentic projects requires resourcefulness and planning by both the teacher and the students, access to various forms of knowledge, tools for collaboration and communication, and support for reflection and authentic assessment (Laffey et al. 1998). Teacher's role in problem-based projects is to model the thinking, aims, working culture and practices typical to experts, and to ensure that these are to be mediated to students' activity. In project work, this is best realised both by supporting students' knowledge construction process by encouraging inquiry and reasoning, and by guiding students to use scientific working methods, strategies and tools (Häkkinen et al. 1997, 1998; Häkkinen 1999).

Project- and problem-based learning does not automatically, of course, lead to deeper level communication, collaboration and knowledge construction. Research on mechanism and processes that support, advance or restrict creation of collaborative knowledge is needed in order to design pedagogically wise environments. Therefore, in the first phase of the study we have examined particularly for possibilities and restrictions of collaborative practices while working in the technology-supported environments. The results will be utilised in the second phase of the study where the aim is to create and investigate virtual environments and their support in high-level learning by the means of case studies and action research. The development of shared knowledge and culture in the virtual environment are to be explored and examined in this study. Especially we are interested in understanding how individuals' mental and developmental processes relate to social and situational factors that influence cognitive performance and learning.

Technologically enriched contexts and collaboration in learning

'Nec manus, nisi intellectus, sibi permissus, multam valent; instrumentis et auxilibus res perficitur.' (Francis Bacon, in Bruner 1996)

Well-integrated uses of technology in learning environment have highlighted some aspects of the constructivist definition of learning. Besides being defined as constructive, cumulative, intentional and self-regulated (De Corte 1993), learning is construed as an activity that takes place among individuals in specific contexts (e.g. Brown et al. 1989). This approach, known as situated or anchored, points out that learning cannot be easily separated from 'where and how it is learned and used'. Situated approaches to knowledge construction emphasise the need to construct learning environments that engage students in meaningful and purposeful activities (Vosniadou 1996). Context is seen integral to understanding; meaning arises from context and the context is an integral part of the meaning (Light & Butterworth 1992). In the virtual learning environment, the context is often seen to include also machines, programmes, communicative and cognitive tools as well as social and emotional processes communicated in shared learning spaces and contents of activities (see Lemke 1998). Technologies and the activities supported by them are viewed as constituent elements of an ecosocial learning environment (Bruce & Hogan 1998).

Following the studies by Vygotsky (1978), a number of researchers – both constructivists and activity theorists – agree that learning is not something that only individuals invent but an activity that has its roots in sociocultural interaction (e.g. Lave 1988; Nardi 1996). People construct knowledge socially, through collaboration and discussion. It is this social process that results in shared meaning and deeper understanding. The implication of this view is that it is important to design learning environments that facilitate social interaction and collaborative learning also in virtual learning environments. When collaborative aspects of learning were earlier seen as a background for an individual activity, the group itself and social interaction of the group has become the unit of learning and analysis which sets new challenges for the research methodology, as well.

Real collaboration seem to occur only if there is a reason and space for negotiation (Dillenbourg et al. 1995, Dillenbourg 1998). Collaboration can be inhibited in trivial tasks where is nothing to disagree upon or where the tasks are obvious and unambiguous which means that there is nothing to misunderstand or argue. Critical reasoning, challenging and counter-challenging other ideas with justifications and alternative hypotheses, is perceived to be important for deeper-level knowledge construction (Mercer 1996). Therefore the best ground for enriching collaboration is usually when participators have a cognitive conflict, they hold different points of view, they are able to share their knowledge and experiences and they are able to construct shared understanding (Häkkinen & Arvaja 1998). Unfortunately in the present learning culture, the problems are often prestructured and without conflicts to argue and to construct the shared deeper-level understanding (Häkkinen et. al. 1998, 1999; Arvaja & Häkkinen 1999).

In our studies on project-based small group interaction in technology enriched learning environments, high level collaboration, i.e. joint critical knowledge building, seemed to be crucially influenced by situational factors such as social relationships and group dynamics among students, the structure of learning tasks, motivational aspects and teachers' support. The results imply that successful collaboration can be promoted by proper group composition and utilisation of real group tasks. Since the lack of motivation and active interaction was one of the central problems in our previous studies (Arvaja et al., 1999), the upcoming study on project-based history learning will apply the role game to activate and motivate students to commit themselves to the group tasks. The students have themselves planned the role characters based on the literature.

At least in the field trial phase, the students have been very enthusiastic and eager to act out the motives of their role characters and to interact with others in the virtual FLE-environment. The networked interaction enabling anonymity makes it easier for the students to be in contact even with the fellow students from other schools. In this history project critical reasoning is supported in the knowledge-building module of the FLE. The module is constructed for supporting higher-level knowledge processing and shared critical reasoning, as well as for directing the students to present their own thoughts and conceptions. Also the learning tasks are designed to support joint critical reasoning, being real problem solving tasks in nature. They are planned so that the students need to take into consideration the role they are playing when discussing the matters. So, the fact that students have to assume different points of view is hoped to create real negotiation situations in authentic tasks (Arvaja 1999).

Promoting authenticity and collaboration through digital portfolios

In learning contexts the meaningful and purposeful activities are often defined authentic. Authentic activities then, are the ordinary practices of the culture (Brown et al. 1989, 34). Vygotsky's theory of human development (1978) suggests that if the aim of education is to provide children with the means of the culture, then they should have access to, and participate in, cultural activities and artefacts similar to those of real life. The artefacts should, however, be modelled according to the children's developmental level and motivational inclinations (Bellamy 1996; De Corte 1993). Characteristic of the authentic learning and assessment activities are the following: ownership by the learner, project- and problem-based activities, collaboration, access to tools and resources, flexible use of time and various environments and contexts for learning (Newman & Archbald 1992; Valencia et al. 1994).

The ordinary practices of the school culture can be made visible for example through digital portfolios. At schools, portfolios have proven to be a promising approach to authentic assessment because they make one's competence, learning and teaching visible and accordingly easier to reflect on and evaluate both by the authors themselves and by the interested others (e.g. Paulson et al. 1991; Linnakylä 1994; Kankaanranta 1998).

Some of the shortcomings of a traditional portfolio have turned out to be the problems with communication and access to information. The paper-based nature of portfolios has made it difficult to show the multiple forms of expertise. One of the worries is also the question of how to store and handle materials collected over several years of studying and working. Solutions for these problems have been searched by constructing, storing and sharing portfolios in the digital form by the means of information technology (e.g. Barrett 1998; Lankers 1998; Linnakylä & Kankaanranta 1999a; 1999b).

At best, a digital portfolio includes realistic and authentic samples illustrating the author's various competencies, their own criteria and goals, but also their actions as a member of the learning or working community. A significant feature of portfolio assessment is its dynamic nature, because the richest portraits of individual learning and teaching are based upon multiple sources of evidence collected over time in authentic settings (Barrett 1998). For example, digital teaching portfolios give possibilities to see areas of expertise, its organisation, teacher's education and philosophical thinking, usual learning and work tasks, collaboration and future envisioning.

In our studies (Kankaanranta & Linnakylä 1999) we have examined the possibilities of digital portfolios published on the web in the collaborative development of teacher and student expertise and in the assessment of teaching and learning. In the explorations of digital student and teacher portfolios we have found essential to emphasise following advantages offered by them in different areas:

- more diverse and enriched documentation and display of competencies by means of hypertext and visual media,
- portraying several aspects and connecting them though links to major collaborators as well as working, teaching and studying contexts,
- interactiveness, co-operation and sharing possibility through computer networks both within the expert community and beyond,
- forming a comprehensive and many-faceted picture of the expert and his development challenges for future,
- opportunity to demonstrate one's knowledge also in information technology as well as creativity and competency in design and
- potentiality for user-oriented sharing and evaluation of portfolios.

Digital portfolios open up the borders of educational fields to many directions locally, nationally and globally. It is most interesting to see the work samples and methods of one's fellow student and teachers in different cultures and work environments. Especially interesting is to compare the selection criteria for these samples as well as the reflections and self-assessments, which often reveal the cultural values relative to national or local education. Access to digital portfolios through computer networks provides an opportunity for feedback and discussion, for negotiation and problem solving among the authors and interested others.

In our action research project 'Collaboration of teachers through networking and digital school portfolios' the main aim is to strengthen collaboration between diverse educational environments and cultures by the means of information technology. Digital teacher and school portfolios and communication networks are used as methods for developing teacher expertise in the area of childhood education. The access to portfolios through networked computers offers possibilities for visibility, sharing and mutual feedback and for the collaborative communication of schools, teachers, children, parents and also teacher students (Kankaanranta 1998a; 1998b; 1999).

In the first phase of our study, it became obvious that a special challenge for the study comes from its action research nature, which encourages participants for continuous development of their own work (Kemmis 1994; Kankaanranta 1998). Teachers have felt encouraged to participation by their need of multilevel collaboration in order to develop qualitative teaching and learning in pre- and primary levels of education. The first phase also showed an enormous need for the teacher support in computer literacy and in the construction of digital portfolios. This is crucial before teachers can become self-confident passengers in the information highways and before they can collaboratively construct their own and their students' expertise in virtual groups and environments (Kankaanranta 1999).

Towards virtual learning environments

Recent research concerning open learning environments has been focused especially on the development of networked, often www-based environments and on the evaluation of their effectiveness in learning. Most learning environments used currently are founded on text-based, mainly asynchronous communication. The basic models of spaces for discussion, conferencing systems, and group work applications have provided the design also for learning environments intended for pedagogical purposes.

There is a special tradition evolved around research on social construction of knowledge in virtual environments. Characteristic to this research community, called CSCL (Computer-Supported Collaborative Learning), is that the research is strongly anchored to the mechanisms and processes associated with collaborative learning and construction of shared knowledge (Koschmann 1996). Research in this field has been recently extended also to various operational contexts of virtual reality (Dillenbourg et al. 1997). The metaphors used in these virtual realities have been borrowed from real-life surroundings and operational contexts such as universities, schools or firms, and the kind of facilities, equipment and operation culture pertinent to these settings. Virtual settings provide their users with various stimuli to support the actions, but leave also room for imagination and for the development of individual or collaborative activities. In order to strengthen the sense of collectivity in a community of learners, attempts are made to promote the user's awareness of the facility and other users. The virtual environments offer opportunities – similar to role-play games – for inviting the learners to participate in experiential activities. In addition, they provide tools for shared online communication and working in order to develop new settings and objects or, for example, to solve open-ended design problems by integrating CAD-utilities in the design environment.

Virtual realities also seek to create opportunities for participating in such activities, which otherwise would be difficult to reach. Many provide simulated analogues of real world experiences: users can visit online museums, galleries, theatres, foreign countries, mountains, oceans or space (Doyle & Hayes-Roth 1998). We can say that a major challenge with respect to these environments is that they should not be confined to offering entertainment but, in particular, ought to support the construction of broad and extensive understanding of the matters to be studied, as well as of their respective contexts. Like any other learning environments, also virtual settings used for this purpose call for careful design regarding the pedagogical models and instructional practices involved (Häkkinen 1999).

Apart from virtual realities, the CSCL research has been expanded to cover the world of possibilities, even unrealities. In the decentralised simulation environments, the students can explore the inside of human body or micro cosmos. A task could be, for instance, to solve complex problems of physics in a micro cosmos. Learning assignments constructed in a simulation environment are usually so complex and overwhelming that a student's possibilities to solve the problems alone are quite limited. Accordingly, the purpose of the environment is to support collaborative learning and especially sharing of the cognitive load between the team of the learners (Scanlon et al. 1997; Smith, 1999).

It is likely that the planning of future learning environments will soon be drawing on the possibilities offered by virtual reality technologies. At present, already, people are talking about illusionary reality, referring to a three-dimensional illusionary settings created by means of computers, where people can act and make observations while the environment reacts to their actions. Illusionary reality can offer meaningful and varied learning environments, where the learner can also go 'inside the pictures' and find him/herself contributing to a dynamic learning event. In the future it is quite possible that virtual settings will be broadening the range of natural human activities in a more and more concrete way, and that people can also construct increasingly interesting illusionary realities by themselves.

We must learn, however, to proportion these technology-driven illusions to our real-life experiences, as we have previously done with textual information. If illusionary images become a new way of writing and experiencing, this medium will not be mastered just by looking or watching but, as with any other medium, we must first learn to read, interpret, analyse and evaluate it critically. Failing to do this, we can get lost in the illusionary reality or be trapped by it. On the other hand, we may also be left standing aside, lacking the fascinating experiences, if we do not have the courage to enter these illusionary settings (Queau 1993). Virtual reality can suck us in, if we are not prepared for it, but when approached wisely it can clarify our views both on the truthfulness of knowledge and on our own reality.

Acknowledgement
This research has been supported by the Academy of Finland (grant no 37189).

References

Admiraal, W. F., Lockhorst, D., Wubbels, T., Korthagen, F. A. J. & Veen, W. 1998. Computer-mediated communication in teacher education: Computer conferencing and the supervision of student teachers. *Journal of Learning Environment Research*, 1(1), 59-74.

Arvaja, M. 1999. *Social processes and knowledge construction in a virtual learning environment of a school history project.* Paper presented in ECER 1999 in Lahti, Finland.

Arvaja, M. & Häkkinen, P. 1999. *Social processes and knowledge-building in project-based face-to-face interaction.* Manuscript.

Barrett, H. 1998. *Strategic questions. What to consider when planning for electronic portfolios. Learning&LeadingwithTechnology.* http://www.iste.org/L&L/Issues/Feature/Body.html.

Bellamy, R. K. E. 1996. Designing educational technology: computer-mediated change. In B. A. Nardi (Ed.) *Context and consciousness.* Cambridge, Mass: The MIT Press, 123-146.

Bereiter, C. & Scardamalia, M. 1993. *Surpassing ourselves. An inquiry into the nature and implications of expertise.* Chigago & La Salle: Open Court.

Bronfenbrenner, U. 1979. *The ecology of human development. Experiments by nature and design.* Harvard University Press.

Brown, J. S., Collins, A. & Duguid, P. 1989. Situated cognition and the culture of learning. *Educational Researcher,* 18(1), 32-42.

Bruce, B. C. & Hogan, M. P. 1998. In D. Reinkin, M. McKenna, L. Labbo & R. Kieffer (Eds.) *Handbook of literacy and technology. Transformations in a post-typographic world.* Mahwah: Lawrence Erlbaum, 269-281.

Bruner, J. 1996. *The culture of education.* Cambridge, Mass.: Harvard University Press.

Csikszentmihalyi, M. 1990. Flow: *The psychology of optimal experience.* New York: Harper & Row.

De Corte, E. 1993. Learning theory and instructional science. In P. Reiman & H. Spada (Eds.) *Learning in humans and machines: Towards an interdisciplinary learning science.*

Dillenbourg, P. 1998. Introduction: What do you mean by collaborative learning? In P. Dillenbourg (Ed.) *Collaborative learning: Cognitive and computational approaches.* Elsevier Science / Pergamon.

Dillenbourg, P., Baker, M., Blaye, A., & O'Malley, C. 1995. The evolution of research on collaborative learning. In H. Spada, & P. Reimann (Eds.), *Learning in Humans and Machines.* Pergamon, 189-211.

Dillenbourg, P., Montandon L. & Traum D. 1997. *Does text-based virtual space impact on collaboration?* Proceedings of the workshop on Collaborative learning/working support system with networking, 8th World Conference on Artificial Intelligence in Education. Kobe, Japan.

Doyle, P. & Hayes-Roth, B. 1998. Guided exploration of virtual worlds. In F. Sudweeks, M. McLaughlin & S. Rafaeli (Eds.) *Network & Netplay. Virtual groups on the Internet.* American Association for Artificial Intelligence, 243-263.

Eteläpelto, A. 1998. *The development of expertise in information systems design.* University of Jyväskylä, Department of Psychology. Doctoral dissertation.

Häkkinen, P. 1999. Collaborative learning in technology-supported environments – two cases of project-enhanced learning. *Journal of Education for Teaching.* In press.

Häkkinen, P., Eteläpelto, A. & Rasku-Puttonen, H. 1997. *Collaborative learning in technology-supported environments: Analysing and modelling interactive processes.* Paper presented at the 7th European Conference for Research on Learning and Instruction, Athens, 26.-30.8.1997.

Häkkinen, P. & Arvaja, M. 1998. Kollaboratiivinen oppiminen teknologiaympäristöissä. [Collaborative learning in technology-based environments] In A. Eteläpelto, & P. Tynjälä (Ed.). *Asiantuntijaksi oppiminen.* [Learning of expertise] WSOY. Manucript.

Häkkinen, P., Arvaja, M., Eteläpelto, A. & Rasku-Puttonen, H. 1999. *Project-based science learning in networked environment: Analyzing cognitive and social processes of collaborative learning.* Manuscript.

Häkkinen, P., Eteläpelto, A. & Rasku-Puttonen, H. 1998. *Project-based science learning in networked environment: Benefits and problems of collaborative learning.* Paper presented at the Annual meeting of the American Educational Research Association (AERA), San Diego, 13.-17.4.1998.

Häkkinen, P. & Järvelä, S. 1998. *Developing a method for analyzing multidimensional process data:* The *dynamics between students' cognitive strategies and motivational interpretations.* Paper presented at the Annual meeting of the American Educational Research Association (AERA), San Diego, 13.-17.1998.

Järvelä, S. & Häkkinen, P. 1998. *Web-based cases in teaching and learning: Reciprocal understanding and perspective taking in conversation.* Manuscript.

Kankaanranta, M. 1999. Portfolioita esi- ja alkuopetuksesta. Päiväkodin ja koulun yhteistoiminnan suuntia etsimässä. [Portfolios from pre- and primary education. Exploring collaboration between kindergarten and primary school.] In M. Kankaanranta, K. Mäkitalo & E. Tiihonen (Eds.) *Esi-ja alkuopetusta kehittämässä ja tutkimassa.* Jyväskylän yliopisto. Koulutuksen tutkimuslaitos.

Kankaanranta, M. 1998a. Towards digital bridges between educational cultures. In H. Jokinen & J. Rushton (Eds.) *Changing contexts of school development.* University of Jyväskylä. Institute for Educational Research, 65-75.

Kankaanranta, M. 1998b. Communication and collaboration of teachers through networking and digital portfolios. In H. Maurer & R. G. Olson (Ed.) *Proceedings of WebNet 98 – World Conference of the WWW, Internet & Intranet.* Orlando, Florida; November 7-12, 1998.

Kankaanranta, M. & Linnakylä, P. 1999. *Mapping collaboration and authenticity in digital portfolios.* Paper presented in CAL99 - Virtuality in education. London, The Institute of Education 28-31 March, 1999.

Kemmis, 1995. *RACGP action research project planning guide.* Stephen Kemmis Research & Consulting.

Khaili, A. & Shashaani, L. 1994. The effectiveness of computer applications: a meta-analysis. *Journal of Research on Computing in Education,* 27, 48-61.

Koschmann, T. 1996. Paradigm Shifts and Instructional Technology: An Introduction. In T. Koschmann (Ed.) *CSCL: Theory and Practice of an Emerging Paradigm.* Mahwah, NJ: Lawrence Erlbaum Associates.

Laffey, J., Tupper, T., Musser, D., & Wedman, J. 1998. A computer-mediated support system for project-based learning. *Educational Technology Research and Development,* 46(1), 73-86.

Lankers, A. M. 1998. *Portfolios: A new wave in assessment.* <http://www. thejournal.com/magazine/98/apr/498trends.asp>.

Lave, J. 1988. *Cognition in practice.* Cambridge: Cambridge University Press.

Lave, J. & Wenger, E. 1991. *Situated learning. Legitimate peripheral participation.* Cambridge: Cambridge University Press.

Lehtinen, E. 1997. Tietoyhteiskunnan haasteet ja mahdollisuudet oppimiselle. In E. Lehtinen (Ed.) *Verkkopedagogiikka.* Helsinki: Edita.

Lehtinen, E. & Palonen, T. 1997. *Asiantuntijaverkosto oppimisympäristönä –projektin loppuraportti.* Turun yliopiston täydennyskoulutuskeskus.

Lemke, J. 1998. Metamedia literacy: Transforming meanings and media. In D. Reinkin, M. McKenna, L. Labbo & R. Kieffer (Eds.) *Handbook of literacy and technology. Transformations in a post-typographic world.* Mahwah: Lawrence Erlbaum, 283-302.

Light, P. & Butterworth, G. 1992. *Context and cognition. Ways of learning and knowing.* New York: Harvester Wheatsheaf.

Linnakylä, P. 1994. Mikä ihmeen portfolio? Arvioinnin ja oppimisen liitto. [What on earth is a portfolio. Merging learning and assessment] In P. Linnakylä, P. Pollari & S. Takala (Eds.) *Portfolio arvioinnin ja oppimisen tukena.* Jyväskylän yliopisto. Kasvatustieteiden tutkimuslaitos, 9 - 31.

Linnakylä, P. & Kankaanranta, M. 1999a. Digitaaliset portfoliot asiantuntijuuden osoittamisessa ja jakamisessa. [Digital portfolios in expressing and sharing expertise] In A. Eteläpelto, & P. Tynjälä (Eds.), *Asiantuntijaksi oppiminen* [Learning of expertise]. WSOY.

Linnakylä, P. & Kankaanranta, M. 1999b. Tietoverkot opettajien pedagogisen asintuntijuuden kehittämisessä. [Networks in developing teacher's pedagogical expertise] In H. Heikkinen, P. Moilanen & P. Räihä (Eds.) *Opettajuuden tragiikka ja komiikka.* [Tragedy and and comedy of teacherhood] Jyväskylän yliopisto. Opettajankoulutuslaitoksen julkaisuja (University of Jyväskylä, Department of Teacher Education)

Littleton, K. & Häkkinen, P. 1998. Learning together: Understanding the processes of computer-based collaborative learning. In P. Dillenbourg (Ed.) *Collaborative learning: Cognitive and computational approaches.* Elsevier Science / Pergamon, 20-33.

Mercer, N. 1996. The quality of talk in children's collaborative activity in the classroom. *Learning and Instruction,* 6(4), 359-377.

Nardi, B. A. 1996. Activity theory and human-computer interaction. In B. A. Nardi (Ed.) *Context and consciousness.* Cambridge, Mass: The MIT Press, 7-16.

Newman, F. M. & Archbald, A. 1992. The nature of authentic academic achievement. In H. Berlak, F. M. Newmann, E. Adams, D. A. Archbald, T. Burgess, J. Raven & T. A. Romberg (Eds.) *Toward a new science of educational testing and assessment.* State University of New York Press.

Paulson, F. L., Paulson, P. R. & Meyer, C. A. 1992. What makes a portfolio a portfolio? In K. Wetzel (Ed.) *Computers and the writing process. Teacher's guide to organizing and evaluating student writing.* International society for technology in education, 87 - 90.

Queau, Ph. 1995. *Lumetodellisuus* [Virtual reality]. Helsinki: Arthouse.

Scanlon, E., O'Shea, T., Smith, R.B. & Li, Y. 1997. *Supporting the Distributed Synchronous Learning of Probability: learning from an experiment.* Proceedings of Computer Supported Collaborative Learning Conference, Toronto, December.

Simmons, W. & Resnick, L. 1993. Assessment as a catalyst of school reform. *Educational Leadership* 50(5), 11-15.

Sinko, M. & Lehtinen, E. 1999. *The challenges of ICT in Finnish education.* Atena-kustannus. WSOY: Jyväskylä.

Smith, R.B. 1999. Kansas: a dynamically programmable multi-user virtual reality. In O. Shea & E. Scanlon (Eds.) *Virtual Learning Environments and the Role of the Teacher.* UNESCO Press. In press.

Stehr, N. 1994. *Knowledge societies.* London: Sage.

Valencia, S., Hiebert, E. H. & Afflerbach, P. P. 1994. *Authentic reading assessment: practices and possibilities.* Newark,

Vosniadou, S. 1996. Representational growth and cognitive flexibility. In S. Vosniadou, E. De Corte, R. Glaser & H. Mandl (Eds.) *International perspectives on the construction of technology-supported learning environments.* Hillsdale, NJ: Lawrence Erlbaum.

Vygotsky, L. S. 1978. *Mind in society: the development of higher psychological processes.* Cambridge, MA: Harvard University Press.

Collaborative Learning of Java Programming in the Graphic-enhanced Videoconferencing Environment: A Pilot Study

Bernhard Ertl, Lai-Chong Law & Heinz Mandl

The supposition that graphic external representations can foster our higher- order thinking is corroborated by many empirical findings. Collaborative learning, of which the basic assumption is that cognition is tool-mediated and socially shared, is presumed to benefit from the use of graphical tools. Nonetheless, different forms of graphic displays have different representational efficiencies for different tasks and can lead to different cognitive effects in different individuals. In the present pilot study, we attempted to investigate how the use of 'whiteboard' (a tool supporting free hand drawing) could influence the extent of conceptual changes of student programmers who solved Java programming problems in the context of videoconferencing. A 2x2 factorial design was formulated. Two independent variables are the communication mode (graphics-enhanced vs. verbal-based) and the nature of the task (visual- vs. text-oriented). Four cases (i.e. dyads) were analysed according to a coding scheme and other methods. A tentative conclusion is that using the graphical tool can enhance the learning of Java programming by fostering explanatory activities of high-level abstraction. The extent of this effect is determined by three boundary conditions, namely the programming expertise, dyadic communication pattern, and nature of the task. Some implications for future research are addressed.

Videoconferencing as an educational tool

Since the introduction of high speed telephone lines like ISDN (Integrated Services Digital Network) in the early 1990s, videoconferencing – which refers to an audio and video connection that allows two or more persons to communicate, regardless of geographical barriers – was considered as the technology of the future. Business travel was regarded unnecessary because videoconferencing seemed to be a much easier and more efficient means of communication. But due to high expenses for the equipment required, the deployment of this technology was mainly confined to the companies which could afford the cost. Currently, because of the growth of the Internet and the power of connected PCs, which nowadays are present in quite a number of private homes, this technology is basically accessible for almost everyone. Sound systems are included in nearly every PC and the extra cost of an image capturing PC-camera is negligible. Nevertheless, with the use of a PC the conference is not restricted to only an audio and a video channel; it is also possible for applications like graphical or textual tools to transmit information synchronously with the other channels. As almost all forms of learning involve multiple representations (van Someren, Reimann, Boshuizen & de Jong, 1998), videoconferencing may thus serve as a promising tool for teaching and learning (Bruhn, 1999).

As a versatile tool, videoconferencing technology can be applied to a broad range of fields (e.g., Finn, Sellan & Wilbur, 1997). Basically it can be useful for people in different locations who have to contact each other. One of the common applications is tele-tutoring. A tutee encounters a problem when working with the computer. The tutor does not have to go to the tutee's working place. Instead, he can establish a video-conference, take over the control of the tutee's screen and show how to solve the problem (Geyken, Mandl & Reiter, 1998). Another application is educating sick children. If sick children have to stay at home for a long time, they will miss a lot of lessons and might fail to follow the courses. Employing private teachers who can help sick children to keep abreast with the learning materials is quite expensive. Besides, it is inconvenient and time-consuming for the teachers to drive around frequently to reach different children. In this case the videoconferencing can be very useful. The teacher can reduce his or her home visits and communicate with the children via videoconferencing. By the same token, if children have any question, they can establish a connection and ask the teacher (Lieutenant, 1999).

Unfortunately, the quality of speech and image of these conferences is sometimes still low. Nonetheless, it is believed that within the next five years the capacity of the Internet will be powerful enough for using videoconferencing in broad educational contexts. That is the motivation for us to research how to ameliorate the videoconferencing technology for yielding better learning results. In this present project we focus on the impact of using graphical tools on collaborative learning. The application domain chosen is object-oriented (Java) programming, given its ever-increasing applicability in handling complex problems, which often entail collaboration among a group of programmers, and the amenability of the programming concepts to graphical representation.

In the ensuing discussion the theoretical assumptions underpinning the cognitive effects of graphical representation and computer-supported collaborative learning will first be delineated. Then, detailed descriptions of our empirical work will be presented. Of particular interest are the meticulous analyses of the four cases. Some intriguing findings were obtained and discussed with respect to the five research questions. Finally, the implications of this pilot study are addressed.

Theoretical Background

Graphics as External Representations
External representations (ERs) play an indispensable role in many of our cogni-

tive activities such as problem solving, reasoning, and decision-making. According to Zhang (1997), external representations are defined as the knowledge and structure in the environment whereas internal representations are defined as the knowledge and structure in memory. Espousing the situated-distributed view of cognition (see e.g., Clancey, 1997; Zhang & Norman, 1994), we believe that internal and external representations co-evolve through ongoing agent-world interactions. Graphs, diagrams, and pictures are typical instances of ERs. Most of contemporary theoretical frameworks for processing of graphical information are derived from Allan Paivio's (1986) seminal concept of dual coding. Put briefly, the dual coding theory assumes that texts (or propositional codes) are processed in the verbal system whereas graphics (or imaginal codes) are processed both in the imagery (or nonverbal) and verbal system.

These two systems – verbal and imagery – are functionally independent but interconnected referentially and interact continuously. Of great relevance is that graphical ERs can enhance higher order thinking. Their cognitive effects, amongst others, include superior memory of dually encoded information (Paivio, 1979), reifying abstract concepts and thereby rendering them more accessible to reflection (Kaput, 1992), facilitating perceptual inferences (Larkin & Simon, 1987; Winn, 1989) and a shift of reasoning mode (Koedinger & Anderson, 1990), fostering construction of mental models (Mayer & Gallini, 1990; Schnotz & Kulhavy, 1994), limiting abstraction (i.e. increasing specificity) and thereby aiding processibility (Stenning, 1999; Stenning & Oberlander, 1995), etc.

In fact, the representation, perception, and comprehension of graphs have been extensively studied since last century (for the review see Tufte, 1990). It is well documented that different forms of graphic displays (e.g. static vs. animated graphics) have different representational efficiencies for different tasks (e.g. problem-solving vs. reasoning) and can lead to different cognitive effects (accreting vs. restructuring existing concepts) in different individuals (e.g. novice vs. expert) (Reimann, 1999; Zhang, 1997). Clearly, it is difficult to isolate the effects of these inextricable factors. In sum, despite the conviction that graphics play a significant role in knowledge acquisition, there are still many questions pertaining to the mechanisms which account for the beneficial effects of ERs in general and of graphics in particular. More research efforts should be invested to explore this specific topic.

Computer-Supported Collaborative Learning (CSCL)
The theoretical framework underlying the research on CSCL, which has been flourishing in the recent decade (1990 – 2000) (see e.g. Koschman, 1996; O´Malley, 1995), is grounded upon the constructivist learning theories. Accordingly, learning is seen as active, social, self-regulated, reflective, contextualized, and situated (see e.g. Weinert, 1996). Furthermore, human cognitive system is assumed to be

distributed over physical objects, semantic tools, and other people (Resnick, Levine & Teasley, 1991; Salomon, 1993). Specifically, the use of ERs, be they verbal or graphical, often represents socially shared cognition (Cox, 1999). The main advantage of collaborative learning is to foster metacognitive skills and this effect is augmented with the use of computer technology, which supports a form of communication transcending temporal and spatial constraints. The basic concepts of constructivism are derived from the ideas of Dewey, Piaget, Vygotsky, and other scholars. In particular, the Piagetian notion of 'social-cognitive conflict' in peer interactions (Piaget, 1974/1976) and the Vygotskian notion of 'cultural-historical activity theory' (Vygotsky, 1978) contribute substantially to the development of collaborative learning model (Dillenbourg, 1999).

However, the two traditions have different assumptions regarding the mechanisms underpinning the cognitive impact of social others (e.g. expansion scheme in Vygotsky's view vs. revision scheme in Piaget's mode; see also Rogoff, 1990). Hence, they have different implications for designing learning environment (Derry, 1992) and varied explications for cognitive change (e.g. Schnotz & Preuß, 1994), equity issue (e.g. Webb, Nemer & Chizhik, 1998), and other phenomena. As an advanced form of CSCL, video-mediated communication (VMC) becomes more common and has a wide scope of applications such as distance learning and teleconferencing (Finn, et al., 1997). However, the claimed benefits of VMC are thwarted by the inconsistent empirical findings (see e.g. Finn, 1997). The compelling question is what kind of group doing what kind of task in which situation will benefit from what sorts of video connections (Olson & Olson, 1997; Fussell & Benimoff, 1995). Tools for evaluating the process of collaborative learning, which usually manifests in form of linguistic expressions, are derived from language sciences, including the grounding process, conversation and discourse analysis (Clark & Brennan, 1991; Schegloff, 1991). A variety of coding methods have been developed in accord with the specific research questions addressed in individual studies. Owing to the lack of canonical methods of analysis, it is difficult to compare the related studies. Nonetheless, the research on CSCL is plagued by a number of theoretical and empirical problems, which might be resolved by future studies.

Empirical Work

Considering the cognitive effects of graphical ERs and collaborative learning, it is assumed that students of computer programming, a domain where graphical ERs are commonly used as a tool for elaborating concepts, can benefit from learning programming in a graphics-enhanced, CSCL environment.

Research Aim

To evaluate conceptual changes of student programmers who solve Java programming problems either in the context of verbal-based or graphics-enhanced videoconferencing.

Research Questions

(Q1) Are there any significant differences in the quality of the joint solution between the verbal-based and graphics-enhanced group?

(Q2) Are there any significant differences in the extent of conceptual changes induced in individual learners between the verbal-based and graphics-enhanced group?

(Q3) Does the use of the graphical tool lead to higher tendency of convergent or divergent understanding?

(Q4) What are the effects of unequal access to the graphical tool on the problem-solving approach?

(Q5) Are there any interaction effects between the nature of the task and the use of the graphical tool on the variables of interest?

Method

Design: A 2x2 design was formulated (Table 1). Two independent variables were communication mode (or precisely speaking, the time-on-task using the graphical tool) and the nature of the task, i.e. visual-oriented (binary search tree) versus text-oriented (linear linked list). Dependent variables consist of the quality of the joint solution, extent of conceptual changes of individual participants, problem-solving approach, communication pattern, and tendency of convergent understanding. Covariates include individual's domain-specific knowledge, verbal and spatial ability.

Mode \ Task	Visual-oriented (V)	Text-oriented (T)
Graphics-enhanced (G)	GV (3)*	GT (1)
Verbal-based (V)	VV (1)	VT (1)

*Note: the digit enclosed in brackets represents the number of dyads in that category

Table 1 – Four experimental groups

Participant: 12 university students of *Technische Universitaet Muenchen* (Germany) took part in the Pilot Study on a voluntary basis. Seven and five of them majored and minored in computer science, respectively. Six of them were female. They were grouped into six dyads; two of these dyads were randomly paired whereas the other four formed by themselves.

Instrument: Two Silicon Graphics Incorporated (SGI) workstations, which support shared video (visual field limiting to head and shoulder), audio (full-duplex), and graphical (whiteboard) communication channels, were employed. In addition, the Unix-based X-Multiplexer (XMX) software, which supports two or more users to access a common x-term window and text-editor (e.g. *emacs*) in parallel, was installed. Furthermore, we used a digital video-camera with its focus centring on the computer monitor to record online interactions.

Procedure: Each dyad attended two sessions. The first session lasted about 1.5 hours in which the participants were required to take three tests on an individual basis, namely a pretest on domain-specific knowledge, an intelligence test, and a questionnaire for learning and programming experience. The second session lasted about 3 hours. In the beginning, the participants were given a preparation training (ca. 25 minutes) through which they could familiarise with the operation of the videoconferencing environment. Then, they were required to solve a programming task collaboratively (ca. 105 minutes). Next, they were asked to take a posttest and fill in a questionnaire for self-evaluation of learning success and motivation on an individual basis. The members of each dyad were seated in two different rooms and they could communicate synchronously via video, audio, and text channels. In addition, the graphics-enhanced groups could use the graphic editor which supports free-hand drawing, whereas the verbal-based group could not. All dyadic conversations were audiotaped and these audio-recordings were transcribed into verbal protocols. Moreover, log files for online programs and graphics were saved as backups.

Analysis and Measurement
To evaluate the variables of interest, we have developed an analytical scheme with three levels, which are defined in terms of grain-size of unit of analysis. For the finest or microscopic level, the unit of analysis is an utterance, which is delimited by dialogical turn taking. Given the huge size of data corpus, it was impractical for us to code every single utterance. Instead, we adopted a systematic sampling method to select protocol segments (Chi, 1997): time (i.e. non-content criterion) and use of the graphical tool (i.e. content criterion). Accordingly, we selected three time slots out of the whole 105-minute collaborative programming session: the beginning phase (1st – 20th minutes), the middle phase (41st – 60th or any 20-minute block encompassing the use of the graphic editor), and the end phase (85th – 105th minutes). Furthermore, with reference to the related works (e.g. Baker, 1994; Roschelle, 1996; Roschelle & Teasley, 1995), we have developed a coding

scheme for analysing the verbal protocols (Figure 1). Basically, each utterance is coded at both the problem-solving and communication level. However, it should be remarked that some utterances can not be categorized, albeit such incidence is rather low, and that some long utterances are assigned more than one sub-categories (for details see Law, Ertl & Mandl, 1999).

For the middle or mesoscopic level, the unit of analysis is a so-called episode, which represent periods of time during which the participants are engaged in a particular activity. The protocol is parsed into chunks or episodes, ranging from a few to tens of successive utterances, and they can be characterised by different categories (e.g. reading, reasoning, exploring). The transitions between episodes identify points where the solution attempts change directions (cf. Schoenfeld, 1992). For the broadest or macroscopic level, the unit of analysis is a block of 20-minute dialogue. Different kinds of observations such as density of interaction, evidence of convergent understanding, and strategic change of role assumption, are derived. Apart from the three-tiered analytical scheme, we have also taken some other important measurements. To observe if there are any conceptual changes with regard to particular data structure, algorithm, and programming language structure, the occurrences and changes in the interpretation of key terms and its variants are tracked down with the use of the whole protocol. The correctness, efficiency, and elegance of the developing computer program is also evaluated with the use of log-files. Besides, the informativeness of each graphic drawn and the time-on-task using the graphic editor are assessed.

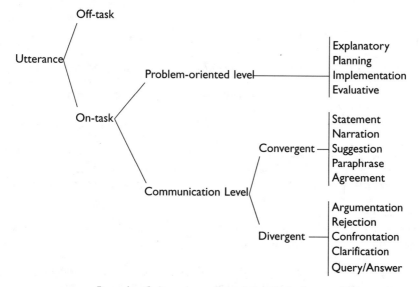

Figure 1 – Coding scheme for verbal analysis of protocols

Preliminary Results and Discussion

Four cases – GV1, GV2, VT3 and GT4 – were meticulously analysed. However, given the limited space for this chapter, only the first two cases – GV1 and GV2 – will be discussed here (for detailed comparisons between the two other cases, see Law et al., 1999). Some interesting findings are summarised in Table 2.

Comm. –Mode Task Nature	Dyad GVI Graphics-enhanced Visual-oriented	Dyad GV2 Graphics-enhanced Visual-oriented
Programming Expertise	A1 – novice B1 - novice (more knowledgeable) Large difference in pre-test (A1=17.5; B1=38.5)	A2 - advanced novice B2 – novice Large difference in pre-test (A2 = 44.0; B2 =22.0)
Partnership	Self-formed (female-female)	Self-formed (male-female)
Social Interaction Pattern	Equitable, (semi-)symmetrical: Mutually guiding (share of control) Begin Phase: A1 was dominant Middle Phase: Equal End Phase: B1 was dominant	Equitable, symmetrical: Negotiating (mutual persuasion) Begin and End Phase: Equal Middle Phase: A2 was dominant
Utterance Density	10.1 utterance /min. (medium)	18.5 utterance/min. (high)
Time using the Graphic Editor	18.7 minutes	11.8 minutes
Application of the Graphical Tool	~ Middle phase (14.7 min): data structures ~ End phase (4.0 min.): progr. concept, algorithm ~ mostly initiated by B1	~ Begin phase (3.5 min.): progr. concepts, data structures ~ Middle phase (8.3 min.): algorithm ~ initiated by both partners
Problem-solving: Explanatory act. Co-planning act.	Concrete except at Middle phase Low	Concrete except at Middle phase High (technical and algorithmic)
Communication: Convergence Divergence	Unpredictable trend Unpredictable trend	Relatively high in all 3 phases Decreasing with the phases
Extent of Conceptual Change	A1 - slight (data structures, programming concepts)	A2 - slight (algorithm) high-level transfer

	low-level transfer	~ externalising ideas with
	~ visual display: para-graphing	graphics in the posttest
	~ gain declarative knowledge	~ misconceptions about the
	(description given in posttest)	'delete' algorithm were clarified
	B1 – slight (data structures,	B2 - detectable
	programming concepts)	(data structures, algorithm)
	low-level transfer	high-level transfer
	~ constructing relationship	~ gain in procedural knowledge:
	between data structures	applying the algorithm
	~ applying the newly learnt	in the posttest
	programming concepts	~ misconceptions about data
	in the posttest	structure and algorithm
		were clarified
	Posttest: A1 = 12.0; B1 = 18.0	Posttest: A2=39.0; B2=20.5
Quality of the joint solution	10% of the tasks given;	80% of the tasks given;
	low quality	medium quality

Table 2 – Comparisons between two case studies – GV1 and GV2

Tendency to use graphical ERs. Both dyads worked under the same conditions (i.e. the four communication channels – video, audio, textual, and graphical – are available) and on the same problem (i.e. construction of a bank account system with binary search tree). Dyad GV1 used the graphical tool more often (i.e. almost 1.5 times) than did Dyad GV2. The two dyads employed the graphical tool in different phases, but both of them used the graphic tool most intensively during the middle phase, albeit for different purposes - discussing data structures (i.e. binary search tree) in GV1 and algorithm (i.e. deleting an element from a binary search tree) in GV2. Interestingly, for GV1, it was B1 (the more knowledgeable partner) who initiated the use of the graphical tool most of the time when she intended to explain something to A1. In fact, B1 was a kind of 'visualiser' (Cox, 1999) who tended to externalise her reasoning with graphical ERs.

This propensity was evident by her drawings in the individual, pen-and-paper pretest. In GV2, both partners took the initiative to use the graphical editor. In some occasions, A2 attempted to convince B2, who tended to adhere to her preconceptions, by verbally explicating the abstract concepts with real-life examples. However, when he failed to persuade B2 by this means, he resorted to using graphical ERs. In the same vein, when B2 failed to understand A2's verbal explanations, she requested A2 to clarify the concepts with graphics. These observations are somewhat in line with Cox's (1999) claims that the tendency to use a form particular of ER depends on users' prior knowledge of ER formalism (i.e. their ER repertoire) and on users' cognitive style (i.e. their preferable modalities and types of ER and the degree to which they are used to externalising their reasoning).

Metacognitive activities and the use of graphical ERs. An intriguing finding was that for both dyads the explanatory activities tend to be at concrete level except in the middle phase when the graphical tool was most frequently used to discuss abstract concepts relating to data structures and algorithms (Figure 2). This observation is somewhat consistent with Stenning and Oberlander's (1995; Stenning, 1999) so-called "specificity theory". They assert that graphics force a determinate representation that is severely limited in terms of the amount of abstraction that can be expressed and therefore aid processibility. The weak expressiveness of graphics makes inferences more tractable. We assume that the more abstract the concepts can be explicated by explanatory activities, the higher the order of thinking can be fostered. The incidences of co-planning activities, which did not appear to coincide with the use of the graphical tool, were low in GV1 and relatively higher in GV2.

The difference might be attributed to their differing social interaction pattern (i.e. share of control vs. mutual persuasion). Evaluative activities, which are related to personal competence, task-related events, or technical aspects, were low in both dyads. According to Schoenfeld (1992), the low incidence of self-regulating behaviours (e.g. assessing and re-considering whether the strategies being adopted are adequate) can partially account for failure in poor problem solvers.

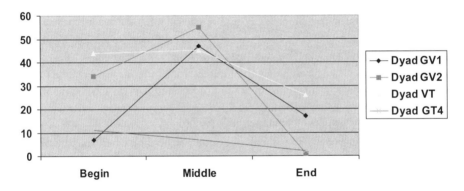

Figure 2 – Explanatory activities of high-level abstraction of the four dyads

Note: y-axis represents the absolute number of utterances. Given that there is no significant statistical correlation between the total number of utterance per block and the incidence of explanatory activities of high-level abstraction, no normalisation is required.

Social-cognitive factors for conceptual changes. As evident by the performances in the online collaborative programming task and offline individual posttest, both partners in GV1 demonstrated less conceptual changes than did the two partners in GV2, although the former used the graphic tool more often than the latter. Clearly, it is the quality rather than the quantity of graphical ERs that accounts for the extent and nature of conceptual changes. The effectiveness of a graphical ER does not only simply rely on its format, which is actually similar for both dyads (i.e. an inversed tree-like structure which is a conventional graphical notation employed in computer science), but more important is how the student relates the two representational systems – linguistic (i.e. natural or artificial languages) and graphical.

According to Cox (1999), ER construction (i.e. the process of externalising a mental model) assists problem solving in numerous ways, e.g., refining mental representation and offloading working memory. In this sense, the effectiveness of ER may be mediated by mechanisms that parallel the ways in which self explanations associated with successful problem solving (Chi et al., 1989). However, we argue that if the student's mental model, on which the process of externalisation is based is inadequate and his or her metacognitive skills are limited, the advantages of constructing ER will be undermined. Conversely, the limited expressiveness of graphical ERs may even limit their thoughts on certain problem-solving possibilities (cf. Greene & Petre, 1992). Given that the graphical ERs generated in the present context are both for sustaining social interaction and self-regulating (cf. A2 used the graphical ERs first as a tool of persuasion and then a mediator of self-explanation), we believe that the effects of the graphical ERs will be optimised if they can elicit feedback from their constructor as well as interpreter. This involves the question of the differential cognitive processes involved in constructing and interacting with one's own ER and reasoning with a pre-fabricated ER (Cox, 1999; cf. Renkl, 1997).

According to Hardy and Moore (1997), two predominant mechanisms for conceptual changes are negotiation and appropriation. The former entails the process of clarification, elaboration, or repair during interaction (cf. Baker, 1994) whereas the latter entails modeling and other sense-making activities (Rogoff, 1990). The apparent differences in the communication pattern between the two dyads are the incidences of disagreement-argumentation and question-answer, whereby GV2 showed a higher rate in both respects than GV1. In addition to these factors, the greater extent (i.e. involving different aspects such as data structures and algorithm) and deeper nature (i.e. procedural vs. declarative knowledge) of conceptual changes demonstrated by GV2 can also be attributed to the relatively high programming expertise of A2. In the beginning and end phase, A2 and B2 were engaged equally in the negotiation process aroused by cognitive conflicts, which might lead to conceptual change (cf. Piaget's theory). However, in the middle phase, A2 dominated the interaction by explaining and demonstrating the implementation of an algorithm when B2 attempted to appropriate his explanation. In this situation, B2 might benefit from A2's modelling by expanding her repertoire of knowledge and skills (cf. Vygotsky's theory).

Similar analysis can be applied to GV1, albeit the quality of interaction between A1 and B1 is comparatively lower. It seems reasonable to assume that some old concepts are replaced whilst some of them co-exist with the newly constructed ones (cf. Magnusson, Templin & Boyle, 1997). This assumption is evident by B2's recurrent misinterpretations of the semantics of a constructor (i.e. a conceptual structure of Java programming), despite A2's explanation and her explicit acknowledgement of understanding. In addition, it is assumed that successful negotiation normally leads to progressive convergent understanding of the topic of interest between collaborators. Hence, a decreasing incidence of divergent understanding with time is expected. This trend was demonstrated by GV2, but not GV1 (Figure 3). This factor may also explain the differences in conceptual changes between the two dyads.

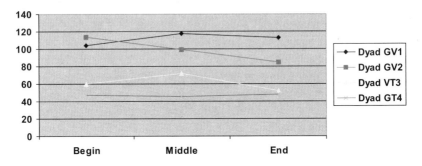

Figure 3:Trends of divergent understanding of the four dyads

Translation between the two representational systems. Grounded upon Stenning and Oberlander's (1995) theory, we can predict that the process of translating from the more expressive, more abstract, linguistic representation to less expressive, less abstract, graphical representation may be more effective than the other way round. This prediction could somewhat be verified by the cognitive behavior of GV2; they could well explain the algorithm of deleting an element from a binary search tree with graphical ERs, however, they showed difficulty in translating the ideas into the programming language and the resulting program segment was incorrect. This observation is not uncommon in student programming behavior in general. Nonetheless, this scenario renders the notion of the internally referential link between verbal and graphical representation questionable (cf. Kosslyn's [1994] 'imagery debate').

Summary
Based on the preliminary findings of our case analyses, we attempt to answer the five research questions we posed earlier in this chapter (section 2.2) and to draw some implications for the further development of our work.

Q1 and Q2: Concerning the questions whether there are significant differences in the quality of the joint solution (Q1) and the extent of conceptual changes (Q2) between the verbal-based and graphics-enhanced group, we could basically refer to the findings of VT3 and GT4 (see Law et al., 1999). However, interesting enough, while the graphic editor was available for GT4, the dyad did not use this tool at all for the collaborative programming task. Moreover, as shown by their performances in the pretest, the two partners of GT4 (A4 and B4) were weak novice programmers. In contrast, one of the partners in VT3 (A3) was an intermediate programmer and his partner (B3) was a very weak novice. It was not surprising that the so-called 'joint' solution of VT3, which was mostly completed by A3, was of much higher quality than that of GT4. In this situation, the differential performance between the two dyads could only be attributed to the level of programming expertise of individual participants (see Schwartz's [1995] comparison between individual and dyadic performance). Whether GT4's performance would be improved if they resorted to using the graphical ERs remains uncertain. All except A3 showed a minimal level of conceptual change. It may be inferred that A3 did not gain anything by merely playing the role of 'resource dispenser' (cf. self-explanation effect). Nonetheless, Q1 and Q2 could also be indirectly answered by GV1's and GV2's performance. We found that the time-on-task of using the graphical tool is not a reliable predictor for the quality of the joint solution or the extent of conceptual change. More important is how the learners relate the less expressive graphical ERs with the more abstract linguistic ERs. We assume that the effectiveness of such a relationship hinges crucially upon the adequacy of mental models, i.e., the programming expertise of individual learners (Remark: there are no significant differences in spatial and verbal abilities between all 8 participants, as shown their performances in the intelligence tests). In addition, the nature of social interaction pattern play an important role in determining the extent of conceptual change. Of particular importance are negotiation strategies, which involve disagreement-repair and question-answer, and appropriation, which entails effective modelling.

Q3 and Q4: With regard to the effect of the use of the graphical tool on the tendency of convergent (or divergent) understanding (Q3) and on the problem solving approach (Q4), some interesting observations were obtained. Based on the findings of GV1 and GV2, it can be inferred that explanatory activities of high-level abstraction are enhanced by the use of graphics. In accord with Stenning and Oberlander's (1995) 'specificity theory', graphical ERs can limit abstraction and thereby aid the processibility of information. On the other hand, the use of graphical ERs seems to have no specific effect on planning or evaluative activities. In fact, graphical ERs are mainly employed as a tool of explanation. In addition, based on the performance of A3 (intermediate programmer), we assume that learners with high domain-specific expertise and thus well-developed mental model seem to be able to explain concepts at high-level of abstraction without relying on graphical ERs. Nonetheless, the effectiveness of the so-called socially-oriented explanation (cf. self-directed explanation) is determined by its level of abstraction and its compatibility with the learning pre-requisite of the explainee. Furthermore, as shown by GV2's performance, it seems that the use of graphical ERs can reduce the level of divergent understanding.

Q5: The relationship between the nature of the task and the tendency to use the graphical tool (Q5) can be derived from our findings. Based on the substantial difference in time-on-task of using the graphical tool between GV1/2 and GT4, it can be inferred that the nature of a task seems to be a crucial factor in determining the tendency of using graphical ERs. In fact, this observation is somewhat consistent with our assumption that text-oriented task (i.e. implementation of sparse matrices with linear-linked list) is less amenable to graphical ERs than a visual-oriented one (i.e. implementation of a bank account system with binary search tree). Nonetheless, it can be argued that the two tasks are different in terms of difficulty and authenticity (or 'real-life-ness', an attribute upheld by the situated learning model, see Gruber, Law, Mandl & Renkl, 1996) and therefore the reliability and validity of the conclusions drawn from the inter-task comparisons can be threatened. As mentioned earlier, different forms of graphic displays have different representational efficiencies for different tasks and can lead to different cognitive effects in different individuals.

Self-evaluation: Based on the subjective evaluations, all participants expressed that they were motivated in solving the collaborative task. Moreover, their subjective assessments of learning success were compatible with the objective observations. The role of the graphical tool in fostering communication of ideas is commonly acknowledged. For instance, A2 of GV2 remarked 'Without graphics, the interpretation of theories would be impossible [and] one could hardly explain anything.' (Remark: translated from German) In contrast, the function of video-channel seems to be primarily emotional-affective, as expressed by B1 of GV1 'The video camera by itself is calming. Thereby I know, with whom I am working here, and I also know, that you [her partner] are there and still alive.' (Remark: translated from German).

In sum, we tentatively claim that the use of graphical ERs can enhance the learning of Java programming. Nonetheless, the extent of the effectiveness of graphical ERs is determined by three interdependent factors: (1) the level of programming expertise of individual problem solvers (i.e. the adequacy of mental models); (2) the pattern of social communication between problem solvers (i.e. predominantly the process of negotiation and appropriation); (3) the nature and demands of the task.

Outlook

Considering the problem of reliability and validity of inter-task comparisons and the difficulty of recruiting sufficient number of participants, we only employed the visual-oriented task (binary search tree) in our main study. In addition, we believe that not only qualitative but also quantitative data are essential for investigating the research questions of interest. Hence, with the relatively larger number of participants in the main study, some relevant statistical tests on the variables of interest will be performed. Thereby, more insights and solid conclusions can be obtained. Apart from these practical improvements, we aim to explore the following theoretical problems more in-depth based on the data gathered in the main study:

- How do learners integrate multiple representations – graphical and verbal (natural language and artificial programming language) – in the collaborative problem solving?
- How the cognitive processes involved in constructing and interacting with one's own graphical ER differ from those involved in reasoning with a pre-fabricated graphical ER generated by someone else?
- What factors contribute to the higher incidence of negotiation and appropriation which can lead to conceptual changes (e.g. gender-combination of dyad, constraints of social etiquette, cognitive style of individual partner, etc.)?
- How does the level of programming expertise relate to the tendency of using the graphical tool (i.e. fine categories of expertise should be developed)?

Some intriguing questions which are worth exploring but not within the scope of our present project:

- Would a structured graphical tool rather than an unstructured one like 'whiteboard' lead to higher conceptual changes?
- Are the effects observed in the present study domain-specific or general across disciplines where graphical ERs are also commonly used (e.g. mathematics, statistics, logic)?
- Would learners benefit more from self-constructed graphical ERs or from interactive graphical representation systems (IGRS) (Reimann, 1999), in which they can enter certain inputs and then observe the corresponding changes of graphics?

References

Baker, M. (1994). A model of negotiation in teaching-learning dialogues. *Journal of Artificial Intelligence in Education, 5*(2), 199-254.

Bruhn, J. (1999). Förderung des kooperativen Lernens über Computernetze. Prozess und Lernerfolg beim dyadischen Lernen mit Desktop-Videokonferenzen [Supporting the cooperative learning over computer networks: Process and learning success of dyadic learning with desktop videoconference] (Unpublished doctoral thesis). München: Ludwig-Maximilians-Universität, Lehrstuhl für Empirische Pädagogik und Pädagogische Psychologie.

Chi, M.T.H. (1997). Quantifying qualitative analyses of verbal data: A practical guide. *TheJournal of the Learning Sciences, 6*, 271-315.

Chi, M.T.H., Bassok, M., Lewis, M.W., Reimann, P., & Glaser, R. (1989). Self-explanations: How students study and use examples in learning to solve problems. *Cognitive Science, 13*, 145-182.

Clancey, W.J. (1997). *Situated cognition*. Cambridge: Cambridge University Press.

Clark, H.H. & Brennan, S.E. (1991). Grounding in communication. In L.B. Resnick, J.M. Levine & S.D.Teasley (Eds.),

Perspectives on socially shared cognition (pp. 127-149). Washington: American Psychological Association

Cox, R. (1999). Representation construction, externalised cognition and individual differences. *Learning and Instruction, 9*, 343-363.

Derry, S.J. (1992). Metacognitive models of learning and instructional systems design. In M.Jones & P.H. Winne (Eds.),

Adaptive learning environments (pp. 257-286). Berlin: Springer.

Dillenbourg (Ed.) (1999). *Collaborative learning: Cognitive and computational approaches*. Elsevier Science/ Pergamon.

Finn, K.E. (1997). Introduction: An overview of video-mediated communication. In K.E. Finn, A.J. Sellen, & S.B.Wilbur, (Eds.), *Video-media communication* (pp. 3-22). Mahwah, NJ: Erlbaum.

Finn, K.E., Sellen, A.J., & Wilbur, S.B. (1997) (Eds.), *Video-media communication*. Mahwah, NJ: Erlbaum.

Fussell, S.R. & Benimoff, N.I. (1995). Social and cognitive processes in interpersonal communication. *Human Factors, 37*, 228-250.

Hardy, I.M., & Moore, J.L. (1997). *The relationship between collaboration and conceptual change during mathematical problem solving*. Paper presented at the Annual Meeting of the American Educational Research Association, Chicago, IL, March, 1997.

Koedinger, K.R., & Anderson, J.R. (1990). Abstract planning and perceptual chunks: elements of expertise in geometry. *Cognitive Science, 14*, 511-550.

Kosslyn, S.M. (1994). Image and brain. Cambridge, MA: MIT Press.

Geyken, A., Mandl, H. &Reiter, W. (1998). Selbstgesteuertes Lernen mit Tele-Tutoring. In Schwarzer, R. (Hrsg,), Multimedia und Telelearning. Frankfurt: Campus

Greene, T.R.G., & Petre, M. (1992). When visual programs are harder to read than textual programs. *Proceedings of the 6th European Conference on Cognitive Ergonomics (ECCE-6)*, Hungary.

Kaput, J.J. (1992). Technology and mathematics education. In D.A. Grouws (Ed.), *Handbook of research on mathematics teaching and learning* (pp. 515-556). New York: Macmillan.

Koschmann, T. (Ed.) (1996). *CSCL: Theory and practice of an emerging paradigm*. Mahwah, NJ: Erlbaum.

Larkin, J.H. & Simon, H.A. (1987). Why a diagram is (sometimes) worth ten thousand words. *Cognitive Sciecne, 11*, 65-100.

Law, L.-C., Ertl, B., & Mandl, H. (1999) Collaborative learning of Java programming in the graphics-enhanced vidoeconferencing environment: A pilot study (Research Report no. 113). München: Ludwig-Maximilians-Universität, Lehrstuhl für Empirische Pädagogik und Pädagogische Psychologie.

Lieutenant, C. (1999). *Distance education and at-home education, definition of infrastructure and example of procedure to establish such a service.* Paper presented at ECER (European Conference of Educational Research) Lathi, Finland, 1999.

Magnusson, S. J., Templin, M., & Boyle, R.A.(1997). Dynamic science assessment; A new approach for investigating conceptual change. *The Journal of the Learning Sciences,*   6(1), 91-142.

Mayer, R.E. & Gallini, J.K. (1990). When is an illusion worth ten thousand words? *Journal of Educational Psychology, 82*(4), 715-726.

O'Malley, C. (1995). Designing computer support for collaborative learning. In C. O'Malley (Ed.), *Computer supported collaborative learning* (pp.283-297). Berlin: Springer.

Olson, G.M. & Olson, J.S. (1997). Making sense of the findings. In K.E. Finn, A.J. Sellen, & S.B.Wilbur, (Eds.), *Video-media communication* (pp. 75-92). Mahwah, NJ: Erlbaum

Paivio, A. (1979). Psychological processes in the comprehension of metaphor. In A. Ortony (Ed.), *Metaphor and thought* (pp. 150-171). Cambridge: Cambridge University Press.

Paivio, A. (1986). *Mental representations: A dual-coding approach.* Oxford: Oxford University Press.

Piaget, J. (1976). *The grasp of consciousness: Action and concept in the young children* (S. Wedgwood, trans.). Cambridge, MA: Harvard University Press (Original published in 1974)

Reimann, P. (1999). The role of external representations in distributed problem solving. *Learning and Instruction, 9*, 411-418.

Resnick, L.B., Levine, J.M. & Teasley, S.D. (1991) (Eds.), *Perspectives on socially shared cognition.* Washington: American Psychological Association

Rogoff, B. (1990). *Apprenticeship in thinking.* New York: Oxford University Press.

Roschelle, J. (1996). Learning by collaborating: Convergent conceptual change. In T. Koschmann (Ed.), *CSCL: Theory and practice of an emerging paradigm* (pp.209-247). Mahwah, NJ: Erlbaum.

Roschelle, J. & Teasley, S.D. (1995). The construction of shared knowledge in collaborative problem solving. In C. O'Malley (Ed.), *Computer supported collaborative learning* (pp. 69-97). Berlin: Springer.

Salomon, G. (1993). (Ed.) *Distributed cognition.* Cambridge: Cambridge University Press.

Schegloff, E.A. (1991). Conversation analysis and socially shared cognition. In L.B. Resnick, J.M. Levine & S.D. Teasley (Eds.), *Perspectives on socially shared cognition.* (pp. 150-171). Washington: American Psychological Association

Schoenfeld, A. H. (1992). On paradigms and methods: What do you do when the ones you know don't do what you want them to? Issues in the analysis of data in the form of videotapes. *The Journal of the Learning Sciences, 2*(2), 179-214.

Schnotz, W., Preuß, A. (1997). Task-dependent construction of mental models as a basis for conceptual change. *European Journal of Psychology of Education, 12*(2), 185-211.

Schnotz, W., & Kulhavy, R.W. (1994). *Comprehension of graphics.* Amsterdam: North-Holland.

Schwartz, D.L. (1995). The emergence of abstract representations in dyad problem solving. *The Journal of the Learning Sciences, 4*(3), 321-354.

Stenning, K. (1999). The cognitive consequences of modality assignment for educational communication. *Learning and Instruction, 9*, 391-410.

Stenning, K. & Oberlander, J. (1995). A cognitive theory of graphical and linguistic reasoning: Logic and implementation. *Cognitive Science, 19*, 97-140.

Part 2
Teacher Education

Establishing a Research/Training Partnership to Facilitate the Professional Integration of Novice Teachers and Help them Become Reflective Practitioners

JACQUELINE BECKERS & GERMAIN SIMONS

Recent studies about how the school context influences the teacher efficacy show that the sense of community, the opportunity for collaboration with other adults, for mutual observation are reliable indicators of the teachers' level of efficacy. The effect of collective efficacy may be especially important for novice teachers as they are socialized into the teaching profession. The research/training program analysed in this paper aims at developing, through a cross-partnership network, a positive form of self-esteem and 'teacher efficacy' in the double sense of Rotter's internal locus of control and of Bandura's perceived self-efficacy. One of the characteristics of the methodological approach of this research/training program is that the teachers involved in the process became in turn *scriptwriters* (creating the experimental didactic sequences) *actors* (playing the script in their own class) the *audience* (observing their colleagues teaching, taking notes and filming) and *critics* (assessing the process and the results of the didactic sequences to improve it). In that way, teachers were encouraged to confront their perceptions of their efficacy as teachers with their partners' observations and with video extracts of their lessons.

The research described and analysed in this paper was carried out in the academic year 1996-1997 in secondary schools of the French Community of Belgium. The partners involved in the project were two researchers from the University of Liège and five novice language teachers who tought Germanic languages in different secondary schools in Liège. Teachers and researchers were all volunteers. This research program was not financed, except for the cost of videotapes and travelling expenses. The research/training program aimed at:
- facilitating the professional integration of novice teachers,
- enabling inexperienced teachers to progressively construct a 'reflective practitioner *habitus*' (Schön, 1982),
- developing, through the partnership, a positive form of self-esteem and 'teacher efficacy'.

When novice teachers enter professional life, they frequently encounter a 'reality shock' (Veenman, S., 1984; Weinstein, C. S., 1988): they have to cope with different kinds of difficulty such as teaching at different schools, 'patchwork' timetables, the lack of communication between colleagues, the 'clash' between their initial perceptions of what should be done in schools ('good' teaching and learning), and what is actually done... Every European teacher has to face this 'reality shock' at the beginning of their career, but we believe it is particularly difficult for Belgian teachers of the French Community because a) the practicum in the preservice training is extremely short: trainees teach only twenty lessons, b) the inservice training is neither compulsory, nor systematized c) there is a terrible gap between preservice training and inservice training.

The transitional period between pre- and inservice training, when the latter exists, is crucial for two basic reasons. Firstly, the way inexperienced teachers negociate this critical period is likely to determine (positively or negatively) the rest of their career as teachers (Huberman, M., 1989; Murnane R. J. *et al.*, 1991). Secondly, novice teachers are still flexible, that is, they are not yet imprisoned in stiff didactic scripts, and their perception of 'efficacy' is not yet deeply rooted, which is important because both phenomena appear to be resistant to change (Clark, C. M. & Peterson, P. L., 1978, 1986; Ross, J. A.,1998).

So it seemed really important to undertake something for these novice teachers and to undertake it at that specific critical period of their career. To reach this aim, we deliberately chose to create *a research partnership network*. Two hypotheses underly this choice:

H1: *The partnership network helps teachers develop a positive personal identity and avoid education burnout.*

H2: *Integrating beginning teachers into research activities is important to develop teacher efficacy.*

The partnership network helps teachers develop a positive personal identity and avoid education burnout

The research/training program we are going to describe aimed at developing, through partnership, a positive form of self-esteem and 'teacher efficacy' in the double sense of Rotter's internal locus of control (1966) and of Bandura's perceived self-efficacy (1977). Recent studies about how the school context influences the teacher efficacy show that the sense of community, the opportunity for collaboration with other adults and for mutual observation, are reliable indicators of the teachers' level of efficacy. All these conditions make up what Bandura defines as *collective efficacy* (1997). The effect of collective efficacy may be especially important for novice teachers as they are socialized into the teaching profession.

> It has been suggested that one of the major causes of education burnout is the absence of a social support network. Teacher training may encourage a cadre who come to view their teaching isolation as autonomy and remain hesistant to discuss educational issues with colleagues. (Samaras, A. P. *et al.*, 1998, p. 716)

> The findings of this study confirm the importance of a collegial school culture to new teachers in urban districts. Controlling for the effect of age, beginning teachers who

were assigned to schools in which they perceived high degrees of collaboration among teachers and administrators reported substantially higher values of change in self-efficacy beliefs than those who worked in schools with little opportunity for collaboration with other adults. (Chester, M. D. & Beaudin, B. Q., 1996, p. 251)

It must be pointed out that most of the studies on the influence of partnership on teacher efficacy were carried out in a specific context in which the partnership is developed *inside* the school. That is what Gather Thurler calls 'the learning organization' (1998). Most of the time, colleague teachers in the same school work together on a specific school project which often focuses much more on the organisational aspects of teaching/learning than on didactic ones. What we wanted to test out was a *cross*-partnership project in which beginning teachers from *different* schools would be led to identify a didactic problem in their class and try to solve it together. Like Hausfather (1996) we wanted to create 'a social environment supportive with models of collaboration and interpersonal activity [...]'. We chose to adopt a Vygotskian approach in which *cognition* is *socially shared* (Vygotsky, L. S., 1978), a methodology in which learning, thinking and knowing arise through collaboration with others.

Integrating beginning teachers into research activities is important to develop teacher efficacy

When we formulated this hypothesis, we immediately added two conditions:
1. It must be a research project *for* teaching and not *on* teaching;
2. It must be a research project *with* teachers and not *through* teachers.

A research project for *teaching*
The approach we wanted to avoid was a positivist one where novice teachers would (simply) have been asked to implement (new) theories, methods or techniques which would have been worked out by researchers. So we decided to start from the problems encountered by the teachers in their classroom and we tried to create a context which would enable them to assess the learning outcomes and the pupils' level of satisfaction. From Guskey's conception (1986, 1989), we hypothesized that novice teachers must experiment with the positive effects of their teaching on their students to be convinced of the interest of the approach and eventually change their initial perceptions and attitudes:

| Staff development | ⇨ | Change in teachers' classroom practices | ⇨ | Change in student learning outcomes | ⇨ | Change in teachers' attitudes and perceptions |

(A model of the process of teacher change. In Guskey, T. R. (1986), 'Staff development and the process of teacher change'. *Educational Researcher*, 15 (5), 5-12.)

A research project with *teachers*

As mentioned above, we were convinced that our research program would not succeed if the novice teachers felt they just had to apply new theories in their class. We then tried to develop a model of partnership in which the teachers would successively be brought to build up an experimental didactic sequence, to test it out in their classrooms, and assess its learning outcomes. Moreover, we thought that if we wanted the teachers to feel they were real partners in the experiment, we had to share the results of the research with them. That is the reason why we asked them to publish a paper on the research and to organize workshops for their school colleagues as well as for our trainees.

Methodology of the research/training process

A research/training program for *teaching*

What stimulated us to propose such a research program was the desire to undertake something for our former students, these novice teachers who have to face, often by themselves, the 'reality shock' mentioned above. The novice teachers involved in the program were all volunteers. This choice, which can be considered 'comfortable', is an important principle of the project and if we had to carry out a similar training program, we would certainly make the same choice because we believe that the willingness to participate in such a demanding and time-consuming project is a necessary condition for its success (see point 4). In fact, the five teachers who carried out the research right to the end were not motivated by external constraints. Neither were they looking for some praise or reward from their school colleagues or headmasters. On the contrary, their motivation was internal and the positive feedback was associated with the feeling of having learnt something and progressed in their teaching practice.

At the beginning of this project we chose ten novice teachers and asked them to list all the difficulties and problems they encountered in their classrooms. We then selected one difficulty which was common to all the teachers and on which it seemed possible to act: the problem of heterogeneousness. So we tried to start from practice and meet the teachers' needs. The solutions to the identified problem were to be searched for and found together through real partnership work.

A research/training program for *and* with *teachers*

Once we had identified the problem of heterogeneousness, we started to build up an experimental didactic sequence which was intended to help the beginning teachers to better understand and, if possible, solve the problem of heterogeneousness. Then we split the group of teachers in two groups: the first group started to teach the experimental sequence in their own classes while the second group was asked to observe them, to take notes and to video record some extracts of the lessons. The next week we organized a workshop which aimed at helping the novice teachers to reflect on their practice (Schön, D., 1982). This workshop was organized in three successive steps:

1. The teachers who had tested out the didactic sequence in their classes were invited to identify the strong and weak points of their instructional practice. Here, we let the teachers express themselves freely. What mattered to us at this stage was their subjective perception of their performance.

2. We confronted their perception of their efficacy as teachers with their partners' observations and with video extracts from their lessons. This confrontation often helped teachers to *reframe* (Schön, D., 1988) their negative perceptions of their efficacy as teachers (see point 4).

3. The whole group was invited to make suggestions to improve the experimental sequence and adapt it to other school contexts.

After the workshop, we tested out the experimental sequence we had just improved. For this second experimentation, we reversed the roles: the teachers who had been the observers became the actors and *vice versa*. After this week of experimentation, we organized a second workshop with the same methodological approach. Finally, the novice teachers were asked to communicate their new knowledge to others by publishing a paper in a review and by organizing lectures and workshops for experienced teachers as well as for trainees. This last step of the methodological approach mattered to us because we wanted the beginning teachers to feel that the research was their property.

The hypothesis underlying this methodological approach is that the research partnership network positively influences teacher efficacy. This influence occurs through a triple mechanism: mutual observation, reflection on practice and feedback session on teaching. Some of the findings from Chester's recent study (1996) on the relationships between change in self-efficacy beliefs, teacher characteristics, and school practices for newly hired teachers in urban schools confirm the importance of observation and feedback on self-efficacy beliefs:

> [...] beginning teachers who were observed multiple times reported substantially higher values of change in self-efficacy beliefs than their colleagues who had not been observed. The findings confirm the self-reported experience of novices: Failure to observe a teacher until late in the year sometimes results in the feeling that the school administrator does not value competence in the instructional domain. (Chester, M. D., & Beaudin, B. Q., 1996, pp. 251-252)

> In addition to the timing and frequency of feedback, the focus of the feedback is an important aspect of the findings regarding supervisor observations. The absence of feedback directed at validating and improving teachers' instructional practices results

in feelings of uncertainty, anxiety, and neglect. (Chester M. D., & Beaudin, B. Q., 1996, p 252)

However, there is one important difference between Chester's findings and our methodological options. The school context described by Chester and Beaudin is defined as a 'collegial school culture' (see quotation, p. 3). In our research program, we deliberately replaced this school culture with a *cross*-partnership network that focused on didactic *research*. Our beginning teachers were not observed by school inspectors, headmasters or administrators but by peers and trainers/researchers. We believe that it definitely made a difference because the attendance at the lessons and the feedback provided during the workshops were never perceived by the novice teachers as an assessment of their teaching. In a recent paper intitled 'Vygotskian interpretation in a teacher education program', Samaras and Gismondi (1998, p. 717) also insist on the importance of collaboration with peers under the guidance of adults. Like us, they point out the fact that learning should occur through assistance and not through assessment.

As we have already pointed out, we hypothezised that our methodological approach based on collaboration and mutual observation was a necessary (though not sufficient) precondition for a redifinition of the teachers' self-perception of heterogeneousness. Like Guskey (1986, 1989) and Tschannen-Moran *et al.* (1998) we believed that the novice teachers' initial representations would change *if* the new practices which had been suggested in the workshops succeeded in the class and thus enhanced student learning:

> [...] professional development workshops give teachers information about the task of teaching. These experiences also provide strategies and methods that can contribute to a teacher's arsenal of skills. But these new skills may not have an impact on self-perceptions of teaching competence until they are used successfully to enhance student learning.
> [...] Social persuasion can contribute to successful performances to the extent that a persuasive boost leads a person to attempt new strategies or to try hard enough to succeed. (Tschannen-Moran, M. *et al.*, 1998, p. 230)

Results

Throughout the research we collected qualitative data from the different partners involved in the training program: teachers, researchers/trainers and students. Moreover, we collected some quantitative data about the students' results showing that they had significantly improved their reading strategies (see appendix, p.10). In this paper we shall mainly focus on the *process* of the research/training. To illustrate this point, we shall relate the results to the theoretical framework we synthetized with the figure presented page 3.

The willingness to participate in such a research/training program is a necessary but not sufficient precondition for the success of the experiment
Ten teachers were contacted at the beginning of the project. Seven of them took part in the research/training experiment and five of them carried out the research to its very end. Among the many reasons which can be put forward to explain this result, there is one which seemed particularly interesting to us. A close analysis of the language used by the novice teachers in their letters of reply to our proposal of research/training enabled us to distinguish *a posteriori* two distinct groups of teachers: those who admitted they had encountered difficulties in their class and were still in a process of questioning, and those who did not. Interestingly, teachers belonging to the first group were the ones who carried out the experiment through to completion. Guskey (1984) had also observed such results. Teachers showing a great deal of confidence may not feel the need for new strategies and so do not attempt to implement what they have learned.

The partnership network has helped teachers to reframe their initial representation on teaching
The group played an important role in the improvement of teacher efficacy. Actually, we identified a lot of examples of *reframing* strategies in the workshops we organized, especially when teachers were led to confront their subjective perception of the success of the different lessons with the notes taken by their peers and with video extracts from the lessons. For instance, one teacher was particularly disappointed with his performance in one lesson which aimed at proposing simultaneously different activities to different groups of students. Confronting this perception of failure to the notes and video extracts revealed that this teacher had focused his attention on one particular event of the lesson (a problem of discipline) which concerned only three out of the twenty-six students in the class. We also noticed some examples of negative reframing (a contrast between the teacher's positive perception of her/his performance and the notes and/or the video extracts revealing that the lesson was not as efficient as it was felt to be) but they were far less frequent than examples of positive reframing.

The partnership network has positively influenced the teachers' self efficacy and contributed to modify their initial representation of the job
When we started to work on the problem of heterogeneousness, teachers believed that it was impossible to organize simultaneously different learning activities adapted to different needs and mastery levels. This negative attitude was best summed up by one of the teachers who wrote in her letter of reply to our research proposal:

> We should adapt our teaching to the students' level but the heterogeneousness of some classes is so important that it is really impossible to do. While we are busy

explaining something to a group of weak students, the others get bored and stop working and *vice versa*.

Surprisingly, when we asked the teachers to assess the training-process at the end of the research program, they all insisted on the fact that it was *possible* to manage the problem of heterogeneousness. It must again be pointed out that this marked gain in self-efficacy is probably due to the success encountered by the teachers in the implementation of the two experimental sequences (see appendix). In other words, we believe, like Guskey and Tschannen-Moran *et al.*, that if teachers had not perceived a general satisfaction from their students with the experimental didactic sequences, and, more important, a clear improvement in their students' learning outcomes, they probably would not have changed their initial representation.

Teacher efficacy has positively influenced the teachers' behaviours
Here we noticed different manifestations of that change in behaviour:

Spontaneous adoption of reflective attitudes: Throughout the research, we identified a lot of examples of reflective attitudes in the novice teachers' behaviours, which is not surprising because the whole methodological approach precisely aimed at encouraging the novice teachers to reflect on their practice. What seems particularly meaningful to us is the *spontaneous* adoption of such a reflective behaviour because one can infer that it is the evidence that this reflective attitude has been *internalized* by the novice teachers.

Here is a striking example of such a spontaneous reflective behaviour: at the beginning of the research program, we intended to use the results of the Xmas examinations to identify the students' needs in writing, reading, listening and speaking. A close analysis of the exam questions and of the criteria used by the teachers to mark their students revealed that these data were not rigorous and accurate enough to diagnose the students' mastery in each skill. At the end of the workshop, we were rather pleased to note that the teachers spontaneously proposed creating a specific test on one of the four skills (reading). The teachers insisted on the fact that the test should be valid; it should enable them to accurately diagnose their students' mastery in reading.

A willingness to experiment with new theories in the class and to further question one's behaviour as a teacherr: Throughout the research, we tried to encourage teachers to adopt an 'actor's attitude'. We wanted them to be ready to take risks, to manage uncertainty, and to accept their possible mistakes. That was certainly the most difficult thing to achieve. However, we found some manifestations of this experimental behaviour. For instance, after the post-test of the second didactic sequence, one of the teachers decided to organize a fifth lesson in her class. With the group's help, she prepared a lesson with four different activities which were intended to meet the needs of four different groups of students in the class. The four activities were organized simultaneously in the class. This teacher had obviously run some risks.

A desire to communicate one's methodological approach and its pedagogical products to the educational community: At the end of the research/training program, we suggested to the five teachers that they communicate the results of the research to their school colleagues. The teachers were very enthusiastic about this suggestion. So we offered them the opportunity to communicate their newly acquired knowledge by publishing a paper in a review and organizing lectures and workshops for experienced teachers as well as for trainees. This last step turned out to be an important one. Writing the paper led the novice teachers to further reflect on their experiential learning and to retheorize it.

Conclusion

We must admit that the research/training program we have described in this paper was really time-consuming. It started in October and ended in June. Fifteen workshops were organized during this period. In addition to the involvement in the workshops, the teachers had to correct their students' copies (pre-test and post-test) and to travel from one school to another to observe their peers. The next year, they had to prepare the lectures and workshops and write a paper. However, all project partners believed that it was worth the time and effort involved. The novice teachers' integration into a group of peers who did not work in the same school but who shared the same apprehension and faced the same difficulties in their class contributed to the construction of a positive professional identity.

However, no system is perfect and it can be interesting for further research to mention one of the risks of this kind of methodological approach. When we started testing out the experimental sequences in the classes, we encountered a problem with one of the five teachers. Most of his students as well as his school colleagues were rather resistant, not to say hostile, to the new pedagogical methods he was led to experiment in his class. We thought that the clash between two diametrically opposite didactic cultures had progressively driven this young teacher to isolation and we feared that this research would have a negative effect on his professional integration. But three years later, he still teaches in the same school. He still tries to work differently with his students and frequently helps us in the preservice training. Recently, he told one of us that without this research-program he would certainly have left the profession, which confirms the findings of many studies in that field:

Teachers are most likely to leave the profession during their early years in the classroom, the first year being the most risky. Teachers who survive this early period are likely to continue to teach for many years. Retaining new teachers beyond their induction year is critical because experience is one teacher characteristic associated with instructional effectiveness. (Chester, M. D. & Beaudin, B. Q., 1996, p. 234)

If this research/training program only contributed to help one novice teacher remain in the profession, then it was worth the time and effort involved.

Acknowledgements
To Barbara, Christelle, Janny, Sylvie, Jean-François, our partners in this research/ training program.

References

Bandura, A. (1977). 'Self-efficacy: Toward a unifying theory of behavioral change'. *Psychological Review*, 84, 191-215.

Bandura, A. (1997). *Self-Efficacy: The Exercise of Control*. New York : W.H. Freeman.

Beckers, J. (1998). *Comprendre l'enseignement secondaire: Evolution, organisation, analyse*. Bruxelles, De Boeck Université.

Beckers, J. & Simons, G. (1997). 'Analyse d'un programme de formation-recherche destiné à favoriser une entrée positive dans la vie professionnelle de jeunes agrégés de l'enseignement secondaire supérieur'. *Puzzle*. Centre interfacultaire de formation des enseignants de l'Université de Liège. Liège, n°3, décembre 1997, pp. 15-19.

Beckers, J., Charlier, J.-F., D'Ornofrio, B., Pecheux, S., Simons, G., Stadler, Chr. (1998). 'Analyse d'un programme de formation-recherche destiné à favoriser une entrée positive dans la vie professionnelle de jeunes agrégés de l'enseignement secondaire supérieur - 2e partie'. *Puzzle*. Centre interfacultaire de formation des enseignants de l'Université de Liège. Liège, n°5, décembre 1998, pp. 8-16.

Chester, M. D. & Beaudin, B. Q. (1996). 'Efficacy beliefs of newly hired teachers in urban schools'. *American Educational Research Journal*. Spring 1996, Vol. 33, No. 1, pp. 233-257.

Clark, C.M. & Peterson, P.L. (1986). 'Teacher's thought processes'. In WITTROCK, M. (Ed.): *Handbook of Research on Teaching*. New York: Mac Millan.

Gather Thurler (1998). 'Rénovation de l'enseignement primaire à Genève : vers un autre modèle de changement. Premières expériences et perspectives.' In CROS, F. *Dynamiques du changement en éducation et en formation. Considérations plurielles sur l'innovation*. Paris, I.U.F.M. de Versailles et I.N.R.P.

Gist, M. E & Mitchell, T. R. (1992). 'Self-efficacy : a theoretical analysis of its determinants and malleability'. *Academy of Management Review*, 17, 2, 183-211.

Guskey, T. R. (1984). 'The influence of change in instructional effectiveness upon the affective characteristics of teachers'. *American Educational Research Journal*, 21. 245-259.

Guskey, T. R. (1986). 'Staff development and the process of teacher change'. *Educational Researcher*. 15, 5, 5-12.

Guskey, T. R. (1989). 'Attitude and perceptual change in teachers'. *International Journal of Educational Research*, 13, 439-453.

Guskey, T. R. & Passaro, P. D. (1994). 'Teacher efficacy : a study of construct dimensions'. *American Educational Research Journal*, 31, 627-643.

Hausfather, S. J. (1996). 'Vygotsky and schooling: Creating a social context for learning'. *Action in Teacher Education*, 18 (2) , pp. 1-10.

Hoy, W. K. & Woolfolk, A. E. (1990). 'Socialization of student teachers'. *American Educational Research Journal*, 27, 279-300.

Huberman, M. (1989). 'Les phases de la carrière enseignante : un essai de description et de prévision'. *Revue française de Pédagogie*, n°86, janvier-février-mars 1989, pp. 5-16.

Murnane, R. J., Singer, J. D., Willett, J. B., Kemple, J. J, & Olsen, R. J. (1991). *Who Will Teach? Policies That Matter*. Cambridge, MA: Harvard University Press.

Pajares, F. (1992). 'Teachers' beliefs and educational research: cleaning up a messy construct ". *Review of Educational Research*, 62, 307-332.

Peterson, P. L. & Clark, C. M. (1978). 'Teachers' reports of their cognitive processes during teaching'. *American Educational Research Journal*, 15, 555-565.

Ross, J. A. (1992). 'Teacher efficacy and the effect of coaching on student achievement'. *Canadian Journal of Education*, 17, 1, 51-65.

Ross, J. A. (1994). 'The impact of an inservice training to promote cooperative learning on the stability of teacher efficacy'. *Teaching and Teacher Education*, 10, 4, 381-394.

Ross, J. A. (1998). 'Antecedents and consequences of teacher efficacy'. In BROPHY, J. (Ed.), *Advances in Research on Teaching* (Vol. 7, pp. 49-74). Greenwich, CT: JAI Press.

Rotter, J. B. (1966). 'Generalized expectancies for internal versus external control of reinforcement'. *Psychological Monographs*, 80, 1-28.

Samaras, A. P. & Gismondi, S. (1998). 'Scaffolds in the field: Vygotskian interpretation in a teacher education program'. *Teaching And Teacher Education*. Vol 14, No. 7, pp. 715-733.

Schön, D. (1982). *The Reflective Practitioner*. New York : Basic Books.

Schön, D. (1988). 'Coaching reflective teaching'. In GRIMMET, P. & ERICKSON, G. (Eds.) *Reflection in Teacher Education*. New York, Teachers College Press, 1988.

Tschannen-Moran, M., Woolfolk Hoy, A. & Hoy, W.K. (1998). 'Teacher efficacy : its meaning and measure'. *Review of Educational Research*, vol. 68, n° 2, 202-248.

Veenman, S. (1984). 'Perceived problems of beginning teachers'. *Review of Educational Research*, 54, 2, 143-178.

Vigotsky, L. S. (1978). In. Cole, M., John-Steiner, V., Scribner S. & Souberman, E. (Eds & trans.). *Mind in Society: The Development of Higher Psychological Processes*. Cambridge, MA : Harvard University Press.

Weinstein, C. S., (1988). 'Preservice teachers' expectations about the first year of teaching'. *Teaching and Teacher Education*, 4, 31-40.

Appendix

As has been explained in the paper we chose to work on the reading skill. To improve the students' mastery in this skill we decided to select two reading strategies: *the content anticipation strategy* and *the compound decomposition strategy*. The first didactic sequence (5 lessons) focused on the content anticipation strategy, the second one (4 lessons) on the compound decomposition strategy.

The content anticipation strategy aims at helping students identify and understand all the elements in or beside the text which are likely to facilitate their further reading. It can be the title of the text, the subtitles, the titles of the different paragraphs, the typography (italic, bold type) but also the photos, the caricatures, the tables or charts which illustrate the written text and give sense to it. All these elements are important clues which enable the reader to make some hypotheses about the content of the text he is going to read.

The compound decomposition strategy aims at helping students understand some compounds in the text without being forced to constantly stop their reading and ask for assistance (teacher's help or use of the dictionnary). Teaching this strategy includes two key-aspects: teaching the basic principle of compound (de)composition (translating an English compound from right to left)* and teaching the meaning of some prefixes and suffixes. In our study, we worked on the prefixes *under/over* and on the suffixes *less/ful*.

To assess the extent of the progress made by the students in these two reading strategies, we organized a pre-test at the beginning of the didactic sequence and a post-test at the end.

* Our study shows that few students understood this basic principle. For example, the compound: 'a bacteria filled world' was often translated into French by: 'une bactérie répandue dans le monde' (from left to right) instead of 'un monde rempli de bactéries' (from right to left).

Assessment of the progress made by the students at the end of the two experimental didactic sequences:
Content anticipation and *Compound decomposition* strategies

Content anticipation strategy				Compound decomposition strategy			
pre-test		*post-test*		*pre-test*		*post-test*	
FAILURE	SUCCESS	FAILURE	SUCCESS	FAILURE	SUCCESS	FAILURE	SUCCESS
42/84	42/84	5/77	72/77	42/84	42/84	11/71	60/71
(50%)	(50%)	(6,49%)	(93,50%)	(50%)	(50%)	(15,49%)	(84,50%)

These results show that most students have progressed in the two reading strategies. Moreover, when we compare the marks of the pre-test with the marks of the post-test we notice that the improvement is significant because the average progress between the two tests is one of 7/20:

Content anticipation strategy (n= 75)			Compound decomposition strategy (n= 68)		
REGRESSION	STABILITY	PROGRESS	REGRESSION	STABILITY	PROGRESS
4/75 (5%)	2/75 (3%)	69/75 (92%)	8/68 (12%)	2/68 (3%)	58/68 (85%)
on average: - 1,37/20		on average: + 7,17/20	on average: - 1,81/20		on average: + 6,75/20

ICT in Finnish Teacher Education – Evaluation with Special Reference to Active Learning and Democracy

HANNELE NIEMI

In 1998 the Finnish Parliament started a large evaluation project with the purpose of examining the impact of ICT on education. This article focuses on a description of the evaluation methods and theoretical background of the measurements in an attempt to present the main results of the review in the area of teacher education. The results are reflected from two perspectives. The first viewpoint is how ICT in teacher education will promote or resist the development of democracy in a society. The second perspective is to consider empirical results as cultural. The aims of this article are to elaborate a theoretical concept model for technological learning environments and a democratic society and to seek the kind of cultural change in teaching and learning that is needed in teacher education.

Finland launched a special information society strategy in the middle of the 1990s. The use of ITC in teaching and learning figured prominently as a key way to accelerate the progress towards the chosen direction. (Sinko & Lehtinen 1999: 7). In 1998 the Finnish Parliament started a large evaluation project with the purpose of examining the impact of ICT on education. The review process covered the whole educational system, from childhood to adult education, taking into account principles of lifelong learning. The evaluation project was divided into five sub-projects, and each of these was further subdivided. As the result of this work, a total of eight reports were produced (Sinko & Lehtinen 1999: 11). One of these subprojects focused on higher education and teacher education as a part of it (Viteli & et al. 1998). The writer of this article was responsible for the evaluation of teacher education (Niemi 1998). The results and recommendations for the development of ICT in teacher education have been presented in a sub-report (Viteli et al. 1998) and an English summary (Sinko & Lehtinen 1999: 145-155).

This article aims to give a description of the evaluation methods and theoretical background of the measurements and to present the main results of the review in the area of teacher education. After the description of the empirical study, the results will be presented from two perspectives. The first viewpoint is how ICT in teacher education will promote or resist the development of democracy in a society. This aspect was visible in many discussions of the evaluation board. The intention was to gain information on how ICT may support and enhance democracy and equity. The aim of this article is to elaborate a theoretical concept model for technological learning environments and a democratic society. Empirical results will be reflected in the light of this model. The second perspective to consider empirical results is cultural. The purpose is to seek the kind of cultural change in teaching and learning that is needed in teacher education. This leads at the end of the article to assess how applications and environments of ICT should be developed in teacher education in the near future. The empirical results will answer the following questions:

– What is the readiness of student teachers to use ICT in their teaching and learning?
– What are the main obstacles to using ICT in teacher education?
– What kinds of innovative practices have been started in teacher education institutions and what can we learn from these experiences?

Data Collection

The important task of the evaluation was to find out how users see ICT's meaning in their teaching and learning and what their capacity is to use new technological environments. The project wanted to see how ICT adds quality in teaching and learning. To answer these questions, quantitative and qualitative data collection methods were used.

A survey

A survey method was applied to obtain a large overview of student teachers' and teacher educators' concepts and experiences in ICT environments. The survey consisted of questionnaires using the Likert scale. Questions on learning quality were based on theoretical assumptions and principles of active learning (Niemi 1997; Stern & Huber 1997). The survey also consisted of questions which aimed to reveal the kinds of skills student teachers and teacher educators have for using ICT and what their greatest obstacles are. In addition to the structured Likert–scale questions, open-ended questions were used. These focused on users' readiness to apply ICT in teaching and learning and the educational needs that different user groups have in ICT environments. Through the survey, data was collected from 581 student teachers and from 254 teacher educators in three universities and two polytechnics. This article focuses only on the student teachers.

Good practices as cases

To have a deeper understanding on the personal and institutional levels, the evaluation project used a case study method. The aim was to get information about innovative projects and good practices in different parts of the country and in different institutions. The evaluation board selected seven cases to give examples of innovative practices of ICT in teacher education.

The information from innovative practices was collected by interviewers who also observed practices in the institutions and analyzed the documents which were available. The case interviewers and writers followed a structural guideline issued by the project board (Niemi 1998). It was planned on the premises of active learning in the institutional contexts. The interviewers were encouraged to also keep their eyes open for other aspects in each case, although they had a common outline. The intention was to make special elements of the innovative practices visible. The innovative cases were published as a separate book (Viteli 1998) within the ICT evaluation project.

Active Learning as the Theoretical Background of the Evaluation

The theoretical framework of the evaluation project focused on the important question: How does ICT promote quality of learning, especially active learning in TE?

Active learning is one of the most important goals in the European scenarios, which include the concept of a learning society. An important characteristic of the learning society is the learners' own initiative and responsibility for their own progress.

Achievement of this goal, however, is not easy or self-evident. Teachers and teacher education are considered as key factors in promoting active learning. The teachers' work is becoming more crucial than ever. (Cochinaux & de Woot 1995: 87; White paper 1995). All pedagogical arrangements should improve the quality of learning, enhance the equality of opportunities for different learners and help prevent social exclusion.

Active methods in teaching and learning have been requested in many educational debates at national and international levels (Stern & Huber 1997). During the last decade, the new meta-knowledge of teaching and learning, new concepts of learning environments and new knowledge of the diversity of the learners have offered several initiatives to seek new practices at schools. However, Monique Boekaerts (1997), as a researcher of self-regulated learning, describes a recent situation in schools and societies in the following way: '…most classrooms are still populated with students who are not self-regulating their learning, and most teachers are not yet equipped to turn students into self-regulated learners. In most cases, teachers are still steering and guiding the learning process, a situation which does not invite students to use or develop their cognitive or motivational self-regulatory skills. Usually, students are expected to reproduce and apply the new information that the teacher has presented or made available.'(Boekaerts, M.1997: 162)

The recent research body on learning does not form any particular unified theory group, but a large variety of different approaches which emphasize a learner's activity (Simons 1997, Niemi 1997). In modern learning psychology many concepts, such as authentic learning, self-directed learning, self-regulated learning, constructivistic learning, independent learning, autonomous learning, problem-solving and active learning, have the same purpose, even though they originate from somewhat different theoretical frameworks. The common feature is a learner's active impact on learning and a learner's involvement in the learning process. This active role may be manifested in individual and co-operative learning strategies (Simons 1997; Slavin 1997; Niemi 1997).

The questionnaires and case study guidelines of the evaluation project were constructed on the following theoretical categories:

Individual learning strategies

Active learning strategies emphasize constructivistic qualities in knowledge processing. These are independent inquiry, structuring and restructuring of knowledge. In active learning, the processing of knowledge also requires a problem-solving orientation, a critical approach and an evaluation of knowledge. The ultimate goal of knowledge processing is that the learner can elaborate on applications of knowledge and s/he may also produce new knowledge using cognitive processes. According to the newest learning theories, quality of learning also depends on learners' abilities to steer their own learning orientation, to develop inquiring skills and to learn to reflect on and control their own learning processes. Metacognitive skills are key concepts. In addition to metacognitive skills, meta-mood skills or motivational strategies seem to play an important role in active learning processes. Learners need skills to manage or steer their own motivation and emotions. These qualities may also be called intrapersonal skills or emotional intelligence (Gardner & Hatch 1989; Goleman 1995). Commitment and inner motivation are usually in mutual relationship to the cognitive factors in a learning process.

Co-operative learning

In the construction of knowledge, social elements have emerged as very important. How we learn and comprehend knowledge depends on our beliefs, attitudes, values and our self-concept as a learner. Learning is related to our social history and interaction with other people. Active learning theories stress the social elements of learning, e.g. the importance of co-operative action, collaborative problem-solving and sharing as tools for attaining deeper processes of learning; and in many cases also achieving better results. Learning has increasingly seen a deepening within a social context and framework (Slavin 1997). Promotive interaction, sharing and reflection are necessary for the learner to work on his personal beliefs, concepts and constructions of knowledge. This means participation in discussions, dialogues and mutually-shared reflections, working in responsible co-operation with other learners. Learner participation is fostered by a supportive atmosphere and an equal partnership among the learners, based on mutual respect. European scenarios of learning emphasize teamwork and networking as important tools for bringing people closer together.

Empirical Results

Student teachers' readiness to use ICT in their teaching and learning
Student teachers' readiness to use ICT practically means that they use computers for word processing and e-mail. The third area in which they use ICT is surfing on the WWW pages. Typical of students teachers is their low capacity to use other applications of telecommunication, such as video conferences, or to use or produce electronic learning materials

	El	Sec	Kind	Voc	Total
Basic skill;s and tools					
Operating systems	3.57	3.53	3.15	3.81	3.55
Word processing	4.16	4.17	3.83	4.13	4.13
Spread Sheet programs	2.47	2.66	2.06	3.14	2.58
Catalog/Database programs	2.12	2.18	1.77	2.32	2.13
Graphics and Draw programs	2.82	2.60	2.57	2.92	2.73
Presentation graphics	2.11	2.01	1.57	2.77	2.10
Telecommunication					
E-mail	3.97	3.85	3.56	3.87	3.88
Web browsing	3.30	3.64	3.04	3.97	3.61
Creating web pages	1.93	1.86	1.42	2.06	1.87
Other Internet use	2.13	2.22	1.83	2.28	2.16
Working group programs	1.56	1.41	1.40	1.80	1.52
Video conferences	1.68	1.42	1.21	1.97	1.58
Use of electronic learning materials					
CD-ROMs	2.74	2.84	2.06	2.44	2.68
Computer-aided teaching programs	2.13	2.08	1.51	1.94	2.03
Web learning material & inf. searching	2.84	2.85	2.17	3.01	2.80
Using Helps of Programs	2.02	2.27	1.72	2.16	2.10
Special applications for working life					
Games (e.g. business games)	1.96	1.88	1.89	1.87	1.91
Simulations (e.g. in production)	1.48	1.46	1.19	1.63	1.47
Business applications	1.63	1.62	1.42	2.20	1.68

Table 2 – Student teachers' readiness to use ICT applications.

Mean values (5 = very high; 1 = very low).
El = Elementary student teachers – *Sec* = Secondary student teachers – *Kind* = Kindergarten student teachers – *Voc* = Vocational student teachers in polytechnics

The trends are very similar for all higher education students, but the results of student teachers are somewhat lower than the mean values for the whole group (Sinko & Lehtinen 1999, 114). If we compare differences between student teacher groups, vocational teachers have the best skills and kindergarten teachers have the lowest readiness. In open answers, all student groups said that they lack ICT skills. The student teachers did not undervalue ICT. They strongly indicated that they need to have more opportunities to practice using ICT, with the first step being relatively easy and flexible access to computers. In addition, the students requested more courses, support and teaching in this area. Student teachers and teacher educators would like to have more education and tutoring in creating meaningful pedagogical environments with computers or other ICT applications. This help should also be given as on-line support, not as traditional courses. There is also a lack of high standard software in Finnish. In addition, student teachers need more skills to produce multimedia material for and with their pupils.

The results confirm earlier evaluations (Niemi & Tirri 1997). In 1995, newly graduated teachers had very low competencies to use ICT and open learning environments. This seems strange in a Finnish context. Finland is one of the top countries developing high tech environments. The numbers of computers and other ICT facilities per capita are the highest or second highest in the world. In addition, there are many high standard ICT pilot projects in all Finnish TE institutions. Why does teacher education not provide new teachers with better skills for ICT?

Main obstacles to using ICT in teacher education
There are differences between student teacher groups, but the main trends are clear. There are too few workstations in the institutions. Lack of software in Finnish is also a problem. There is also a great need for pedagogical support. The serious problem seems to be that neither students nor student teachers have the time to learn new skills and there is no space for it in the full-packed courses

There is a clear relationship between the available technical infrastructure and user readiness, which means that ICT skills cannot be learned without an effective infrastructure, but also that the need for technology grows along with experiences in open learning environments.

The meaning of ICT in student teachers' learning
The main target of the project was to get new knowledge about what the value of ICT is for student teachers. How does it add quality of learning? The summary of the results are described in Table 4. ICT really is an important aid for many students. The value of ICT is first and foremost in the support it offers in doing tasks and assignments related to studies. It adds self-directed learning. ICT is also important in processing information and getting new information and source

					Total
Amount of student teachers' workstations	3,59	3,71	3,92	2,93	3,58 ***
Lack of skills to create electronic learning material	3,56	3,52	3,52	3,25	3,50
Lack of time of student teachers	3,57	3,44	3,43	2,96	3,43 **
Lack of ICT support to student teachers	3,41	3,34	3,55	2,82	3,32 ***
Too little instruction and in courses of ICT	3,40	3,21	2,92	2,79	3,22 ***
ICT skills of student teachers	3,38	3,11	3,37	2,74	3,20 ***
Lack of time of teacher educators	3,10	3,27	2,86	3,13	3,14
Server capacity	3,21	3,04	3,08	2,76	3,09 *
Student teachers' ICT at home	3,12	3,11	2,86	3,02	3,08
Curriculum contains too small units	3,32	2,94	2,85	2,73	3,07 ***
Lack of pedagogical ICT support to teacher educators	3,06	3,25	2,83	2,69.	3,06 ***
Timing problems in courses	3,11	3,04	3,06	2,48	3,01 **
Lack of technical ICT support to teacher educators	2,91	3,14	2,64	2,60	2,93 ***
Deficiencies in teaching methods	3,01	2,94	2,98	2,42	2,91 **
Pedagogical ICT skills of teacher educators	2,87	3,12	2,94	2,28	2,89 ***
ICT skills of teacher educators	2,75	3,11	2,69	2,48	2,84 ***
Objectives of courses	2,98	2,84	2,57	2,41	2,83 **
Lack of electronic teaching and learning material	2,80	3,00	2,58	2,64	2,83 *
Reserve attitudes of teacher educators	2,60	2,91	2,61	2,36	2,68 **
Reserve attitudes of student teachers	2,52	2,44	2,59	2,46	2,49
Numbers of Licences	2,39	2,60	2,21	2,53	2,47
Numbers of teacher educators' work stations	2,34	2,63	2,17	2,49	2,45 *
Teacher educators' ICT at home	2,31	2,46	1,93	2,80	2,39 ***
Library and information services	2,17	2,11	2,20	2,09	2,14
Telecommunication nets in HE institutions	2,21	2,09	1,84	2,21	2,13
Telecommunication from HE institutions	2,23	2,06	1,80	2,15	2,12

Table 3 – Obstacles to using ICT in teacher education. Mean values (5 = highest; 1 = lowest)

material. Another dimension in the use of ICT is communication with the learning community. The picture becomes more clear with combined variables, which were formed after factor analysis. They were named as:
1. Planning and organizing TE studies,
2. Working on assignments
3. Combining studies and working life and
4. Communication in the learning community.

The mean values show that ICT is an important tool to prepare essays, reports and other homework. ICT is also a good tool for communication, but not yet well used as an organizer of tasks or as a tool in connecting studies with different contexts and partners including working life.

Variables	Mean	Std Dev
Learning in a self directed way	4.45	.88
Writing project or research reports	4.25	1.02
Preparing reviews, essays or presentations	4.20	1.00
Information processing	3.78	1.20
Searching for new knowledge and information sources	3.73	1.11
Communication with members of learning community	3.68	1.35
Working in groups	3.47	1.24
Making studies more effective	3.43	1.21
Speed up studies for graduation	3.35	1.26
Planning for teaching practice	3.15	1.25
Delivering new knowledge and information sources	2.86	1.24
Connecting studies with practical work	2.81	1.18
Elaborating new ideas	2.74	1.17
Implementing personal study programs	2.71	1.27
Getting feedback from studies	2.59	1.15
Planning studies with other students	2.59	1.20
Assessing peers' achievements	2.57	1.15
Combining working life with studies	2.55	1.24
Giving feedback from study programs	2.52	1.14
Communication with working life	2.52	1.28
Finding suitable timing in own life context	2.42	1.29
In self-evaluating	2.39	1.07
In evaluation of validity and quality of knowledge	2.32	1.05
Planning personal study program with teacher educators	2.25	1.13
Getting supervision	2.13	1.01

Table 4 – Meaning of ICT in student teachers' learning. (5 = extremely important; 1 = not at all important).

Combined variables	Means	SD	Cronbach alpha
Planning and organizing TE studies	2.61	.84	.92
Working on assignments	3.91	.80	.82
Combining studies and working life	2.58	1.02	.83
Communication in learning community	3.42	1.01	.76

Table 5 – Meaning of ICT in student teachers' learning. Combined variables after factor analysis.

The project revealed much evidence that the frequency of using ICT and considering it as an important aid was highly correlative. This means that those who used it saw it as a meaningful tool and vice versa. Earlier research which described teacher education in 1995 (Niemi & Tirri 1997), shows that the most common form of active learning has been the student teachers' intensive work with their assignments. They had learnt to set objectives for themselves and for their learning. Students worked in groups with problem-solving tasks and they self-evaluated their own products. The use of electronic nets to seek information for student assignments, however, was a very rare learning process at that time. Now the new evaluation in 1998 shows that the use of ICT is much more usual. But student teachers still seldom have opportunities to plan and carry out fairly large projects, or to plan and organize, together with their peers, the contents and methods of study units. Also, they seldom applied ICT in their teaching practice. It seems that in teacher education students have active learning experiences with fairly closed tasks. They are not used to planning and building their own learning tasks and environments. We must ask critically, if students could use more ICT, would they also see it as more important in areas which are now less valued?

Innovative Practices and Cultural Change
Although there seem to be numerous shortcomings in teacher education, a number of relatively innovative projects are under way in several places. For the purpose of assessing TE, we therefore tried to find practices where ICT has been used in an innovative way and where a new kind of teaching and learning culture has been developed. The seven case studies describe innovative practices of ICT in teacher education within different application areas:

ICT and distance learning
  – Language teaching was provided in a very remote school in Lapland by a
    university teacher-training school in Helsinki, through its student teachers.
  – A co-operative project, involving a university teacher-training school, a
    teacher education department and local schools on a remote island,
    offered instruction and optional courses to pupils who otherwise lacked
    these opportunities.

ICT in teaching practice
  – A telematic teaching-practice pilot project guided student teachers' work
    in remote rural schools and had active supportive networks with supervi-
    sors and student teachers though different telematic tools.
  – Teaching practice, with high quality information technological observa-
    tion tools, gave student teachers an opportunity to have immediate
    feedback on their teaching. Video was connected with information-
    processing programs, giving different summaries of the students'
    behaviour as a teacher. This provided a remarkable basis for reflections
    on professional development.

How to integrate ICT into teacher education programmes
  – Educational technological courses for student teachers were organized
    virtually by three universities. It also provided authentic experiences of
    co-operation and electronic learning environments.

– Communication and information technological studies for teachers was a pilot study in which student teachers worked in flexible, open and learner-centred learning environments.
– Business and entrepreneurial study modules were integrated in teacher education using new technology. The project was in co-operation with the local business life and a university teacher education institution.

Typical of the pilot projects were the active networks through ICT, for partnership between teacher education, local schools and also with the business life. Experimentation and new practices, where ICT has been courageously applied to teacher education, have been motivating and important experiences for the participants. One of their foremost merits has been the co-operation of teacher education departments and their practice schools with partners outside the university. The projects have usually been launched through the initiative of enthusiastic individuals, and they have required relatively substantial resources for the necessary technology, as well as management and co-ordination. Many of the projects have only become possible through the support and partnership of the outside partners (Niemi 1998; Sinko & Lehtinen 1999: 154-155).

These pilot programmes provide hope for teacher education and schools to find a new culture of active learning. Their problem is, however, that they remain projects within small active groups. Very often they are isolated from other schools or the TE community. The culture of these pilot projects is different from what is usual in these institutions. They work with a flexible timetable, they allow for individual choices, they have contacts with other institutions and partners. The projects are very rewarding for participants, but they have difficulties to become integrated with the traditional school life or TE practices. There is a danger that the projects and innovative practices only enrich their participants, without enabling other students or teachers to benefit from the experiences gained in the projects. The innovative ICT projects set a clear need for schools and TE institutions to change their cultures.

ICT, democracy and active learning
The empirical results revealed that there is much lacking in teacher education using ICT. To gain a more comprehensive picture, a theoretical concept model has been constructed in which ICT is connected with active learning and democracy in a society. The crucial questions are:
– How does ICT promote and maintain equity and democracy in a society?
– How does ICT promote quality of learning, especially active learning?

The two components are closely interconnected, but they set different demands on the use of ICT. The aims of future development may be illustrated by Table 6, in which the theoretical components are set at three levels of life: society, culture and the person. The levels used refer to the structural components of Habermas' 'Lifeworld' concept (Habermas 1987: 138). Society is used for the legitimate orders through which participants regulate their memberships in social groups and thereby secure solidarity. The term culture is used for the stock of knowledge from which participants in communication supply themselves with interpretations as they come to an understanding about something in the world. By the person we understand the competencies that make a subject capable of speaking and acting, that put him into a position to take part in processes of reaching understanding and thereby to assert his own identity.

Society level means people's belongingness to a certain group. We may include or exclude people on different bases. We may ask for what reasons people are included or excluded by ICT. The evaluation of TE revealed that the first and fundamental reason is whether or not people have access to ICT. If they do not have real chances they will be excluded. The second point at the society level is what kinds of systems and structures for communication and co-operation are available through ICT. Are users being included or excluded in these structures? The problem of innovative projects was forming insider groups. It created gaps between other students and teacher educators. TE communities should evaluate their own structures (such as curriculum, working schedules, teaching modules and teaching loads). They should ask whether they prevent people from gaining those advantages that ICT can provide and whether there are structural barriers for communication and co-operation which would be essential preconditions and also consequences for ICT applications.

Active learning plays an important role in a democratic society. The theoretical basis of active learning raises two important aspects of learning: individual learning strategies and co-operative learning. A human being is seen as an active constructor of knowledge, and learning also has a social component. At the societal and community level, active learning requires conditions which provide chances to share knowledge, to work in teams, to have joint learning projects and to be responsible as a group for the learning result. ICT may be a good tool for this kind of learning. There is a mutual interaction between democracy and active learning. If society can provide flexible structures and equal opportunities for communication by also using new technology, people will use them more and more if they have internalized active learning strategies in their life. But this demands that they really have opportunities to learn and apply co-operating working methods at different level of the educational system.

Cultural level refers to the fact that people are an integral part of their cultural surroundings. How they understand their own roles and identity depends on the cultural stock of their social communities. People's interpretations grow out of their culture, but they also play an active role in forming new interpretations.

When something changes in an earlier unifying horizon, they need to form new
concepts and find new ways to act. ICT has brought new elements into people's
lives, both locally and globally. It has increased opportunities to obtain more information and to participate more effectively in society. At the same time, we may
see many Western countries turning from a representative democracy to a more
participatory model. We could say that ICT may strengthen people's opportunities to participate in a society if they have access to ICT and a society that supports their participation with structures and facilities. But to become participatory in a society also demands high quality learning abilities, above all knowledge
management. They must learn to choose, process and evaluate information and
knowledge. They must find the essential points in the information and they must
learn to express their own knowledge to others. Active learning in schools is not
a purpose in itself, or something which makes learning more attractive. A learning
culture has a clear connection with participatory democracy in a society.

Person level of the concept model means competencies that people need in
their lives. The teacher education evaluation project revealed that many new teachers
lack the technical and pedagogical skills to use new environments. To utilize technological environments, basic skills are needed. In these contexts, communicative
skills are also necessary. In earlier studies of active learning we have learnt that
both teachers and students lack metacognitive knowledge and skills. To have ICT
as a tool for democracy in a society, educational systems should provide more
competencies which make people more empowered in the learning processes
through metacognitive skills. The conceptual model of components of ICT, democracy and active learning is summarized in Table 6.

	Democracy	Active Learning
Society	Equal access and availability of ICT	More opportunities for communication in educational communities
Culture	Participatory culture through ICT	More knowledge management
Person	Technological and communicative competencies	More empowerment in one's own learning through metacognitive skills

Table 6 – Theoretical components of ICT, democracy and active learning

Coming back to the empirical results of the evaluation project, we may summa-
rize that, before teachers can promote democracy in a society through ICT, they

must have the opportunity to use the new technology. It is a challenge to TE to provide the *equal access and availability* of ICT, which means the availability of computers and other tools for students in TE institutions. They need more workstations and knowledge of how to use the new programs and software. But democracy cannot be obtained only through technological infrastructures. Teacher education also needs a new learning culture and a new professional teacher culture, where communication and co-operation have a more vital role than at present.

The second task is to promote *participatory culture* in TE. ICT can promote communication and co-operation between different partners in TE. It will increase their opportunities to participate in planning and development of the learning environments and other fields of their lives. The precondition of participatory culture is that educational systems also provide more opportunities for knowledge management, which helps people to prepare themselves for communication.

The third challenge concerns *person level competencies*: teachers and their students require the competencies needed in ICT environments, especially the basic skills for technological environments and communicative competencies. But in addition, they need more metacognitive knowledge and skills for becoming more empowered in their own learning.

Conclusion: How to Anticipate the Future?

The results indicated clearly that schools and teacher education departments are in the middle of a cultural change in using ICT. The evaluation study revealed that attitudinal resistance has been overcome in teacher education. Student teachers and teacher educators, however, have a fairly narrow readiness to use ICT environments. The main application areas are word processing and the use of e-mail or WWW pages for communication. Students and teacher educators are not very familiar with either applying, producing or developing electronic learning material or using open and distance learning, e.g. video conferences or network programmes. Their competency areas should be broadened. Student teachers also need more skills to produce virtual and multimedia material for and with their pupils.

The need for pedagogical knowledge to apply ICT is obvious. Student teachers and teacher educators would like to have more education and tutoring in creating meaningful pedagogical environments with computers and other ICT applications. There is also a lack of high standard software in Finnish. The differences between student teachers were statistically significant in many skills. There is a clear relationship between the available technical infrastructure and user readiness, which means that ICT skills cannot be learned without an effective infrastructure, but also that the need for technology grows along with experiences in open learning environments. There is also a lack of knowledge about active learning methods and strategies with ICT. Student teachers do not have enough experience of using metacognitive skills in the context of ICT.

Although Finnish teacher education has succeeded in many respects, there are still many problems which need to be taken seriously. It seems that teachers are educated for a stable world. Teachers have a good readiness to work in classrooms, but the readiness for ICT and for relationships with partners outside the university is weak. The results raise the question of how teacher education culture really gives space for ICT. Teacher education institutions have a culture of time pressure, fully-packed courses, fairly inflexible time schedules and ready-made task settings. More open, communicative and participatory working culture should be the direction towards which they are aiming.

New technology has provided rich opportunities to seek, handle and produce information. New technology also creates open learning environments, which provide enormous learning opportunities. However, these environments require new learners' skills. The learner must have abilities to use these opportunities. New technology is producing innovations which accelerate changes in economic life, societal structures and production. The serious problem is that there are many people, young and old, who do not have the opportunities or readiness for new ICT. There is a growing gap between those who can and those who cannot. This has been seen as a serious threat to democracy in societies. Technological innovations, together with social, political and cultural dispersion, are producing new forms of knowledge and culture. We must be aware of the dysfunction of the information society, and we cannot close our eyes to the future, into which a new generation is entering. It will be much more complicated, multi-valued and full of tensions and dilemmas. Teachers will be key persons in supporting different learners to find their opportunities in a society. To add quality in learning and democracy in a society requires that teachers themselves have access to ICT and they can grow to use the advantages that it provides.

Democracy is never a fixed state. It is a continuous process. This means that people must be conscious of their rights. There are many hidden barriers to democracy. To many people, the hidden barriers in our century, and in the coming century, are unequal opportunities and the lack of skills to use ICT. Giddens (1998: 79) emphasizes that democracy means something other than the orthodox voting process of a nation. Democracy should give real space and tools to people to become more active and participatory. John Dewey wrote at the beginning of this century: 'A society which is mobile, which is full of channels for the distribution of a change occurring anywhere, must see to it that its members are educated to personal initiative and adaptability. Otherwise, they will be overwhelmed by the changes in which they are caught and whose significance or connections they do not perceive. The result will be a confusion in which a few will appropriate to themselves the results of the blind and externally directed activities of others' (1916: 88).

References

Boekaerts, M. (1997). Self-Regulated Learning: A New Concept Embraced by Researchers, Policy Makers, Educators, Teachers, And Students. *Learning and Instruction* 7 (1), 161-186.

Cochinaux, P., & de Woot, P. (1995). *Moving towards a Learning Society.* A CRE - ERT forum report on European education. Geneve: CRE and Brussels: ERT.

Dewey, J. (1916). *Democracy and Education. An Introduction to the Philosophy of Education.* New York: Macmillan.

Gardner, H. & Hatch, T. (1989). Multiple Intelligences Go to School. *Educational Researcher* 18 (8).

Giddens, A. (1998). *The Third Way. The Renewal of Social Democracy.* Oxford: Polity Press.

Goleman, D. (1995). *Emotional Intelligence. Why It Can Matter More Than IQ.* New York: Bantam Books.

Habermas, J. (1987). *The Theory of Communicative Action. Volume 2. LifeWorld and System: A Critique of Functionalist Reason.* Translated by McCarthy, T. United States: Polity Press.

Niemi, H. (1998). Opettajankoulutus. In Finnish. (ICT in Teacher Education). In Viteli, J. (eds) & Collan, S. & Kauppi, A.& Niemi, H. & Vainio, L (1998) *Yliopistojen ja ammattikorkeakoulujen tilanne ja tulevaisuuden näkymät.* In Finnish. *(Scenarios of Universities and Polytechnics).* Helsinki: Sitra 189, .

Niemi, H. (1997). Active learning by teachers. In Stern. D., & Huber, G. L.(Eds), *Active Learning for Students and Teachers. Reports from Eight Countries.* OECD. Frankfurt am Main: Peter Lang. 174-182.

Niemi. H. & Tirri. K. (1997). Niemi, H. & Tirri, K. 1997. *Valmiudet opettajan ammattiin opettajien ja opettajien kouluttajien arvioimina.* Readiness for Teaching Profession Evaluated by Teachers and Teacher Educators. (In Finnish, Abstract in English). Reports from the Department of Teacher Education in Tampere University A 10.

Simons, P.R. J. (1997). Definitions and theories of active learning. In Stern . D., & Huber, G. L. (Eds),. *Active Learning for Students and Teachers. Reports from Eight Countries.* OECD. Frankfurt am Main: Peter Lang, 19-39.

Sinko, M. & Lehtinen. E. (1999). *The Challenges of ICT in Finnish Education.* Juva: Atena

Slavin, R.E. (1997). Co-operative learning among students. In Stern, D. & Huber, G. L.(eds.) *Active learning for students and teachers. Reports from eight countries.* OECD. Frankfurt am Main: Peter Lang 159-173.

Stern, D., & Huber, G. L. (1997). *Active learning for students and teachers. Reports from eight countries.* OECD. Frankfurt am Main: Peter Lang.

White Paper on Education and Training. (1995). Brussels: Commission of the European Communities.

Viteli, J. (ed.) (1998). *Esimerkkejä ja kokemuksia korkeakoulumaailmasta.* In Finnish. *(Examples and experiences from higher education.* ICT in Teaching and Learning. The Evaluation Project of Sitra). Helsinki: Sitra 190.

Viteli, J. (ed.) & Collan, S. & Kauppi, A.& Niemi, H. & Vainio, L (1998*). Yliopistojen ja ammattikorkeakoulujen tilanne ja tulevaisuuden näkymät.* In Finnish. *(Scenarios of Universities and Polytechnics.* ICT in Teaching and Learning. The Evaluation Project of Sitra). Helsinki: Sitra 189.

Teachers' Discourses in Social Learning

Maria A. Martínez Ruiz & Narcis Sauleda Parés

Nowadays, social learning discourses are not only in profusion, but also prevalent. However, the analysis of this educative practice tends to suggest that authentic collaborative learning strategies are rarely enforced in the classroom. This is due to the inconsistency that derives from educators´ diverse and dissonant discourses. It is also due to the fact that the majority of activities of professional reconstitution in which the educators participate, do not influence their own course of thought nor their own practical reasoning. The most frequent situation in the lecture room is that the educators receive the theory related to social learning in a theoretical scenery characterized by individual study. This means that through university education, the situative perspective is rarely set out. Our previous research has identified educators' thoughts related to the process of learning through the analysis of their metaphors. After having examined the interpretation of their narratives closely, we have reached the conclusion that the more frequent perspective of learning is ambiguous, although individual traits are prevalent in it. Paradoxically, this research based on biographical narratives shows that new educators seek, almost desperately, personal and professional support from their colleagues, for their own personal, professional and political development. In this context, we consider that the educators will assume the relevance of developing a learner's framework for each other inside the classroom, especially if they take into account the way in which they value the outspoken and well-founded support of their colleagues. Furthermore, we feel that the educators' ability to assume the importance of learning as a social process depends on whether they work inside a culture of learning in which the conceptual tensions are resolved through dialogue, discussion and conversation with their colleagues as well as with others.

At present, the social structure is characterized by the networks which support the dynamics of fluxes of information and of materials which result from human activity. The interconnections within the networks and the close links and interdependencies between the social, political and economical spheres have all opened a door towards an era characterized by the generation, diffusion and exchange of knowledge. In the existing society of networks (Castells, 1994, 1996, 1997, 1998), which lacks a centre and is characterized by interdependence, education is not an island, but part of culture (Bruner, 1996) and the student is not an isolated agent which acquires knowledge, but an individual in a subcommunity of learners. In this new society of networks and fluxes, neither individual learning nor individualist action are going to solve the problems which emerge. As a result, our first assertion is that the educator's own education should develop the disposition in all educators to learn how to collaborate in the generation of knowledge in order to resolve the authentic problems which arise inside the classroom and inside the educational communities. This means that investigatory projects which assume that learning is essentially a process of social collaboration correspond, in a closer way, with the new concept of society (Day, 1997, 1999). Resounding with this perspective is the idea that these educators must evolve from an individual conception of professional learning towards a theory of initiation and participation in both the network as well as in professional and social communities. In this sense, the idea of an educator as an isolated agent does not work, although this does not mean that it is not necessary to promote a culture which facilitates the strengthening of personal identity. Faced with 'the increasing distance between globalization and identity, between the net and the self' (Castells, 1996, p.23), we tend to incline towards the recurrent integration between global culture and the culture that enactuates an individual's identity.

Assuming that the educator's education depends on a process of interdependence and collaboration between humans and non-humans, we are also accepting that both social and individual learning should be integrated by means of a circularity of recursive interactions. The intensification of interdependence between social and individual learning should be able to respond to the antagonism which, in the world, or in what Castells calls the chaotic jungle, currently emerges from the forces which tend towards the standardization and globalization, and also from those forces which favour the assertion of identity itself. In comparison with the emphasis we place on collaborative learning perspectives, our previous investigations (Martínez and Sauleda, 1997, 1998, 1999) have led us to hypothesise that prospective educators tend to assume that learning is basically an individual process of conceptual acquisition or development. As a result, educators very seldom tend to introduce these strategies based on participation in their classes.

The participation in the discourse of a community as the nucleus of professional reconstitution

Parting from an analysis of the learning theories present in the current panorama, Ann Sfârd (1998) has synthesized the different views of several authors into two metaphors. One metaphor evokes learning as the process through which knowledge is acquired (Anderson, Reder and Simon, 1996), while the other considers learning to be, basically, a process of participation (Lave, 1998; Rogoff, 1990; Lave and Wenger, 1991; Cole and Engerström, 1993; Greeno, 1997). In a similar way, Salomon and Perkins (1998) and Cobb and Bowers (1999) have also differentiated a group of learning theories which emphasize the acquisition of knowledge and the individual development of cognitive skillls, from another group that interprets learning as a process similar to that of an apprentice's work (Rogoff,

1990). These metaphors of social learning, together with the vast number of publications which refer to models based on participation (Antil, Jenkins, Wayne and Vasady, 1998) are clear evidence of the present prevalence of theories based on collaboration and distributed cognition (Salomon, 1993). Even Popkewitz (1998, 1999) argues that currently, not only systematic theories, but also critical ones, assume the learning perspective as a collaborative process.

As a counterpart to the prevalence of social learning theories within the circle of educational researches, educators do not seem to organize their classes around a community of practice (Brown and Campione, 1995; Day, 1999). The model of the isolated teacher in the heart of a community of education has been well documented over the years (Lortie, 1975; Hargreaves, 1994), and evidence of educators' fragmented professionality still continues to be presented. The dissonance between, on one hand, the relevance in literature of situated or collaborative perspectives of learning and, on the other hand, the apparent absence in the classroom and in educators' conceptions of the philosophy and the premises of social learning and the distributed cognition, has led us to hypothesize that the organisation of courses orientated towards the education of educators themselves, in a situative and cooperative scenario facilitates the change of status in educators' conceptions in favour of a situated perspective.

In short, the arguments in favour of distributed practice and action, by which people solve problems not in an isolated way, but jointly with the available tools; and, furthermore, the vision by which it is not only the 'person-solo' who learns, but the 'person-plus' the whole network of interrelated factors (Perkins, 1993), has inclined us to offer educators who are registered in our courses, the opportunity to participate in social learning situations. For this purpose, we have put emphasis on methods orientated towards the creation of a community of distributed work in our academic activities, and have generated an atmosphere and discourse characterized by the participation and cooperation of all the agents. We aim towards a harmonic interaction of the forces derived fom students' proclivities and personal experiences, with co-laboured actions with others and with different resources, and from beliefs and cultural practices. In brief, our aim is to achieve a community of discourse where synergetic interconnections between social and individual aspects of learning take place, in a sort of recursive circularity (Salomon and Perkins, 1998; Sfard, 1998; Martínez and Sauleda, 1998).

Study case: Educator's narratives

Recent investigations (Martínez and Sauleda, 1999) carried out in the context of educational actions directed towards prospective educators in the framework of this University, have shown that, in spite of the fact that the educators tend to value collaborative work highly, very few actually enforce it in a regular way. Usually, educators restrict the process of social learning to activities that are supposed to be more ludic rather than instructive, and which are directed as a complement to individual learning. In this context, our main concern has been the institutionalization of a learning situation in which prospective educators can promote their disposition to participate in a more cooperative way in the development of their own professional knowledge. We have, therefore, tried to generate a culture of learning in which these prospective educators can directly experience themselves, by means of their own actions of learning and the meaning of cooperative learning; and can critically co-reflect on the implications and foresee and discuss their ideas on how they think their future students should learn.

With this aim in mind, we have enacted a learning culture connected as much as possible to the complex and authentic problems that the active practice of the teacher inside the classroom entails. Together with the participants, we have tried to portray a scenario which accepts and assumes that the invention of knowledge depends on the social process of experience exchange in the heart of a split culture. In the first phase of this process we consider starting with a joint reflection on the participants' personal, professional and political narratives, discourses and metaphors to be essential. The study of educational metaphors, particularly in relation to the prospective educator's process of learning, has been presented in a different paper (Martínez and Sauleda, 1999). This investigation focuses on the analysis of the biographical narratives which refer to the network of the participants' educational and professional careers. The aim of this paper is to work out the nodes of experience or thought which guide their beliefs and values. A subsequent research will be orientated towards the stimulisation of the recognition of participants' educational thoughts through a joint reflection of the class community.

The complexity of the world at present has persuaded us to approach a line of investigation that recognises cultural plurality and diversity and which assumes that comprehension makes it essential to take multiple ideas into account (Calderhead 1996; Castells,1996). Thus, our research has tried to build a framework for the nodes of investigation by means of different discourses. Instead of being unidimensional and deductive, the approach has been open and polytopical. The final results and conclusions are the result of the process of recursive feedback and feedforward between the empirical data and the theoretical scenary which exists at present. In general terms, the interpretation of the narratives can be diverse and can be affected both by the background in which they are inscribed as well as the foreground of the historical contingencies which have affected these. In this sense, we have tried to be aware of the cultural frame in which the discourses are attributed. In the interpretation of the narratives we have taken into account the segmentation of time which the narrator has assigned, due to the fact that temporal discontinuties usually give an indication of the events which the author has considered as being human and professionally important in his/her biography. The interpretation of partial segments of the narrative has been carried out in all the classes by means of contrasting the parts belonging to the narrative with that of the whole of the discourse. The meaning of the fragments that are partial can be interpreted from the rest of the narrative's meaning, as well as from the meaning of the text as a whole. However, our intention has never been directed towards the pretension that all the segments belonging to the narrative can harmonize together with the apparent global meaning of the narration. Our assumption is that professional thought depends on a group of discourses that are built together in the same framework, but which are not always assimilated together with the rest. For this reason, we have looked for the convergences that exist between the different discourses. In the narratives we have tried to be critical towards keeping in line with the verisimilitude and credibility that they show, and in this sense the final interpretation is a result of a process of triangulation. Only certain information obtained has been included in this article, and in this sense the rest of the data and resulting categories obtained in the classification process will be considered in a later publication. Our line of thought ressembles that of Popkewitz (1998) in the assumption that there is a relation between the accumulation of data and the theoretical frame. As Popkewitz has pointed out, the information that is selected responds to the theoretical dispositions that determine the investigation of one thing or another. The categories have not been previously decided upon, although they are related with our own perspective and with the network in which we continually develop ourselves, minute by minute, time and time again. In this sense, the categories have not been organized attending to preconceived responses, but instead have been enacted by means of a reverberation process between the empirical data and the theoretical frame.

Within the conceptual frame of learning conceived as a social participation, and especially from our own conviction that learning implies a development of the complex network which exists between humans and non-humans, in which each participant inhabits and lives, this investigation has analysed the biographical narratives that were thought of and written at the beginning of an educational course for practising educators. The aim of this activity was directed towards the achieving of a specialization in child education. The group of participants included 24 educators (23 women and 1 man). At the beginning of the educational programme we asked the students as a group to think about and discuss their most relevant educational and professional experiences. It was expected that amongst others, these transitions would include their university education (teacher training studies or other degrees), a master, and/or other courses specializing in professional development and professional training experience in schools. After the participants had discussed these issues, each had to think and narrate by themselves their own experience in a written discourse. In some ways, at this stage, the discussion and conversation continued in the sense that their own personal reflection could be interpreted as a dialogue between the I and one's self. Our study has placed particular emphasis on the relations that the participants' narratives have set between their own learning experiences in their initial university studies and their professional experiences in relation with their own professional, personal and political development.

Interpretation of the results

As a consequence of the recursive interaction between the results obtained and the theoretical frame, we have chosen to classify the data in three basic categories. The first focuses on assessing the importance of the educator's initial university studies in relation with their own professional education. The second includes the evaluation of their own personal experience inside the classroom and school centre in relation with their education as an educator. Finally, the third category shows the group of opinions which refers to the importance that professional collaboration with their colleagues and with experts, within the centres, has had in their own education.

1. In relation to the evaluation that the educators gave in their biographical narrative to the impact that their initial studies had had on their own reconstitution as professionals inside the classroom; most of the discourses tended to reflect the idea that the impact of their university studies had been of little significance. Different subgroups can be distinguished inside this group.

A large group of educators (41%) have explained their conviction that the influence of their initial studies in their professional development has been of little significance. The majority have underlined that the least interesting feature of their initial university education has been the 'theoretical' character of the curricular programme. Many of these reports also point out the fact that there has been a clear lack of context between the notions given in the university and the authentic problems that arise inside the school classroom. The participants tend to consider that the insignificant value of their initial studies has been particularly put to evidence when they have had to enact solutions to the complex problems that arise inside the frame of the school centre, and that, in these cases, they have realized that their initial education has not helped them to enact the right modifications needed. In short, the conviction that their initial education had been of very little value is also connected to the feeling of helplessness that they experimented in their first year of practice as professionals.

My first encounter with teaching was in a nursery school. After three months I began to realize that what I had studied was not really of any use. (Mª. Carmen)

My first class of work was that of disenchantment. As an inexperienced school teacher and faced with a difficult group I wondered where the average student was, to whom I could apply what I had learned in my degree. Real children do not have the characteristics described in books. (Remedios)

Nearly half of the educators (45%) do not consider their experience as an educator in relation to their university degree as being amongst the relevant episodes and processes in their professional reconstitution. This group avoids any reference to their initial educational studies. On the other hand, not one of the educators evaluates in a completely positive manner their initial studies. The only teacher that qualifies her initial studies as being relevant immediately goes back on the meaning of the term by stating that teacher training studies were not sufficient.

I learned what I had expected in my teaching degree and I think that, in general, I can consider what I learned as being valuable, but not sufficient. (Remedios)

The only systematical exception in the conviction of the participant on the fact that her initial studies had not been of any use is consistent and resounds with her own negative evaluation of theoretical education. We are referring to the fact that in their university curricular programme the only thing that the participants tend to put forward and emphasize as being extremely relevant and interesting is their training practice (*Practicum*), which is the only part of the programme that actually takes place outside the university lecture rooms. Taking into account that the *Practicum* is carried out in the final stage of the syllabus, we believe that it can be asserted that the participants' evaluation of their two and a half years of 'theoretical' studies is clearly negative. Some of the participants (12%) have expressed with convinced assertions that the *Practicum* has been the period of their initial education with the greatest influence in their own personal, professional and political development. The deep emotional and intellectual mark that the practice has left in their lives is clearly reflected in different narratives.

It was in my practical period that I began to enjoy myself with children (...) I remember my teacher from the practicum, I learned a lot of things from her, and I can still remember her calmness and the way in which she looked at the children. I would like to mention the 'Aneja' school and the teacher and the innovating way of working from this practical course which have helped me through my professional career. (Mª.José)

In short, the narratives inscribe a practically unanimous disconsideration of the participants' careers in relation to their studies that are negatively qualified as being entirely theoretical. In their discourses, the term 'theory' is equivalent to something void of any value or meaning. In clear consistence with what has already been stated, the majority of the discourses emphasize the participants´

desire that their initial education should have been centred in the professional reconstitution in the school classroom.

> The schooling that I received was excessively theoretical, what I really needed was more contact with what really goes on inside the classroom and with everyday experience. (Yolanda)

When the prospective educators look back on the impact their initial studies had in relation to their practical action in the school classroom, the majority coincide in pointing out that their induction in the classroom made them come to terms with the insecurity and uncertainty that existed in relation with the 'adequacy' of their professional preparation. The opinion that their initial studies had been deficient for their professional reconstitution is restated by the majority of the participants.

> By working at the school, I realized that I didn't know what I thought I did about education. (Eulalia)

> The first year of work we found it quite difficult. Although we had studied Bloom's taxonomy, and all the areas of knowledge of the theoretical art of teaching, we didn't know what to do with the children inside the class. (Josefa)

In combination with what Börger and Tillema (1993) state in relation with the problem of transposing knowledge to practice and experience, most of the participants define their incapacity to enact appropiate strategies in order to resolve the problems that arise inside the classroom not as a lack of knowledge, but due to the ignorance of the strategies and techniques needed in each concrete situational action. The perception of the difference between the knowledge acquired and the lack of capacity to use is especially evident in the educators during their first professional phase. Faced with this difficulty, we propose trying to deal with these first periods, in a specific way, by means of professional induction strategies.

The consciousness of the lack of the necessary minimal information is also laden with a strong and frustrating emotional component. The sense of worry and helplessness in the first year diminishes or grows in function of the human support received.

> In my first job, I didn't find any help in the school centre, I had a terrible time because I never received any sort of guidance (...) During the following years I met colleagues with more experience (...) we formed a work group together with a specialist (...) They were really rewarding years because we worked a lot together. (Lamberta)

> During that course (nursery education) I was scared, but I found a brilliant colleague and met some marvellous children. (Montse)

2. In relation with the self-evaluation that the educator's have made with regard to the influence of their personal experience considered as a source of knowledge; it can be confirmed that only a few of the participants (8%) have refered to it without associating it to collaborative experience. Most of the narratives (92%) never categorize their own experience as a source of knowledge without connecting it to the collaboration received from the rest of their colleagues.

> My attitude was to learn from each mistake, looking for help in colleagues that had more experience in order to increase my formation. (Remedios)

> We were all working provisionally (as beginners) and helped each other. (Asunción)

Many educators locate the beginning of their professional education in their first contacts with the school instead of in their initial university education.

> During the first four years of work I learned a lot, although I had studied a lot in my teacher training studies, everything seemed very theoretical and it's when you step inside a classroom that you come face to face with reality. (Mª. Carmen)

> I finished my studies with a very confused vision of what a school was and how you were supposed to work with children. The preparation had not been properly focused on (...) It was when I started to work that I really realised the difference that existed between theory and practise (...) and I learned a lot. (Mª. Teresa)

> All the different levels I have taught in have shown me something (...) I have learned bit by bit with the help of my colleagues. (Milagros)

Many of the participants emphasize the education received in the school frame as the main source of their own professional development. Some have highlighted the importance of experimental learning (by trial and error for example), while others have underlined learning mechanisms more centred in reflective processes (although there are actually few explicit and appropriate references towards reflection itself).

> In that school, I learned as much or more than my students did. (Julia)

> From a professional point of view all the classes and levels that I have taught have shown me something. (Milagros)

> I learned (...) by correcting my mistakes. (Vicenta)

> Reflecting on the negative and complicated experiences has been a source of learning for me, (...) Professional reestructuring classes have helped to confirm and reorientate the concepts acquired through experience. (Remedios)

3. The assesment of the social participation and the collaboration as an element of professional learning is shown in three quarters of the participants (75%), all of whom consider it indispensable. In short, the relevance of working in col-

laboration with colleagues is highlighted by practically all of the participants.

> In practically all of the schools I have been in, the working relation with my colleagues has been crucial for my own development in the area of teaching (...) especially in the last few years which is when I have most perceived and valued the importance of the coordination between colleagues. (Julia)

> I have learned bit by bit with the help of my colleagues. (Milagros)

In the opposite pole, the lack of support is perceived as being the hardest professional problem to overcome.

> In my first job, I didn't find any help in the school centre. I had a terrible time because I never received any sort of guidance. (Lamberta)

> I started to work last year (...) I had a difficult class but the rest of my colleagues really helped me. The way they treated me was wonderful and I was sad to leave. (Encarna)

In many cases the importance of the figure of an expert colleague is highlighted as the initiator and catalyst for one's own professional expertise.

> I started in a unitarian school, lost off the beaten track, but with a colleague older and more experienced than myself who gave me a hand and helped set me in the right direction in order to carry out my work. (Mª. Carmen)

In this sense, many participants underline the positive impact that the presence of the good work ways of a colleague has had in their own professional reconstitution, as well as their colleague's capacity to make them enthusiastic and to encourage them by setting a professional goal.

> The following year I met a colleague who was really nice, whenever I could I would go to her class and watch her work. It really made an impact on me and I thought that if she could do it then so could I. (Mª. Carmen)

> During that period I worked with nursery school teachers who were really enthusiastic about their work. It was a very positive experience. (Mª. Carmen)

We feel that it is worth highlighting the importance that the participants give to the emotional and personal support received from their colleagues. In many cases professional support is relegated to a second position.

> I remember the warmth, the companionship and the support from all the people that I met that year. (Concepción)

> There was a good atmosphere of teamwork in the school. (Milagros)

> There is a good team of colleagues in the school centre, and I have enjoyed my work there very much. (Montserrat)

I spent my best years as a professional surrounded by a good group of colleagues where I learned most of what I know now. (Vicenta)

In line with what we have already stated, many of the narratives emphasize the importance of being part of a community in their practice training.

I would like to work (...) with a group of colleagues, I have always had to work by myself as I was the only English teacher in the school. (Isidra)

When I started working in a public school (...) I felt that I belonged to a group. (Mª. Carmen)

Some of the narratives inscribe, in a short text, a synthesis of the points that our interpretation considers as being essential for this study. Firstly, the initial studies are recognized as being theoretical and of irrelevant professional significance. Secondly, the experience and practical knowledge forms the appropiate process of learning. And thirdly, the collaboration inside a community of practice training is considered as indispensable.

Once your studies are over there is a lot of theory left in the air that you don't actually use (...), in our teacher training studies we were never shown how to programme and we had never seen a curricular adaptation programme, so what was the use of knowing its definition? (...) I learned with the help and support of the pyschopedagogue (advisor/specialist) and the coordination of the teachers which formed a team together (...) and by correcting my own mistakes. (Vicenta)

The insight that we have carried out between the participants' narratives sets us in context to assert that the conscious of prepared professionals depends on the participation carried out in the process of development. In the same way, Carter and Doyle (1996) have pointed out that the mastery of education requires a long period of time and dedication.

Conclusions

The first and most important conclusion is that this investigation confirms that the narratives that inscribe the educators' reflections on the transitions that have influenced their professional reconstitution the most, are a decisive element in their education. For this reason, we have put forward the idea that the educators´ reconstitution is influenced by their co-reflection about their actual discourses in an ocean of discourses belonging to the school culture and the social community. Our conclusion is consistent with the assertions of Calderhead & Gates (1993), Liston and Zeichner (1996), Zeichner (1996) and Bain, Ballantyne, Packer and Mills (1999) in relation to the idea that the reflection that is based on the most profound elements of a person's history has more possibilities of transforming the educator's previous conceptual scenary, because it is produced from spheres that deeply affect the emotional and private memories. We would like to highlight the fact that the narratives encourage the educational imagination and increase the educator's aptitude to reflect in a deliberate and critical manner. The narratives embody the way in which the social space and the contingencies can influence our beliefs, values and fears. We agree with Martha Nussbaum (1998) in stating that the narratives allow us to see beyond the stereotypes that make human beings invisible and that narrative imagination is essential for a moral reconstitution. It goes without saying that the art of writing a narrative is in relation with the way in which we interpret life, as the texts that we write invent the person we are and give sense to our biography as educators. On the basis of this, we consider it necessary to educate by taking into consideration the narratives of the actual protagonists, and by doing so through the dilemmas situated in a social and spatial sphere. We assume the narrative as an educational strategy linked to the dialogical discourse in such a way that the participants' dispositions are inclined to *co-contrast* different versions of a same incident or problem, or, in other words, they to tend towards a joint metacognition. In short, in our opinion the personal, social and cultural reconstitution implies the transformation of the culture belonging to the educators and the educational community. Furthermore, we interpret this as being in accordance with Elliot's idea (1998) that 'the pedagogical change mainly implies the collaborative reconstruction of the teacher's culture through the growth of discursive consciousness.'

In second place, our revelations differ from Elliot's assertion (1998), at least in part, in relation to the idea that educators do not have a clear perception of the effectiveness of the coalitions and consortiums that exist between different institutions and groups, and that they prefer courses organised by professionals outside the university. We can state that, in the majority of cases, the nursery educators' narratives of the group studied all show their conviction towards the collaboration with their companions, including their expert colleagues, as having been crucial for their professional development. We would like to remember here that the group studied was composed entirely by female educators with just one exception, this means that we have not been able to consider the question of gender in this study. In contrast with the emphasis that the educators put in the importance of collaborating in a community for their professional development, we have found (Martínez and Sauleda, 1999) that when the educators reflect together on the most appropiate perspective of learning for their students they are inclined to interpret learning as an individual process of acquisition or reconstruction and they tend to avoid the perspectives of social learning. That is to say, whilst the narratives incorporate the essence of dialogical communication and the participation inside a community, their metaphors (Martínez and Sauleda,

1999) related to learning tend to evoke this as a process of the individual acquisition of learning. The high reiteration of the educators' metaphors related to learning as an individual process, as we have previously discovered in our research, suggests that this idea has a coherence and depth larger than what would be expected. This basically implies that educators assert in a redundant way that their most relevant professional learning has emerged from a social process of participation inside a community but, that in contrast with what we have previously said, the same educators assume and apply organizational models of individualistic nature when they are working with students and tend to forget the perspectives which focus on participation. On the basis of what has been stated, we propose that the relevance that the educators award in their narratives towards participative learning should be converted into a privileged node inside the network of the development of their own vision of learning to the extent that it increases their predisposition towards perspectivs that focus to include social learning in a more emphatical manner.

In third place, the educators' narratives tend to inscribe in a redundant and categorical way, that the initial 'theoretical' education that they acquire in the framework of their university studies have a scarce influence in their development as educators. This radical negation of the value of the curricular programme of their initial studies includes just one exception, the *Practicum*. This means that the educators agree in a unanimous way that only the knowledge acquired in their training practice has been of interest. This conclusion, which is explicitly borne out in many of the narratives' fragments as well as the totality of them, is also put into evidence by the educators´ tendency to divide the actual length of their universitary studies into two parts: a significative one – the *Practicum* – and another without any relevance – the rest, which is qualified as 'theory'. In this sense, the narratives also isolate the first year of professional practice as an important event for the process of the development of their idea in relation to the mission that corresponds to education. Furthermore, they have also assumed the fact that the educator's education should be focused on practical knowledge – craft knowledge – and they have insisted on a curricular programme centred in practice. The perception that educators learn through their practice hands-on can be found in Dewey and in all the tradition of craft knowledge. We agree with Retallick (1999) in that the workplace learning of educators might be given greater recognition in their overall professional development, although we would like to specify that our perspective does not assume the educator's development as exclusively having to shut oneself away in the study of practical knowledge. In this way, we are inclined to assume, as a desirable tendency, the idea of doing away with the traditional epistemological lack of consideration towards practical knowledge that is derived from inside the school frame. In the same way, we consider that the strong school cultures that arise from the intersubjective resolution of authentic problems should be acknowledged and recognised through professional development networks that create the necessary conditions to expand and share practical knowledge (Hargreaves, 1996). University education should not forget the importance of learning through situated problems and should develop alternative methodologies that assume collaboration as a systematical form of work. It is essential to reshape the relations that exist between those that are inside and outside the school frame (Hargreaves and Fullan, 1998). This collaboration should also be expanded to the consortium of educators and centres (Yinger, 1999). In this sense, we agree on the necessity of social learning, although this present study and our own thoughts assume the fact that the participation of educators should affect the educators' own personal thoughts. The educators are not simple agents, for they are conscious of their actions and intentions. For this reason, we consider the development of the communitary educational culture as a valuable intention, although we have studied it through the assumption of the necessity of the educator's own personal reconstitution.

Finally, we would like to emphasize that, almost unanimously, the educators' narratives associate their professional reconstitution to the importance of the emotional support received from their colleagues. In a previous report (Martínez and Sauleda, 1998) we have already highlighted the importance of the emotional dimension in the educator's professional reconstitution. Although we consider Morin's assertion (1997) refering to the fact that 'intelligence and affectivity are related together' (p. 60) as being excessively lineal, we do concur with the author mentioned in the fact that the multiplicity of affectivity is necessary for developing a person's intelligence. The coexistence and cohabitation inscribe a complex, but essential relation of negotiation between all the participants which chaotically alternate between antagonism and acceptance. The essence of educational negotiation implies a process full of emotional charge. For this reason, we consider as being crucial the fact that emotional reconstitution is not separated from but integrated in global transformation at a personal, professional and political level (Day, 1997). Speaking in terms that we realize are not very appropiate, we could suggest that in any educational level, the illiteracy that should worry us the most is emotional illiteracy. Our conviction towards education as a negotiation allows us to clarify that our pespective of learning rejects and abominates the notion of learning as a way of penetrating inside the child's mind and tends towards the idea of learning as a mutually consented process of the search for knowledge through the other. This search must occur in a complex network. Inside this labyrinth the meaning of complexity assumes the notion that the networks fold up upon each other. The multidimensional netting is woven with extremely varied threads of diverse origins. We understand that the very same intelligence(s) (Gardner, 1983, 1999) is not shut away inside our heads but distributed in human networks–friends, colleagues, educators-and nonhumans–books, computer programmes, personal notes, data bases and the individual's own world. For this reason, we can conclude that educational reconstitution depends on the dialogical interactions that flow inside the network in which the educators participate. This network tangles and untangles itself in a resourceful manner, with other human and nonhuman networks. As a final note, we would like to recall that the main purpose of this research, which will be continued, is to generate an alternative culture of professional reconstitution in which the narratives and metaphors that belong to perspective educators play an important role. This investigation therefore forms part of our search for an alternative learning culture, which has been created and recognized both by ourselves as well as our students. In this sense, it is a practical research that does not overlook epistemological arguments, but is not centred in them.

Acknowledgements
We would like to thank Christopher Day and Dolf van Veen. We have benefited from thoughtful support of the two named researchers.

References

Anderson, J.R., Reder, L.M. & Simon, H.A. (1997). Situative versus cognitive perspectives: Form versus substance. *Educational Researcher 26,* 18-21.

Antil, L.R., Jenkins, J.R., Wayne, S.K. & Vadasy, P.F. (1998). Cooperative learning: Prevalence conceptualizations, and the relation between research and practice. *American Educational Research Journal, 35,* 419-454.

Bain, J.D., Ballantyne, R., Packer, J. & Mills, C. (1999). Using journal writing to enhance student teachers' reflectivity during field experience placements. *Teachers and Teaching: Theory and practice, 5,* 51-74.

Brown, A.L. & Campione, J. (1995). Concevoir une communauté de jeunes élèves. Leçons théoriques et practiques. *Revue Française de Pedagogie, 11,* 11-33.

Bruner, J. (1996). *The culture of education.* Cambridge, MA: Harvard University Press.

Calderhead, J. (1996). Teachers beliefs and knowledge. In D.C. Berliner & R.C. Calfee, *Handbook of Educational Psychology,* 709-725. New York: Simon and Schuster Macmillan.

Calderhead, J. Y Gates, P. (1993). Introduction. In J. Calderhead & P. Gates (Eds.), *Conceptualizing reflection in teacher development.* London: Falmer Press.

Carter, K. & Doyle, W. (1996). Personal narrative and life histoy in learning to teach. In J. Sikula, T.J. Buttery & E. Guyton, *Handbook od Research on Teaching,* 120-142. New York: Simon & Schuster Macmillan.

Castells, M. (1994). Flujos, redes, e identidades: Una teoría crítica de la sociedad informacional. In M. Castells, R. Flecha, P. Feire, H.A. Giroux, D. Macedo & P. Willis, *Critical education,* 37-64. Madrid: Ediciones Paidós Ibérica, S.A.

Castells, M. (1996). *The information age. Economy, society and culture. The rise of the network society. Vol. I.* Oxford: Blackwell Publishers Inc.

Castells, M. (1997). *The information age. Economy, society and culture. The power of identity. Vol. II.* Oxford: Blackwell Publishers Inc.

Castells, M. (1998). *The information age. Economy, society and culture. The end of millenium. Vol. III.* Oxford: Blackwell Publishers Inc.

Cobb, P. & Bowers, J. (1999). Cognitive and situative learning perspectives in theory and practice. *Educational Researcher, 28,,* 4-15.

Cole, M., Engestrom, Y. & Vasquez, O. (1997). *Mind, culture, and activity.* Cambridge: Cambridge University Press.

Day, C. (1997). Teachers in the twenty-first century: Time to renew the vision. In A. Hargreaves and R. Evans, *Beyond educational reform,* 44-61. Buckingham: Open University Press.

Day, C. (1999). *Developing Teachers. The challenges of lifelonglearning.* London: Falmer Press.

Gardner, H. (1983). *Frames of mind: The theory of multiples intelligences.* New York: Basic Books.

Gardner, H. (1999). *The disciplined mind.* New York: Simon & Schuster

Greeno, J.G. (1997). On claims that answer the wrong questions. *Educational Researcher, 26,,* 5-17.

Elliot, J. (1998). *The curriculum experiment.* Buckingham: Open University Press.

Hargreaves, A. (1994). *Changing teachers, changing times: Teachers' work and culture in postmodern times.* New York: Teachers College Press.

Hargreaves, A. (1996). Transforming knowledge: blurring the boundaries between research, policy, and practice. *Educational evaluation and policy analisis, 18,* 105-122.

Hagreaves, A. & Fullan, M. (1998). *What's worth fighting for in education?* Buckingham: Open University Press.

Lave, J. (1988). Cognition in practice: *Mind, mathematics, and culture in everyday life.* Cambridge: Cambridge University Press.

Lave, J. & Wenger, E. (1991). *Situated learning: Legitimate peripheral participation.* New York: Cambridge University Press.

Liston, D.P. & Zeichner, K.M. (1996). *Culture and teaching.* Mahwah: Lawrence Erlbaum Associates, Inc.

Martinez Ruiz, M.A. & Sauleda, N. (1997). The professional development of teachers by means of the construction of collaborative thinking. *British Journal of In-service Education, 23,* 241-252.

Martinez, M.A. & Sauleda, N. (1998). Teacher education research in the framework theory of the conceptual change as a social construction: a case study. Paper presented to the ECER 98. Ljubljana

Martinez, M.A. & Sauleda, N. (1999). Collaborative Teacher Education in an Inclusive University Setting. Paper presented to the International Study Association on Teachers and Teaching-ISSAT99 Conference. Dublin. Ireland.

Morin, E. (1997). *Amour, poèsie, sagesse.* Paris: Éditions du Seuil

Nussbaum, M.C. (1997). *Cultivating humanity.* Cambridge, Massachusetts: Harvard University Press.

Perkins, D. (1993). Person-plus: A distributed view of thinking and learning. In G. Salomon (Ed.), *Distributed cognition: Psychological and educational considerations,* 88-110. Cambridge: Cambridge University Press.

Popkewitz, T.S. (1998). The culture of redemption and the administration of freedom as research. *Review of Educational Research, 68,* 1-34.

Popkewitz, T.S. (1999). A social epistemology of educational research. En T.S. Popkewitz & L. Fendler, *Critical theories in education,* 17-44. New York: Routledge.

Retallick, J. 1999. Teachers' workplace learning: towards legitimation and accreditation. *Teachers and Teaching: theory and practice, 5,* 33-50.

Rogoff, B. (1990). *Apprenticeship in thinking: Cognitive development in social context.* Oxford: Oxford University Press.

Salomon, G. (1993). No distribution without individuals' cognition: A dynamic. In G. Salomon (Ed.), *Distributed cognition: Psychological and Educational considerations,* 111-163. Cambridge: Cambridge University Press.

Salomon, D. & Perkins, D.N. (1998). Individual and social aspects of learning. *Review of Research in Education, 23,* 1-24.

Sfard, A. (1998). On two metaphors for learning and the dangers of choosing just one. *Educational Researcher 27,* 4-13.

Yinger, R.J. & Hendricks-Lee, M.S. (1998). Proffesional development standarts as a new context for professional development. *Teacher and TeachingTheory and Practice, 4,* 273-298.

Zeichner, K.M. (1996). Educating teachers for cultural diversity. In K.M. Zeichne, S. Melnik & M.L. Gomez, *Currents of reform in preservice teaching education,* 133-175. New York: Teachers College Press.

Using E-mail to Promote Reflection in Teacher Education

Torlaug L. Hoel & Sigrun Gudmundsdottir

This paper presents a project trying out one-to-one communication via e-mail between student teachers out on teaching practice and their university professors. The paper describes how the students reflect over episodes from the classroom in a structured interaction with their university teachers. The theoretical framework for the study are theories from Vygotsky and Bakhtin and their followers. The e-mail messages were analyzed in correspondence with the ALACT-model for reflection. On the basis of our research findings, we believe that structured e-mail communication can make important contribution in teacher education.

This paper presents a part of a larger European research project, the REFLECT Project (1996-1997). The project was a research co-operation between four European universities: Exeter in England, Utrecht in the Netherlands, Barcelona in Spain, and Norwegian University of Science and Technology (NTNU) in Norway (Gudmundsdottir & Hoel 1996). The aim of the project was to use telematics and teleguidance to promote reflective skills among student teachers. The partners tried out different technological approaches: video-conferencing, list-serve, and, as in the Norwegian part of the project, one-to-one e-mail interactions between student teachers while on teaching practice and their tutors at the university campus. A number of case studies describe how student teachers learn in a structured interaction with their tutors to reflect over episodes from the classroom. This structured interaction is an essential part of a pedagogy of interactive technology.

Theoretical framework

The ALACT model

The theoretical model that is the foundation for our work is a reflection model, the ALACT model, which is developed by a research team at the University of Utrecht (Korthagen 1985, 1988). The word ALACT consists of the first letters in the five steps in the model: action, looking, awareness, creating, trial. It describes the spiralling process of reflection over practice. It proceeds in five steps that each has two dimensions, students' and teachers': For the students, step one is a description of the action. Here student teachers describe in detail a concrete episode in the classroom. The teacher assists by helping in coming up with the relevant experiences. Step two for students involves 'looking back' at the event. Teachers' role is acceptance of the students' contribution while steering them towards practice. Students' step three is identifying fundamental pedagogical principles in that episode. Teachers' contribution here is assisting the student in connecting implicit vague feelings to the here and now in explicit and concrete terms. Step four for students is generating alternative strategies, while the teachers continue their support. Step five brings both teachers and students back to step one of a new cycle. The five steps of the model suggest a path that the reflection process might take in approaching the goal of the reflective practitioner.

The zone of proximal development, internalizing, and scaffolding

The spiralling reflection process can be understood in terms of Lev Vygotsky's *zone of proximal development* (ZPD). The zone of proximal development is

> the distance between the actual problem solving level as determined by independent problem solving and the level of potential development as determined through problem solving under adult guidance or in collaboration with more capable peers (Vygotsky 1978:86).

Vygotsky founded his theories about ZPD mainly on research on child and grownup dyades, but his construct applies to learning at all ages. To understand learning in the zone, three concepts are important: situation definition, intersubjectivity, and semiotic mediation. Observing events in the classroom, student teachers and experienced teachers have been known to define the situation differently, that is, deciding what is going on in an particular classroom situation (Berliner & Carter 1989). Experienced teachers appear to be more perceptive to what is important in classroom situations than novice teachers, and they show more sensitivity to subtle characteristics of classroom tasks than their less experienced colleagues. The teacher training situation establishes the basis for the zone of proximal development in learning to teach. Out in the schools, on a teaching practice assignment, student teachers work with experienced teachers who supervise them. In addition they hav a university tutor who also often sees classroom events in a different way.

Once the student teachers reach an understanding that enables them to define situations that is in tune with the experienced teachers' and tutor's definitions, they have achieved intersubjectivity. This is not merely a matter of adding up knowledge; it is a qualitatively different understanding of the situation than that which was previously held. Intersubjectivity is negotiated through semiotic mediation, i.e. through a dialogue between the experienced teachers and tutors on one hand, and the student teacher on the other.

In the ZPD, the theory of *internalizing* is important. A person is first part of a joint activity between two or more persons, in an interpersonal relation. Using the cognitive functions which are developed by taking part in the joint activity, the person then carries out the activity on her own. The conversion from the social to the individual, or from the intermental to the intramental process takes place in the ZPD. Learning takes place through interaction between the individual and the world around. A crucial point in a socio-cultural approach to thinking and learning is that thinking develops according to the types of activity people in a given culture engage in. Through engagement in culture specific activities people develop higher mental processes that are appropriate in solving culture specific tasks (e.g. Tulviste 1991; Wertsch 1991). Classroom activities take place within a special cultural context that embodies them with meaning. Reflection is also a kind of higher mental process, what is often called an 'intellectual tool', enabling teachers and student teachers to systematically think about and reflect on what they did. It takes place in a context, in a particular classroom and over a specific episode or a series of episodes.

Scaffolding as an instructional principle is first and foremost associated with Bruner (Wood, Bruner & Ross 1976). Scaffolding can be described as an aid to cognitive and social development. As an instructional principle it is based upon the belief that when students have progressed far enough in their development, the scaffolding becomes superfluous. But when students liberate themselves from one scaffold, they face new challenges, new problems, new learning processes, new ZPDs, which require new scaffolding.

The concept of scaffolding has its background in Vygotsky's theory of ZPD. A more systemathized approach to progression through the ZPD is found in Tharp and Gallimore (1988). They suggest that the progression through the zone of proximal development goes through two stages and beyond that into another two stages to achieve mastery. Stage I is called 'assistance provided by more capable others'. In our situation the co-operating teachers are 'the more capable others' that the student teachers observe and with whom they discuss. The university tutors, with whom they communicate via e-mail are also 'the more capable others'. Student teachers are only able to attend and experience a limited amount of classroom life at the beginning of the teaching practice period. It is a sign of mastery to comprehend the complexity of classrooms (Gudmundsdottir and Shulman 1987, Gudmundsdottir 1996. Typically in an apprenticeship situation, the master gradually fades into the background and the apprentice takes more responsibility for planning the unit and teaching it. Eventually essential teaching routines become 'internalised, personalised, adapted and owned' by the novice (Tharp & Gallimore 1988, page 252).

Stage II is when 'assistance is provided by the self'. The responsibility for the task has shifted from others to the self. Teaching functions are not fully automatic. Tharp and Gallimore claim that stage II is a stage intermediate between external regulation and full individual competence (automaticity). It may also be seen as a stage in which the 'voice' of the regulating other is gradually acquired by the learner, so that the regulations may be stated by self to self, gradually taken 'underground', transmuted into thought, and eventually discarded as the behaviour becomes fully developed and adaptively automatic (op.cit. page 253). In daily life, this process is easily observed, as individuals 'talk themselves through' some new skill, often in the very words of coaches and instructors.

Stage III starts when the relevant skill is automatic and the 'voice falls silent'. At this stage the tasks are carried out in a flexible way. Support from others is no longer necessary because the apprentice has developed routines and ways for dealing with the task. Vygotsky applies the word 'fossilizing', which means that the psychological processes have been repeated so often that they have become automatic (1978 page 63). The lifelong learning by any individual is made up of regulated ZPD sequences – from other-assistance to self-assistance – recurring over and over again for the development of new capacities. For every indidvidual, at any point in time, there will be a mix of other-regulation, self-regulation and automatic processes. Another important consideration is that de-automatization and recursion occur so regularly that they constitute a stage IV of the normal development process. What one formerly could do, one can no longer do (Tharp & Gallimore 1988, page 39). After de-automatization, for whatever reason, if capacity is to be restored, then the developmental processes must become recursive.

The ALACT model serves as a kind of useful scaffold for the student's process through the last part of stage I and the whole of stage II of the Tharp and Gallimore model for development through ZPD. It is also a tool for student teachers and their teachers to construct the interaction in their written messages. For example: The tutor asks the student to describe an incident in the classroom (I), at stage II the tutor asks the student to look back at the incident and tell what it means to her or him. The ability to see fundamental aspects, other perspectives, make new interepretations, processes that are related to stage III, are the core of the reflection process.

Language as a mediator for thought
Language plays a central role in the internalization of higher mental processes. Vygotsky considers language as an important tool for thought and problem solving. 'Thought is not merely expressed in words, it comes into existence through them'(Vygotsky 1986:128). The thought becomes explicit when it is expressed in language. Through language we are able to examine thought, clarify it, explore connections or discover lack of connections. Language is not only our most important mode of communication, but also our most important aid in structuring and examining our inner worlds.

Inspired by Vygotsky, contemporary linguistic theory differentiates between two functions of language: language as a mode of thought and language as a mode of communication. It is important to keep in mind these two functions when one is using writing as a tool in developing thought. When we are writing to develop our thoughts the reader is just ourselves. This kind of writing is exploratory by nature as well as fragmentary, spontaneous, and unfinished. When we are writing for someone else the aim is to communicate ideas, beliefs and points of view. In this mode of writing, the text needs to have internal logic, be consistent and grammatically correct. The two different functions of language also represent different relationships to the most important stress factor for writing namely a critical reader. The student teachers' e-mail messages to their tutors will often be explanatory and unfinished, and not always grammatically correct. It is important to clarify this for the participants. It is imperative that they should understand that the reader of the texts they write on e-mail is a friendly reader, not a critical one.

In writing, the author enters into two kinds of dialogue. One is the dialogue between the author's inner being and the words that are put down on paper. The other is between the author and an external reader. This involves ever changing and expanding perspectives, and can therefore lead to increased insight and understanding. The written dialogue between the student and tutor can be compared to what happens in a conversation. It is a collective process where partners enter into turn-taking roles both as senders and receivers, the one who speaks and the one who listens, and a dialogue develops through these turn-taking roles. The product of a dialogue is a joint product, albeit put together by individual contributions, but each individual's contribution is dependent upon others and influences the others, and the result is a wholeness which is more and something else than the sum of the parts. In this project the e-mail messages had a double function. Firstly, the writing in itself was intended as a tool for the students' own thinking. Secondly, e-mail is intended to enable communication between the student teachers and their tutors. The first aspect is rooted in Vygotsky's view on language as an important tool for thought and problem solving.

The student teachers should be introduced to the different functions of writing and they should be encouraged to use writing as a tool in sorting out impressions in the reflection process, not just with a reader in mind, but also with themselves in mind. As they gain experience in this way of working, they will in turn eventually be able to encourage their students to use writing as a tool for developing thoughts and reflections and getting new insights.

Introduction to and preparation of students

The introduction of the project to the students specified that they would be expected to use e-mail as a log-book during teaching practice reflecting upon the following: Experiences in the classroom; teaching, learning, students, themselves, subject matter; episodes, actions, situations, interactions that surprised them, both negative and positive experiences; their ideas about advising, conversations with colleagues, or departmental meetings in school, their ideas about preparation, reflection and anything else they wanted to discuss. The introduction covered three aspects: (1) Using the computer and Eudora e-mail software. (2) Writing as a tool for the development of thought and for communication. (3) The reflection aspect and the ALACT model.

Hanne: a case study

Hanne had her teaching practice in Norwegian language and literature in a first-year upper-secondary-school. The main themes of Hanne's e-mail correspondence were (1) Teaching literature and using a log book. (2) Writing as a tool for reflection. Hanne has a meta-perspective on writing and its value as a promoter of reflection and conscious thinking. This theme engages her considerably and she frequently returned to it in her e-mails. (3) Her own development from pupil, student and undergraduate to a teacher. This development may be traced in her e-mail messages, where she draws on her experiences from her own period as a student and undergraduate. She utilizes these to understand her students, their reactions and her own behaviour better. Previous experiences are tied to the situation here and now. Hanne is very honest and sincere in her description of herself. She puts down on paper experiences, emotions and thoughts that many people would think twice about letting somebody else see. We have chosen to base our analysis on the teaching of literature.

Hanne was to teach literature and wanted to include short story writing. Her first e-mail casts a quick glance back to her own literature classes when she was a student at an upper-secondary school:

> We were never allowed to write our own short stories. We exclusively analyzed literature. We never created anything ourselves as it were, we only produced what we believed was a «correct interpretation» of the text (e-mail 06/03).

In Torlaug's (her tutor), response she dwelled on this point. She wanted her to develop further and examine more closely the idea she proposed in her e-mail, partly by considering her own experience as a student in the light of the present situation:

> What did you think/experience concerning how literature was taught, for example when working with short stories, when you were a student? How do you look at these experiences now, when you teach Norwegian? (e-mail to Hanne, 07/03).

Torlaug also asked her questions concerning her situation as a teacher. She was going to teach literature – what did she want to give her students, and how? (e-mail to Hanne 07/03). In her next e-mail Hanne presented her thoughts about teaching literature during her own schooling and also what she as a teacher wanted to emphasize:

> Much too little weight was given to the personal experience of reading, I'm sure. The teacher had his interpretation of the short story, and we students were intended to approach this by means of certain criteria... We were more or less absolved of any obligation to think for ourselves... I am very concerned that my own interpretation should shine through. Therefore, I consider it important that the students are allowed to offer their own views, and we draw no conclusions on what is correct or incorrect, only on what is probable or less probable (e-mail 09/03).

In the quote above Hanne starts at steps two and three in the reflection model. Towards the end she moves up to step four: She discerns an alternative approach to literature teaching which she wants to employ, this being that students must be permitted to offer their own ideas irrespective of the teacher's interpretation. She does not offer any explicit explanation for choosing this, but her reason is implied in what she has related from her own experiences: She wants students to learn to think independently, in this case in relation to a literary text. Because of this she as a teacher wants to keep her own interpretation to herself, and she emphasizes that interpretations may be probable or less probable.

In Torlaug's answer to Hanne she again attempts to have Hanne dwell on the theme of literature teaching, and in Hanne's reply she returned to this theme, this time by relating it to her own university experiences. Even there she was accustomed to having the text presented in a 'complete interpretation by a lecturer'. In this e-mail she elaborates on what she wrote in her previous e-mail about letting student's encounter the text based on their premises:

> They [the students] encounter the text with totally different expectations than I do. Now everybody reads into a text what he wants, to a certain extent at least. Everything depends on age, background, experience, and knowledge. In brief, everything that distinguishes us as humans and makes us different (e-mail 15/03).

Behind Hanne's writing, we perceive reception theory, theory of literature pedagogy and learning theory, even if she does not explicitly refer to these in her e-mail messages. She did, nevertheless, do so in a previous e-mail. What she said about reading and interpreting texts may also be extended to general theories of learning (constructionism). The concrete event which caused the issue of literature teaching to be raised (in the e-mail dated March 6th) was then relegated to the background, and Hanne moved to a stage where she supplied reasons for certain pedagogical principles she believed were important for literature teaching.

The interaction with the individual student and the whole class is important to Hanne. From day one she noted groups in the class, especially the silent ones and those who were vocal. She told about one class where she concentrated especially on the active ones, the vocal students, explaining her choice by stating that in this particular lesson she felt uncertain and thus especially dependent on student response. She was also afraid to ask the silent ones, because they might be dreading to be called on. Halfway through the teaching assignment she noticed development in herself: Initially she was most concerned with the active students, but gradually she held the entire class in view including those who never appeared willing to speak (19/03). 'A long-term goal for me is to have more people speak,' she wrote (22/03).

At the time of Hanne's first e-mail she had taught two lessons, and she admits that she was feeling very nervous, but she was surprised at how much the students knew, and that allowed much of the lesson '...fortunately to be created by the students themselves, as they offered their contributions to the questions I posed' (06/03). Letting the students be creative within the framework necessary to govern teaching and learning is something she developed during her teacher-training assignment in a reflective and professional manner.

Hanne oriented herself in the direction of her new role as a teacher. One typical feature of Hanne's e-mails is that during this process she continually drew on her experience as a student and as an undergraduate studying the subjects she now is teaching, using this both for her practical methodological arrangement of teaching and as a source of reflection. Her experiences contributed to shaping the teacher and student roles she wanted to establish. She looked back at herself as a high school student and the student role she was allocated there, then at her undergraduate role. She was very aware that she wanted another teacher role and thus also another student role than what she herself had experienced.

One interesting trait of Hanne's teacher training is that she drew attention to events and episodes she had felt uncomfortable with, where she had fallen short or done something 'stupid', as she herself states, and then used these to develop. This is a general trait of problem solving and learning from experience. However, what makes this typical of Hanne is her honesty and the fact that she allows even the more uncomfortable episodes from her teaching assignment into her e-mails. Other student teachers may have similar experiences, but they do not choose to make them public. It is obvious that it is not the experience itself, which is decisive, but rather the way it is *interpreted*.

Discussion

The analyses, interpretations and the more overarching ideas build on an interactional principle (Hoel 1995:13). Everything, all phenomena, in one way or another are interconnected, they interact and affect each other. Some belong in a larger whole, one detail always joins a larger context, one moment in time is part of a time span, a person always exists in relation to other people, in relation to her closest social context, and to the larger historical and social context she belongs in. The individual interacts with her surroundings, with the social and cultural context, which she is a part of. This also applies to cognition, thinking and reflection. Cole (1988) defines the interplay between the individual and the larger context thus: 'The zone of proximal development: where culture and cognition create each other' (page 146).

An interactional or dialogic view of communication implies that utterance, message, meaning 'is completely inseparable from intercourse, ...meaning ... is built between them (the partners) as a kind of ideological bridge, is built in the process of their interaction' (Bakhtin & Medvedev, 1978, quoted from Nystrand et al. 1993:295). Concentrating the analysis exclusively on the students' e-mails would be like analyzing a telephone conversation based only on what one person on one end says. An analysis of reflection and thought development should also include the factors that initiate such processes, those that enhance development and promote changes in thinking, and those that inspire new thoughts. In e-mail communication thought development and reflection are largely connected to the dialogue between the student and the e-mail partner, to the interaction process itself.

An interactional standpoint also yields consequences for the view on thinking and reflection. In the living reality, reflection is not an abstract, isolated phenomenon. Reflection is always connected to a 'something' or one or more 'some ones', and it is always connected to one or more contexts. One of the contexts in this study is the one created through the e-mail communication. Another is the pedagogical content knowledge lectures. A third is the individual student teacher in the classroom with her pupils and interacting with her supervisor.

The case studies show how difficult it is to isolate one episode with its subsequent reflection. A single episode always belongs in a context and is part of a further context, as it is also linked both to the past and the future. In order to understand Hanne's development one should know such things as whether she have already assessed a number of approaches to the concrete subject material, and that the alternatives she has chosen are the result of experiences, testing and evaluations at an earlier stage in her professional teaching careers.

Traditional cognitive problem solving theory regards problem solving as a linear step-by-step process where one step must be completed before the next can be entered. We have chosen to consider the model in the context of a dynamic and cyclical view of problem solving. A phenomenon or problem is usually inter-linked with others, and the more complex it is, the more complex is the solution. A problem never remains unambiguous and constant, our perception and interpretation of it change continuously. During the process new conceptions about the problem are being formed, as well as possible solutions and new perspectives on the correlations between the individual parts and the whole. Problem solving, comprehension and creation of meaning are dynamic processes where the problem, the players and the context continually interact (Hoel 1995, page 227). When the boundaries of the immediate development zone have been reached after addressing a problem or phenomenon, attempts to solve the problem from other angles may be made, or the problem might be left on the shelf, as it were - consciously or in the subconscious – until it again can be processed within the range of the immediate development zone. This is one of the reasons that the solving of complex problems often takes the form of spirals or cycles, not as a linear process.

The case studies show that the bad experiences, or rather, an episode where one has the subjective feeling of not having succeeded, or of having come up short, often are necessary in order to dwell on the episode and use it as a stepping stone to further development. One seldom pauses to reflect on the successes. It is also quite common that when student teachers feel they have failed, the failure tends to take on extra dimensions as they are inclined to search for the causes of their problems and failures in themselves on the personal level. Part of what both the supervisor and the e-mail partner want to attempt is to assist the student teacher in sorting and analyzing phenomena, thereby putting the causes where they belong.

Nevertheless, problems or cognitive conflicts are means of development. A perceived problem causes a cognitive conflict, which in turn constitutes an intellectual need, which requires satisfaction through finding answers or solutions. Becoming aware of a problem causes intellectual and emotional engagement, the problem follows its own innate course towards a solution (Hoel 1995, page 226). An obvious task for the e-mail partner is to attempt to assist the student teacher in solving problems. Another task is, paradoxically, to make the student teacher see problems she has been unable to see.

Concluding remarks

The theoretical framework of the project especially emphasizes the role of written and spoken language in development, problem solving and learning. In the study the two researchers have been exploring the pedagogical implications of information technology. Our interests are focused on the message, not so much on the medium. We have chosen this medium because we are able to give almost immediate feedback. Previously, student teachers out on teaching practice got feedback on their journal several days later, which was too late to be able to make meaningful learning experiences from critical episodes from practice. Our view on writing as a tool for reflection, is strengthened by the project.

On the basis of our research findings, we believe that structured e-mail communication can make an important contribution in teacher education. Although, one-on-one communication requires so much time that it will probably not be feasible to offer this to every student teacher, it may be appropriate for those student teachers who appear to need a supplement to the individual supervision they are given at the school where they are on teaching practice. Within education in general, e-mail communication has a place everywhere where novices are having field experiences in order to connect theory to practice. Also, we see the place for one-to-one communication in distance teaching and the in-service education of experienced teachers.

References

Bakhtin, M. M. and Medvedev, P. N. (1978). *The formal method in literary scholarship: A critical introduction to sociological poetics.* Cambridge, MA: Harvard Univ. Press.

Berliner, D. & Carter, K. (1989). Differences in processing classroom information by expert and novice teachers, in J. Lowyck & C. Clark (Eds) *Teacher Thinking and Professional Reflection.* Leuven: Leuven University Press.

Cole, M. (1988). The zone of proximal development: Where culture and cognition create each other. In Wertsch, J.V. (Ed): *Culture, communication, and cognition: Vygotskian perspectives.* Cambridge, NY: Cambridge Univ. Press, pp 146-161.

Gudmundsdottir, S. (1996). The teller, the tale and the one being told: the narrative nature of the research interview. *Curriculum Inquiry,* 26(3), pp 298-306.

Gudmundsdottir, S. & Hoel, T.L. (1996). *The REFLECT Project. Four case studies of reflection chains.* NTNU November 1996.

Gudmundsdottir, S. & Shulman, L. (1987). Pedagogical content knowledge in social studies, in J. Lowyck & C. Clark (Eds). *Teacher Thinking and Professional Reflection.* Leuven: Leuven University Press, pp 23-34..

Hoel, T. L. (1995). *Elevsamtalar om skriving. Responsgrupper i teori og praksis.* In English: Students' discourse on writing. Dr.art.dissertation. University of Trondheim.

Korthagen, F. (1985). Reflective teaching and pre-service teacher education in the Netherlands. *Journal of Teacher Education,* 36(5), pp 11-15.

Korthagen, F. (1988). The influence of learning orientations on the development of reflective teaching. In J. Calderhead (ed.) *Teachers' professional learning.* London: Falmer Press, pp 35-50.

Nystrand, M., Greene, S. & Wiemelt, J. (1993). Where did composition studies come from? *Written Communication,* 10(3), pp 267-333.

Tharp, R. and Gallimore, R. (1988). *Rousing minds to life.* Cambridge: Cambridge University Press.

Tulviste, P. (1991). *The cultural-historical development of verbal thinking.* Commack, NY: N o v a   Science Publishers.

Vygotsky, L. (1978). *Mind in society. The development of higher psychological processes.* Cambridge, Mass. & London: Harvard Univ. Press.

Vygotsky, L. (1986). *Thought and language.* Cambridge: MIT Press.

Wertsch, J. (1991). *Voices of the mind. A sociocultural approach to mediated action.* London: Harvester Wheatsheaf.

Wood,D.; Bruner, J.S. & Ross, G. (1976). The role of tutoring in problem solving. *In Journal of Child Psychology and Child Psychiatry, 17,* pp 89-100.

Part 3
Intercultural issues

Ethnography of Education in the Waldensian Valleys: Analysis of the Relationship between a Religious Minority Identity, its Cultural History and Current Educational Experience

FRANCESCA GOBBO

This paper presents the findings of ethnographic fieldwork in the Waldensian valleys northwest of Turin (Italy). The research aimed to understand (1) the meaning of education and schooling within this minority, and (2) the relationship of education and schooling to the group's religious identity and to the members' status as Italian citizens. 15 fifth year school students at the Waldensian high school were extensively interviewed. Findings indicate that that high school provides students with an identity as *students* rather than as Waldensian, while the *minority* identity is transmitted and acquired in out-of-school contexts, both religious and secular ones. The educational experience is also described as relevant to the students' *component* identity, i.e. as Italian citizens, but not to higher education future choices. Findings interpretation took into account the *diffused* local cultural and educational 'environment', the Waldensians' reflective inquiry on the relationship with the Italian nation-state, and the minority's educational tradition.

Current educational discourse centers on culture and diversity in an effort to account for changes in post-industrial societies, as a consequence of demographic and occupational changes occurring there. More specifically, in continental Europe the discourse of intercultural education declares the intention of getting to know and to understand women, men, children of different cultural/religious/ linguistic/ethnic origins as desirable, especially when such intention makes the 'natives' look at their own society with a 'new', i.e. critical, eye (Gomes 1998, Sclavi 1999, Gobbo 2000). The latter attitude has prodded educators and anthropologists to point out that a multicultural Europe existed well before the arrival of immigrants (Perotti 1994, Marazzi ed. 1996). Furthermore, some of them also suggest that the awareness of multiethnic and multicultural societies – be they in Europe or in other continents – should be paralleled by that of interculturalism and multiculturalism as an everyday, normal experience (Goodenough 1976, Gibson 1976, Wolcott 1996, Gobbo 2000).

However, it must be acknowledged that regardless of the rhetorical emphasis placed on mutual recognition and respect for differences, little is often known about the latter. This happens even where, as in Italy, different types of minority groups have achieved official acknowledgment by the republican Constitution. It can be hypothesized that this is so because minority groups and minority identity have usually been assigned to the private realm of life. Within the latter, such an identity is relevant to everyday interactions, it can be freely expressed, and passed on to the younger generation. As researchers and as educators we need to know how a minority group's identity succeeds to persist within the national culture, and how diversified the latter is as a result of minority groups' capacity to adapt to it while at the same time they remain and are perceived as different.

My concern with religious diversity and with the topic of home/school discontinuity made me decide to study the relationship between schooling and religious identity among the Italian Waldensians[1]. The aim was to learn how history, tradition and faith influence the community's, families', individuals' educational decisions and *vice versa*, and to question current descriptions of Italian 'multiculturalism'.

Purpose

The purpose of the research was to explore how Waldensians conceive and respond to their history, how they define themselves in relation to the church, to Italian society at large, and to schooling in particular, in the hope that this will allow cross-cultural comparison in the future. The focus of the research was on the process of identity formation and maintenance, its ties with ideas and beliefs about education and personal commitment, and perceptions of and responses to the cultural and social situation, both in the Waldensian valleys and in the rest of the country.

Background

My research falls within the realm of 'anthropology of education' which developed about thirty years ago in order to understand and interpret minorities' educational experience through an ethnographic approach and anthropological theories (Gibson ed. 1976, Ogbu 1996a). Anthropology traditionally described the ways in which in oral societies parents and adults transmit knowledge, skills, values and appropriate behaviors to their young ones. Such informal educational activities, not necessarily related to oral societies (cfr. Wolcott 1996), have an even greater relevance today both for anthropologists and educators as discontinuity between the different cultural orientations present in multiethnic and multicultural societies has been interpreted as the origin of unsatisfactory school performance by many researchers (cfr. Emihovic 1996, Gomes 1998). Anthropologists' focus is on the minorities' meaning and perceptions of education and schooling, and on the ways in which such meaning is connected to the group's culture and to its members' projects for the future. Anthropologists also inquire about the conflictual relation between the group's culture and the 'culture of the school' (Florio-Ruane 1996).

In order to better understand the relationship between educational outcomes and minority status, anthropologist John U. Ogbu (Ogbu 1978, 1981, 1990, 1999, Ogbu eds. 1991) calls attention 'to different histories of the people who make up the larger category referred to as minorities' (Ogbu, Simons 1998: 164). In his approach, the different groups' histories account for different theories about schooling and success in life as adults that are generated within the minority groups (i.e. emic theories). Minority groups' members are seen as 'autonomous human beings who actively interpret and respond to their situation' (*idem*: 158) and who thus construct their social and cultural environment. Because not all minority groups are alike, the cultural continuity, family's and community's beliefs and trust in schooling, as well as the students' status and expectations are pursued differently on the basis of the group's own dual cultural frame of reference, generating different levels of 'accomodation' to the majority's cultural framework[2].

Immigrant minority groups and groups such as the American-Indians or the Afro-Americans have been the most extensively studied because of their poorer educational outcomes. Similar attention has not been paid to religious minorities. The notable exception has been the well studied Amish (Hostetler 1974, 1993, Hostetler, Huntington eds. 1992), who represent an interesting case of cultural 'resistance' and symbolic separation from the rest of U. S. society, that is achieved by being faithful to their religious beliefs, by rejecting technology, by practicing a style of life respectful of nature's rhythm and needs, and by resisting and fighting against the too many years of school attendance that compulsory schooling requires.

In Ogbu's definition, religious minorities are 'people who belong to groups that are small in number. They may be different in race, ethnicity, religion, or language from the dominant group. (…) Although these groups may suffer discrimination, they are not totally dominated and oppressed, and their school achievement is no different from the dominant group' (Ogbu, Simons 1998: 164). Like other minorities, the religious ones understand or interpret their world, and act in it, according to a cultural frame of reference characterized by their own 'theories of 'making it' (and role models), degree of trust of …[the majority] and …[its] institutions, and beliefs about the effect of adopting' (*idem*: 169) majority ways on minority identity. Religious minorities are present in every modern nation-state – in fact, such as the Jews or the Waldensians within the Italian context, for instance, have been there for centuries – contributing to the contemporary diversity in societies, and succeeding in maintaining their distinctive religious and cultural identity even when they appear to be socially, politically and culturally integrated[3] in the curriculum and values of an educational system which leaves little or no room for differences in general, and for religious differences in particular. In the case of the Waldensians, discontinuity between the school and the home can be hardly described in terms of conflict, nevertheless some does exists, not only in relation to the religious instruction in school but to the religious behavior and organization within the Italian wider society.

The Waldensians: history and identity

The historical accounts about the Waldensians, written by Waldensian historians, narrate events and figures distinctive of this people-church that are linked in an uninterrupted, conflicting relationship with the Catholic Church and the Catholic powers (such as the King of France and the Dukes of Piedmont) for which the Waldensians soon came to represent the *other* and to be described in a very negative manner. The name that designates them since the 14th century refers to a man – probably a rich merchant – known as Valdès, Valdesio, or Pietro Valdo, from Lyon, who had had a deep spiritual crisis around the year 1170. Because of the crisis, he dedicated his life to poverty and to bringing the Word to people. Other men and women joined him and were soon known as the Poor of Lyon. They moved to Lombardy at the beginning of the 13th century, but because of heretics' persecutions later they sought sanctuary in the long and narrow Piedmont valleys near the French border, where they lived the meager life of mountain-farmers. This was the first of many dramatic changes that Waldensians had to make in order to survive as a people and as religious community, which Waldensian historians interpret as an original way to attain religious and cultural continuity through the discontinuity brought by historical decisions.

Waldensians joined the Reformation in 1532 and became a Reformed community in the midst of Catholic Piedmont that tolerated them for almost a century. But this situation changed dramatically in the second half of the XVII century when, after being attacked by the Piedmont army (1655) and after having resisted as long as they could, they were defeated. They were captured and then sent to exile in Geneva (1686). However, in 1689 they decided to return to their valleys through a hard trek across the Alps known as 'the Glorious Recovery'. The return brought them against the French and the Piedmont armies once more. Just when they were going to be defeated again, the Duke of Piedmont decided it would have been better to secure the Waldensians' help so as to limit the ambitions of France. With the Duke's decision, it began the so called 'ghetto period', during which Waldensians lived peacefully and somewhat successfully in their valleys. However if they wished to do business or to pursue higher education they had to migrate to a different nation-state.

Such a situation ended in 1848, after Waldensians were granted civic rights by the Prince of Piedmont, on February 17th. Since then they are said to have become more and more 'Italian' (Tourn 1973, 1993). The latter process gained momentum when many of them chose 'to move into' Italy to proselytize in the poor, backward areas of the country where they founded schools (Mannucci 1989) as the main way to carry out their mission. Almost a century later, many of them left the valleys again – this time for the industrial areas of Piedmont (thus resuming the migration that in the previous decades had taken them to the Americas) where they shared the working life common to other Italians. This 'diaspora' had important though not positive effects on the human and natural environment of the valleys.

The goal to keep and to transmit the memory of historical events such as the 1655 persecutions and the 'glorious Recovery' of 1689, as well as the Waldensians' strenuous efforts to live according to their faith in spite of overwhelmingly opposing forces, prodded XIX and XX century Waldensians to devise innovative ways by which to realize it. At first, these methods were novels and dramatic plays staged on February 17th by the local youth associations. Then, they used museums, recently renovated, a magazine, a publishing house, a Waldensian cultural center, and the organization of cultural and historical meetings as vehicles to maintain their history. All of these emphasize a distinctive identity wrought out of the successful struggle to remain loyal to the faith, on the one hand. On the other they represent an original form of educational process, thanks to which Waldensian identity could and can persist and be passed on to younger generations.

Education and Schooling among the Waldensians: historical perspective

Education has always been fundamental for Waldensians. It is one of the main duties of the Church. At the beginning of the group's history, education meant literacy in order to read the Bible without mediator. In the early XIX century education meant schooling, i.e. the system of 'little schools' (envisioned by the retired British general Beckwith) managed by the Church itself. Today, only the Waldensian high school (the *Collegio della Santa Trinità*) remains in Italy. It was founded in 1831 and since 1836 it has remained in the same building.

The *Collegio* was under the direct responsibility of the Waldensian Church until thirty years ago, when such responsibility was taken by a Committee on which the school principal and other elected members from the Waldensian community sit. This Committee makes curricular decisions, hires teachers and manages the school finances, but it is also accountable to the Church. Though the *Collegio* is a privately financed school, it has shared the curricular programs of Italian state high schools since the end of the last century. Originally established to prepare church ministers who would otherwise have had to study abroad, it soon became a school where non-Waldensian students were also welcomed. During Fascism, the school faculty took an openly critical stance against dictatorship, and some of its teachers fought and died in the Resistance. In 1968 the question should the *Collegio* continue to exist divided the Waldensians: some of them objected to it believing that the Church should no longer maintain what appeared as an élite institution. Others shared such criticism, but they also thought that the *Collegio* should continue to represent the community and its strong, traditional belief in education. What resulted from the debate were structural changes, innovative curricula which attracted a progressively greater number of Waldensian and non Waldensian students appreciative of the high quality of education offered by the *Collegio*. The latter's new educational opportunities now include a 'European' course of study described as in 'ideal continuity' with the Waldensian and school history by the *Collegio*'s self-presentation *brochure*. In fact, the community's longstanding investment in education can be considered one of the basic elements of the Waldensian identity and one that helps explain its continuity in time.

Consequently, the belief in the importance of education for the community and its youth is repeatedly emphasized and made visible by the many locally organized initiatives. Publishing, journalism, scholarly colloquia, teachers' in service training, libraries and archives, seminars on literature, debates, characterize and enrich the valleys' intellectual 'environment' and everyday life. In my view, books and articles on past and contemporary events should be considered not only as interventions in the ongoing debate and research on Waldensian history, but also as a fundamental contribution to the social construction of the group's identity, so that such 'diffused educational environment' is a specific cultural way to support and strengthen this people's sense of continuity and distinctiveness.

Methodology

Context

The research was carried out in Torre Pellice, the main town in the Val Pellice, one of the three Waldensian valleys that lie west of Turin, the capital of the Piedmont region. Torre Pellice is the seat of the Waldensian Archive, of the Waldensian Cultural Center and Library, of the Museum, and of the *Collegio*. The town also has a hospital, a hostel for the many visitors who visit the area, and a home for the elderly. All these institutions (with the partial exception of the *Collegio*) are run by the Waldensian church which has thus become one of the major sources of employment and economic growth in the valleys, while it offers the opportunity to realize one's own religious vocation by answering the needs of fellow human beings.

In Torre Pellice temple, the church Synod takes place every year in August. There discussions take place about important issues for the life of the church and of civic society, and decision are made during a week long public assembly. There again, the Waldensian Cultural Center publishes a magazine on the history and culture of the Waldensians, and it organizes many scholarly events and meetings.

Although Torre Pellice is perceived and described as a Waldensian town, more than half of its population is not Waldensian but Catholic. The cathedral, the Catholic pre-school and the parish playground stand at the entrance of the town, and the Catholic oriented weekly, published outside the valley like the Protestant one, is regularly distributed and read.

Procedure and Data Collection

In my research I took an ethnographic approach to the context and the topics I intended to explore. In other words, I lived in Torre Pellice and participated in as much as I could of its social, cultural and religious life[4] in order to carry out fieldwork. This started in February 1994 and ended in December 1996, although I did not stay there continuously. While there, I was a resident of the Waldensian hostel, where I had the opportunity to talk at length and informally with the members of the family in charge of it, to meet many Italian and foreign visitors, to participate in the social and religious events held in the big assembly hall. The hostel's sitting room also provided a quiet area to interview members of the community.

Another place I often visited for research purpose was the library of the Waldensian Cultural Center where I gathered information from the newspaper's and youth magazine's articles, historical essays and books, and the Synod's proceedings. Today, and unlike the past, the anthropological unit of analysis is often a group with a written tradition which should be attentively considered by the researcher if various situations are to be understood. This has certainly been the case with the Waldensians who claim to have 'produced' more historians than theologians (and for good theological reasons – they add).

If published history books and research narrate what Waldensians have pursued, accomplished and suffered, they are also meant to provide a lasting inspiration for future generations. A highly respected historical researcher and a church minister writes that 'he who doesn't have a past has no future, a community who loses its memory doesn't know what course of action to take in the present, it lacks a perspective and a vision of the future' (Tourn 1995: 4). My reading 'sessions' had thus a major role in understanding the Protestant point of view on education and school tradition in the valleys, its perceived relationship to religious minority identity, and the minority's cultural frame of reference – the way they see and interpret events, the reasons they give in arguing about identity and minority condition.

Interview Questions

I developed the interview questions partly from Ogbu's theoretical framework, and partly from what I had learned through participant observation and inter-

views of older students, community representatives, ministers and historians. In order to gather data to be compared, in all the interviews I explored the following points:
- choice to enroll and attend the *Collegio* (reasons, expectations, role of the family)
- evaluation of their choice at the end of the five year school experience (had expectations been met, for instance)
- meaning of the educational and school experience (with regard to teaching and teacher-student relations) and perceived difference with regard to other schools
- perceived specificity of Waldensian culture (educational tradition, current worries about possible deschooling, Waldensian 'institutions')
- perception of Waldensian culture and identity (from the point of view of non Waldensians as well)
- Waldensian identity and choice of faith (within the Church: Sunday school, catechism, 'confession' and confirmation; within the community: youth groups, theater groups, choir, etc.)
- meaning of education (for the students and their families).

Findings

All[5] 15 fifth year *Collegio*'s students (age 18-19) were interviewed[6]: 8 defined themselves as Waldensians, 5 as Catholic, and 2 of them stated they did not practice Catholicism. The interviews were carried out in a small room of the *Collegio*, at the end of classes or by appointment with the students whom I had met during their class of Italian language and literature in order to introduce myself and the theory and methodology of the research[7].

The opening question was about whether the *Collegio* – being the only Waldensian high school in Italy – was still considered a place where the process of education fosters the sense of belonging and membership in a different history, faith and tradition, and whether this was the reason for enrolling in it. The students' answers stress the importance of the *Collegio*'s local dimension which is described as a network of personal relations favoring and supporting their choice, rather than as the Waldensian historical past and traditions. They also emphasize how the school was the challenging and fulfilling experience friends, relatives, and siblings had foretold them. Parents are described to have supported enrollment at the *Collegio* because they wanted quality of education for their children.

> The people I knew spoke highly of this school (…) but to be sure, I asked my friends who had already attended this school. My parents convinced me [to enroll] by pointing out to me that it was a small sized school, that there were more opportunities for a dialogue with teachers.

Furthermore, students state that parents believe the *Collegio*'s teachers can help, support and understand young people but also treat them as adults, albeit in a familiar and friendly way. For parents, quality of education means not only the teachers' good academic training, but also their capacity to listen to students' learning and everyday difficulties.

In their children's narratives, parents are described as willing to trust and to invest in an educational institution which does not make students feel alienated, as if they were 'just a number', but that instead aims to reduce undifferentiated mass schooling' as well as the possibility of conflicts with teachers.

> It's the teachers' quality that matters: teachers are more or less the same everywhere, but here they pay more attention to us, there is one teacher for every ten students.

Not surprisingly, students respect their teachers because the latter understand and help them to become responsible persons.

> This school aims at making us more mentally open towards other countries. (…) Here I have experienced a cultural enrichment process … And the way the school achieves this is by giving a sense of responsibility to the persons.

The style of student-teacher relations, which is described as also promoting new, different situations in which the young people have an opportunity to test themselves, is perceived as what insures the *Collegio*'s continuity, rather than its history or the Waldensian educational tradition. However, an important connection with such tradition can be found here, precisely because of the great significance the *Collegio* attributes to an educational experience understood in the widest sense. For instance, teachers are perceived to stay at the *Collegio* because of their commitment to this kind of educational tradition.

The school experience is described in terms of a 'culture' based on cooperation, sharing, *ésprit de corps*, whose transmission and acquisition takes place not only in the classroom but also in out-of-school enterprises, such as the organization of rock concerts, Christmas parties, various initiatives to raise money for the school, and the 'study abroad' program. Such 'school's culture' includes interpersonal expectations (personal growth, cultural enrichment, ability to confront and solve problems) and values (responsibility, independence of judgement, balance).

> I have just come back from a month in Germany. I find a very important aspect the fact that we are prepared to accept the different cultures, and different ways of living; anyway, having such exchanges gives us the opportunity to live like our peers do in Germany, England, France.

Some students criticize this 'school's culture' since they fear it might make them believe they belong to an enlightened minority, protected by the valleys' network, so 'far from the madding crowd' of the bigger high schools in the towns nearby.

This high school is very European, open to European states; but I think we are not as open toward Italy … At the level of [students'] protest … we do very little … We're a bit isolated. We're a minority, a minority, a minority, we're all together, we stay close to one another … and then this minority becomes an enclave … and it remains so.

Choice of faith, membership in the Church, and religious identity are apparently not seen as relevant to the school experience in general, but to contexts other than the school's, where Waldensian students can construct their identity as members of a religious minority.

[Unlike some years ago], now I like to go to meetings where we all sing together, we get to know each other, enjoy each other's company, even though those I meet there are not the friends I see during the week.

That *Waldensian* minority identity is constructed outside the Waldensian high school[8] means for instance that a good part of these young people's life is devoted to activities within the Church. Furthermore some of them state their interest in the diaconate, the Church's sector in charge of social care and assistance. There, those who have a strong sense of social and community responsibility and strong feelings for the people in need, or with problems, can find work opportunities, that will also allow them to return to work and to live in the valleys.

I plan to become a deaconess. … It's a choice related to my interest in theology, not to this high school. … I believe that it is extremely important to maintain this Waldensian identity, the Waldensian faith which is a minority religion.

Among these students the strong sense of being Waldensian is not described in terms of any form of culturally marked behavior. Yet the bonfires, the communal festive meals, the choir, and the February 17th dramas all play an important symbolic function, though they may be perceived as sign of difference/separation by non Waldensian peers. In the realm of faith, ministers, rather than teachers, constitute Waldensian students' reference point with whom to discuss one's ideas about theological issues.

[What I know of the Waldesian history] I have learnt it in school, but also in my family; subsequently, for personal interest, I've read some books, and I've attended catechism, and the Waldesian community cultural events. (…) I am part of the 'Coretto' [the local choir] now by many years, I am very tied to it. I am also part of the theatre of Angrogna and last year I performed my first part. It was a minor one, but I felt good and it was a very very beautiful experience.

Waldensian students have many commitments within the community: they attend youth and theater groups' meetings, religious activities and seminars, and sing in the local choir.

I go regularly to the Coppieri [a local temple] and my best friends are there. (..) We do many things together besides having fun: we read the Bible, we discuss current issues, we read the papers, and discuss the news which interest us the most … Then we do other things such as organizing the neighborhood meetings, the bonfires, the plays, or fund raising events … We sing in the choir.

Such meetings and activities affirm spiritual and secular meanings which are neither described nor are perceived as being in competition or antagonistic to other everyday ways of life and behaviors. Rather, they also stress that Waldensian students are, at the same time, Italian citizens.

This is a secularized school, if it can be so defined, in any case it is not a religious school. But it is important for the culture of the valleys, just like all the other [Waldensian] institutions that there are here – the hospital, the home for the elderly, the library (…) Perhaps, like other minority groups we have a greater sense of being a community … the Sunday spent being together, the community dinners, the youth associations. … We're more involved in the nation's culture …

Attending the *Collegio* has been a rewarding educational experience; however, the relation between this experience and the minority identity is not a simple one. The emphasis on responsibility, autonomy and investment in high quality of learning is seen as relevant not only to Waldensian individuals but to *individuals* capable of playing an active part within their own community of faith *and* Italian society. In fact, as the young citizens that they are, students are eager to participate in, and to understand the issues and problems that characterize Italian society at large. Yet, regardless of the *Collegio*'s high quality education, they way they talk of the future is not very optimistic.

I don't have the courage to attend the faculty [art history] that really interests me because I've realized that if I were to do so, afterwards I wouldn't find a job, it isn't easy, this in fact is the reality. Among us, we talk about the usual things, but in recent years above all we have talked about our fears of not being sure to find an employment. Are we worried?… yes and no. But we often discuss this problem, what the future will be like, our prospects. Personally, I am a bit worried because the way things are going … they're not so great.

Their feeling of uncertainty, though, is in no way related to being members of a minority group, but it's instead connected to the unsatisfactory prospects in Italian society in general.

I chose to study foreign languages because it gives one more opportunities in terms of jobs. If I were to start school all over again I would make the same decision and come to this high school again. (…) As a person I'm rather concerned about the future … I'm concerned about being able to find a job. (Ll.)
[Speaking of work], I reckon we all imagine we'll have to cope with difficulties and

obstacles, because even here work isn't easy to find, it's necessary to go away to find a job [even if one has attended a technical high school]. (…) For sure, if I don't find a job it doesn't mean I won't do anything but complain … I will work as a volunteer somewhere, until I find a job.

Discussion

These findings[9] allow us to understand (1) the emic perspective on schooling, learning and minority identity elaborated by the *Collegio*'s Waldensian students and within the Waldensian community, and (2) the different strategies by which such an identity is acquired, transmitted and enriched, together with the cultural meanings attached to it. The interviews' findings indicate that the *Collegio*'s educational experience provides students with more than high quality school learning. Students describe themselves as challenged by the out-of-school enterprises they organize and as aware of the greater sense of responsibility and cooperation they have thus acquired. As *students,* they identify with the 'cultural enrichment process' they underwent and believe it created a bond among *all* students.

Waldensian students do not see their identity as fostered by the *Collegio*'s history and tradition. Instead, these students' perceptions and behaviors as *Waldensians* are more influenced by the historical and cultural factors outside the school. On the one hand, the history of this minority group and of its relation with Italian society is characterized by past persecutions. On the other hand it is influenced by the great respect that Protestant nations and individuals had for the Waldensians (Spini 1959). The latter's firm faith and their love for education won them wide admiration. Furthermore, notwithstanding the persecutions and the isolation, i.e. the 'ghetto period', Waldensian demanded to be recognized as citizens and, once being granted their rights, they moved into 'Italy' – thus perhaps becoming the first minority group to care for the needs of the poor in the majority population. The valleys were, and still are, considered a symbolic motherland for the Waldensians. There are places high on the mountains that have a deep historical meaning for this minority group and which preserve the memory of the XVII century dramatic events. When the Waldensians of the 'diaspora' return to the valleys, they return to a context where the *minority identity was, and is, enacted* (or externalized, cfr. Hannerz 1992) *in the public realm of life.* The February 17th celebrations, or the Synod, for instance, are collective and deeply felt events which involve a few non Waldensians as well. As for the many educational, social and cultural initiatives, they reverberate beyond Torre Pellice and into the other valleys. The theater group which is located in a nearby town attracts people from other areas, as does the Torre Pellice based choir. It can be said that all these initiatives, as well as those addressing local needy people, continue a long tradition of innovative ways to transmit and enrich the minority identity.

But the valleys and the mountains also remind residents and visitors of the cause of the Resistance and of those who died for it, during World War II. Many of them were Waldensian and their decision to fight can be related to the Waldensians' love for freedom. Yet the same decision can be interpreted as that of citizens who defended their country from both an internal and an external enemy. Students elaborate on their identity as Italians on the one hand by speaking of their interest for national political issues and how to confront them. On the other hand they underline the uncertainty and the difficulties awaiting for them in the near future. In their answers, Waldensian students implicitly acknowledge their *component* identity, as it has been called by this minority's historians and intellectuals. Such a notion defines Waldensians as part and active members of Italian society. By declaring themselves a *component* of Italian society, Waldensians stress that they share many values, concerns and ways of life with the rest of Italians, but that the Waldensian values and style of life still persist and distinguish them as a religious minority *vis à vis* Italian society.

Conclusion

This research shows that education and schooling have still a major role to play in the process of maintaining and broadening both the *minority* identity and the *component* identity. In fact, though the *Collegio* is not perceived as an institution responsible for transmitting the religious minority identity, such institution continues to be considered as a place where the sense of belonging to a tradition of educational and cultural innovation is transmitted to the young people *studying* there. Such sense of belonging is reinforced by participation in what I have defined as a *diffused educational environment*. For instance, in the students' interviews there are echoes of the ongoing debate on minority identity and its relationship to Waldensian history and tradition, as well as on its relationship with Italian civic and religious life. The diffused educational environment promotes an awareness of this people's history of endurance and resistance and of its relationship with the religious majority, but it also fosters and enhances a pluralistic and intercultural approach to the public realm of life.

References

Emihovic C., "Continuità e discontinuità culturale in educazione", in Gobbo F., a cura di, *Antropologia dell'educazione. Scuola, cultura, educazione nella società multiculturale*, 1996, Milano, Edizioni Unicopli, pp. 85-103.

Florio-Ruane S., "La cultura e l'organizzazione della classe scolastica", in Gobbo F., a cura di, *Antropologia dell'educazione. Scuola, cultura, educazione nella società multiculturale*, 1996, Milano, Edizioni Unicopli, pp. 171-189.

Gibson M. A., *Approaches to Multi-Cultural Education in the United States: Some Concepts and Assumptions*, in "Anthropology and Education Quarterly", 1976, 7, 4, pp. 7-18.

Gibson M. A., *Introduction. Anthropological Perspectives on Multi-Cultural Education*, in "Anthropology and Education Quarterly", 1976, 7, 4, pp. 1-4.

Gibson M. A., Ogbu J. U. eds., *Minority Status and Schooling: A Comparative Study of Immigrant and Involuntary Minorities*, 1991, New York, Garland.

Gobbo F., *Educazione, cultura, identità: il caso della minoranza religiosa valdese*, in Gobbo F., Gomes A. M. eds., *Etnografia nei contesti educativi*, in "Etnosistemi", 1999, 6, pp. 21-49.

Gobbo F., *Pedagogia interculturale. Il progetto educativo nelle società complesse*, 2000, Roma, Carocci.

Gomes . M., *"Vegna che ta fago scriver". Etnografia della scolarizzazione in una comunità di Sinti*, 1998, Roma, CISU.

Goodenough W. H., *Multiculturalism as the Normal Human Experience*, in "Anthropology and Education Quarterly", 1976, 7, 4, pp. 4-6.

Hannerz U., *Cultural Complexity. Studies in the Social Organization of Meaning*, 1992, New York, Columbia University Press.

Hostetler J. A., "Education in Communitarian Societies. The Old Order Amish and the Hutterian Brethren", in Spindler G. D. ed., *Education and Cultural Process. Toward an Anthropology of Education*, 1974, New York, Holt, Rinehart & Winston, pp. 119-138.

Hostetler J. A., *Amish Society*, (I ed 1963), 1993, Baltimore, The John Hopkins University.

Hostetler J. A., Huntington G. E., *Amish Children. Education in the Family, School and Community*, (I ed. 1971), 1992, Fort Worth, Harcourt, Brace Jovanovich College Publishers.

Mannucci A., *Educazione e scuola protestante*, 1989, Firenze, Manzuoli.

Marazzi A. a cura di, *L'Europa delle culture*, 1996, Milano, I.S.MU..

Ogbu J. U., *Minority Education and Caste: the American System in Cross-Cultural Perspective*, 1978, New York, Academic Press.

Ogbu J. U., *School Ethnography: A Multilevel Approach*, in "Anthropology and Education Quarterly", 1981, 12, 1, pp. 3-29.

Ogbu J. U., *Minority Status and Literacy in Comparative Perspective*, in "Deadalus", 1990, 119, 2, pp. 141-168.

Ogbu J. U., "L'antropologia dell'educazione: introduzione e cenni storico-teorici", in Gobbo F., a cura di, *Antropologia dell'educazione. Scuola, cultura, educazione nella società multiculturale*, 1996, Milano, Edizioni Unicopli, pp. 1-47.

Ogbu J. U., *Una teoria ecologico-culturale sul rendimento scolastico delle minoranze*, in Gobbo F., Gomes A. M. a cura di, *Etnografia nei contesti educativi*, in "Etnosistemi", 1999, VI, 6, pp. 11-20.

Ogbu J. U., Simons H. D. *Voluntary and Involuntary Minorities: A Cultural-Ecological Theory of School Performance with Some Implications for Education*, in "Anthropology and Education Quarterly", 1998, 28, 2, pp 155-188..

Perotti A., *La via obbligata dell'interculturalità*, 1994, Bologna, EMI.

Sclavi M., "Il sapere delle emozioni e il tocco dell'umorista: l'esperienza etnografica come *savoir faire* nella complessità", in Gobbo F., Tommaseo Ponzetta M., a cura di, *La quotidiana diversità*, 1999, Padova, Imprimitur, pp..

Spini G., "Riforma italiana e mediazioni ginevrine nella Nuova Inghilterra puritana", Cantimori D., Firpo L., Venturi F., Vinay V., a cura di, *Ginevra e l'Italia*, 1959, Firenze, Sansoni, pp. 453-489.

Tourn G., *Una chiesa in analisi. I valdesi di fronte al domani*, 1973, Torino, Claudiana.

Tourn G., *I valdesi. Storia singolare di un popolo-chiesa*, (I ed. 1977), 1993, Torino, Claudiana.

Tourn G., *Perché la storia*, in "la beidana", 1995, 11, 1, pp. 4-7.

Wolcott H., "Trasmissione e acquisizione culturale", in Gobbo F., a cura di, *Antropologia dell'educazione. Scuola, cultura, educazione nella società multiculturale*, 1996, Milano, Edizioni Unicopli, pp. 49-64.

Notes

[1] While there are many historical studies about the Waldensians and about education among them, none had been carried out from an anthropological point of view.

[2] Empirical research does show that some groups are able to maintain a certain *level* (sometimes quite a high one) *of cultural continuity*, even when at the same time they succeed in integrating themselves into the mainstream society by learning most of the specific behaviors and the language spoken in it. In the first place such learning is intended to make it possible to attain a good job, a new residence – in other words, they attempt to acquire whatever equal opportunities are available as well as opportunities for social mobility.

[3] My analysis addresses problems of continuity/discontinuity among Italian Protestants in present times, even though it will go deeply into history; I am fully aware that racial laws and confinement and death in concentration camps for the Jews proved that in totalitarian societies difference is considered something to be disposed of regardless of the degree of integration or assimilation achieved by the minority group.

[4] I went to the Synod in summer 1996, the bonfires in February 1994 and 1996, the communal meal on the civic liberties anniversary, the Spring 'confession' of faith at the temple, the end of the year live rock music concert, the local arts and crafts fairs, the school year inauguratio. I also went to a play staged by the local Waldensian theatrical association, and to many concerts organized by the local radio station and by the Torre Pellice choir.

[5] The *Collegio*'s total student population was less than a hundred in 1995-96.

[6] Although all students were interviewed, only the answers elaborated by the Waldensian ones will be taken into consideration and discussed here. The interviews were recorded and transcribed by myself; my interpretation is not based on any computer assisted coding system. Instead, I drew the young people's emic theory on identity and education by personally singling out and highlighting the passages which best expressed their point of view.

[7] In that same occasion I asked students to give consent to be interviewed.

[8] In this sense, the *Collegio* is the place where students learn what they have in common regardless of the religious difference

[9] For a more comprehensive analysis, see Gobbo 1999.

The Multicultural Issue in Portuguese Schools: Seeking Justice or Another Morality?

José Manuel Resende & Maria Manuel Vieira

In recent years, the concepts of multi and intercultural education have made a sudden appearance in reflections upon the school universe, in Portugal. These reflections have become more and more linked to the exposure of injustices practised by a public school in a space of differentiated social relations, where not all are treated equally. The arguments involved and the models of justification that they reveal is the aim of this article.

From emigration to immigration: the social visibility of the inter-multicultural issue

From studies of emigration to immigration

The issue of multiculturality only gained visibility in the Social Sciences in Portugal during this decade. In fact, the issue of multiculturality is necessarily related to the impact that the major popular movements taking place in the past few decades have had on the Portuguese social structure. Indeed, the end of the 80s are marked by the growing importance of immigration amongst us, representing a novel change in traditional migratory tendencies in national territory and consequently in the type of issues it raises for the Portuguese society.

During the 60s emigration is the focus of studies then being carried out in this field of the Social Sciences. As an economically peripheral country, Portugal is part of the chain of working force exportation then typical of South European countries heading for the growing markets of the North. Challenged by the size of this phenomenon the reflections produced by the Social Sciences at the time are strongly marked by that decade's dominant economic point of view.

Independence of the former Portuguese colonies in Africa in 1975, on the one hand and, on the other, policies supporting the return of the immigrants on behalf of more developed European countries following the economic crisis brought on by the petrol crisis, create a dramatic turn in the popular movements occurring in Portugal in the second half of the 70s. This in turn implies a change in the relevance of the objects for study. Now it is the return (of colonists or emigrants) which captures researchers' attention.

In the 80's, however, when Portugal enters the European Economic Community in 1986, it is provided with economic development and the advantages of belonging to an economically, socially and politically privileged space. This transforms its old vocation for rejection and grants it the ability to attract working force. Despite the fact that today Portugal still holds a small percentage of foreigners in comparison to its peers in the European Union , it is clear that the country has been witnessing an increasing demand as a destination for countless citizens from the former African colonies and from Brazil.

However, these foreign communities are not distributed regularly over national territory. On the contrary, they are mainly concentrated in the area surrounding the capital and to a smaller extent in the more developed districts of the south and north, which favours their visibility as a group.

Space as a form of representing social groups: central and peripheral construction in the case of politically problematic groups

In fact, another dimension for analysing the public visibility of inter-multiculturality is the spatial distribution of the sub-populations included in the group, that is, checking the location of their residential neighbourhoods and briefly describing their living conditions. The reasons behind these things are essential for the spatial distribution of social groups is not random nor does it happen due to a more or less arbitrary voluntary determination. In a way, we may say that the location of residence is an important indicator for measuring distinctions between groups with uneven resources or, in other words, to grant them their own social identity.

Their concentration in certain neighbourhoods contributes decisively towards the objectivation of this category. Issues referring to disputes, clashes and even violent conduct of different intensities occurring in these neighbourhoods are usually brought up when security, violent conflicts and illegal conduct are publicly discussed. These issues produce generalised forms of judgement regarding these actions, directly affecting the processes of social construction of these categories, both in terms of the creation of stigmas and in terms of stressing differences through naturalistic remarks as well as in terms of maintaining postures which are strongly marked by one-sided evaluations, which are almost always rooted in ideologies, especially those found in certain culturalistic conceptions. In other words, residential areas are seen by sociologists as spaces of their inhabitants' social representation.

The 'immigrants' social issue: contributions and interrogations concerning actions of the respective representation systems

One important aspect of this paper is to find reasons for the growing interest of the Educational Sciences in Portugal concerning studies on the issue of inter-multiculturality. In short we may consider two reasons. On the one hand, there are reasons of a moral nature: acknowledging the extent and intensification of discriminatory practices, namely ethnic and racial ones.

On the other hand, there is a reason that is more about matters of educational policy. Though as a school reality racism is seen as something happening only occasionally 'and problems are limited to matters of underachievement due to language deficiencies and lack of cultural integration' (Cortesão and Pacheco, 1991:39) this does not mean that such 'problems' will not manifest themselves in certain 'aggressive forms of segregation' (ibidem:39).

However, another set of reasons helped transform 'immigrants' into a social issue. Programs to fight poverty certainly contributed to bring this cause into public visibility. Some of these studies in Portugal identified, among many others, a 'extremely vulnerable to poverty' – a group generally known as 'ethnic and cultural minority groups' (Capucha, 1998).

Other events related to these groups also made the headlines and in some cases became an even more important cause because of the attention given by certain non-governmental organizations (S.O.S. Racism) as well as other associations and groups of actors. The fact is that they played an important role in including the issues of racism and the entry of immigrants born in former Portuguese colonies, in the political and civic agenda. However, the press does not only publish news of this sort. Other press reports show different views on the 'reality' of teenagers belonging to these groups, suggesting pattern behaviours and life styles linked by the 'deviation' and transgression of social norms.

It is in the full picture resulting from different sources and brought to public knowledge by several formal and informal means, that a reality is depicted in which the boundaries between 'good' and 'evil' are defined by the points of view of those who sketch this seemingly simple reality and, above all, easily understandable for those who do so to give their assertive and final opinion.

The place of inter-multiculturality in the Educational Sciences and in the Sociology of Education – from equality to difference

The 70s and particularly the implementation of democracy in Portugal in 1974, opens the door to a more active and diverse questioning of the State. Treated in an implicit way and mitigated during the dictatorial regime, the issue of school democratisation takes on a central role around which all debates regarding the educational field orbit.

The issue of the social inequalities that the school is confronted with, seen through the interpretation originally made by the social scientists of the previous decade, in other words, the inequalities in the access by the different social classes to the educational system, is now the object of unequivocal confirmation, further enriched by the theoretical contributions and by the instruments of scientific research offered by the sociological science, hereafter institutionalised among us. In a context characterised by rapid structural changes with the tendency to construct a more equalitarian society, the identification of mechanisms of inequality in the Portuguese society gains priority in the scientific agenda. Following the articulation of education with the economic development of the country as well as the civic legitimacy attributed to an ample school democratisation, there is an intensive effort to dismantle, on all the levels of the system, the mechanisms and factors responsible for the production of inequalities among the different social classes regarding the school culture, with the aim of revealing and (hopefully) eradicating them from the fair and equalitarian society trying to be built at the time.

This analytical position remains until the beginning of the 90s. In a direct or indirect way, the relation between the different classes and sub-classes and the School is maintained as one of the analytical priorities for the Sociology of Education, although it is now integrated in a different context generated by new educational policies established by the democratic regime in force.

Indeed, the persistent denunciation by the Educational Sciences of the unequal character of the system inherited from the previous regime, namely the drastic selection made in the premature orientation of students towards one of two relatively limited school directions – a technical path, strongly associated to practical knowledge, and a state path, clearly oriented towards intellectual work – had urged the political power emerging from the revolution to promote the unification of the school system, moving to a more advanced level of studies similar to that of vocational guidance. By adopting this measure, it was believed that the system would gain the necessary conditions to promote full equality of opportunities. In the 80s, the political power takes this principle one step further, increasing the duration of compulsory education from six to nine years of unified studies. Formally, access by all to a common cultural denominator was finally ensured, thus eliminating any institutional obstacles to the promotion of equalitarian schooling of the population. In other words, the process of mass teaching in Portugal had begun.

Therefore, it is in a context of formal access by all to the same education that the question is raised regarding the relation established by the different social classes with the School. In this case, it becomes quite obvious that granting equal opportunities in the access to the educational system becomes a necessary but in no way sufficient condition for the success in the attainment of the cultural privilege which the School intends to supply to all citizens. This way, it is now within the school, where all social classes formally meet, that we will try to understand the social processes responsible for the maintenance of the inequalities of school success; in other words, to understand the production of those 'internally excluded' (Bourdieu and Champagne, 1993) from the system. The selected branches of knowledge and codes of discourse involved in their transmission as well as the articulation between the contexts of family socialisation, the pedagogical practices in the classroom and even the constitution of student groups and youth subcultures in the school space have been strongly explored analytical dimensions in the last two decades. But until the beginning of the 80's, we are dealing with an exclusively autochthonous and national school reality.

In fact, the issue of inter-multiculturality in the school space invades the field of the Educational Sciences during the 90's. Its emergence is linked to the numerical increase of the multiethnic population which is, as we saw, strongly concentrated in spatial terms.

Actually, this issue witnesses a change in the type of analysis used up to this point, replacing a class-related perspective traditionally brought forth in debates about the School's functions and aims with a dominating culturalist perspective. We move from demanding equal opportunities of access to one education for all, which is the essential condition for fighting the school inequalities found among different *social classes*, to demanding equal opportunities of achievement considering the unquestionable respect for different *cultural identities* living side by side in the school. This change constitutes a completely 'new battle' declared by the School, 'in which it [the School] defines itself as a space for the meeting of cultures, defending cultural diversity more than a homogeneous and "monocultural" equality' (Valentim, 1997:85).

The truth of the matter is that the school massification now taking place does secure principles of social equity considered essential for building a civic school at the service of all citizens, but nevertheless it raises new questions concerning the quality of the public service rendered. However, this concept is full of semantic connotations, as is proved by different studies and essays produced over the decade, revealing 'a certain tension between a democratic/equalitarian position (...) and another more meritocratic or elitist position that focuses on quality and promoting merit' (Valentim, 1997:78).

Finally, the efficiency of mass schooling in dealing with the 'differences' it shelters presently is also seen in the light of the quality of public service rendered by the educational system. In many of these studies the quality of this service undoubtedly implies abandoning the cultural 'monolithism' that traditionally characterises school, considered to be inefficient, and replacing it with a school open to cherishing the cultures before it (Stoer, 1993; Correia and Correia, 1993; Guerra, 1993; Cardoso, 1996a; Cortesão and Stoer, 1996; Pacheco, 1996), in which the teacher is a privileged actor (Cardoso, 1993 and 1996b). Only this way can the school be successful in the democratic mission it has been entrusted with. In other words, in this perspective, emancipation of the (culturally and ethnically) disfavoured.

In this sense the issue of school inequalities and their opposite is still an important point in the discussion about school justice. Everything seems to show that the problem of underachievement continues to be a clear manifestation of the injustices practised by the School. On top of this it is the students born in the more socially and economically disfavoured domestic groups, including immigrants and gypsies, that most feel shut out. It was in this internal and external atmosphere that a project of Intercultural Education (PREDI) was born in 1993, related to activities of the Ministry of Education and lasting two years (1993 to 1995). Under the general motto of 'multiethnic, multiracial and multicultural' integration (Diálogo Entreculturas, 1993:1), the State Secretary of Elementary and Secondary Education briefly presented the reasons that led the Ministry to support this project. One of them refers to the 'racial and cultural conflicts that took place recently in suburban schools of Lisbon and in other parts of the country', revealing 'once again, the importance and good timing regarding the inauguration of the "Entreculturas [Between Cultures]" Department by the Ministry of Education.'

In short, we may state that the emergence of studies on inter-multiculturalism in schools is closely related to two fundamental dimensions. On the one hand, to the dynamics of internal and particularly external popular migrations, including all consequences in terms of their settlement and living conditions. On the other hand, to the typical social experiences of these groups of immigrants, particularly those of children and teenagers in public schools, which greatly contributes to the construction of judgements of distinct origins about subjects related to these groups.

However, most of these studies rotate around two central concepts – 'culture' and 'ethnicity' – whose unquestioned and therefore often indiscriminate use has consequences on the analyses that are performed.

From the critical theory to the sociology of criticism: justification models regarding the social issue of inter-multiculturality in mass school contexts

Since the 60s the school universe has become a favourite target in terms of criticising modernism. Sociology also contributed to this debate. More specifically, the Sociology of Education analysed theories from the 60s onwards which, although conceptually divergent, were aimed at explaining the bases of school inequalities.

In democratic societies, these sociological paradigms led to a constant debate on the nature of school justice and its influence on citizens' education, from two complementary points of view. The first dealt with the civic participation of school pupils. The second dealt with acceptable behavioural civic models, that is to say, civilly agreed upon and justified, transmitted through school socialisation.

Studies on the issue of inter-multiculturality in Education reveal elements that make it imperative that a constructive approach towards them be developed. On the one hand, it is possible to typify analyses that are created as *guides* for teachers who deal with problems resulting from school massification on a daily basis, namely with problems arising from the entry of pupils labelled as being part of the 'ethnic minorities'.

Analytical guides and their main targets give most of their attention to the latter problem, due to two complementary aspects. The first aspect consists of the problems related to the cognitive learning of students belonging to 'ethnic minorities' in comparison to other students' learning. The second aspect concerns the problems related to these students' behavioural patterns, which are normally considered deviant and therefore subject to long, complicated disciplinary procedures or steps taken towards cognitive compensation and integration. These measures are usually looked upon with suspicion by these students' teachers, as far as their efficiency is concerned.

On the other hand, we have the analyses of the *problem of inter-multiculturality and the phenomenon of educational massification*. This topic is set within the context of another social problem – the inequalities of school access and achievement – although here this problem is studied in a wider, more analytical perspective.

The reasons presented in some of these writings enter the realm of justification models in relation to the activities which should be accounted for by the intervening policy-makers in this social field, by the teachers who deal with problematic students belonging to 'ethnic minorities' within their pedagogical practice and also by the problem-students themselves, who should change from the objects of action into the subjects of critical, demanding and participating action. Defending a critical concept regarding the effects of globalisation upon school socialisation, these writings invoke the wish that all those involved in the educational circle participate in establishing a chain of solidarity that resists the consequences of homogenisation brought about by globalising messages and practices, particularly those born in organisations that are called upon to protect this movement (International Monetary Fund, World Bank, etc.).

The issues generally raised in these analyses direct their analytical and methodological premises in a similar manner to that of the *civic justification model* created by Boltanski and Thévenot (1991). Having diagnosed the problem of school inequalities as a result of the unfair functioning of the school system, the authors question the pedagogical space as the place for cognitive learning and school socialisation. They identify it as being organised to respond to the requests of economically and culturally privileged social groups. As a result, they denounce the fact that the disadvantages in these two areas, endured by the students from migrant families (African, gypsy, etc.), are not only not overcome in school but are still subject to mechanisms and procedures that reinforce them.

The learning difficulties due to a deficient grasp of the Portuguese language also imply difficulties in understanding and memorising knowledge transmitted in the different subjects. However this problem is not limited to the problems related to cognitive learning, objectified through bad school grades and therefore in an increasing amount of underachievements.

The learning problems themselves lead to other problems that are not taken seriously enough, given the functions and goals of the school public service. Among them, we may highlight their relation to indisciplinary behaviours regularly attributed to these 'bad' students. Behavioural disturbances have other implications, both in terms of integration in the area of school sociability and in terms of integration in the area of public sociability.

Similarly to the case of cognitive learning, the causes of the problem regarding indiscipline are found in the way the school institution works. In a certain way, school indiscipline and subsequent school violence are two phenomena that are related to a maladjustment between the school and this only recently integrated 'public'. Therefore, the main problem lies in the old-fashioned school norms that are, at best, simply not adjusted to the social and cultural features of these students. In short, the school institution has not been shaped to answer the needs of these minorities. This is why it is doubly unfair: it fails the disadvantaged more often – particularly the 'minorities' – and in doing so aggravates their emotional and behavioural instability that already existed due to their deprivations.

The previous description is regarded by the Educational Sciences as an unbearable situation, in human and civic terms, in the current democratic and developed societies. Therefore this situation cannot go on, without some form of immediate public intervention. Actually, its diagnosis alone is sufficient reason for action at several levels: organisational, administrative, pedagogical, technical, social, etc. This way, both the analytical argumentation and the post-modern scientific concepts present in these studies are very close to the civic justification model. The authors of these studies seek the basis for the collective mobilisation of the school actors through the ideas underlined in this model.

On the one hand, they look to teachers as the fundamental pillar for the success of these transformations. Conceived as intellectual transformers, teachers play an important role in solving problems that arise due to inter-multiculturalism. In order to do so, they need pedagogical-organisational training programs that work around this new problematic. However, these training programs will only succeed if pedagogy is seen as an instrument of a critical nature, whether in terms of mental habits, routines or, ultimately, socio-cultural-material models that are not adapted to this new reality.

On the other hand, they try to increase the students' awareness of the need to change these undesirable situations. The success of this implementation depends on a reduced interference by higher hierarchies. This is the direction of every goal in this fight against resignation, as well as the requests for a general mobilisation to defend these principles, namely transforming object-students into subject-active-participating-critical students.

All political-technical-organisational goals, all legislative decisions, every political program, whichever its field of influence, should be connected to a concept of Education that includes the majority's solidarity towards the minorities without, however, jeopardising the general public's interests, that is, the interests of the weaker and dispossessed, among them the migrant groups.

In order to reach these political goals, it is necessary to involve people, discuss ideas, projects and resolutions, join wills, adjust positions – in other words, to gather all forces for this purpose. Therefore the call for mobilisation is not restricted to teachers and students. It spreads throughout the whole educational community, particularly households and political and economic local powers.

It is quite appropriate to assert that one of the roles played by the critical and resistance theory of the Educational Sciences has been that of a vehicle of mobilisation for groups involved in school issues. The success of this task implies the acceptance of its guidelines in favour not only of the Public School, but also of a certain opinion regarding the functions and goals of mass public schooling in post-modern societies.

Both these movements are essential for understanding how, beyond doubt and simultaneously, their defenders can justify the following:
- on the one hand, defending two rights of the general public's interest – equal opportunities and national identity – transformed into two public service duties on behalf of the State directed towards placing the general public's interest above individual interests;
- on the other hand, defending features linked to the minorities of migrant populations, inside the country and abroad, related to preserving their local and specific identities – rights which the State must protect with equal commitment, but which are directed towards placing individual interests above the general public's interests.

The latter seems to oppose the civic justification model. It is at this intersection of apparently irreconcilable ideals that the analytical proposals related to the cause of the inter-multiculturalistic movements come closer to other models of justification (Boltanski and Thévenot, 1991), namely the *inspired world* and the *domestic world* models.

In relation to the *inspired world*, its link is through two related facts. First, the fact that this movement was created through the planning of intellectually and politically informed minorities, some close to the minorities directly related to the intellectual movement of the critical and resistance theory of the Educational Sciences, others closer to minorities that are generators of organised movements against racial, ethnic, religious, cultural and sexual discrimination as well as that of women.

On the other hand, the fact that they belong to resistance movements against national and global dynamics of homogenisation that they violently criticise. Their political and analytical efforts are such that their political and civic intervention agendas are not necessarily those of unions with leftist ideals.

As for the *domestic world*, its link is through the 'tension between the principles that ensure the purity *of the mass beings* based on a *cause* and unique relations that grow from one person to another' (...) (Boltanski and Thévenot, 1991:312). This tension is resumed by the complicated compromise between the will of the general interest and the will of individual interests.

The tense relations between the organs that represent the general will and those that represent the individual will are even more pronounced when dealing with social issues based on public accusations related to individual cases. The State does not always succeed in solving these situations, through its regional and local branches, without having to compromise because of external pressures placed on it by individual interests opposing the general public interests. These tensions can be felt in many social movements and are often the object of accusations brought forward by the defenders of the critical and resistance theory.

The School is precisely an organ of the Republic destined to eradicate the prejudices through school socialisation. This function aims to enforce general will over discriminatory prejudices associated with individual interests.

The same line of thought applies to the issue of tense relations between learning the national language taught at School and the particularities of the languages and linguistic terms brought to this space by students born and socialised in different linguistic contexts. Once again, there is a conflict between two interests and wills, which cannot always be reconciled.

Learning the language is of great importance due to its connection to the problem of school access and success. This is why one of the pedagogical issues that is always present in reflections upon inter-multiculturality is precisely to determine the most adequate modalities for these students to learn the language of the host country.

How is it possible to reconcile the function planned by the School of the Republic, that of educating citizens regardless of their backgrounds, with the need to preserve individual identities and differences? How is it possible to guarantee that students will preserve their ethnicity, so strongly marked by the constant presence of the mother-tongue, among many other dimensions, in the presence of another language which is initially totally unfamiliar to them?

Isn't the separation of local, regional and domestic bonds one of the functions of the School of the Republic? How is it possible to guarantee the freedom and autonomy that are so essential to citizenship education without opposing all modalities of dependency of an individualistic nature?

Finally, the adoption of the civic model gives most of these authors a chance to direct a series of critical observations at the followers of the *mercantile* and *industrial* justification models. As for the *mercantile world*, the authors cannot guarantee the individualistic and competitive nature created within it. The expansion of these values at every level of teaching within schools worries their fiercest opponents. Moreover, the growth of these individualistic and competitive conducts are obvious signs of how this institution depends on the interests of the middle classes.

Instead of adopting them as type values, the School must replace them with others, such as solidarity, mutual help, justice, equity, joint effort, group or teamwork, etc. Only with these values is the School prepared to fight wilfulness, merit, individual initiative, etc. Parting with this model's reasons is what makes it possible to overcome the learning and integration difficulties of these student cultural minorities.

As for the second universe – the *industrial world* – the authors criticise the excessive dependency of the school system's goals concerning the logic imposed by the economic-industrial space. On the one hand, the school's organisational modalities seem to be an almost mimed re-translation of the reasons of business management. On the other hand, the complexity and centralisation of the decisions and their logic of action, within the educational system and in terms of the new school management model, are not too different from the technoburocratic and enormous organisational schemes that exist in commercial and industrial firms.

In short, schools are metaphorically pointed out as factories that produce mass students or else they are metaphorically pointed out as large warehouses where parents leave their children every day. With this double dependency on forms of logic that are contrary to civic aims, how can this institution pay attention to the expectations of students belonging to minorities and, in this way, meet their main difficulties efficiently and immediately, both in terms of learning and in terms of their social integration?

References

AAVV, (1968) - Problemas do pessoal docente universitário, *Análise Social*, 6 (20-21), 254-267.

A.C.R.A. (1989) - *Os angolanos em Portugal*, Lisboa, Associação Cultural e Recreativa Angolana.

Alarrcao, A. (1964) - Exodo rural e atracção urbana no continente, *Análise Social*, 2 (7-8), 511-573.

Almeida, C. C. (1973) - Sobre a problemática da emigração portuguesa: notas para um projecto de investigação interdisciplinar, *Análise Social*, 10(40), 778-789.

Almeida, C. C. (1975) - Movimentos migratórios, espaços sócio-culturais e processos de aculturação, *Análise Social*, 11(42-43), 203-212.

Almeida, J.C.F. (1968) - Situação e problemas do ensino de Ciências Sociais em Portugal, *Análise Social*, 6 (22-23-24), 697-729.

Almeida, J. F. (1964) - A emigração portuguesa para França: alguns aspectos quantitativos, *Análise Social*, 2 (7-8), 599-622.

Almeida, J. F. (1966) - Dados sobre a emigração portuguesa em 1963-65: alguns comentários, *Análise*

Social, 4 (13), 116-128.

Almeida, J.F., Capucha, L., Costa, A.F., Machado, F.L., Reis, E., Nicolau, I. (1992) - *Exclusão Social - Factores e Tipos de Pobreza em Portugal*, Oeiras, Celta Editora

Almeida, J. F. (1995) - *Introdução à Sociologia*, Lisboa, Universidade Aberta.

Amado, R. R. (1985) - Reestruturações demográficas, económicas e socioculturais em curso na sociedade portuguesa: o caso dos emigrantes regressados, *Análise Social*, 21(87-88-89), 605-677.

Ângelo, V.(1975) - O ensino discriminatório: liceu e escola técnica - resultados de um inquérito, *Análise Social*, 44, 576-629.

Anido, N., Freire, R. (1976) - A existência de ciclos emigratórios na emigração portuguesa, *Análise Social*, 12 (45), 179-186.

Anido, N., Freire, R. (1977) - Análise de alguns ciclos emigratórios da emigração portuguesa, *Análise Social*, 13 (50), 451-459.

Antunes, M. L.M. (1970) - Vinte anos de emigração portuguesa: alguns dados e comentários, *Análise Social*, 8 (30-31), 299-385.

Araujo, H.C., Cortesao, L., Stoer, S. (1992) - *Educação e diversidade cultural: para uma sinergia de efeitos de investigação*, Porto, CIIE, Faculdade de Psicologia e de Ciências de Educação da Universidade do Porto.

Bairrao, J. (1968) - O ensino da Psicologia em Portugal: situação e perspectiva, *Análise Social*, 6 (22-23-24), 682-696.

Benavente, A. (1976) - *A escola na sociedade de classes,* Lisboa, Livros Horizonte.

Benavente, A. (coord.) (1996) - *A literacia em Portugal - resultados de uma pesquisa extensiva monográfica*, Lisboa, Fundação Calouste Gulbenkian.

Benavente, A, Correia, A.P. (1981) - *Obstáculos ao sucesso na escola primária*, Lisboa, Instituto de Estudos para o Desenvolvimento.

Benavente, A., Costa, A.F., Machado, F.L., Neves, M.C. (1987) - *Do outro lado da escola*, Lisboa, Teorema.

Boltanski, L., Thevenot, L. (1991) - *De La Justification: les économies de la grandeur*, Paris,Gallimard.

Bourrdieu, P. , Champagne, P. (1993) - Les exclus de l'intérieur, In P. Bourdieu (dir.) (1993) - *La misère du monde*, Paris, Éd. du Seuil.

Cabrita, Felícia, (1997) - Histórias de Gangs,*Expresso-revista*, n°1267, 28 junho, 25-32

Caporale, C. (1965) - Custos e lucros das migrações internacionais, *Análise Social*, 3 (11), 295-312.

Capucha, L. M.A. (1998) - Pobreza, exclusão social e marginalidades, in Viegas, J.M., Costa, A.F. (org) *Portugal, que Modernidade?*, Oeiras, Celta Editora.

Cardoso, C.M.N. (1993) - O professor em contextos multiculturais, *Forma*, 47, 14-16.

Cardoso, C. M. N. (1996a) - Referências no percurso do multiculturalismo: do assimilacionismo ao pluralismo, *Inovação*, vol. 9, 1/2, 7-20.

Cardoso, C. M. N. (1996b) - *Educação multicultural - percursos para práticas reflexivas*, Lisboa, Texto Editora.

Castro, P. , Freitas, M.J. (1991) - *Contributos para o estudo de grupos étnicos residentes na cidade de Lisboa*, Lisboa, LNEC-ITECS-9.

Certeau, M. de (1993, 1ª ed 1974) - *La Culture au Pluriel*, Paris, Éditions du Seuil.

Correia, C.A.P., Correia, M.C. (1993) - Apoios educativos e minorias étnicas, *Noesis*, 27, 39-40.

Cortesao, L., Pacheco, N. A. (1991) - O conceito de educação intercultural. Interculturismo e realidade portuguesa, *Inovação*, vol. 4, n°2/3, 33-44.

Cortesao, L., Pinto, F. (org.) (1995) - *O povo cigano: cidadãos na sombra - processos explícitos e ocultos de exclusão,* Porto, Afrontamento.

Cortesao, L., Stoer, S. (1996) - A interculturalidade e a educação escolar: dispositivos pedagógicos e a construção da ponte entre escolas, *Inovação,* 9, 35-51.

Cortesao, L., Stoer, S. R. (1997) - Investigação-acção e a produção de conhecimento no âmbito de uma formação de professores para a educação inter/multicultural, *Educação, Sociedade e Culturas*, 7, 7-28.

Costa, A.B., Pimenta, M. (coord) (1991) - *Minorias étnicas pobres em Lisboa*, Departamento de Pesquisa Social do Centro de Reflexão Cristã, Lisboa, Policopiado.

Cruzeiro, M.E., Antunes, M.M. (1976) - O ensino secundário em Portugal (I), *Análise Social*, 48, 1001-1046.

Cruzeiro, M.E., Antunes, M.M. (1977) - O ensino secundário em Portugal (II), *Análise Social*, 49, 147-210.

Cruzeiro, M.E., Antunes, M.M. (1978) - O ensino secundário: duas populações, duas escolas (I), *Análise Social*, 55, 443-502.

Cuin, C.-H., Gresle, F. (1995) - *História da Sociologia*, Lisboa, Publicações D.Quixote.

Derouet, J.-L., (1992) - *École et Justice. De l'égalité des chances aux compromis locaux?*, Paris, Éditions Métailié.

Emediato, C.A. (1978) - Educação e transformação social, *Análise Social*, 14 (55), 443-502.

Esteves, M. C.(org.) (1991) - *Portugal, país de imigração*, Lisboa, Instituto de Estudos para o Desenvolvimento.

Ferreira, V. M., Nunes, A. S. (1968) - O meio universitário em Portugal: subsídios para a análise sociológica da sua estrutura e evolução no período 1945-1967, *Análise Social*, 6 (22-23-24), 526-595.

Ferreira, V.M.(1969) - Inventário analítico da imprensa estudantil em 1945-1967, *Análise Social*, 7 (25-26), 223-281.

Franca, L. de (coord), (1992) - *A Comunidade Cabo-Verdiana em Portugal*, Lisboa, Instituto de Estudos para o Desenvolvimento.

Gracio, S.(1997) - *Dinâmicas da escolarização e das oportunidades individuais*, Lisboa, Educa.

Gracio, S., Miranda, S. (1977)- Insucesso escolar e origem social: resultados de um inquérito piloto, *Análise Social*, 13(51) 721-726.

Guerra, I. (1993) - Contexto e enquadramento do projecto de educação multicultural, *Forma*, 47, 10-13.

Guerra, I. (1996) - Reflexões em torno de um projecto de educação multicultural, *Inovação*, 9, 83-97.

Guerra, J.P.M.(1968) - Tradição e modernidade nas Faculdades de Medicina, *Análise Social*, 6 (22-23-24), 639-667.

Guerra, J.P.M., Nunes, A.S. (1969) - A crise da universidade em Portugal: reflexões e sugestões, *Análise Social*, 7(25-26), 5-49.

Lopes, J.T. (1997) - *Tristes escolas - práticas culturais estudantis no espaço escolar urbano*,Porto, Afrontamento.

Machado, F.L. (1992) - Etnicidade em Portugal. Contrastes e politização, *Sociologia - problemas e práticas*, 12, 123-136.

Machado, F. L. (1994) - Luso-africanos em Portugal: nas margens da etnicidade, *Sociologia - problemas e práticas*, 16, 111-134.

Machado, F. L. (1996) - Minorias e literacia: imigrantes guineenses em Portugal, in Ana Benavente (coord.), *A literacia em Portugal - resultados de uma pesquisa extensiva e monográfica.*, 171-238.

Machado, F. L. (1997) - Contornos e especificidades da imigração em Portugal, *Sociologia - problemas e práticas*, 24, 9-44.

Machado, F. L., (1998), Da Guiné-Bissau a Portugal: imigrantes e luso guineenses *Sociologia - Problemas e Práticas*, nº26, 9-56.

Machado, F. L. (1999) - Imigrantes e Estrutura Social, *Sociologia - Problemas e Práticas*, nº 29, 51-76.

Machete, R. (1968) - A origem social dos estudantes portugueses, *Análise Social*, 6 (20-21), 213-247.

Maravall, J.M. (1972), *La Sociologia de lo Posible*, Madrid, Siglo XX.

Martins, I. F. (1967) - A migração dos trabalhadores rurais para a indústria, *Análise Social,* 5 (18), 298-302.

Melo, A. (1975) - Educação e capitalismo: uma certa economia política de educação recorrente, *Análise Social,* 11(41), 105-117.

Miranda, J. D. (1969) - A população universitária e a população portuguesa: um confronto da sua composição social, *Análise Social,* 7 (25-26), 158-166.

Miranda, S. (1978) - Insucesso escolar e origem social no ensino primário: resultados de um inquérito na zona escolar de Oeiras-Algés, *Análise Social,* 55, 609-625.

Monica, M.F. (1977) - Correntes e controvérsias em Sociologia da Educação, *Análise Social,* 13(52), 989-1001.

Monica, M.F. (1997) - *Os filhos de Rousseau - ensaios sobre os exames,* Lisboa, Relógio d'Água

Moais, A.M., Neves, I., Antunes, H., Fontinhas, F., Medeios, A., Penada, D., Reis, E. (1996) - Práticas pedagógicas e aprendizagem científica: um estudo sociológico, *Revista de Educação,* 5 (2), 69-93.

Moura, F.P., Filipe, C.A. (1968) - Uma experiência de colaboração professores-alunos, *Análise Social,* 6 (22-23-24), 510-525.

Murteira, M. (1965) - Emigração e política de emprego em Portugal, *Análise Social,* 3 (11), 258-278.

Naysmith, J., Souta, L. (1996) - A diversidade linguística e étnica em Portugal, *Multicultural,* 4 (6), 5-6.

Nazareth, J. M. (1976) - O efeito da emigração na estrutura de idades da população portuguesa, *Análise Social,* 12 (46), 315-362.

Nazareth, J. M. (1978) - A dinâmica da população portuguesa no período 1930-70 *Análise Social,* 14 (56), 729-800.

Neves, I., Morais, A.M. (1993) - A orientação da codificação no contexto da socialização primária - implicação no (in)sucesso escolar, *Análise Social,* 121. 267-307

Nunes, A. S. (1968a) - O sistema universitário em Portugal: alguns mecanismos, efeitos e perspectivas do seu funcionamento, *Análise Social,* 6 (22-23-24), 386-474.

Nunes, A. S. (1968b) - A população universitária portuguesa: uma análise preliminar, *Análise Social,* 6 (22-23-24), 295-385.

Nunes, A.S. (1968c) - O ensino das Ciências Económicas em Portugal e os objectivos da Universidade, *Análise Social,* 6 (22-23-24), 682-696.

Oliveira, M. J. C., Pereira, R. S. (1967) - Envelhecimento e vitalidade da população portuguesa: uma análise distrital, *Análise Social,* 5 (17), 23-56.

Pacheco, N. (1996) - Da luta anti-racista à educação intercultural, *Inovação,* vol. 9, 1/2, 53-62.

Pais, J.M. (1993) - *Culturas juvenis,* Lisboa, Imprensa Nacional-Casa da Moeda.

Pereira, R.S. (coord.) (1968) - O ensino da Engenharia: contribuição para a sua reforma, *Análise Social,* 6 (22-23-24), 763-784.

Pinto, J.M. (1994) - *Propostas para o ensino das ciências sociais,* Porto, Afrontamento.

Pires, R. P., Maranhao, M.J., Quintela, J., Moniz, F., Pisco, M. (1984) - *Os retornados. Um estudo sociográfico,* Lisboa, Instituto de Estudos para o Desenvolvimento.

Poinard, M. (1983a) - Emigrantes portugueses: o regresso, *Análise Social,* 19(75) 29-56.

Poinard, M. (1983b) - Emigrantes retornados de França: a reinserção na sociedade portuguesa, *Análise Social,* 19 (76), 261-296.

Pontes, M. L. B. (1968) - A crise do ensino superior: relações com o ensino secundário, *Análise Social,* 6 (20-21), 147-162.

Portas, N., Barata, J.P.M. (1968) - A Universidade na cidade: problemas arquitectónicos e de inserção no espaço urbano, *Análise Social,* 6 (22-23-24), 492-509.

Portela, A.F.(1968) - A evolução histórica do ensino das Ciências Económicas em Portugal, *Análise Social,* 6 (22-23-24), 787-836.

Prata, F.X.P. (1968) - A transformação dos métodos pedagógicos no moderno ensino superior, *Análise Social*, 6 (20-21) 163-212.

Reis, M., Nave, G. (1986) - Camponeses emigrados e emigrantes regressados - práticas de emigração e estratégias de regresso numa aldeia da Beira Interior, *Sociologia - problemas e práticas*, 1, 67-90.

Resende, J. M., Vieira, M.M. (1992) - Subculturas juvenis nas sociedades modernas: os hippies e os yuppies, *Revista Crítica de Ciências Sociais*, 35, 131-147.

Rocha-Trinidade, M. B. (1976) - Comunidades migrantes em situação dipolar: análise de três casos de emigração especializada para os E.U.A., para o Brasil e para a França, *Análise Social*, 12 (48), 983-997.

Rocha-Trinidade, M. B. (1986) - Longitudinalmente diferente ou o discurso polémico de luso-descendentes, *Análise Social*, 22(92-93), 609-618.

Rocha-Trinidade, M. B., Baptista, L. V., Mendes, M.L., Teodoro, V. D. (1988) - *População escolar directa e indirectamente ligada à emigração*, Lisboa, Projecto Universidade Aberta.

Saint-Mauice, A. de (1997) - *Identidades Reconstruídas - Cabo Verdianos em Portugal*, Oeiras, Celta Editora

Santos, A. R. (1978) - Emprego e migrações na Europa: perspectivas para os anos 80, *Análise Social*, 14 (56), 801-816.

Santos, M.L.L. (1988) - Questionamento à volta de três noções (a grande cultura, a cultura popular, a cultura de massas), *Análise Social*, 24 (101-102), 689-702.

Santos, I. S. (1965) - Aspectos da política emigratória espanhola, *Análise Social*, 3 (12), 533-547.

Santos, I. S. (1967) - Algumas considerações sobre o retorno de emigrantes, *Análise Social*, 5 (18), 288-298.

Secretariado Coordenador dos Programas de Educação Multicultural (1993) - Projecto de educação intercultural, *Forma*, 47, Dezembro, 3-7.

Secretariado Coordenador dos Programas de Educação Multicultural (1993), *Diálogo entreculturas*,n° 3, Fevereiro.

Secretariado Coordenador dos Programas de Educação Multicultural (1993), *Diálogo entreculturas*, n° 4, Abril.

Secretariado Coordenador dos Programas de Educação Multicultural (1993), *Diálogo entreculturas*, n° 5, Junho.

Secretariado Coordenador dos Programas de Educação Multicultural (1993), *Diálogo entreculturas*,n° 6, Setembro.

Secretariado Coordenador dos Programas de Educação Multicultural (1993), *Diálogo entreculturas*,n°7, Dezembro.

Serra, E. (1975) - O operário emigrante português na sociedade industrial capitalista, *Análise Social*, 11(41), 67-102.

Serrao, J.(1970) - Conspecto histórico da emigração portuguesa, *Análise Social*, 8 (32), 597-617.

Sousa, A. (1968) - Algumas reflexões sobre a democratização do ensino superior, *Análise Social*, 6 (20-21), 248-253.

Sousa, A. T. (1972) - Os trabalhadores portugueses na região de Paris: condições de habitação e de trabalho, *Análise Social*, 9 (33), 11-78.

Sousa, A. T. (1973a) - Trabalhadores portugueses e sindicatos franceses na região de Paris: contribuição para o estudo das suas relações, *Análise Social*, 10 (39), 508-551.

Sousa, A. T. (1973b) - Trabalhadores portugueses e sindicatos franceses na região de Paris:uma tentativa de interpretação das suas relações, *Análise Social*, 10 (40), 703-733.

Souta, L. (1991) - A educação multicultural, *Inovação*, 2-3, 45-52.

Stoer, S. R. (1993) - Educação inter/multicultural e a escola para todos, *Correio Pedagógico*, 73, 12-13.

Stoer, S. , Araujo, H.C. (1992) - *Escola e aprendizagem para o trabalho num país da (semi)periferia europeia*, Lisboa, Escher.

Stoer, S., Cortsesao, L. (1994) - Educação inter/multicultural crítica e o processo de transnacionalização: uma perspectiva a partir da semi-periferia in *Dinâmicas multiculturais: novas faces, outros olhares, Actas do III Congresso Luso-Afro-Brasileiro de Ciências Sociais*, vol.II, Lisboa, Instituto de Ciências Sociais, 22-33.

Tavares, M.V. (1998) - *O insucesso escolar e as minorias étnicas em Portugal*, Lisboa Instituto Piaget.

Valentim, Joaquim Pires (1997) - *Escola, igualdade e diferença*, Porto, Campo das Letras.

The Role of Western Universitiesin the Development of a New Generation of Researchers in Education in Lithuania

PALMIRA JUCEVICIENE

To ensure the effectiveness of the educational reforms, Central and East European countries, including Lithuania, have to rely on the knowledge of contemporary education. The aim of this paper is to reveal the role of Western universities in influencing the development of the young generation of researchers in education in Lithuania. Based on the experience of Lithuanian universities, as well as on the analysis of documents and data on Lithuanian higher education, the importance of links with Western universities in influencing the development of educational science and researchers is revealed. The study enabled to conclude that Lithuania faces the problems related to realisation of certain research conditions at doctoral studies. Lithuanian Educational Research Association, together with EERA which it recently joined, could make a significant contribution to the development of the new generation of researchers in Lithuania, as well as to the integration of the European academic community.

'...Europe is not only that of the Euro, of the banks and the economy; it must be a Europe of knowledge as well. We must strengthen and build upon the intellectual, cultural, social and technical dimensions of our continent. These have to a large extent been shaped by its universities, which continue to play a pivotal role for their development.' ('Joint Declaration on Harmonisation of the Architecture of the European Higher Education System', Paris, 1998)

To ensure the effectiveness of educational reforms, Central and Eastern European countries, including Lithuania, logically have to rely on the knowledge of contemporary education. Meanwhile isolation of these countries from Western theoretical and practical experience hindered the development of empirical pedagogy into contemporary multidisciplinary knowledge in education, i.e. into educational sciences as they are interpreted, for example, by Mialeret (1985).

The problematic situation in Central and Eastern Europe after 1990 was declared in the seminars and conferences of NESA (Network of Educational Science, Amsterdam), where scholars in education from the West and the East emphasised the importance of acquisition and creation of the new quality educational knowledge in the countries that are in the process of transition (Sting, Wulf, 1994). The need for the development of competence of Lithuanian researchers in education in the period of transition from pedagogy to educational science was analysed in my earlier works (Juceviciene, 1997).

Great expectations in this respect are related to the development of the new generation of researchers in education with particular emphasis on doctoral studies. This raises the question for Lithuania, facing the above-mentioned problems: what would be the most rational way to educate the young generation of researchers possessing the contemporary knowledge in education and capable on this basis to create new knowledge?

This question calls for special discussion which would undoubtedly reveal the problems related to researchers' development in Lithuania as in the country in transition. My paper *is targeted* at the constructive side of the problem - to reveal the role of Western universities in influencing the development of the young generation of researchers in education in Lithuania. The author hopes that this problem is of great importance also to other countries in transition. The discussion of this problem will hopefully contribute to the development of European integration processes. The research was based on the following methodology:

Doctoral studies as the highest stage of university studies have to fulfil the general educational aims of higher education. At the stage of contemporary doctoral studies new knowledge is created and future researchers are educated. Doctoral studies are looked upon as a special educational process for which certain organisational conditions for research realisation are necessary (Clark, 1995; Kerr, 1994). The basic conditions for research in doctoral studies, based on the traditional values of higher education (Barnett, 1990), are the following: institutional autonomy, search for objective knowledge and truth, open and non-biased discussion, liberal education, and academic freedom. Also, the discussion will be based on the components of these basic conditions which were specified in earlier works (Juceviciene, Milisiunaite, 1998).

Methods. Discussion is based on the experience of Lithuanian universities in realisation of doctoral studies, and in particular of the University X described in the case study, especially in respect to co-operation with Western partners. Other methods used include analysis of documents and management facts of Lithuanian higher education, meta-analysis of data on doctoral studies (Bitinas, Vaiciunaite, 1998), and in-depth interviews with doctoral students and their supervisors. All these methods enabled to reveal the importance of links with Western universities and scholars for influencing the quality of researchers' education and for the development of educational science.

The logic of discussion is as follows. First of all, I will attempt to analyse current situation in doctoral studies in Lithuania and to reveal the reasons which caused the situation. Then I will try to outline the ways of improving it and the possible role of Western universities in doing that.

The paper consists of five sections. The *first section* deals with the controversial situation regarding the autonomy of Lithuanian universities which is very important for ensuring the quality of doctoral research. The *second section* emphasises the significance of Western experience in search for objective knowledge and truth within the context of two approaches to social research – normative and interpretative. Also, the importance of co-operation between the European and Lithuanian universities for creation of the integrated European knowledge area is revealed. The *third section* reveals that open and non-biased discussion and liberal education are still lacking in doctoral studies in Lithuania. The possible contribution of Western universities to solving this problem is discussed. The *fourth section* deals with the problem of academic freedom faced by Lithuanian scholars and doctoral students. Some positive changes and recent problems are revealed. The *fifth section* is devoted to discussion why it may be beneficial for European universities to consolidate their efforts in helping Lithuania to develop young researchers in education and how they could do that.

The problem of university autonomy in realisation of doctoral studies

University autonomy is one of the preconditions for realisation of doctoral studies. In this section, I will try to reveal the problem of ensuring this precondition in Lithuanian universities. This problem is related to attempts of emphasising the process instead of the result in young researchers' education.

Legislative basis of doctoral studies in Lithuania

After reestablishment of independence in 1990, the reform of higher education was initiated in Lithuania. The legal system guaranteed academic freedom and autonomy for universities, and the goals were set to strive for integration of research and studies and to liberalise education. Three levels of studies were introduced – bachelor, master and doctoral. The new generation of researchers is educated at the level of doctoral studies. Doctor's degree is the first degree designating researcher's qualification.[1]

In Lithuania the Government grants the right to universities to offer doctoral studies and to confer doctor's degree, following the approval of its main expert – Science Council of Lithuania. Also, the Government sets general requirements to this degree and to the process of its acquisition, i.e. to doctoral studies. It also regulates the registration of doctor's diploma.[2]

Certainly, some decisions are left to the universities. These include, for example, the number of doctoral students to be admitted, selection of the candidates, relationships between the students and their doctoral committees, etc. In order to attain higher quality of doctoral studies, co-operation between universities is encouraged. As a result, often several universities are granted the right to jointly organise doctoral studies.

Concluding discussion on the legislative environment of doctoral studies in Lithuania, it is correct to say that the state regulates acquisition and acknowledgement of doctor's degree. This suggests that for Lithuanian universities, which are

legitimately granted the autonomy, the true autonomy is yet the goal to be attained. Is this situation created by the objective reality? Does this help to achieve
the desired quality?

*Doctoral studies in social sciences in Lithuania: non-traditional solutions and the reasons
behind them*

According to Haworth (1986), the idea of the institutional autonomy embraces
the ideas of independence (freedom from restrictions) and self-control (freedom
to (values). Apparently, independence is the necessary precondition for conducting research. According to Barnett (1990), 'searching for the truth' should be
protected from any outside pressures. This could have a positive impact on the
objectivity of knowledge and on the university mission of influencing society
development by creating and disseminating the new knowledge. Doctoral studies
are unimaginable without research. Logically then, the institutional autonomy is
the necessary precondition for realisation of doctoral studies.

The idea of self-control or 'freedom to (values)' in the broad sense is related
to the ability of the institution's intellectual potential to act as a self-governing
organisation (Haworth, 1986; Berdhal, 1990). In case this ability is not sufficient,
granting of the institutional autonomy can have very negative effects on the process of 'searching for the truth' and on the quality of studies, and consequently –
on the development of knowledge and society. The author of this paper has
accomplished analysis of the number of higher education institutions of Europe
and the US. It enabled to conclude that only highly competent universities have
full autonomy, while others are to a greater or lesser extent controlled by different
expert institutions, of course avoiding the detailed administration (Juceviciene,
1995).

What features must be present in the higher education institution to be considered as one of the high competence, i.e. to be capable to be autonomous? It is
commonly accepted that this institutional competence is determined by the competence of institution's researchers and by the quality of research and by the level
of studies performed by this institution. According to classification of the US
Carnegie Council (1973), such institutions of higher education generate the new
knowledge of high level and educate highly competent researchers.

Obviously, the way to becoming such an institution is a long process. It is
'nourished' by knowledge creation and young researchers' education which takes
place in the academic community of the given country, and first of all at the
universities already possessing high competence.

Let's turn to the controversial situation of social sciences in Lithuania. In this
country, essential reconstruction of this knowledge area was started only in this
decade. These changes were brought by the newly opened Western scientific experience. All Lithuanian higher education institutions faced the beginning of trans-

formation being in similar starting positions. The reformers of higher education pondered upon the question: is it possible already in the beginning of this process to educate a completely new generation of researchers? Influencing the changes in social life strongly needed the new scientific competence; educational reforms in particular required people competent in contemporary education. The major question was whether the first priority should be development of the competence of the current researchers.[3] What if this process will be very slow and inefficient? It was concluded that this reconstruction would become faster when stimulated by education of the new generation of researchers. This would in turn lead to the more rapid development and growth of the competence of current researchers, members of the doctoral studies committees. It was doubted whether both educational processes (education of the new researchers and development of the competence of existing scholars), while at the same time related to the creation of new knowledge, would stimulate each other without any outside control.

For this reason, a non-traditional solution was found. The right to offer doctoral studies was granted to higher education institutions which met formal requirements, while at the same time doctoral studies were more strictly regulated and their result was more strictly controlled. In this way, the universities which were allowed to organise doctoral studies did not have full autonomy in this respect.

Responsibility for supervision of the quality of doctoral degrees is assigned to the Science Council of Lithuania, the key expert of the Parliament and Government in science and studies. It registers doctor's diploma subject to the approval of the dissertation summary and public defence record by its experts. The question is whether these controlling actions restricting the autonomy of universities can have a significant effect on the future competence of Lithuanian social scientists? I will attempt to answer this question.

Firstly, no clearly defined and exhaustive criteria for evaluating the competence and dissertations of the new researchers were approved on the national level in Lithuania. Evaluation criteria are very abstract, which leads to the possibility of different evaluations of the same dissertation.

Second problem is related to experts and their competence. Lithuania is too small country to have a sufficient number of experts of the adequate competence. Consequently, research in education is often assessed by experts from other unrelated areas, for example from medicine, forestry, etc.

Third problem is related to the scope of doctoral studies and to the process or researchers' development. In 1998 nearly two thousand doctoral students (1897, to be precise) were enrolled in Lithuanian universities. Almost one third of them were working in social sciences, over thirty percent of whom (almost 200) were doctoral students in education (Bitinas, Vaiciunaite, 1998). All of them were led along the way to becoming a doctor by doctoral studies committees consisting of five researchers. So, the process of every researcher's education involved 6 people, including the doctoral student. Thus, it can be concluded that in 1998 about 1.2 thousand actors were involved in education of the new generation of researchers in Lithuania (certainly, the scholar can be a member of several committees, however in every particular case he/she can be considered as a different actor involved in the process). All of them made their contribution to the process of the *researchers' development*. Through this complex process individual values and skills are developed, and they will determine the academic capacity of the new generation of researchers.

Thus, ensuring the quality of this process is much more important than controlling the product – doctoral dissertation, which only to a limited extent reflects the result of this process (especially, the control which at present is performed in Lithuania). This would enable not only to impact the quality of researchers' education, but also to foster the autonomy of universities.

Certainly, a more considerable support to this process is possible only through the group of researchers working in the field who run this process. The efficiency of this support will be determined by readiness of this group in terms of its values and competence to accept it. Is it possible to declare that this condition has already been met in Lithuania? To answer this question, even individual cases of group competence can be important. Several such groups could serve as 'active radicals' of the support network targeted at the development of researchers in education nationwide. These radicals would use their experience of going along the non-easy way of development.

Case study of the research group in education at Lithuanian university X: an example of the development of competence and doctoral studies

The research group in education (let us call it RGE) at one of the largest Lithuanian universities (let us call it the university X) responsible for realising doctoral studies in the field, was formed in 1992. The number of scholars was increasing almost proportionally to the number of doctoral students. At present, the group involves four professors, habilitated doctors, 15 associated professors, doctors and 30 doctoral students. 12 new doctors completed their dissertations during the period of 1992-1999.

Already in the very beginning, the group has formulated the research competence development strategy targeted at the transition from pedagogy to contemporary educational science. The strategy aimed to influence the development of the knowledge area in education in Lithuania. It also promoted active adoption and analysis of Western information as well as its comparison with the existing knowledge. The combined Western and Eastern scientific experiences were expected to result in the synergetic effect, i.e. in creation of the new knowledge in the field of education.

The tactics for implementing this strategy was as follows. Both researchers and doctoral students participated in creation of the new knowledge in the overlap of Western-Eastern and especially European-Lithuanian knowledge. However, the emphases in the roles of doctoral students and their supervisors in the process of competence development had some differences. Doctoral students were actively seeking Western scientific information, while their supervisors provided methodological input into knowledge analysis, its comparison, formulation and solution of research problems. Research conducted by both supervisors and doctoral students was targeted at expanding the area of educational knowledge in Lithuania. Doctoral students, therefore, were urged to choose the topics requiring deep conceptual analysis and interpretative research rather than solving narrow problems based on the empirical research, normative research strategy and obsolete knowledge.

For this reason, co-operation with Western and Lithuanian scholars was of a particular importance. To this end, research visits of scholars and doctoral students to Western universities (six out of twelve new doctors were involved in the long-term internship programmes) and giving papers at the international conferences were encouraged. As participation at international conferences was limited by the lack of financial resources, the University organised two international conferences attended by Western and Eastern scholars from more than ten countries. These events resulted in numerous publications (monographs, collections of works) and discussions at the standing methodological seminar. Publication of the scientific periodical 'Socialiniai mokslai' ('Social Sciences') was initiated in order to promote wider discussions and co-operation with foreign scholars. It received recognition of the Science Council of Lithuania. RGE initiated Lithuanian Educational Research Association aimed at uniting the efforts of Lithuanian researchers in education.

The researchers' group established contacts with Network of Educational Science Amsterdam (NESA) which unites more than 50 American and European universities. It is worth mentioning that although NESA had no official goals to provide assistance to the Baltic partners, their contribution was considerable. Comparing the comments on the dissertation summaries, one may notice that Western universities were more active than Lithuanian ones: 54 comments against 13.

Scholars from abroad were invited to deliver courses or individual lectures in the doctoral studies. RGE received assistance from Lund University, Florida International University; University of Cambridge provided constant support. As the outcome of this process, all twelve young doctors are using their competence working at the Lithuanian universities and reforming national education. Their performance in Lithuania and comments made by foreign partners confirm the high competence of young researchers.

So, the RGE received considerable support in various forms from Western universities. However, as illustrated by case study, this support was actively sought by proving to Western partners that the group is ready to accept this support and that it will be used in the competent way for the advancement of the country's knowledge in education. Despite all its achievements, the University X group faces some problems in researchers' education. A better organised support would enable to deal with these problems more efficiently. Group's performance suggests that it is fully mature for efficient use of such support.

This case study proves that in case a better organised framework of support to the process of doctoral studies in Lithuania is established, it would be possible already now to find 'active radicals' who are especially receptive to this support, have rich experience in competence development and are able to spread it among other members of the network in Lithuania.

Therefore, the quality of the development of young researchers in education would be more effectively ensured by influencing the **process** of doctoral studies - not by administering it, but by highlighting the problem areas and providing support, especially in the form of professional competence. It would also be an effective way of promoting the autonomy of universities. Support from European universities and their researchers in education - individual, or preferably associated (for example, in the European Educational Research Association) would be very valuable and appreciated.

Searching for objective knowledge and for the truth as precondition for researchers' education
Being educated by senior researchers, doctoral students also take part in knowledge creation. Nowadays knowledge, due to its higher importance to society, is increasingly used for expressing social interests. In the information society, the problem of knowing becomes the problem of power (Lyotard, 1993). This brings the issue of legitimisation of knowledge to the centre of attention.

Lithuania, similarly to other countries trying to erase the tracks of the Soviet regime, pays particular attention to the knowledge in social sciences. Increasing understanding of the significance of education to the future of the society causes special significance of the knowledge in educational science. The task of researchers in education lies in creating knowledge on education of the free individual, and not in shaping the knowing which meets interests of certain social groups striving for the priority status. This task is especially conceivable to the Lithuanian researchers in education because the scholars of the older generation of this country experienced the compulsion of *serving* in the Soviet period.

Truth and objectivity are the two criteria of knowledge recognition in higher education, and the very process of doctoral studies means searching for the objective knowledge and the truth. However, it is not easy to answer the questions: What knowledge is objective knowledge? What are the criteria for its determination? Based on what criteria knowledge is recognised? Who sets them?

Philosophy offers several conceptions of the truth, based on which the academic community has split itself into different epistemological groups. As we know, search for the truth in natural sciences is based on the theory of correspondence, according to which the truth is perceived as correspondence between thinking and its objects. In certain disciplines of these sciences, the truth is based on the pragmatic theory relating it with its benefit to human activities and with their practical efficiency.

Social sciences, as well as philosophy, humanities, mathematics and logic, emphasise the coherence theory which sees the truth as the idea of the systemic whole. According to this theory, objectivity of knowledge is related to its non-contradiction to the existing system. If the new proposition contradicts the system, it can be rejected as erroneous, or it can be acknowledged as correct and used to change the system in such a way that, having accepted this new proposition, the system remains non-contradictory (Nekrasas, 1993).

This logic of searching for the truth, followed also by the educational science, brings to light two problems:

1. Every country as a peculiar social system has to some extent unique structure of the knowledge in education (or at least a part of this structure is unique).
2. It is very important to ensure that Lithuanian young researchers in education acquired the contemporary knowledge in education. This makes creation of this knowledge of utmost importance.

Certainly, even being unique, educational knowledge structures of different countries interact with each other. This is best reflected in the vision of contemporary Europe. Deep understanding of this vision is expressed in the 'Joint Declaration on Harmonisation of the Architecture of the European Higher Education System' (Paris, 1998) signed by four Ministers in charge of higher education for France (Claude Allegre), Germany (Juergen Ruettgers), Italy (Luigi Berlinguer) and the United Kingdom (Tessa Blackstone). Also, this understanding is fully reflected in the Joint Declaration of the European Ministers of Education 'The European Higher Education Area' (Bologna, 1999).

European area includes not only Western states, but also European countries formerly occupied by the Soviet regime. Lithuania was one of them, with a special structure of knowledge. *Firstly*, it contains certain special national knowledge in education preserved through all painful historic developments, i.e. the works by Lithuanian classics. *Secondly*, it also contains some valuable knowledge created during the Soviet period but free of one-sided ideological influence. This knowledge is based on the theories which for a long time were little known in the Western world and which recently became very popular (e.g., some teaching concepts based on the theory of Vygotsky). Also, it covers the theories developed on the basis of Western ideas, e.g. the theory of modular instruction. *Thirdly*, this knowledge area also contains the knowledge shaped under the influence of one-sided ideology. This knowledge does not meet the criteria of the truth of the contemporary pluralistic society.

These three types could be found in the structure of knowledge of any country influenced by the Soviet ideology.

What should be the strategy of creating the integrated European knowledge area? It should be created by efforts of every European country, while their knowledge structures in education, as the existing systems, should be supplemented by the new value – the scientific experience of other countries. In this way, according to the coherence theory, the country's system of scientific knowledge will inevitably be encouraged to reorganise itself.

I believe that the European area of knowledge in educational science will be *integrated* in terms of the possibilities to use the information accumulated in this area, i.e. educators of every European country will be able to easily access and understand the information significant for education. At the same time, this will not deny the possibility for every country to have to some extent unique knowledge structure corresponding to its national identity. Certainly, this knowledge area will be accessible to researchers from other countries.

In Lithuania, the area of contemporary knowledge in educational science is created in three directions: 1) by essentially reviewing the knowledge created under the influence of one-sided ideology; 2) by preserving the knowledge meeting the criteria of the truth; 3) by adopting the knowledge created in the West, i.e. by integrating it into the existing system and, when necessary, modifying it or reorganising the system itself. This causes the problems of terminology. Moreover, some theories developed in the West have different implications in Lithuania (Falk, Barczyk, Juceviciene, 1996; Rinkevicius, 1998). Only following further research on validity of these theories in our conditions (i.e. further development of these theories), they can be integrated into the knowledge structure of our country.

In the context of the integrated European knowledge, the Lithuanian structure of knowledge in education, after completing its restructuring, can be valuable to other countries and serve as the object of their researchers' studies.

So, how could Western universities contribute to the creation of the contemporary knowledge in educational science in Lithuania as a part of the European educational science area? How would these universities benefit from such contribution? Western universities could help Lithuania by offering the essential information on their contemporary knowledge in education. This should not be the one-way process: Lithuania would also offer Western researchers its best scientific experience. In the optimal situation, merging the information from both sides in joint discussion could produce a particularly new knowledge as a result of synergetic effect.

While developing contemporary knowledge in educational science, and especially when working on doctoral dissertations, Lithuanian researchers encounter problems related to research methodology and expert evaluations. Researchers in social sciences, including education, clearly perceive that contemporary knowledge area in this sphere is created based on pluralistic methodological approach recognising both interpretative paradigm and qualitative research methods and normative paradigm and quantitative research methods. Meanwhile, as I already mentioned, in our country dissertations in educational science are often assessed by experts in natural sciences who emphasise the normative paradigm and the quantitative research methods. Consequently, research in education based on the interpretative paradigm is not properly understood and even gains negative evaluation from these experts. Moreover, discussions with some of these experts suggest that they have a limited understanding of educational science as focusing merely on the teaching process.

This fact can seriously hinder searching for the contemporary educational truth in Lithuania, threatening to compliance of doctoral dissertations and of young doctors' competence to contemporary European and world-wide standards. One possible way to solve this problem is to encourage open and non-biased discussion.

Open and non-biased discussion and liberal education: their role in developing the new generation of researchers in Lithuania

Referring to the consensus theory developed by Habermas (1978), Barnett (1990) emphasised open and non-biased discussion as the paradigm of searching for the objective truth. According to the consensus theory, the truth is determined by common interests of many people. Habermas (1978) named discussion caused by wish to understand, based on facts and calling for arguments, a *discourse*. The aim of discourse is consensus, i.e. the agreement achieved by means of discourse. According to Barnett, real knowledge is the result of discourse negotiations. The objective truth is the matter of consent not only in social sciences and humanities. The laws of physical world are not the subject of discussion, but the objectivity of theories based on these laws can always be discussed (Barnett, 1990).

However practice shows that Lithuanian experts in natural sciences are not always open to discourse when assessing work of researchers in education. Perhaps this problem could be dealt with by presenting the results of Lithuanian educational research to a broader discussion, especially on the European scale. The experience shows that European scholars' comments on doctoral dissertations are taken seriously by the Lithuanian Science Council. So, support from European universities is very important in protecting Lithuanian researchers in education from exaggerated influence of the normative research strategy.

The results of Lithuanian educational research, especially that of doctoral students, should therefore be discussed in European conferences and publications. However, Lithuanian researchers in education have to be ready for these activities. Unfortunately, until recently one could feel lack of such discussion. The author of this paper has analysed 160 articles of social scientists published in Lithuania in 1995-1997. The analysis showed that certain studies are lacking reference to other scholars' research results and do not contain attempts to further develop their ideas (Juceviciene, 1999). This, to a greater or lesser extent, was the case with 91 out of 160 articles reviewed. This can cause certain problems in the development of the field.

I tried to determine the reasons of this phenomenon. The most plausible explanation was lack of critical thinking, which is not surprising because during the Soviet regime it was not one of the values in education. This resulted in quite common phenomenon of scholars lacking this quality and, consequently, having difficulties related to developing it in their doctoral students.

However, some recent facts allow to hope that development of this quality has a more favourable environment. This hope was inspired by the initiative of researchers in education, especially of the young ones, to establish the Lithuanian Educational Research Association (1998) and to discuss the important issues within it. Positive changes can also be noticed in publications of doctoral students. I analysed the publications of two conferences of Lithuanian doctoral students in education and their supervisors. These conferences took place in 1997 and 1999. Publications of the first conference were marked by lack of discussion. Meanwhile in papers of the second conference some attempts were made to discuss the theories, to interpret empirical data and, almost in all works, after drawing conclusions to engage in their discussion.

This and other facts illustrate significant positive processes in Lithuanian educational science. However, European universities could considerably speed up these processes by providing their support. Among other things, this support could help to call the experts in natural sciences for discourse, not only focusing on methodology of educational research, but also encouraging new attitudes towards research in natural sciences.

Thus, the networks of European and Lithuanian universities would be really beneficial to both sides. These networks could encourage development of critical thinking and open and non-biased discussion by the following means:
- permanent methodological seminar which can be run in electronic form;
- discussion of research results during conferences, including electronic ones;
- written comments on dissertations (they are especially important for Lithuanian side).

Liberal education

Also, it is important to ensure internal conditions in doctoral studies for developing critical thinking, rationality, independence – all that Barnett (1990) called emancipation. These qualities could be developed when the process of doctoral studies is based on the *conception of liberal education*. In doctoral studies it implies *creative research climate, close co-operation between doctoral students and their supervisors, multidisciplinary courses based on interactive teaching methods, clearly defined requirements to doctoral dissertations and clear criteria of their evaluation* (Juceviciene, Milisiunaite, 1998).

In order to determine the attitude of students and their supervisors towards these aspects of doctoral studies, the author of this paper and then doctoral student Milisiunaite surveyed 24 doctoral students and 8 supervisors using the in-depth interview. To get a broader view based on such a small number of respondents, we surveyed doctoral students from 4 different research areas (6 from each area): educational science, economics (social sciences group), computer science, and environmental engineering (physical sciences group). The average age of the surveyed doctoral students was 30.7 years. Over a half of them (14) had families, the rest lived on their own or with parents. Most of these respondents (18) were in the last years of research (3rd, 4th, 5th year), 4 were in the middle (2nd year), and 2 were in the first year of doctoral studies.

Our first interest was in the respondents' motivation for joining doctoral studies. Interestingly, most of the respondents, except doctoral students in education, as the major reason of joining doctoral studies indicated social problems – unemployment and housing difficulties for young people (registration for doctoral studies entitles them to the room in dormitory). Doctoral students in education indicated a different motive related to acquiring competence and self-actualisation. It should be noted that the requirements of admission to doctoral studies are quite high. They will become even higher, as the number of applications to these studies increases.

Most of the surveyed doctoral students gave positive evaluation to their creative and intellectual abilities, i.e. to characteristics which they indicated as crucial for researcher.

Importance of creative research climate. The importance of the research group as the necessary environment of doctoral studies was admitted both by doctoral students and their supervisors. However, respondents from physical sciences (computer science and environmental engineering) emphasised research group and its creative climate as the factor stimulating the development of research skills and mastering of research methods. Meanwhile respondents from social sciences (educational science and economics) saw research group and its climate first of all as preventing intellectual and social isolation. Some supervisors also emphasised the role of university traditions as contributing to the new researchers' integration into academic community, professional responsibility and ethics.

Co-operation between doctoral students and their supervisors. When commenting on the roles of doctoral students and their supervisors, the supervisors emphasised that doctoral dissertation is the result of co-operation between them. While admitting that the aim of doctoral studies is to educate young researchers, most of the supervisors identified themselves more with 'inspectors' than with 'educators', seeing the development of would-be researchers as more or less self-contained process. Incidentally, this attitude is quite common in the world-wide practice of researchers' education (Clark, 1995; Gumport, 1993).

Already in the beginning of doctoral studies supervisors expect doctoral students to have certain research competence. Meanwhile they do not possess it yet, or it is quite modest. We identified one more serious factor limiting closer co-operation between the two and confirming that supervisors are not always willing to take the responsibility for the competent education of researchers. This is determined by the fact that supervisor is sometimes working in a different research problem, which means that doctoral student can hardly expect in-depth discussions and advice. On the other hand, according to both supervisors and doctoral students, often the obstacle to closer co-operation is lack of the students' responsibility in performing their duties related to research and studies. (Due to financial difficulties most doctoral students have other jobs which are often unrelated to university activities).

Multidisciplinary courses. Supervisors emphasised the importance of providing doctoral students with knowledge in their research area. However, both groups of the respondents indicated that it is important to achieve a more advanced level of this knowledge. Also, both supervisors and doctoral students emphasised the importance of multidisciplinary and specialised courses to forming the theoretical background of the students and indicated their lack. It can be explained by insufficient financial and intellectual resources (information, supervisors' scientific experience in given research topic, etc.).

Active teaching methods, clearly defined requirements to doctoral student's work and its evaluation criteria. These ways of encouraging doctoral students for consistent (disciplined) research work were emphasised by all surveyed supervisors. However, at the same time they admitted that due to lack of time they do not pay to them enough attention. Also, supervisors indicated that committees of doctoral studies do not always perform the role of consultant and appraiser. Some doctoral students also expressed this view.

However, both groups of the respondents indicated insufficient financing of Lithuanian higher education, including doctoral studies, as the major reason of these problems. Lack of resources resulted in the inadequate base of scientific information and in doctoral students and supervisors rushing about between several jobs.

Summarising the results of the in-depth interview, certain problems related to realisation of liberal education can be identified. The key problem is lack of resources and of supervisors' knowledge in certain narrow research areas. However, the study indicated that supervisors', and especially doctoral students' attitude towards liberal education is positive. Certainly, it is not attempted to apply this conclusion to all programmes of doctoral studies in education in Lithuania, and by no means to doctoral studies in all areas. However, the revealed facts encourage to think of the ways of enhancing liberal education of young researchers.

Of course, the existing financial and economic situation creates certain conditions for actions. Reacting to the above-mentioned problems, Lithuanian Educational Research Association developed and distributed guidelines regarding the methodological standards of educational research. These guidelines define possible areas of educational research as *basic and applied research*, discuss the relationship between qualitative and quantitative research methods, define the standards of researcher's competence, research ethics and characteristics of the research results presented in the form of doctoral dissertation.

These guidelines could serve as a basis for the universities and Science Council of Lithuania for developing detailed requirements to young researchers' competence and education. However, all these rules could be defined as 'hardware', while the 'software' is the culture of co-operation between supervisor and doctoral student, doctoral student and his/her committee, doctoral student and university. Shaping of this culture requires considerable time and efforts. This could be done by following good examples, e.g. of British and other European universities with long traditions in liberal education.

The idea of networks of European and Lithuanian universities could be further developed by planning the two-side mobility of doctoral students and researchers within these networks, conducting joint research, delivering lectures and seminars to doctoral students. The idea of mobility is strongly supported by Leonardo da Vinci programme.

Academic freedom as precondition of doctoral studies

Academic freedom is the right of professionals (Haworth, 1986). It guarantees to the members of academic community the intellectual freedom to search for the truth without danger to their status which could be caused by the originality of their ideas (Shils, 1991). Analysing academic freedom in the context of doctoral studies, Milisiunaite (1998) splits it into three components – intellectual freedom, academic duties and the conditions of their performance.

Unquestionable is author's argument that performing of intellectual activities in doctoral studies requires the freedom of choice of research problems, methodologies and methods, the right to originality in data interpretation and analysis, the right to the results publication and unrestricted exchange of opinions during open, non-biased discussion. However, regarding doctoral studies as the process of researchers' education, it remains unclear what is the relationship between the above-interpreted academic freedom of doctoral student and his/her supervisor? Academic freedom is the right of professionals, meanwhile doctoral student does not yet possess doctor's competence. Of course, undeniable is the argument that doctoral students, like all students, have the right to the objective assessment and respect to their personal interests and that they are not obliged to agree with any indoctrination, religious or racial discrimination, sexual harassment and non-professionalism of professors.

Another question is ensuring intellectual freedom in the broad sense. It pertains both to doctoral students and to their supervisors. Does anyone have the right to exert influence on them in choosing the research topic, e.g. arguing that it must meet pressing national needs and inviting to focus on applied instead of fundamental research problems?

Academic duties imply the right of doctoral students, supervisors and other members of doctoral studies committees to meet their main obligations related to research and studies, and to take responsibility for them. As indicated by research using the in-depth interview, realisation of the academic duties as the right in some cases is hindered by insufficient financial and physical resources. On the other hand, however, both doctoral students and their supervisors admitted that they should perhaps show greater responsibility towards their work.

Academic community has significant impact on deeper and broader understanding of the researchers' academic freedom, their firmness in its protection and perception of the obligations raised by this freedom. Important role in the development of academic freedom in Lithuania could be played by Lithuanian Educational Research Association aided by EERA.

Why it may be beneficial for European universities to consolidate their efforts in helping Lithuania to develop the new generation of researchers in education

Having declared the idea of the European Higher Education Area (Bologna, 1999) and having expressed resolution to create the integrated European knowledge, European universities will have to solve the above-mentioned problem of knowledge area reorganisation. This problem is partly caused by interaction with the scientific experience of Eastern and Central European countries. To overcome this problem, European universities will definitely have to consolidate their efforts in analysing and comparing high volumes of knowledge. Strategic solution to this problem is related to answering these questions:

How to make this process more efficient and productive? Maybe this task should be addressed by joint efforts of researchers from Eastern and Western Europe? Who from Eastern Europe would be most interested and capable to work in this integrated knowledge area?

The logical answer is – young doctors in education. They are going to live in the integrated Europe with common knowledge area. In this case, wouldn't it be beneficial for European universities to influence the quality of education of these doctors? If yes, the major targets for this influence are the problem points in the process of doctoral studies. Thus, consolidation of universities' efforts for creating the integrated European knowledge also means consolidation of their efforts for education of contemporary doctors in education.

Conclusions

The above discussion on the development of the new generation of researchers in education enabled to draw the following conclusions:

1. Creating common European knowledge area basically requires from the countries in transition the following: (i) knowledge reconstruction, and (ii) ensuring the quality in the process of education of young researchers.
2. Development of young researchers in education is implemented through doctoral studies. Lithuanian universities face certain problems related to realisation of research conditions in these studies, i.e.: institutional autonomy, search for objective knowledge and truth, open and non-biased discussion, liberal education, and academic freedom.
3. Realisation of these research conditions could be enhanced by developing contemporary competence of Lithuanian scholars, which calls for essential reconstruction of the knowledge in education. However, these two processes are closely related and form a certain vicious circle which could be broken by certain advanced Lithuanian researchers in education. As indicated by the case study of University X, they already exist in Lithuania, having reached their level of advancement with support from Western universities.
4. Better consolidated efforts from Western, and in particular from European, universities would be more effective and beneficial, especially now, when necessary organisational conditions for taking advantage of these efforts have been created. Important factors of these conditions are the establishment of Lithuanian Educational Research Association and the emergence of competent researchers' groups which can serve as 'active radicals' in the common network of European and Lithuanian universities. Universities from other countries in transition would be welcome to join it.

Possible activities of this network could be the following:
  (i) joint research targeted at creating the integrated European knowledge
       area and developing the competence of Lithuanian researchers;
  (ii) making accessible to the European academic community the valuable
       national knowledge in education created by Lithuanian scholars by
       translating their works into European languages;
  (iii)discussions in various forms: conferences, seminars, publications in
       European and Lithuanian scientific press;
  (iv)comments on Lithuanian doctoral dissertations by European experts in
       education;
  (v) mobility: from Europe to Lithuania – for research on the unique experi-
       ence of the country in transition; from Lithuania to Europe – for gaining
       familiarity with the European knowledge area and for close observation
       of liberal education in doctoral studies at European universities, in
       particular of the culture of co-operation between supervisors and
       doctoral students; also aimed at encouraging members of the Lithuanian
       academic community for stronger appreciation of academic freedom.

By helping to solve these problems, European and Lithuanian universities would
contribute to ensuring the future of the common European knowledge area.

Post Scriptum
This paper was given at the Research Partnerships in Education Network of
ECER'99. It has initiated the discussion involving Conference participants from
United Kingdom, Canada, Lithuania, Estonia and other countries. The discussion resulted in developing joint project 'Changing Role and Paradigms of Educational Research: Were are Baltic Countries in Western Context?' Within this
project seminars involving Western scholars and Baltic researchers and doctoral
students will be held, also inviting Lithuanian researchers from other areas to join
them in methodological discussion.

References

Barnett R. (1990). *The Idea of Higher Education.* London: SRHE.
Berdhal R. (1990). Academic Freedom, Autonomy and Accountability in British Universities. In
    Studies in Higher Education, London: SRHE, 15(2), 169-180.
Bitinas B., Vaiciunaite J. (1998). *Doctoral and Master Studies in Education in Lithuania.* Vilnius.
Clark B. R. (1995). *Places of Enquiry. Research and Advanced Education in Modern Universities.* Los Angeles:
    University of California Press.
Falk G., Barczyk C., Juceviciene P. (1996). How Generalizeable is Herzberg's Two Factor Theory?
    Selected Papers of the International Conference on Upgrading of the Social Sciences for the Development of

Post-Socialist Countries, pp. 37-44. Kaunas: Technologija.

Gumport P. J. (1993). Graduate Education and Research Imperatives: Views from American Campuses. In *Clark B. R. (Ed.), The Research Foundations of Graduate Education. Germany, Britain, France, United States, Japan*, pp. 261-196. Los Angeles: University of California Press.

Habermas J. (1978). *Knowledge and Human Interests*. London: Heinemann.

Haworth L. (1986). *Autonomy*. New York and London: Yale University Press.

Joint Declaration on Harmonisation of the Architecture of the European Higher Education System. 25 May 1998, Paris.

Juceviciene P. (1999). Lithuanian Universities on the Way to the World-wide Academic Community: The Problems of the Development of Critical Thinking and Research Skills. *Selected Papers of the International Conference 'The Role of Social Science in the Development of Education, Business and Government Entering the 21ˢᵗ Century*, pp.121-125. Kaunas: Technologija.

Juceviciene P., Milisiunaite I. (1998). The Features of Doctoral Studies in Lithuania in the Context of World-Wide Trends. *Social Sciences: Education, 2 (15)*, 81-90.

Juceviciene P. (1997a). *Development of Educational Science: From Pedagogy to Contemporary Education*. Kaunas: Technologija.

Juceviciene P. (1995). The Prospects of the Development of Lithuanian Higher Education in the Context of Contemporary World-wide Tendencies. *Report to the Science Council of Lithuania on Research Visit as a Fulbright Scholar to the Purdue University Calumet*. Kaunas: Kaunas University of Technology.

Kerr C. (1994). *Higher Education Cannot Escape History. Issues for the Twenty-First Century*. Albany: State University of New York Press.

Kraujutaityte L. (1998). *Democracy of Higher Education: World-wide Experience and Situation in Lithuania*. Doctoral Dissertation, Kaunas University of Technology.

Lyotard J. F. (1993). *Postmodern Existence*. Vilnius: Baltos Lankos.

Mialeret G. (1985). Introduction to the Educational Science. UNESCO.

Milisiunaite I. (1998). *Researchers' Education in Doctoral Studies. World-wide Tendencies and Their Reflection in Lithuanian Higher Education*. Doctoral Dissertation, Kaunas University of Technology.

Nekrasas E. (1993). Filosofijos ivadas. Vilnius: Mokslo ir enciklopediju leidykla.

Resolution No. 1317 of 13 November 1996 of the Government of Republic of Lithuania *'Regarding the Approval of General Regulations of the System of Academic Degrees and Titles in Lithuania'*.

Rinkevicius L. (1998). *Ecological Modernisation and its Prospects in Lithuania: Attitudes, Expectations, Actions*. Doctoral Dissertation, Kaunas University of Technology.

Shils E. (1991). Academic Freedom. In *Altbach P. G. (Ed.), International Higher Education. An Encyclopedia*, vol. 1, pp. 1-22. New York and London: Garland Publishing.

Sting S., Wulf C. (Eds.) (1994). *Education in a Period of Social Upheaval. Educational Theories and Concepts in Central East Europe*. WAXMANN.

The European Higher Education Area. Joint Declaration of the European Ministers of Education Convened in Bologna on the 19ᵗʰ of June 1999.

Notes

[1] The Lithuanian system of academic degrees has the second degree – habilitated doctor. However, this degree is conferred to scholars who already have doctor's degree, not for completing a certain programme of studies but for significant research results. The habilitated doctor's degree is not the subject of this paper.

Part 4
Values in Education

Participative Education: An Incomplete Project of Modernity

JOE HARKIN

This paper advocates the concept of critical modernity, in contradistinction to that of postmodernity, in orientating the practice of education. It draws on work in anthropology, and the writings of Habermas, Giddens and Rorty in support of a re-vivified project of modernity for education. The paper takes the view that the concept of postmodernity is based on an agonistic view of human language in which the possibility of bridging the gap between persons is remote. An alternative, more communicative and convivial aspect of language use is ignored because it does not sit comfortably with the thrust of the concept of postmodernity and it is in recovering this aspect of language that I believe the defence of the incomplete project of modernity in education lies most tellingly.

A defence of the concept of modernity as a foundation for educational practice was made in Harkin (1998b). This paper extends the argument, drawing in particular upon the work of Rorty (1999). Formal education systems reflect the nature of the society in which they exist. As such, their deficiencies are in micro the deficiencies of the wider society of which they form a part. When children fail to become literate, or drop-out of school prematurely there are usually societal factors at play, such as poverty, unemployment, and deprivation. Schools and teachers may be blamed for it is convenient to governments that this should be so, and there are failing teachers and failing schools, but a fundamental link between the nature of a society and the nature of its education provision is demonstrable (ALBSU, 1995; Holtermann, 1996; Cohen and Long; 1998 Ball, 1998).

It is important, therefore, to ask what sort of society would constitute a 'good' society? For in answering this question we cast light on what we would take to be a 'good' formal education. The answer to this question at any time varies from place to place. The Taliban's idea of the 'good' society will differ markedly from that of Feminists'. Rorty (1999), following Dewey, believes that Western Liberal Democracy, represented by the United States, is about as good a society as the world has ever known. This may be gauged pragmatically by a relatively free press, or the average per capita income, or the fact that so many people outside America would like to move there, or the popularity of American clothes, drinks, food, and music. The same holds true, perhaps to a greater degree, of the United Kingdom. It does not follow, of course, that these societies are perfect. They may have very many faults but these are open to public debate and potentially, through a democratic political process, to redress.

If we take as an hypothetical starting point when discussing a 'good' education in the UK that it should reflect the nature of Western Liberal Democracy, upon what democratic principles should that education be based? Following Dewey (1933), it should be experiential, in the sense of engaging the interests of the learner; it should be reflective, in encouraging people not just to gather facts but to make connections and to critique knowledge. Following Habermas (1987) - and Rorty to an extent – it should allow relatively open communication, free as far as possible from domination.

Habermas distinguishes internal and external features of communication. Internal features include that what we say is comprehensible, true, right and sincere. This co-operative view of language is supported by other commentators (Grice, 1975; Aitchison, 1996). External features, such as who has the power to determine what can be talked about, and who is privileged to speak, systematically distort the internal, communicative features of language. In education it is easy to see that teachers have a powerful role in controlling the externals of communication. You do not have an ideal speech situation, although the ideal may always be rare or impossible. That is why it is an ideal.

It is important to evaluate whether educational experience, in a Western, Liberal Democracy, tends towards or away from open communication. Is there an acknowledged endeavour to create relatively open communication between teachers and learners? If not, we should question the health and the sustainability of our Democracy. Education that reflects, promotes and sustains a Democratic society will have democratic features, such as relatively open classrooms, relatively autonomous learners, and attention to the Deweyan emphases on experience and reflection. In turn, the valuing of certain kinds of learning experience gives rise to particular kinds of teaching, in which teachers shape knowledge for the benefit of learners in ways that help them to co-construct knowledge for themselves.

Experienced learners have a sound grasp of these features of teaching. Using a Kellyian (1955) approach, the constructs were elicited that 17-19 year old students in Norway and England use routinely and informally to evaluate their teachers (Johannessen, 1997; Harkin, 1998a). The research showed a consistency of student views across different learning programmes and between the two countries. Students identified the primary factor in effective teaching as human warmth, shown by behaviour such as respect for students, listening and responding to students, sharing a joke, knowing the students' names. That is, all the normal features of natural, co-operative language use. The second factor, statistically of much less importance, was leadership, shown by behaviour such as being well organised, understanding the syllabus and its assessment requirements, setting reasonably high standards of work, and being fair in marking.

The endeavour to develop education along democratic lines is a modernist one. In a Habermassian sense, it is held to be possible to reach a consensus about what is the case, rather than the 'facts' being imposed through domination. The possibility of consensus is vested in natural language (Habermas, 1980) and is the fundamental principle upon which Western Liberal Democracies and democratic education are based. Postmodernist positions, such as that articulated by Usher & Edwards (1994). tend to betray the delicate balances inherent in the endeavour to develop education on democratic principles. They do so by drawing on the work of Derrida, Foucault and Lyotard who stress a different conception of language that emphasises difference, agonistic challenge and ludic parology

Young (1995) pointed out that 'Derrida honours the other, Foucault honours the self, both effectively stumble when they reach toward the possibility of bridging the gap between persons'. (p. 17) Lyotard (1984) based his analysis of contemporary knowledge on the metaphor of language as game – 'what is needed if we are to understand social relations…is not only a theory of communication, but a theory of game which accepts agonistics as a founding principle.' (p.16). He holds a pessimistic view of the splintering of language, holding that those within a particular game, such as science, may reach consensus, but that each game is separate from other people's games. Even 'In the ordinary use of discourse – for example, in a discussion between two friends – the interlocutors use any available ammunition…questions, requests, assertions, and narratives are launched pell-mell into battle.' (p.17) For Lyotard, human communication is war.

This agonistic endeavour may be linked to a concentration upon language as divisive discourse and an alternative, more *communicative and convivial* conception of language is ignored because it does not sit comfortably with the thrust of the concept of postmodernity. It is important to acknowledge the communicative nature of natural language in all areas of democratic life. This is particularly important in education where communities of people, drawn often from different backgrounds, come together for a common endeavour. For some teachers and learners language use may be a war, in which games are played, including oppressive discourses of teacher power, and self-protecting games of student disaffection and revolt. However, this is not the practice in most classrooms, especially in post-16 education, where interaction is marked by the normal conventions of language use (see Catan *et al*, 1996). Following Habermas, it is clear that we are far from establishing an ideal speech community but importantly we should be endeavouring to complete the project of modernity by making classrooms more open to natural language practices.

The term 'modernism' is now sometimes used by academics as a catch-all term of abuse, made to stand proxy variously for the shortcomings of reason and the Enlightenment, the absence of universal Truth, the domination of the world economy and culture by the West, the power of men over women, the failings of education to meet the needs of all people. All that is complacent, selfish and too materialistic may be dubbed 'Modern', as if by some magic hidden in the term 'postmodern' a step is then taken to remedy any of these defects.

Lurking like a palimpsest in postmodernist positions there is, paradoxically, a grand narrative, in which the status quo of education is seen as oppressive. Education should be subverted by constant questioning, in the interest of uncovering and highlighting difference (what an American scholar (Grubb, 1996) described as the tendency of British sociology of education to be footnotes to the work of Willis). Now that Communism is no longer tenable, there has been a flight of some academics into postmodernist mantras which serve the same oppositional endeavour as Marxist critique.

Rorty (1999) dismissed the term postmodernism as being almost meaningless and 'too fuzzy to convey anything' (p.262) and criticised intellectuals who use it because,

> Whereas intellectuals of the nineteenth century undertook to replace metaphysical comfort with historical hope, intellectuals at the end of this century, feeling let down by history, are experiencing self-indulgent, pathetic hopelessness. (p.263)

For Giddens (1991a), 'Rather than entering a period of postmodernity, we are moving into one in which the consequences of modernity are becoming more radicalised and universalised than before.' (p.3) The reflexivity of modernity is unsettling because it subverts the idea that we can gain certain knowledge and presumes 'wholesale reflexivity', including the reflection upon reflection itself. The concept of 'critical modernity', which Giddens also refers to as 'utopian realism' can lead to individual and collective acts to bring about change. The institutional dimensions of modernity, the global abstract systems that seem like an uncontrolled juggernaut, can be guided by human agency. The site of struggle, in each case, may be seen in terms of human communication. Although Giddens (1991b, p.213) held that Habermas's theory of communication leaves open how this may work in practice, Giddens' own work indicates the importance of dialogue in controlling the juggernaut of modernity. Late modernity, far from being a time of fragmentation of human experience, 'produces a situation in which humankind in some respects becomes a "we", facing problems and opportunities where there are no "others".' (p.27)

In a later work, Giddens (1994) agrees with Rorty that a post-traditional order opens the possibility of "a cosmopolitan conversation of humankind" (p.100), and identifies only four ways in which value disputes can be resolved: *embedding of tradition*, which in modernity is undermined; *disengagement*, the possibilities of which are limited; *discourse*; or *violence*. (p.105)

Bauman (1998) from a different perspective reached a similar conclusion. He criticised the postmodernist narrative of 'globalization' for failing to convey the complexity and sharp contradictions tearing the world apart. He quotes the Polish anthropologist Wojciech Burszta,

> Former peripheries clearly go their own way, making light of what the postmodernists tell about them. And they [the postmodernists] are rather helpless, when facing the realities of a militant Islam, the ugliness of Mexico City hovels or even the black squatting in a gutted South Bronx house. (p.101)

How can we find hope, engagement, and a sense of agency in such a world? Not through a flight into solipsistic language games, or self-indulgent mantras of difference but through a recognition of the potential for consensus given in natural language. Habermas (1980, 1986) expressed it thus:

> The human interest in autonomy and responsibility is not mere fancy...what raises us out of nature is the only thing whose nature we can know: language. Through its structure, autonomy and responsibility are posited for us. Our first sentence expresses unequivocally the intention of universal and unconstrained consensus. (p.314)

Education should be rooted firmly in this view of language. This is not to ignore or elide differences or to be complacent about how open and communicative educational practices are. Differences of gender, culture and outlook should be celebrated as part of a democratic endeavour. However, it should be acknowledged that there is more that unites human beings, at a fundamental level, than divides us. This has been shown, for example, in language studies and in anthropology.

Lukes (1990) reported that,

> The upshot of . . . language-cognition research . . . is not favourable to the Sapir-Wharf hypothesis. It has been observed that "the fascinating irony of this research is that it began in a spirit of strong relativism and linguistic determinism and has now come to a position of cultural universalism and linguistic insignificance". (pp. 267-8)

Horton (1990), in studying the thought systems associated with peoples of sub-Saharan Africa and Western Europe found a 'common core' of rationality, central to which,

> ...is the use of theory in the explanation, prediction and control of events. Central too is the use of analogical, deductive and inductive inference in the development and application of theory....the high cognitive yields of modern Western science is nothing more than the *universal rationality* operating in a particular technological, economic and social setting. (pp.256-257 - Horton's emphasis)

For Habermas, (1987) postmodernist writers, paradoxically, find themselves hopelessly emeshed in the Enlightenment thinking that they set out to subvert:

Heidegger and Foucault want to initiate a *special discourse* that claims to operate *outside* the horizon of reason without being utterly irrational . . . Those who would like to leave all paradigms behind along with the paradigm of consciousness, and go forth into the clearing of postmodernity, will just not be able to free themselves from the concepts of subject-centred reason. (pp. 308-9 - Habermas's emphasis)

This does not mean that Habermas is complacent of the enlightenment tradition. As Lemert (1997) pointed out,

Habermas is critical of the Enlightenment tradition with its dangerous temptations to essentialise all humanity into a one-dimensional totality shorn of real differences. Yet, this position is a radical *modernism* because it seeks critically to discover the liberating potential in modern culture.' (p. 43 - Lemert's emphasis)

Habermas returned to the Enlightenment tradition of western philosophy to uncover a road not taken and to advocate a 'transition to the paradigm of mutual understanding.' There is no privileged understanding for an individual but, as expressed by Thomas McCarthy (Habermas, 1987),

If situated reason is viewed as social interaction, the potential of reason has to be realised in the communicative practice of ordinary, everyday life . . This orientation of communicative action to validity claims admitting of argument and counter argument is precisely what makes possible the learning processes that lead to transformations of our world views . . .the defects of the Enlightenment can only be made good by further enlightenment. (p. xvi-ii)

Habermas holds that we took a wrong turn in the road of enlightenment, asking 'How can I know that something is true?' rather than 'How can members of a community come to an agreement that something is true?' He believes that a revival of the public sphere of democratic decision making requires 'the organisation of social communication in a way approximating to an unconstrained dialogue' (Outhwaite, 1994, p.26), and 'the development of norms which could fulfil the dialectic of moral relationships in an interaction free of domination.' (ibid, p.16)

We need to hold a concept of the ideal speech community in order to form judgements about our society and about education as a feature of society. Rorty believes that this introduces a metaphysical element, but how otherwise do you judge between the views of women held by the Taliban and by feminists? Rorty knows the many shortcomings of American democracy and exhorts academics to critique these using Socratic methods. What else are they critiquing if not the failure of American Liberal Democracy to live up to the ideals of its founders and the Declaration of Independence? Rorty, and American democracy, operates from a strong sense of an ideal speech community.

I also take a different view than Rorty to the role of schooling as distinct from higher education. He believes that schooling should concentrate on inculcating the 'facts' currently taken as the norm by society; while higher education should focus on critique of these 'facts' by a community of academics free from societal restraint. It seems to me that a healthy democracy should prepare for participation *through* participation, and that Rorty's view would lead to an elitism that is fundamentally dangerous to a participative, as distinct from a representational, democracy.

At what age should children be encouraged to take part in a Socratic dialogue in which their views are taken seriously? At three when they have a sophisticated grasp of language use, including equivocation (Swann, 1992). At eight when according to the Catholic Church they have reached the age of reason? At fourteen when they are young adults who have reached puberty and may procreate? At eighteen when in the UK they may vote? Or later still when they are deemed to be 'mature'?

Surely the practice of democratic participation should begin as early as possible? Just as we expect that studies in all subjects will deepen with age and experience, there is no reason that the participative process of education should not begin at the earliest possible age and deepen towards maturity.

Unfortunately, the ideal speech community does not exist in education, not even in Western Liberal Democracies. As Darling-Hammond (1996) pointed out in the United States, and many studies have shown in the UK (Barnes, 1969, Rutter, 1979, Bennett, 1984, Rodenburg, 1992, Keys & Fernandez, 1993) that in many classrooms learners are relatively passive recipients of teaching, even when they are organised in groups. Young (1992) pointed out that in much educational practice students 'are seen as individuals who must simply be made to reproduce the point of view being advanced, by whatever means seem expedient and economical. This is already well on the way to treating students like things.' (p. 36)

The silence of learners is profound. There is something terminally wrong with our education system which may be a portent that, if we are not careful, there is some deeply amiss with our democracy too. Rorty believes that within a hundred years it is unlikely that we will still have liberal democracies. I hope that he is wrong and I believe that the practice of education along democratic processes is one way to keep democracy alive.

It is important to travel hopefully. To endeavour to make classrooms more participative places that model democracy. To acknowledge that there is more that unites people than divides us. The rhetoric of postmodernity does nothing to help these endeavours. It is important to re-vivify the incomplete project of critical modernity.

References

ALBSU (1995) *Parents and their Children: the Intergenerational Effect of Poor Basic Skills*. London: ALBSU.

Aitchison, J. (1996) *The Seeds of Speech*, (Cambridge, Cambridge University Press).

Ball, M. (1998) *School Inclusion: The school, the family and the community*. (York: Joseph Rowntree Foundation).

Barnes, D. (1969) *Language, the Learner and the School*. (Harmondsworth, Penguin).

Baumann, Z. (1998) *Globalization:the Human Consequences*, Cambridge, Polity).

Bennett, N., Desforges, C., Cockburn, A., and Wilkinson, B. (1984) *The Quality of Pupil Learning Experiences*. (London, Lawrence Erlbaum).

Catan, L., Dennison, C., & Coleman, J. (1996) *Getting Through: Effective Communication in the Teenage Years* (London, the BT Forum).

Cohen, R. & Long. S. (1998) Children and Anti-Poverty Strategies, *Children and Society*, 12,2, pp.73-85.

Darling-Hammond, L. (1996) The Right to Learn and the Advancement of Teaching: research, Policy, and Practice for Democratic Education, *Educational Researcher, 25, 6*, pp.5-17.

Dewey, J. (1933) *How We Think*. Boston, Heath.

Giddens, A. (1991a) *The Consequences of Modernity* (Cambridge, Polity).

Giddens, A. (1991b) *Modernity and Self-Identity* (Stanford, Stanford University Press).

Giddens, A. (1994) Living in a Post-Traditional Society in U. BECK, A.GIDDENS, and S. LASH (eds) *Reflexive Modernization* (Cambridge, Polity Press).

Grice, P. (1975) In P. Cole and J. Morgan (eds) *Syntax and Semantics, III: Speech Acts* (New York, Academic Press).

Grubb, N. Comments by Professor Norton Grubb of the University of California, Berkeley, at the 'Future of Training and Vocational Education in the Global Economy' symposium, Hanover, October 1996.

Habermas, J. (1980) Modernity - an incomplete project, speech on receiving the Adorno prize, Frankfurt, September 1980.

Habermas, J. (1986) *Knowledge and Human Interests* (Cambridge, Polity Press).

Habermas, J. (1987) *The Philosophical Discourse of Modernity* (Cambridge, Polity Press).

Harkin, J. (1998a) Constructs Used by Students In England to Evaluate their Teachers', *Journal Of Vocational Education And Training* 50, 3, pp. 339-353.

Harkin, J. (1998b) 'In Defence of the Modernist Project in Education', *British Journal of Educational Studies*, 46, 4, pp. 404-415.

Holtermann, S. (1996) The Impact of Public Expenditure and Fiscal Policy Britain's Children and Young People, *Children and Society*, 10,1, pp. 3-13.

Horton, R. (1990) Tradition and Modernity Revisited. In M. HOLLIS & S. LUKES (eds) *Rationality and Relativism* (Oxford, Blackwell).

Johannessen, T., Gronhaug, K., Risholm, N., & Mikalsen, O. (1997) What is important to Students? Exploring dimensions in their evaluations of teachers, *Scandinavian Journal of Educational research*, Vol. 41, No. 2, pp. 165-177.

Lukes (eds) *Rationality and Relativism* (Oxford, Blackwell).

Kelly, G.A. (1955) *The Psychology of Personal Constructs* (Norton).

Keys, W. and Fernandez, C. (1993) *What Do Children Think About School?* (Slough, NFER).

Lemert, C. (1997) *Postmodernism is Not What You Think* (Oxford, Blackwell).

Lukes, S. (1990) Relativism in its Place. In M. HOLLIS & S. LUKES (eds) *Rationality and Relativism* (Oxford, Blackwell).

Lyotard, J-F. (1984) *The Postmodern Condition: A Report on Knowledge* (Manchester, Manchester University Press).

Rodenburg, P. (1992) *The Right to Speak* (London, Methuen).

Rorty, R. (1999) *Philosophy and Social Hope* (London, Penguin).

Rutter, M., Maughan, B., Mortimore, P., and Ouston, J. (1979) *Fifteen Thousand Hours: Secondary Schools and Their Effect on Children* (London, Open Books).

Sapir, E. (1929) The Status of Linguistics as a Science, *Language*. 5. 209.

Swann, J. (1992) *Girls, Boys and Language*. Oxford: Blackwell.

Usher, R. & Edwards, R. (1994) *Postmodernism and Education* (London, Routledge).

Young, R. (1992) *Critical Theory and Classroom Talk* (Clevedon, Multilingual Matters).

Young, R. (1995) Liberalism, Postmodernism, Critical Theory and Politics. In Post-compulsory Education, *The Journal of Further and Higher Education*, 20,1, pp. 25-35.

Lifelong Learning Strategy Calls for Equity in Education

Reijo Laukkanen

The world economies face challenges of globalisation, population ageing, new demands in working life and increased marginalization of people from the main stream society. The OECD has analysed those issues from the view of different policy sectors. In education policy OECD has consistently advised the governments that broadening access to education and improving the quality of learning is a paramount must. This is evident in the conclusions of the OECD education ministers' meetings held in 1978, 1984, 1990 and 1996. Current OECD arguments in favour of realizing lifelong learning for all reflect a commitment to values of equity and equality. However, behind these humanistic values are cold numbers of economy, too. Preserving today's material and social well-being necessitates increased participation of people as productive members of their societies. Education is the most important instrument for diminishing exclusion and involving all to the societies; it is a vital policy for ensuring social inclusion. Keywords: education policy, equity, lifelong learning, inclusion

Governments are increasingly facing the challenge of change. Over the past two decades it has become more and more difficult to predict what knowledge could be capitalized in the future. Therefore, the governments are compelled to adopt a twin strategy to complement their efforts to look into the future, with strategies to adapt more flexibly to the changing circumstances when needed.

As knowledge has become a driving force of economies, human capital has become a key to wealth in modern societies. But for many reasons societies are short of this welcome form of capital, knowledge. This makes education more important than ever, from the view of not only education policy makers, but also those responsible of economic, social and employment policies.

This article, using communiques of OECD education ministerial meetings held in 1978, 1984, 1990 and 1996, analyses the changing context of modern societies and seeks to identify the values directing approaches to education. They are seen to reflect the common values and concerns of OECD member countries in education policy.

What have the ministers wanted to gain?

Education policy reflects the values of a society at a given moment and its strategies for adapting to change. This is to say, the history of education reflects the history of societies at large: past experiences, expectations and ideals, pragmatic responses to current needs and the resources available. The statements of OECD ministers mirror this history.

Ministerial meetings are important for directing the work program of OECD. As these discussions have led to sharing of policy goals, they have directly affected national policy making, too. The Ministerial Communiqués reveal, over the years, continuity and progression in policy goals.

Education for all

The first meeting of the education ministers in the OECD was held in 1978. The ministers discussed four major themes: (i) enchancing the quality of education, (ii) the pursuit of equality of educational opportunity, (iii) combatting the marginalization of young people, (iv) the development of democratic and efficient management of educational system (Papadopoulos 1994, pp. 144–145).

According to Papadopoulos this ministerial was the political manifestation of the OECD's concern with addressing the social consequences of economic recession (Op. cit., p. 145). The meeting also provided a forum for debating the implications of developments internal to education. The drop in the birthrate had led to a steady decrease in enrolments. At the same time democraphic changes were leading to the ageing of the population. Although that marked an opportune moment to reallocate resources in education, there were thus pressures to cut more from the education sector.

Equal opportunities

The 1984 meeting of education ministers discussed three issues: (i) the role of education in the social, cultural and technological changes necessary for long term economic growth, (ii) the quality of basic education essential to cultural and economic progress, and (iii) the need for a wide range of education and training opportunities to help people into working life and adults to adapt to structural change (OECD 1984).

Ministers stressed the cultural and economic roles of education and its importance as a prerequisite for an equitable and just distribution of opportunities. They underlined the importance of the goal of educating each child to the limits of his or her ability. Rapid economic change and the spread of new technologies called for reexamination of the role of education in preparing youth for working life. Ministers said that education should be organized so that it allows citizens periodic access to learning throughout their lives. Students should be helped to develop self-reliance and the capacity to learn.

Quality of education

In their 1990 meeting, ministers discussed the main challenges of the 1990s, their priorities in the light of these, and the strategies and options available to meet them (OECD 1990). They expressed their understanding that the 'human factor' is fundamental to economic activity, competitiveness and prosperity. Many countries reported shortages of labor and relevant skills, but also unemployment was high. Disparities in educational attainment levels and continuing poverty exacerbated the danger of socioeconomic polarization. Increasing movement of labor and migration shaping international skills market called for adequate education to integrate migrants in the new cultures. Learning of values was seen important because of changes in family, community, and social structures. The ability to learn and relearn were seen as most important.

Ministers focused on policies to improve the quality, structure and flexibility of education and training, emphasizing the urgent need to open access, to allow all to achieve their full potential, to overcome failure, and to realize lifelong learning. They identified eleven policy orientations. Among these were the crucial role of initial education and training in support of lifelong learning. The educational system should be open throughout life. Education 'for all' implied that priority be given to reaching the educationally 'under-served'. The continued existence of illiteracy must be ended. Minsters argued for greater coherence and focus to avoid curriculum overload, and improved quality and attractiveness of teaching in education and training systems. Evaluation and assessment were identified as integral components of policy and practice.

Lifelong learning for all

In the 1996 meeting, education ministers discussed on the strategy of 'making lifelong learning a reality for all' (OECD 1996a). They agreed that lifelong learning was essential for everyone as societies moved into the 21st century and that action was needed to make it accessible to all. For the meeting the OECD Secretariat prepared a background report and a ministers' communiqué was published (OECD 1996b). This publication is thus an interesting combination of political statements and analysis of societies.

Ministers agreed to: (i) strengthen the foundations for learning throughout life, (ii) promote coherent links between learning and work, (iii) rethink the roles and responsibilities of all partners who provide opportunities for learning and (iv) create incentives for individuals, employers and those who provide education (Op.cit., 21).

The background report defines lifelong learning, its purposes, and implications. It discusses the following: (i) social and educational changes in member countries, (ii) aims, barriers and strategies of lifelong learning, (iii) establishing the foundations for lifelong learning, (iv) improving pathways and transitions, (v) managing autonomy and choice, (vi) using goals and standards to steering education systems, and (vii) strengthening the resources and financing lifelong learning. It was presented as a concept that broadly coincides with education policy interests in OECD countries.

The policy conclusions of the analysis enable countries to interpret them according their own historical and social contexts. For example, as the background report discusses the foundations of lifelong learning (Op.cit., 121–122), it says that the curriculum of primary education should be revised to concentrate on core skills for further learning. The factual content at primary and lower secondary levels should be reduced in favor of cross-curriculum competencies, social competence and information retrieval and processing skills. In secondary education, there should be continuing emphasis on metacognition and the teaching of core subjects at the upper secondary level. At all levels there is a need for foreign language training. Specific vocational preparation should be postponed, at least until the upper secondary stage. Particular attention should be given to students with special needs. Young people and adults should be permitted to return to regular secondary schools and other institutions of secondary education at a later stage, and to join particular classes. It is stressed that lifelong learning presupposes continuity between initial education and training, and the organized learning experiences that take place thereafter, during working life. The philosophy of the lifelong learning strategy requires reshaping the formal and informal education systems.

The history of the lifelong learning concept backs to the concepts of recurrent education and permanent education that were prevalent 1970s. A detailed description is given by Georges Papadopoulos (1994, pp. 112–115). The former concepts emphasized that school education should be provided on a recurring basis, involving the alternation between work and study, and opportunities for this should be available to all individuals throughout their active life. The main focus was on post-compulsory and adult education. Coordination of various sectors of education – formal and informal, vocational and general – was seen important. In their 1975 meeting, the OECD ministers suggested a twin strategy: Vertical coordination of educational systems by opening bottlenecks and offering people opportunities to exercise their educational rights; and horizontal coordination of education with other policies like manpower and employment policies. This double challenge given then to governments has not been realized yet, but today's lifelong learning philosophy includes similar elements.

What do those statements reflect?

OECD countries have accepted the principle that education policy is an important element of a government's overall policy to increase the standard of living, but that education also is seen a goal unto itself. However, education policies are not totally independent. Governments also use them to solve societal problems and to produce the kind of social benefits they want to achieve. These policies are based on economic, social and cultural values and contexts. Education policies both reflect these and respond to them.

OECD countries are facing major challenges of globalisation, ageing of populations, high unemployment, labour market uncertainties and changes at work. These necessitate new approaches by governments including in the area of education policy. As the education ministers' statements from 1978 to 1996 reveal, policy makers have long seen these trends.

Globalisation is a reality

Globalisation creates both risks and challenges. Goods, investments, information and people cross borders. Problems arising from pollution, economic crises, disruption to energy supply, as well as demographic trends and migration. The world has become a global village. Thus one problem is how to ensure stable development of a society when globalisation might change the context very quickly.

Jacques Delord has said that humanism accepts market economy, but it does not accept market society (Delors 1999, pp. 18–19). He insists on the need for rules for competition, as well as for national social responsibility. Bill Jordan (1999, p. 24) agrees, noting that there is no stable economy without social stability and vice versa. This would suggest that social stability would be of great interest for researchers trying to understand why some economies develop well and others do not. One view is that peoples' trust and their active acceptance of societal values are important elements in stable growth. This concept of 'social capital' (Woolcock 1998) is interesting, because alongside the concept of human capital (OECD 1998a), it offers the potential for further insight into the role of individuals and social structures in growth. The concept has been advanced mostly in research by the World Bank. Recently the OECD has started to examine the relationship between social capital and sustained growth. The concept of social capital reminds us that education has always had a twin objective: to reform and to preserve.

Populations are ageing

The problems posed by ageing populations in OECD countries has prompted the OECD to find new policies to meet this demographic change in positive ways. Production of goods and services, income, and standards of living depend on numbers of people at work and their productivity (OECD 1998b, pp. 10–12). The demographic trend in OECD countries leads to a declining number of people at work. The worst vision is that after the year 2030 material well-being will be halved. A dramatic change will be seen after 2010 when the relative number of people aged 65 or more begins to increase dramatically. In 1960 there were more than four people at work for every one on pension; today the ratio is 3 to one; by 2030 there will be two at work for each one on pension.

This offers big challenges to labor, pension and social policy agendas. The OECD (1998c) has suggested that governments should support active ageing (OECD 1998c). The older part of population could stay longer than today as active working members of society. This would require new incentives for people to choose this option, better arrangements for health care and continuing education. There is a need for increased emphasis in educational research on education needs of older people and adult education in general.

Unemployment is an urgent problem
At the moment unemployment, and the risk of social exclusion connected with it, is the biggest problem facing OECD countries. All OECD governments have ambitious programs to diminish unemployment, but less than one forth of them has actually reduced unemployment in the last ten years (OECD 1999a). Young people are in the worst situation. The unemployment level of people 15–24 years old grew from 11.5 per cent in 1990 to 12.8 per cent in 1998. In the European Union area, this share is now 22 per cent.

Unemployment is expensive for society and puts social stability – an important objective for governments – at risk. More people are needed in the labor force. Governments are therefore seeking active employment policies instead of using passive ones (OECD 1997a). Much hope is set on education: Dropping out of upper secondary education should be stopped. The quality of educational attainments should be improved. Students should get help at the moment symptoms of the risk of exclusion can be detected. Links between vocational and general education should be increased and tightened. Planning of educational goals and programs should be done in cooperation with employers. Links between education ad working life should be broadened, and education evaluations are needed.

Work has become knowledge intensive
The structural change in working life continues. In all OECD countries we have seen the change in the relative weight of the agriculture, industrial production and services industries (OECD 1999b, pp. 16–17). The service sector has grown rapidly and all the OECD (1999c) forecasts tell that new jobs grow just in this sector. Another trend is the rapid pace of change of product development. Due to growing competition, the life cycle of products gets shorter, and companies use increasing resources for research to produce new products.

The input of knowledge in the economies of OECD countries is roughly ten per cent of their GDP. This includes research and development, investment in software and private and public investment in education. (OECD 1999d.)

OECD reports characterize the importance of knowledge by saying that economies have become knowledge-driven or knowledge-based (Drake 1998; Foray &

Lundvall 1996). Knowledge can refer both to institutional and personal factors. Institutions can have longer memories than individuals. Institutions have records and traditions that can be utilized although people working in them change. However, human ability to adapt to the knowledge society is crucial.

Conclusions

In its analyses OECD relates education and training to the broader economic, social and cultural environments in its member countries. This provides OECD governments a better understanding of the needs of societies and the role of education in developing them. The role of education is not seen as subordinated to economic growth, but as an important element of it and as the means to maximize educational benefits for individuals.

All four OECD education ministers' statements address educational equality, stressing the importance of broadening access to education. They call for better quality of educational outcomes. They seek to broaden opportunities for education in support of the concept of lifelong learning. They highlight the need of more effective practices for helping students in transition from school to work. Special attention is given to in avoiding social exclusion.

When an organisation like the OECD, whose main mission is to further economic development, gives particular attention to values like equity, equal opportunities and high quality education for all, it is worth of noticing. Reasons are humanistic and economic. Both are important in the OECD deliberations. The value of economic growth is important, because only growth quarantees sustainable well-being of the societies. However, in the light of the trends today, this cannot be achieved without increased participation of all people of their societies. The OECD societies totally agree to the need to take care of their most vulnerable members. However, there is a great concern as to how to continue sustained development, if the lack of human capital still persists or even increases. Therefore education has become more important than ever. The justifications are pragmatic. The focus is on inclusion.

The educational systems alone cannot solve the problems of societies, but they must have their own strategies on how to contribute in solving them. The OECD (1997b, pp. 105–109) analysis written by David Istance gives a good summary of the policies needed in education. Governments must take responsibility for education of the whole population and guarantee that all education is 'good'. Special investments must be done for those who have been under-achievers. Reasons for under achievement are various, so there is a need to use combinations of policies, also using financial resources of different ministries. Teachers are key persons in innovations needed. Governments should concentrate working through them. Their possibilities to effect innovations should be broadened. The implementation of lifelong learning strategy demands for coherent policies coordinating efforts of different actors. Therefore the government as the whole rather than different ministries separately should take the main responsibility for its planning and implementation.

References

Delors, J. Economic Governance and Globalisation. In *TUAC 1948-1998. Proceedings of the 50th Anniversary Symposium*, pp. 17–21. 1999. Paris: TUAC.
Drake, K. Firms, knowledge and competitiveness. *The OECD Observer*. April/May (211), pp. 24–26. 1998.
Foray, D. & Lundvall, B.-Å. The knowledge-based economy: From the economics of knowledge to the learning economy. In *Employment and growth in the knowledge-based economy*, pp. 11–32. 1996. Paris: OECD.
Jordan, B. Financial stability is not possible without social stability. In *TUAC 1948-1998. Proceedings of the 50th Anniversary Symposium*, pp. 23–26. 1999. Paris: TUAC.
OECD. Meeting of the OECD Education Committee at ministerial level. Communique. PRESS/A(84)64. 1984. Paris.
OECD. Communique. Meeting of the Education Committee at ministerial level. High quality education and training for all. SG/PRESS(90)69. 1990. Paris.
OECD. Meeting of the Education Committee at ministerial level. Making lifelong learning a reality for all. SG/COM/NEWS(96)7. 1996a. Paris.
OECD. *Lifelong learning for all*. 1996b. Paris: OECD.
OECD. Meeting of the Employment, Labour and Social Affairs Committee at ministerial level. Communique. 15 October 1997a. Paris.
OECD. *Education and equity in OECD countries*. 1997b. Paris: OECD.
OECD. *Human capital investment*. 1998a. Paris: OECD.
OECD. *Maintaining prosperity in an ageing society*. 1998b. Paris: OECD.
OECD. Meeting of the Employment, Labour and Social Affairs Committee at ministerial level on social policy. SG/COM/NEWS(98)70. 1998c. Paris.
OECD. *OECD Employment outlook: June 1999*. 1999a. Paris: OECD.
OECD. OECD in figures – 1999 edition. Suplement to the *OECD Observer*, No. 217/218, July. 1999b. Paris.
OECD. *Implementing the Jobs Strategy: Assessing performance and policy*. 1999c. Paris: OECD.
OECD. The knowledge-based economy: A set of facts and figures. Meeting of the Committee for Scientific and Technological Policy at ministerial level 22–23 June 1999. 1999d. Paris: OECD.
Papadopoulos, G. S. *Education 1960–1990. The OECD perspective*. 1994. Paris: OECD.
Woolcock, M. Social capital and economic development: Towards a theoretical synthesis and policy framework. *Theory and society* 27, pp. 151–208. 1998.

Ethical Dilemmas in Mixed Ability Grouping

Zdenko Kodelja

The question of whether or not to group students according to academic ability represents one of the most difficult problems facing educators today. Some research provides evidence against ability grouping, while some point in the opposite direction. If it is true that ability grouping is harmful to many students, and, if at the same time, it has positive effects on gifted students, then an ethical dilemma occurs. The presence or absence of ability grouping would always be harmful to someone, for the majority of students, if it is present, and for the minority of gifted students, if it were absent. In such circumstances it seems acceptable and defensible to choose the lesser of two evils and act in accordance with the utilitarian principle, which obligates us to act against ability grouping because it can be reasonably expected to produce the least harm. But, what is a good solution from the point of utilitarian ethics is not acceptable from the point of deontological ethics. It is known that Kant's later formulation of the categorical imperative says that we must always treat persons as ends in themselves, and never merely as a means to the ends of others.

The question of whether or not to group students according to academic ability represents one of the most difficult problems facing educators today. Many researchers in different countries have tried for decades to find answers to the following questions about ability grouping: 'Does anyone benefit from it? Who benefits most? Does grouping harm anyone? How? How much? Why?' (Kulik, 1992) Unfortunately, the meta-analyses and the reviews of research literature about ability grouping show that outcomes of research are ambiguous and often contradictory. Some research results provide evidence against ability grouping, some point in the opposite direction 'and many show that there is little difference that can be ascribed *only* to the type of grouping.'(Harlen, 1997) However, despite the lack of conclusive evidence for or against ability grouping, it is possible to identify a considerable agreement between opponents and proponents of ability grouping concerning some findings about particular forms of ability grouping. Of course, agreement on findings is not necessarily the same thing as agreement about positive or negative effects of ability grouping. Therefore, such disagreement about ability grouping can remain, even though an agreement about findings was reached. In this paper, I am going to take into consideration just such a case.

There is quite wide agreement, based on the findings of meta-analyses and reviews of research, that ability grouping, which is often called tracking or streaming, has both negative and positive effects.[1] On the one hand, the findings show that such forms of ability grouping, where students are allocated to homogenous separate classes for much of the school day, and tend to remain in the same stream or track throughout their school years, are academically ineffective, harmful to many students, and damaging to democratic society.[2]

On the other hand, the findings clearly demonstrate that such forms of ability grouping with appropriately differentiated programs and instruction, compared with mixed ability grouping,[3] have significant positive effects on the achievement of highly talented and gifted students. The findings from studies suggest that talented and gifted students benefit from learning together, and need to spend the majority of their school day with others of similar abilities (Rogers, 1991; Feldhusen, 1989 and Kulik, 1992). They profit greatly from work in accelerated programs and their academic achievement is significantly better than their achievement in heterogeneous classes (Kulik and Kulik, 1989).

If it is true that ability grouping is harmful to many students, and, if at the same time, it has positive effects on talented and gifted students, then an ethical dilemma occurs.[4] In this context, I am using the term 'dilemma' both in its practical and logical sense. I mean, as a synonym for a practical moral 'problem', and as a designator of the specific form of argument,[5] in which this practical moral problem can be recognised as a real ethical dilemma. Usually we say that we are faced with a dilemma whenever we have to choose between mutually exclusive alternatives. But, according to some interpretations, not every dilemma is already an ethical dilemma. In the more strict sense, ethical dilemma means, 'to have to choose between *equally* morally unacceptable alternatives', therefore, 'between evils' and not 'between goods' (Hursthouse, 1995). If so, then a practical problem whether to group students according to academic ability or not, can be understood as an ethical dilemma, irrespective of the fact that both, ability and mixed ability grouping, are understood as something good, on condition that each is discussed separately. Why is this possible? Why would choosing between goods be an ethical dilemma in its more strict sense? The answer to these questions could be this: because we have to choose between ability and mixed ability grouping, even if we know that whichever we choose, we choose something bad. Namely, if we choose ability grouping, then the students of low ability will suffer, and on the contrary, if we choose mixed ability grouping, then gifted and talented students will suffer. Therefore, the presence or absence of ability grouping would always be harmful to someone, for the majority of students, if it is present, and for the minority of gifted and talented students, if it were absent.

In such circumstances, it seems morally acceptable and defensible to choose the lesser of two evils, therefore, mixed ability grouping. From the utilitarian point of view, such a decision would be a morally right decision because it is in accordance with the utilitarian principle which says: 'An act is right if, and only if, it can be reasonably expected to produce the greatest balance of good or the least balance of harm.'(Beauchamp, 1991). For several types of utilitarianism as a consequentialist ethical theory, the rightness or wrongness of action and practice depends only on their good or evil consequences. 'What makes an action morally right or wrong is the total good or evil it produces.'(Beauchamp, 1990).

But, what is a good resolution to the mentioned ethical dilemma from the viewpoint of utilitarian ethics is not acceptable from the viewpoint of deontological ethics, which asserts that the rightness or wrongness of action should not be judged by its results or consequences. For deontological ethics, some acts are right or wrong in themselves. They must be done regardless of their consequences.[6] So, they are not right or wrong because of their consequences, but because they are required or forbidden by particular moral principles. One such principle is Kant's categorical imperative.

It is known that Kant's second formulation of the categorical imperative in *The Foundations of the Metaphysics of Morals* says that we must always treat persons as ends in themselves, and never only as a means to the ends of others.[7] Therefore, in this context the argument against ability grouping, which is based on supposition that grouping gifted and talented students in separate classes is in itself harmful to other students, because they need gifted and talented students in the classroom to act as role models, is morally unacceptable.[8] Namely considering Kant's second form of the categorical imperative, the minority of gifted students should not be treated *only* as a mean to the ends of other students. This does not mean that we should never treat gifted students as a means to achieve particular educational aims. They can serve, for example, as a positive role model to other students, but only if they are at the same time treated as ends in themselves, as persons with their own ends, educational needs, and interests. But, according to some research results, they cannot be treated in this way if they are in mixed ability classes during the majority of the school day.[9]

If it is also true, that the forms of ability grouping within the mixed ability class (for example, cluster grouping) cannot replace the separate ability classes with accelerated and enriched programs for gifted and talented students,(Winebrenner and Devlin, 1996) then another ethical dilemma occurs. We have to choose between two alternatives: To treat talented and gifted students for the majority of their time spent in school only as a mean to the ends of other students or as ends in themselves as well. The first alternative is morally unacceptable from Kant's point of view, the second is morally unacceptable from the utilitarian point of view, if it is true that the previously mentioned thesis, which states that the absence of talented and gifted students from the mixed ability classes is more harmful for the majority of low and average ability students than their presence. Of course, if this thesis is not true, as some empirical research results permit to suppose, then this practical ethical dilemma seems to be resolvable. Namely, the talented and gifted students can be in the separated classes for the majority of their time spent in school without harmful consequences for other students. In such circumstances, I think the separation of the gifted and talented students from the mixed ability classes would be justified in regard to Kant's second formulation of the categorical imperative and the principles of social justice, on condition, that the gifted and talented students 'would *not* receive sameness of treatment if put in an ordinary mixed ability group.'[10]

In this case, the first ethical dilemma, whether to choose mixed or ability grouping, would also be resolvable because we could choose both without harmful consequences for anyone.

References

Allan, S D (1991)"Ability Grouping Research Review: What Do They Say about Grouping and the Gifted", *Educational Leadership*, 48, 6, pp. 63-64

Bailey, C and Bridges, D (1983) *Mixed Ability Grouping: A Philosophical Perspective*, George Allen and Unwin, London, p. 35.

Beauchamp, T L (1991) *Philosophical Ethics*, McGraw-Hill, New York, p.129.

Beauchamp, T L (1991) *Philosophical Ethics*, McGraw-Hill, New York, p. 128

Beauchamp, T L (1990) *Philosophical Ethics*, p.130

Beauchamp, T L (1991) *Philosophical Ethics*, p. 199

Feldhusen, J (1989) "Synthesis of research on gifted youth", *Educational Leadership*, 46, 6, pp. 6-11

Harlen, W (1997) "Making Sense of the Research on Ability Grouping", *Research in Education*, Spring.

Hursthouse, R (1995) "Fallacies and Moral Dilemmas", *Argumentation*, 4, November, pp.618-619.

Kulik, J A (1992) *An Analysis of the Research on Ability Grouping: Historical and Contemporary Perspectives*, Storrs, CT The National Research Center on the Gifted and Talented, University of Connecticut.

Kulik, J A and Kulik, C L (1989) "Effects of Ability Grouping on Student Achievement", *Equity and Excellence*, 23, 1-2, pp. 22-30.

Rogers, K (1991) *The Relationship of Grouping Practices to the Education of the Gifted and Talented Learner*, Storrs, CT: The National Research Center on the Gifted and Talented, University of Connecticut

Sukhnandan, L (1999) *Sorting, sifting and setting*, NFER News, Spring 1999

Slavin, R E and Braddock III, J H (1993) "Ability Grouping: On the Wrong Track", *The College Board Review*, No. 68, Summer, pp. 11-17

Schunk, D H (1987) "Peer models and children's behavioral change", *Review of Educational Research*, 57, pp. 149-174

Smart, J J C "Extreme and Restricted Utilitarianism", in: P. Foot (ed.), *Theories of Ethics*, Oxford University Press, p.171.

Winebrenner, S and Devlin, B (1996) *Cluster Grouping of Gifted Students: How to Provide Full-Time Services on a Part-Time Budget*, ERIC EC Digest #E538 EC304950 August.

Notes

[1] Similar negative effects could have also the use of setting as a system of grouping students by ability (Sukhnandan, 1999). This does not mean that all forms of ability grouping have negative

effects. On the contrary, there is an agreement on findings that some forms of ability grouping, which can be organised within mixed ability classes, are helpful for at least some students. (Slavin and Braddock, 1993). For this reason, these forms of ability grouping are not problematic for either opponents, or proponents of ability grouping.

[2] "Tracking is ineffective. It is harmful to many students and inhibits the development of interracial respect, understanding, and friendship. It undermines democratic values and contributes to a stratified society" (Slavin and Braddock, 1993). "It has also been found that low ability pupils who are placed in sets, compared with low ability pupils who are taught in inmixed ability classes, are less likely to participate in school activities, experience more disciplinary problems and have higher levels of absenteeism."... (Setting also) "reinforces exiting social divisions by segregating pupils in terms of social class, gender, race and age (season of birth). As a result, low ability groups tend to contain a disproportionately large number of pupils from working-class backgrounds, boys, pupils from ethnic minority and summer-born children" (Sukhnandan, 1999).

[3] A good philosophical analysis of the arguments justifying mixed ability grouping is presented in the book written by C. Bailey and D. Bridges (*Mixed Ability Grouping: A Philosophical Perspective*, George Allen and Unwin, London 1983).

[4] "Dilemmas occur whenever good reasons for mutually exclusive alternatives can be cited. These reasons are usually rooted in conflicting principles that seem to obligate a person to perform two mutually exclusive actions in circumstances in which only one can be performed" (Beauchamp, 1991).

[5] Dilemma is in its logical sense "a form of argument, like *modus ponens*, or *reductio ad absurdum*, its form is (basically) p or q, p implies r, q implies r, so r" (R. Hursthouse, "Fallacies and Moral Dilemmas", *Argumentation*, No.4, November 1995, p. 618).

[6] All deontologists do not support Kant's assertion that an action is morally right or wrong regardless of particular consequences. Utilitarian critics stress "deontologists covertly appeal to consequences in order to demonstrate the rightness of action. John Stuart Mill argues that in Kant's theory the categorical imperative demands that an action be morally prohibited if "the *consequences* of (its) universal adoption would be such as no one would choose to incur."" (Beauchamp, 1991).

[7] One of the four examples, which Kant uses to illustrate this form of the categorical imperative, is failing to develop one's abilities. If someone performing an action following the "maxim of neglect of his natural gifts", that action would involve treating a person as a means, and not an end. Therefore, such a maxim could not be a categorical imperative because performing such action leads to a contradiction when trying to will such maxim as a universal law of nature. According to Kant a man cannot possibly will that such a maxim should be a universal law, because he, "as a rational being, necessarily wills that his faculties be developed, since they serve him and have been given him, for all sorts of possible purposes" (I. Kant, *Fundamental Principles of the Metaphysic of Morals*, trans., by T. K. Abbott, p. 44). For this reason the maxim, which can be a categorical imperative, is this: "Work to develop your abilities".

[8] This supposition, which is very often used in support of mixed ability grouping, is very important because, as Allan said, "the thorniest issue concerning grouping and the gifted is whether the gifted are needed in regular classroom to act as role models for other students and whether this "use" of

gifted students is more important than their own educational needs" (Allan, 1991). Her answer to the first question is based on findings from research on modeling (Schunk, 1987), which show that the mentioned supposition is very problematic. Namely, students of low and average ability do not model themselves on gifted students. It seems that gifted students cannot be effective role models for students of low and average ability, because they differ too much in ability from them. The students of low and average ability prefer to "choose" as a role model the successful students with similar abilities. Her answer to the second question is similar to what I would derive from Kant's ethical theory with application to his second formulation of the categorical imperative. She says: "While there is nothing inherently wrong with serving as a positive role model on occasion, it is morally questionable for adults to view any student's primary function as that of role model to others" (ibid.).

[9] Namely, the findings show that gifted and talented students can realise their educational needs and interests only on condition that they spend the majority of school day together (Rogers, 1991), then it is clear that they must do so.

[10] (Bailey and Bridges, 1983) If "deviations from the mixed ability datum are only justified, it must be stressed, when *not* to deviate means that some pupils do not get equal valuing in terms of educational treatment if they remain in mixed ability groups", then such justification can be "achieved by demonstrating that pupils with certain specific characteristics cannot possibly receive equal valuing as purposive agents within the basic mixed ability group" (ibid., pp. 36-37). Such pupils are, for example, the "deaf children" and "children with severe learning difficulties" (ibid., pp. 35-36). It seems that such pupils might be gifted and talented children as well. They also need special programs, differentiated curriculum and teachers with special teaching skills (Winebrenner and Devlin, 1996.) as a condition to get equal valuing in terms of educational treatment, I mean equal opportunities to satisfy their educational needs and realise their aims and purposes as all other students. In addition to similarities between two groups of children with exceptional educational needs, there are also big differences. The pupils in the first group are at the most disadvantaged position in school. In this case, the deviation from mixed ability grouping is not problematic from the point of view of Rawls's theory of social justice, because it improves the long-term expectation of the least favoured. If this end is attained, by the deviation from mixed ability grouping in the case of gifted and talented students, then such deviation seems to be permissible because it would be in accordance with Rawls's difference principal. Considering the polemics, which have begun between Rawls and Nozick about "talents", it is clear that such deviation would be more problematic, if such an end were not attained. But, if it were true that talented students may be used for the benefit of the most disadvantaged students, would this not be in contradiction with Rawls's rejection of utilitarianism on the basis of Kant's second formulation of the categorical imperative? (cf. Ph. Van Parijs, "Rawls face aux libertariens", in: *Individu et justice sociale*, Éditions du Seuil, Paris 1988, pp. 200-201).

Educational Expansion and Labour Market Changes in Spain: Integration and Polarisation

Luis E. Vila

Labour market integration and labour market polarisation have been proposed as possible, and often as opposed, labour market effects of a process of educational expansion. Within a job-competition framework, I develop a structural procedure to simultaneously test for both effects in terms of a) upgrading shifts in the requirements for educated workers; and b) changes in the allocation of educated labour to different occupations. The results obtained for Spain over the last two decades, a period of rapid educational advance of the labour force and profound economic changes, indicate that remarkable integration has taken place though, at the same time, there is evidence of increasing polarisation of the market in terms of job-opportunities.

During the last two decades, Spain has experienced a period of profound transformations affecting the political, the social, and the economic systems. The most noteworthy changes have been the consolidation of democratic institutions, the entrance into the European Union, and the shift to an urban, service-based economy. These changes occurred during a period of remarkable advances both in the size and in the educational attainment of the workforce. The baby-boom in Spain came about ten years later than in other European countries, so the labour force grew rapidly during the 1980's and the 1990's. New entrants were also much better educated than retiring workers as a result of the increase in post-compulsory schooling, and the extension of higher education to more inclusive social groups (González and Dávila, 1998). However, the returns to formal schooling did not show significant decreases despite the expansion in the supply of educated labour (Vila and Mora, 1998), which suggests that the demand for educated labour shifted as well.

In the research debate about the effects of a rapid educational expansion on the match between education and employment, two main approaches are found (Teichler and Kehm 1995): the integration approach, and the polarisation approach. Both of them consider that the educational system must be responsive to the needs of the employment system, providing the supply of qualified workers that would match the demand for qualified labour. However, their predictions about possible changes in the labour market during the period of educational expansion are rather different, though partially compatible. The integration approach predicts that the demand for qualified workers would shift upwards as a result of higher requirements of qualifications by the production system. The idea is that existing jobs become in general more complex, and that new job-opportunities requiring highly qualified workers would appear in developing fields. On the other hand, under the polarisation view the composition of the pool of jobs would evolve towards a more polarised structure, with more jobs and positions requiring highly qualified workers, fewer middle-qualification jobs, a greater proportion of low-skill jobs, and higher unemployment.

The patterns of match between education and employment in the economy emerge from the interaction between labour supply and labour demand. Since both the demand for, and the supply of, qualified labour evolve over time, changes in the match of education and employment would provide evidence to analyse whether and how the labour market reflected the educational changes.

Section two develops a procedure to simultaneously address the integration and the polarisation hypotheses in terms of structural change in the coefficients of a sharing model for the match between education and employment. The results obtained for Spain comparing labour market structures in 1977 and 1997 are reported in section three. Finally, section four summarises the conclusions of the analysis.

A sharing model for the labour market match

According to standard economic theory, the labour market matches labour demand with labour supply through wage competition. Nonetheless, job competition has been proposed as an alternative mechanism to explain the allocation of workers to jobs, especially when wages are rigid and unemployment is persistent (Thurow and Lucas, 1972). Within a job-competition framework, the demand for labour is determined by jobs requiring workers with diverse qualifications in terms of talents, training, and education. The qualification required for a given position depends on job-characteristics such as the complexity of the tasks and the level of responsibility associated to the job. People in the labour force constitute the supply of labour. The educational attainment of potential workers, combined with other factors, shapes the qualifications they bring into the market. Assuming that the labour market allocates workers to jobs by matching the required qualifications, the interaction between labour demand and labour supply may be expressed through a sharing model, since the cross-structure of any pair of economic aggregates can be captured in a model of that class (Fontela and Pulido, 1993).

Let matrix Z_t represent the labour market match, in absolute terms, between jobs of m different types, and workers with n different qualifications, at time t, and let denote by Z^*_t the augmented $((m+1)xn)$ matrix which include an extra row of unemployed workers. From Z_t, a matrix of employment shares by demographic group across occupations, A_t, may be calculated. Matrix A_t represents the relative demand for workers with different qualifications across occupations. Accordingly, a ((m+1)xn) matrix B_t of employment situation (i.e., working in one of m occupations, and being unemployed) across demographic groups may be calculated from Z^*_t. Thus, matrix B_t represents, in relative terms, the allocation of the supply of educated workers to different occupations and to unemployment. It is worth noting that matrices A_t and B_t estimate, respectively, the distribution of workers' characteristics conditional to occupations, and the distribution of employment situation conditional to worker's characteristics[1].

The labour market match may be represented through the following equations:

$$x'_t = y'_t A_t + u'_t \qquad (1)$$

$$y^*_t = B_t x_t \qquad (2)$$

where x'_t is a vector of potential workers by demographic group (1xn), y'_t is a vector of jobs by type of occupation (1xn), u'_t is a vector of unemployed workers by demographic group (1xn), and $y^*_t = [y'_t \mid \sum_i (u_i)_t]'$ is a vector of workers by employment situation ((m+1)x1).

The changes in the coefficients of A_t between two time periods may suggest which groups of workers have experienced significant increases (decreases) in demand by the employment system after monitoring for the occupational change. If the proportion of jobs performed by workers of a given group tend to increase (decrease) across occupations over time, the demand for labour with the corresponding level of education has necessarily shifted upwards (downwards), irrespective of changes in the composition of the pool of jobs. Similarly, changes in the coefficients of B_t may suggest to which occupations has been preferentially allocated the supply of educated workers during the period. If the proportion of workers allocated to given occupation tends to increase (decrease) across all levels of education, job-opportunities within the occupation have become more (less) frequent than in the past, irrespective of educational changes.

Changes in the labour market match in Spain between 1977 and 1997

The differences in the match between education and employment for the 1977-1997 period in Spain have been summarised in Table 1, in absolute terms, using data from the Labour Force Survey corresponding to the second quarters of 1977 and 1997.

The aggregate expansion of labour supply has been wide, since the total number of people working or looking for a job has risen by 3,1 million. Moreover, potential workers have on average much better credentials in 1997 than in 1977: the number of college graduates in the labour force has increased by 1,7 million, whereas the number of workers with post-compulsory education has grown by 3,6 million people. Contrarily, the number of workers in the labour force with only primary education or less has declined by 4,5 million[2].

The aggregate demand for labour has also risen between 1977 and 1997, though with lower figures. The total number of jobs in the economy has increased by only 0,9 million and, consequently, there are 2,1 unemployed workers more over the period. At the same time, there has been a structural shift away from the agriculture and the manufacturing sector to the services sector, so the composition of the pool of jobs has changed markedly. The number of operators, fabricators, labourers, and other blue-collar employees has declined by 1,6 million. To the contrary, there are 1,2 million new jobs in clerical and other service occupations, and 1,1 million new positions have appeared in technical occupations[3]. On the other hand, there are nearly 0,3 million new entrepreneurs, and 0,25 million people working in professional specialties, while the number of other self-employed (mainly craftsmen and farmers) has decreased by 0,4 million.

The evolution of the Spanish labour market described above may have had significant effects on the qualifications required to be employed in different types of jobs (Burke and Rumberger, 1987), and on the distribution of job-opportunities among educated workers (Matzner and Wagner, 1990). These effects may be

Table 1
Changes in the match between education and employment. Spain 1977-199
(Thousand workers)

	Iliterate	No Studies	Primary	Lower Sec.	Upper Sec. Academic	Upper Sec. Vocational	Higher Educ. Short Cycle	Higher Educ. Long Cycle	All Levels
Entrepreneurs	-0,7	13,4	-12,0	156,9	45,7	33,5	21,7	14,5	272,9
Professional Specialities	0,0	1,5	13,0	43,9	27,0	22,3	40,1	97,9	245,7
Other self-employed	-88,6	-180,6	-819,7	498,8	92,0	60,9	24,9	12,6	-399,7
Managerial in public sector	0,0	0,3	0,3	0,5	7,1	1,8	8,7	14,4	33,1
Managerial in private sector	-0,3	-3,1	-12,6	14,2	17,2	11,0	14,0	31,4	71,9
Technical in public sector	0,0	0,0	-1,3	5,9	-30,2	22,9	269,0	265,7	532,1
Technical in private sector*	0,0	3,1	24,1	103,8	80,1	82,3	140,5	192,2	626,1
Civil servant middle-level	0,0	-1,3	-34,6	-22,4	-27,9	-0,4	-12,3	-3,1	-102,0
Clerical in public sector	-0,6	-1,4	-66,0	65,2	99,7	35,7	60,4	55,5	248,6
Clerical in private sector	-2,7	-12,3	-435,1	218,3	135,4	209,3	100,4	75,2	288,5
Other service occupations	-53,8	-30,6	-143,7	660,2	135,0	98,6	35,5	16,6	717,7
Foremen	-0,1	1,8	-21,1	30,6	10,0	14,5	3,6	2,5	41,7
Operators and fabricators	-48,9	-249,7	-1704,0	899,9	87,5	126,7	10,0	5,9	-872,7
Labourers	-139,5	-230,3	-390,8	339,7	32,1	36,8	4,9	1,7	-345,4
Other occupations	-19,7	-37,0	-362,9	-0,8	-2,1	4,9	1,4	5,0	-411,1
Employed	-355,1	-726,4	-3966,3	3014,	708,7	760,8	722,9	788,0	947,2
Unemployed	2,4	120,0	473,7	980,0	212,6	160,6	109,2	103,4	2161,
Labour force	-352,7	-606,4	-3492,6	3994,	921,3	921,4	832,1	891,3	3109,

* Including related support occupations
Source: Own calculations. Data from Labour Force Survey (INE, 1977 and 1997)

addressed empirically in terms of structural stability of the coefficients defined in the previous section: coefficients of relative demand for diverse types of workers, A $_p$, and coefficients of workers' allocation to diverse occupations, and to unemployment, B $_r$.

Table 2 shows the results of Osblom's test for structural change over the differences in the employment coefficients by demographic groups across occupations[4]. As a rule, the relative demand for workers with lower levels of education declined, the reduction being more significant for workers with only primary education. Consistently, positive changes are found for all educational levels above primary. However, the significance of changes depended crucially on the level of education completed, and on the age-gender group.

Table 2.
Changes in the coefficients of relative demand by educational level and demographic group, 1977 - 1997.
Ostblom's statistics (p-values in italics).

	Women				Men			
	16-29 yr.		30-64 yr.		16-29 yr.		30-64 yr.	
Iliterate	-1,317	*0,209*	-1,860	*0,084*	-1,488	*0,159*	-1,424	*0,176*
No Studies	-1,353	*0,198*	-1,094	*0,293*	-2,295	*0,038*	-1,964	*0,070*
Primary	-2,842	*0,013*	-1,756	*0,101*	-3,681	*0,002*	-4,834	*0,000*
Lower Secondar	1,326	*0,206*	3,700	*0,002*	2,250	*0,041*	1,685	*0,114*
Upper Secondary Academic	-1,283	*0,220*	1,743	*0,103*	-0,239	*0,814*	1,261	*0,228*
Upper Secondary Vocational	1,920	*0,076*	3,114	*0,008*	2,938	*0,011*	4,147	*0,001*
Higher Education Short Cycle	0,124	*0,903*	2,517	*0,025*	-1,078	*0,299*	1,842	*0,087*
Higher Education Long Cycle	2,307	*0,037*	2,509	*0,025*	-0,488	*0,633*	0,903	*0,382*

Source: Own calculations. Data from Labour Force Survey (INE, 1977 and 1997)

During the 1977-1997 period, the requirement for workers with lower secondary education has increased, the variations being more significant for men aged 16-29, and for women aged 30-64. So, labour market demand for those with lower secondary education has improved for young male workers, and adult female workers. The outcome reflects two facts. First, young women are more likely to take post-compulsory education than young men because their chances of employment are worse (Mora,1996). Second, increasing numbers of adult women, many of them with compulsory education only, joined the labour market for the first time during the period (Martínez et al. 1995). The requirement for workers with vocational secondary education has grown significantly in all age-gender groups. The need for relatively more workers with a vocational degree has had two main sources. First, new positions requiring such graduates have appeared in administrative and support occupations, including clerical and sales jobs, as a consequence of the expansion of the service industry. Second, many manufacturing jobs require vocationally trained workers because of the increasing complexity of the products and production processes. Contrarily, the demand for workers with comprehensive secondary education shows much lower variations.

The requirement for workers with a college degree has also grown during the 1977-1997 period in Spain, reflecting the increasing importance of higher education as a tool in getting a job. The expansion of the labour market demand for higher education graduates has been based on two main factors. First, the rapid growth of the service sector, which has generated more positions in executive, managerial and technical occupations. Second, the expansion of the public sector, including local governments and local administrations, which fostered the recruitment of graduates during the 1980's and early 1990's. However, the significance of changes in the demand for higher education graduates depended crucially on the type of courses completed, and on the age-gender group. The changes in the demand for short cycle graduates have been more significant for adult workers than for younger workers. Regarding long cycle graduates, changes in the coefficients of demand have been noticeably greater for women than for men and, as a consequence, women's participation both in higher education and in employment increased during the period.

In brief, structural change in relative demand for educated labour shows that the market provides much better chances of employment for educated workers in 1997 compared to 1977. In particular, the relative demand for higher education graduates and for workers with a vocational degree has clearly improved after monitoring for the effect of the changes in the composition of the pool of jobs. Accordingly, chances of employment have worsened for those with poor educational attainment. The outcome also suggests that labour market integration has been more significant for educated women than for educated men. Additionally, the integration has been less significant for younger workers than for older workers, reflecting that the transition from education to employment is more difficult in the late 1990's than twenty years before.

Nonetheless, conditions and standards of living for new entrants to the market depend crucially on the distribution of new job-opportunities among educational and demographic groups. Consequently, changes in the coefficients of allocation express the opportunities offered to those entering the labour market in 1997 compared to those who entered in 1977. The results of testing for structural change over the changes in the allocation coefficients to diverse occupations across demographic groups are shown in Table 3.

EDUCATIONAL RESEARCH IN EUROPE

Table 3.

Changes in allocation coefficients to occupations, 1977-1997.
Ostblom's statistics (p-values in italics).

	t-statistic	P-value
Entrepreneurs	2,018	*0,063*
Professional Specialities	0,137	*0,893*
Other self-employed	0,595	*0,561*
Managerial in public secto	2,539	*0,024*
Managerial in private sector	-1,13	*0,276*
Technical in public secto	-3,44	*0,004*
Technical in private sector*	-1,57	*0,138*
Civil servant middle-level	-3,62	*0,003*
Clerical in public sector	0,680	*0,508*
Clerical in private sector	0,556	*0,587*
Other service occupations	2,724	*0,016*
Foremen	0,645	*0,529*
Operators and fabricators	-1,01	*0,328*
Labourers	2,986	*0,010*
Other occupations	-4,18	*0,001*

* Including related support occupations
Source: Own calculations. Data from Labour Force Survey (INE, 1977 and 1997

The coefficients increased significantly[5] for managerial occupations in the public sector, on the one hand, and for labourers, and the group of other service occupations, on the other. It is clear that, in relative terms, new job-opportunities have appeared only in occupations that are associated either to high-status positions or to low-level jobs. In contrast, results show significant declines in job-opportunities for three occupational categories which include large proportions of both high-level and middle-level jobs: technical positions, both in the private and in the public sectors, middle-level civil servant positions, and the group of other occupations.

. Thus, the pattern of structural change in the allocation of workers to jobs over the period of educational expansion indicates a remarkable polarisation of the labour market in terms of job-opportunities. The allocation of workers to middle-qualification jobs has declined in relative terms, whereas relatively more workers have been allocated either to high-qualification positions or to low-skill jobs. This suggests that job-opportunities tended to concentrate on both ends of the job-ladder, and that substantial bumping, as defined in Fields (1974), may have occurred during the period since new entrants to the labour force were much better educated than retiring workers. However, the employment of better educated workers in occupations previously performed by workers with lower educational attainment does not necessarily imply underemployment of educated workers, because the complexity of tasks and the level of responsibility associated with jobs of a given type would have shifted upwards over time, as it is suggested by the tests over the coefficients of relative demand.

Concluding Remarks

Between 1977 and 1997, a period of profound changes in the economic structure and in the educational attainment of the workforce, the labour market in Spain has experienced some structural change. By analysing the differences in the match between education and employment, the evidence indicates: a) increased participation of women, both in the labour force and in employment; b) increased demand for workers with vocational education; c) increased demand for women with higher education across occupations, but not for male workers in the same conditions; d) lower proportion of middle-level job-opportunities, e) selective new high-level positions; f) more job-opportunities at the bottom of the job ladder, and g) higher unemployment affecting especially youth, women and less educated people.

The outcomes indicate that the educational expansion and the changes in the economic structure have had two major effects on the labour market structure over the last two decades. First, the labour market integration of increasing numbers of better educated people has been intense. The employment system has been able to absorb large numbers of educated workers, specially women. The demand for workers with a college degree and for those with vocational education clearly expanded. At the same time, labour market integration of young workers has been slower than the integration of adult workers, providing evidence for longer periods of job-search than in the past. Accordingly, there is evidence of a general upgrading shift on the labour-market needs of qualifications, though only workers with very specific personal characteristics and/or curricula have become relatively more demanded by the production system. Although employment of better educated workers has grown in absolute terms, the increase in the demand has been lower than the expansion of the supply, resulting in increasing unemployment rates. Second, the labour market shows a more polarised distribution of jobs, with more low-skill jobs, creation of new high-level jobs, and with fewer middle-qualification positions remaining. Since cohorts entering the labour market were more numerous and better educated than retiring cohorts, employment chances for young people are in general worse than twenty years ago. Nonetheless, labour-market conditions are much better for educated workers than for workers with low educational attainment, because only the former have a real chance of getting high-status jobs.

Summarizing, the changes in the match between education and employment during the 1977-1997 period evidence that the educational expansion in Spain has reduced the gender gap both in labour force and employment participation, and higher education has proven to be the best investment for young people, and women, in obtaining status equity through better jobs and positions. The influence of the public sector as an equal opportunity employer has been a major factor in the labour market integration of the expansion of qualifications, since it has been the main employer of higher education graduates over the last two decades. Nonetheless, the current polarisation of job-opportunities, along with higher unemployment, indicates an increasing risk of general polarisation of society in terms of earnings and living conditions. The current situation will influence the educational choices of younger cohorts and induce new changes in the conditions required to become employed, as well as changes in the expectations of income and social status, in the future.

References

Burke, G. and Rumberger, R.W. (Eds.) (1987) *The Future Impact of Technology on Work and Education*. (London, Falmer Press).

Fields, G.S. (1974) The Private Demand for Education in Relation to Labour Market Conditions in Less-Developed Countries. *The Economic Journal*, 84,336, pp. 906-925.

Fontela, E. and Pulido, A. (1993) *Análisis Input-Output. Modelos, Datos y Aplicaciones*. (Madrid, Pirámide)

González, B. and Dávila, D. (1998) Economic and Cultural Impediments to University Education in Spain. *Economics of Education Review*, 17,1, pp. 903-103.

Martínez, R., Mora, J-G, and Vila, L.E. (1995) Los Rendimientos Internos de los Estudios Postobligatorios. *Estudios de Economía Aplicada*, 1, pp 475-483. (Granada, University of Granada Press).

Matzner, E. and Wagner, M. (eds.) (1990) *The Employment Impact of New Technology: The Case of West Germany*. (Aldershot, Avebury).

Mora, J.G. (1996) The Demand for Higher Education in Spain. *European Journal of Education*, 31, 3, pp. 341-354

Ostblom, G. (1989) Change in Technical Structure of the Swedish Economy. *Paper at the Ninth International Conference on Input-Output Techniques*. (Keszthely).

Teichler, U. and Kehm, B. M. (1995) Towards a New Understanding of the Relationships between Higher Education and Employment. *European Journal of Education*, 30, 2, pp. 115-131.

Thurow, L. C. and Lucas, R.E.B. (1972) *The American Distribution of Income: A Structural Problem*. (Washington, DC., U.S. Congress Joint Economic Committee).

Vila, L.E. and Mora, J.G. (1998) Changing Returns to Education in Spain during the 1980's. *Economics of Education Review*, 17, 2, pp. 173-178.

Notes

[1] Elements in matrix A_t are calculated as ratios of the elements of Z_t to the sum of the corresponding row, so they add up to one by the row. Accordingly, the elements of B_t are the ratios of the elements of Z^*_t to the sum of the corresponding column, so they add up to one by the column.

Part 5
Pupils' Perspectives

'They can be Fawning if They Please, I won't Interfere': Transitions in School Life as Critical Incidents for Young People

Anders Garpelin

What do we know about transitions in school life as critical incidents for young people? This question is focussed in the research project 'Young People Meet the Lower Secondary School', a longitudinal comparative case study of two school classes in Sweden, carried out with an interpretive approach and a relational interpretation perspective. In this paper some preliminary findings are presented, where the transition to the lower secondary school functions as an example of the phenomena. The purpose of this paper is to try to deepen our understanding of the phenomenon, transitions in school life as critical incidents for young people. The analyses are mainly based on a data material (62 students, age-group 12-13), collected with qualitative research interviews, influenced by the life-history tradition. When young people with their different background, meet in the lower secondary school, to continue their individual school careers and as a collective forming a school class, there are differences concerning what happens in the two school classes as well as the role and importance of the transition for young people as individuals. The purpose of this paper is *to try to deepen our understanding of transitions in school life as critical incidents for young people*. The first focus in the following analyses will be on transitions as critical incidents, when young people with their different backgrounds meet at the next stage of their individual school careers and as a collective forming a school class. The second focus is on individual experiences of the transition to the lower secondary school as a critical incident from a life perspective.

In the transition to the lower secondary school, young people are at the beginning of a 3-year period of coexistence. During this period they will experience both the process by which a school class is formed and the development of new and old relationships and school perspectives. Swedish school authorities often use the transition as an opportunity to intervene in young people's lives. This may be interpreted as if the people working in secondary schools lack confidence in primary school teachers´ ability to handle 'trouble makers' and 'destructive relations' among their students, although most commonly other reasons are officially presented for these kinds of interventions.

In this study, both secondary schools have a policy of, not allowing students from the same former school classes to continue together in their transition to the new school. Their strategy is to make the primary schools take responsibility for allocating students to the new school classes themselves. The young people in this study have different experiences from school as well as from other parts of life, differences obvious both between the individuals and between the groups from the various primary schools. Hence this period is critical for the relationship between what is happening in the classroom and what is happening in other areas of their lives.

Parallel with the ambition to create conditions by which all students have equal opportunity, one must in addition take into account students' individual differences. This comprises, on the one hand their intellectual and physical developmental level, and, on the other hand, their cultural, emotional and socioeconomic environment, so that they enter the new school with different requirements.

Research about students' careers in school and other parts of life (Lindblad, 1993) indicates that education given by the teachers doesn't take into account the differences between the social groups that the children come from. In spite of this, the outcome is a stratification, by virtue of the fact that children with different requirements are exposed to education. There is an expectation in school that young people manage to understand the codes their teachers embody (Brice Heath, 1982; Calleweart & Nilsson, 1980).

Some researchers from the US (Talbert, McLaughlin and Rowan, 1993) bring to the fore, the question that research in education seldom focuses on the link between processes in the classroom and factors in the local environment inside or outside the school. In a study related to this problem some researchers (Phelan, Davidson & Cao, 1991) describe how different groups of students experience more or less drastic transitions between the different worlds they encounter every day. Some enjoy a reasonably smooth transition between the worlds of their home, their school and their leisure time. For them, there is more of similarity between the codes of these worlds, while for others, there are huge gaps.

For many young people, the transition to the lower secondary school seems to take place at a critical time. Therefore, to study young peoples' meaning perspectives of this phenomenon – transitions in school life as critical incidents – can be a successful way to form a deeper understanding of young peoples' lives as students from a life perspective.

The case study

'Young People Meet the Lower Secondary School' (Garpelin, 1999) is partly based on data material collected within a former research project (Lindblad, 1992; see also Garpelin, 1997; Garpelin & Lindblad, 1994; Garpelin, Lindblad & Sahlström, 1994). The interpretive approach and the relational interpretation perspective, initially presented in the author's thesis (Garpelin, 1997), are developed further in the case study referred to here (Garpelin, 1999). The interpretive approach (cf Erickson, 1986; Mehan, 1992; Karlsson, 1993) has been chosen in order to penetrate and understand young peoples' meaning perspectives on their life as students, not limiting the analysis to what is explicitly but also to what is implicitly expressed. Applying the interpretive approach means that interpretations are made from a consciously chosen perspective. The relational perspective used here emanates from the work of some internationally and/or nationally well-known researchers (Asplund, 1987; Goffman 1959, 1961, 1963, 1967; Jonsson, 1967; Laing, 1971; Mead, 1934; Schutz, 1967).

The data collected in the above-mentioned ethnographic case study (Lindblad, 1992), and the published (i.e. Garpelin, 1997) and unpublished analyses made so far, serves as a presupposition in analysis made in this paper. However, the main source for the analysis made here are interviews with students during their first term in the lower secondary school (62 students, age group 12-13). The interview guide for the interviewees was tested out in a pilot study (Garpelin & Lindblad, 1993). The students were asked to give a picture of important persons and events along a 'main road' prior to the interviews, and then this road was used as a point of departure during the interview. The interview approach was influenced by the life-history tradition (Berteaux, 1981; Bron-Wojciechowska, 1992; Elgqvist-Salzman et al., 1986; Thomas & Znaniecki, 1918). The students, parents and teachers involved were informed and were positive about participating (Garpelin, 1997).

Taking the points of departure in the interviews, a comparative analysis is presented that examines how the young people in these school classes experience the transition from their former rather small primary schools to the bigger secondary school. It concerns the process by which a school class is formed and the development of new and old relationships and school perspectives. The students own accounts with the primary school in 'the rear-view mirror' constitute the basis for the analysis.

We deal with two school classes, one at Saga school and the other at Field school, two lower secondary schools situated in the suburbs of a large Swedish town. The school districts are both characterised, on the one hand, by an area with modern blocks of flats, detached houses and some houses, and on the other hand, a short distance away, by a village with surrounding countryside and scattered houses. In spite of these similarities, the two school classes quickly revealed themselves to be quite different; one was regarded as a class full of crammers and the other as one with a more disorderly atmosphere.

Saga vs. Field

The principle question of this paper is: What do we know about transitions in school life as critical incidents for young people? They are expected both to continue their individual school careers and, as a collective, participate in the formation of a school class. In this part, the focus will be on what happens when young people with their different backgrounds meet in one of the lower secondary schools, Saga. A comparison will be made with Field class regarding some of the aspects analysed.

Ending up in a school class full of crammers or...
The students in the new school class 7C came from four primary schools in the Saga school district: Alma (5 students), Berta (8 students), Cilla (6 students) and Stoneridge (12 students). You can compare the groups of students from the primary schools with different teams, acting on the classroom stage and elsewhere as team members. From the former schools they bring notions about their position as students inside and outside the classroom, influenced by classmates as well as teachers, by friends in their own team as well as by people outside the institution of school.

The eight girls from Stoneridge were very active when they encountered their new school mates at the Saga Secondary School, whereas the four boys were more passive. The girls came forward, introduced themselves and indirectly made clear the attitudes the other students should adopt in relation to teachers, other classmates and schoolwork, thus forcing the others to choose an attitude.

At Stoneridge they had had a tradition of taking the initiative, taking responsibility for their work and having their ways on matters that served their own interests. Then the students had objected to the plans of the authorities to make them go to Saga School one year earlier, the last year of primary school. Just as they succeeded then, the students now had their way when it came to class formation, contrary to the plans of the authorities. All the team members that wanted to continue together were placed in the same school class. The whole class had embraced this spirit, which was founded on the teacher's authority and the prevailing class hierarchy, all playing their parts. Students with minor parts supported those with major parts in this play. Every member was accepted and Madeleine who arrived as a new girl in the 6th form told us:

> It was smashing there, the best school I ever went to /.../ One big family. Super! We all knew one another /.../ Everyone is much happier there /.../ When I first got there. My God! What a small school! /.../ Everyone stood up and said good morning. /.../ Everyone was so kind, and we worked more freely, some lessons were not really planned in detail, you could choose. /.../ I made a lot of new friends, and I didn't miss my old school, not one bit, really. /.../ I didn't have so many friends there..

How were these students accepted when they displayed their attitudes in the new class at Saga? The students from the other schools agreed they were much more alike, but nevertheless they let the Stoneridge-students take the initiative, and Leo told us how they succeeded in implanting their set of attitudes in the class:

> Those from Stoneridge are always answering and putting up their hands, and of course it's good for them, really. Those from Stoneridge outnumber us, yes, half of the class are from Stoneridge /.../ so they have taken a lot, introduced routines they have to the teachers.

How was this possible? Most of the Alma students were on the whole positive to the attitudes the Stoneridge students stood for, and the two girls from Alma were rapidly assimilated into the team. The eight boys from Berta comprised one team when it came to leisure and break situations, but they were divided and had little in common with regard to their attitudes concerning classroom proceedings. Those boys from Berta, who were mainly concerned with achieving good results and preferred a peaceful and quiet study environment, had their way without having to take any initiatives, wheras the Stoneridge girls had been extremly active in doing just that.

The students from Cilla Primary School and some of the boys from Berta could not adjust that easily, as they had been used to a disorderly atmosphere. Helen said:

> I come from a really noisy class, then I landed up in this class, and I had a shock when I first realised I was to be in this class, because here they are studying dead hard. /.../ The average marks are gigantic, and they are not fun to be with either, boring they are. They can talk math during breaks. It´s not normal /.../ I would rather change classes, really, I used to talk a lot during class, I always did, but now we stand out much more, cause everyone is like that, sitting there studying, and the pace is so fast, you have to follow, I wish I could slow down. /.../ Somebody must slam on the brakes.

Most students had accepted the Stoneridge attitudes before any alternatives had turned up. Most students from other schools had been rather pleased with the quiet, pro-study climate, so the students wishing to oppose the teachers' plans had a very difficult time.

Above all, ending up in a class full of crammers like this was quite a shock to the Cilla students, especially as they found themselves at a school which in other respects was rather tough. They did not react to individual crammers' attitudes, but to the fact that the Stoneridge spirit was allowed to saturate the soul of the new class. They felt as if they were playing on foreign ground, humiliated and partly rejected. Even if they previously had not belonged to the disorderly groups, even disliked what was too disturbing in their former primary school class, they had, through their attitudes in this new class, become conscious of being looked upon as the dissenters or 'chatters' of the class.

The Cilla students and some of the boys from Berta showed different ways of reacting to the new situation. Most of them were not directly negative to the teachers´ projects, but said, that it was not necessary to be so enthusiastic, syco-phantic, and ingratiating as the Stoneridge people were, and they chose to stay in the class under protest. Some of these students both refused to accept the rules and to be loyal to the new class in front of their old classmates. They took their attitudes, including norms and values from groups outside the classroom to whom they felt they belonged. Tommy had much to tell us about his feelings when he came to the new class:

> When you get into such a quiet class, you'll be noticed. It's very hard. /.../ I thought I'd freak out, no mates from other schools. /.../ I myself can't follow this class, that's my opinion. /.../ It's so different from the old one, and the first thing they did was creep for the teacher, and me and Steff have been friends for a long time and we're a bit noisy, and then we observed some others and we thought we're not going to cope, it's difficult to follow. /.../ They work so fast and quietly and so on. /.../ In my class, I'm the only one that's told off, the others just work. I don't babble very much, I'm rather quiet too, but I'm the one they hear /.../ Many crammers came to my class /.../ and they talk and talk about – 'How far have you got?' – 'How did your test go?' – and so on /.../ They can be fawning if they please, I won't interfere.

The rest of the class, together with the teacher, caused these students to become norm-breakers and rule-breakers when they behaved according to what was accepted by their old class-norms. They missed their world, their traditions and felt alienated. They were young people previously accustomed to certain accepted attitudes, but now looked upon as dissenters if they persisted in their attitudes to classmates, teachers, and education. Thus, they could be forced to choose attitudes that badly harmonised with their former school career and life project.

The group process at the beginning of the formation of the Saga school class apparently shows that there is not room for everyone in this process, at least as the opponents look upon the situation themselves. There may be severe problems for those not willing to join in in the cramming atmosphere. If they are too aggressive in their opposition and resistance, there might be risks of exclusion, later manifested by a drop out. Thus, the meeting with others in the lower secondary school might have a strong influence on their personal development from a life perspective. What would have been the outcome if they had been students in a class with a more disorderly atmosphere?

Even if it is obvious, in the way the Stoneridge girls made such a strong impact, that they acquired a great deal of influence over the spirit of the new class, there is no guarantee that, this situation will remain unaltered. The very existence of some new school mates that could by no means cope with their ingratiating attitude, serves as a source of unrest that might easily cause resistance in the future ...one with a more disorderly atmosphere. Those young people ending up at Field Secondary School were more exposed to active interventions from school authorities, compared with the Saga students.

For the Field students there had been more difficulties in having more than one schoolmate with them from the old class, if any. There seemed to have been a systematic splitting up of peer-groups, especially among boys. There was only one pair of friends among the boys (13 boys), with six pairs or groups with three among the girls (17 girls) eleven boys and three girls were more or less without any best friends. For the Saga students, the situation was quite different. They had managed to bring along groups of eight mates in two cases, one with boys and the other with girls. In addition, the others had been allowed to have one or two mates with them. For three boys the situation was similar to the one for many boys at Field, coming without any mutually chosen friend.

While the students at Saga came from five different school classes and four different primary schools, the comparative situation in Field school was seven classes and five schools. The Saga students were allowed to choose desks freely as they entered the new school classroom, thus the class formation process was a matter for the young people themselves. The situation for the Field students, on the contrary, continued with a more active intervention from the adult world, as they were told where to sit in the classroom.

Compared with the Saga class, there was no corresponding single group that managed to predominate in the Field class. This class was looked upon as a school class with a more disorderly atmosphere. When the students met in the new class, many of the pairs seemed concentrated on holding on to one another, while the singles sought contact with someone else. One can understand the frustration when one member of a pair discovers how some outsider tries to take over his/her best friend. In the formation of the Field class, much uncertainty character-ised the world of the young people as new secondary school students. This school class went through a dynamic start, in which some of the students suffered se-verely.

In the Field class, both groups of girls with three members appeared to be the most active in performing in the front region of the classroom, making clear to others their views on how to behave in relation to teachers, other classmates and schoolwork. These groups represented different attitudes towards school, one more ingratiating and the other more oppositional, though neither as extreme as the Stoneridge girls or the Cilla boys. Around both of the three-member constel-lations, a couple of other girls hovered, more or less intensively. Two other more loosely composed groups were formed, one with all of the boys and the other with most of the remaining girls, both groups with little status among the rest of the class mates as well as among themselves. There was a clear hierarchy between the groups as well as within them.

The groups seemed in many respects to be existing without much contact with one another, interesting since the four groups all were composed of stu-dents from two to five primary school classes in the Field district. Still there was some interaction with others, mostly either in contact with a couple of girls not belonging to any of the groups or with some of the boys. Being placed in this more disorderly functioning school class, such as the one at Field school, could be easier for some students but more problematic for others.

The right to intervene in other peoples' lives

Linked to the process of transition, many feelings were expressed by the young people in both of the school classes examined in this study. For some, the feelings were merely positive: leaving childhood, a bigger school, subject teachers, new acquaintances, more challenges and so on. For others, the feelings were more mixed. There were also those students who experienced very strong negative feelings attached to the transition. In the latter case there were those giving expression to being cheated, misled, deserted or even rejected, either by teachers or schoolmates. For these young people the transition to the secondary school was a critical incident, not only from a student perspective but also from a life perspective.

Double-crossed
In the following sequence we can follow how one of the boys at Field school experienced the intervention of school authorities. Before the transition something happened that made him lose a great deal of confidence in the trustworthiness of grown-ups, especially grown-ups related to school. Fred expresses a feeling of betrayal:

> The only guy joining me from my former class, it was Sven Andersson, and I haven´t anything in common with him at all, we never speak with one another and we are never together /.../ It just turned out that way. A pal of mine, Peter, he too, he is, although he, I, we were allowed to choose those who were to join us, and he and I chose one another as first choices. But then there was another guy in the class that had chosen him as first choice, and then, as Peter had chosen him as third choice. But then the teacher thought that he couldn´t make it if he hadn´t any pal from the former class, but she thought that I could make it, but really, I don´t know /.../ I'm still cross with her about this. It's like three years I have ahead of me here. /.../ They weren't allowed to create such big groups. /.../ Field school had decided that. /.../ You almost need another boy as a pal if you come to a new class /.../ I thought it was really rotten, and I haven't found, in this class, I think most of them, there are hardly any decent guys here. /.../ I don't talk with anyone in my new class during lunch break, there's always someone from my old class around, in my old class everyone was really decent, it was really a, it was such a terrific dream class. /.../ [about the teacher:] I thought, I liked her very much when, but yeah, no, I think it was bloody rotten of her. /.../ I don't think they, I don't think they realise, what shall I say, that we shall be here for three years, I, actually you need a good pal. /.../ Mum, they talked to the teacher, but the teacher she said that she won´t change things anyway. /.../ They asked if I couldn't

get a pal from the old class. Well, it's dead hard when you live like this in the countryside, then you really need a pal who, you can hardly make a friend in the town when you don´t live in the town yourself. It's hard.

Fred and his classmates were informed that they were allowed to choose among their classmates those that they would prefer to have with them, when they were transferred to the lower secondary school. In this case, the school authorities did not stick to the premises they themselves had stipulated.

Fred gave expression to having experienced a deep sense of betrayal. Especially in relation to his former primary school teacher he felt double-crossed. Before this crisis he had liked her very much. She had been very important for him during the last three years. This betrayal was hard to deal with, as he had had a great deal of confidence in her. Now she had let him down. She didn't support him when he most needed it. Fred and his best pal Peter had been placed in two different school classes, although they had both chosen one another as first choices. He had obviously lost his confidence in the former teacher and school as an institution.

As his parents without any result had tried to make his position clear, he learned how powerless even they had turned out to be in their relation with the school authorities. This seemed to have deepened his mistrust. The school representative the parents had met was the teacher that had been deeply engaged in the upbringing of their son for several years. Now she refused to discuss the issue, already having made up her mind.

From a life perspective the experiences resulted in some insights that Fred gave expression to: First, his parents are no longer able to protect his interests in relation to the outer world, appearing to be as powerless as he himself. Second, someone that he had believed in for a long time had let him down, when he was most vulnerable. Third, teachers and other representatives from school authorities do not keep their promises. They are not reliable, and so they might double-cross you at any time. Fourth, in a conflict, in the final analysis, those in power will act according to their own plans and interests, regardless of what the man on the street has to say. Fifth, can you trust grown-ups at all.

Reflection

Fred left primary school for three years at Field school, while Tommy and Helen went to Saga. What odds do they have in coping with the challenges they will meet during their time in lower secondary school? The start did not seem auspicious. These young people express a feeling of rebellion. One could expect further mistrust, opposition and in the long run perhaps drop out, voluntarily or involuntarily. Whereas Fred feels he is alone, Tommy and Helen have a few close friends from their former school. When feeling a need to demonstrate their attitudes, Tommy and Helen can make a performance as members of small but well-known teams, even if they act in a class with a cramming atmosphere. Even though Fred is in a more disorderly class with a diversity of attitudes, at the same time he experiences much of uncertainty and lack of trust, and yet he has not found a possible classmate worth approaching.

Both Tommy and Fred have solved their dilemma by relying on groups of mates in other classes, mostly classmates from their former primary schools, functioning as their group of references. By this they seem to have a breathing space during their school day. Tommy always makes these contacts with others together with his team-mate, while Fred acts on his own. Helen on the other hand mostly sticks to her team in the class, a team composed of three girls from the former primary school, even if they almost always feel exposed.

In these young people, there is a great deal of opposition, defiance and bitterness, but at the same time you can see their pride, self-confidence and fighting spirit. In the interviews they show examples of an ability to analyse the situations they are confronted with during the transition.

This is an example of the benefit of making an interpretive study. Naturally there is a lot of information that is impossible to present in this kind of paper, but nevertheless the interpretive approach has some advantages. Hugh Mehan (1992) has put it this way:

> …culture is not merely a pale reflection of structural forces; it is a system of meaning that mediates social structure and human action. Social actors no longer function as passive role players, shaped exclusively by structural forces beyond their control; they become active sense makers, choosing among alternatives in often contradictory circumstances. Schools are not black boxes through which students pass on their way to predetermined slots in the capitalist order; they have a vibrant life, composed of processes and practices that respond to competing demands that often unwittingly contribute to inequality. (Mehan, 1992, p 3)

In order to understand the phenomenon of rebellious students, traditionally it is common to rely on structural forces such as social class, genus or ethnicity to explain peoples' actions. As an interpretive researcher one does not deny the existence of for example different socioeconomic conditions, serving as preconditions that limit the potential courses of action that people can select from. But in seeking structural explanations the specific nature of the actions as well as the meaning perspectives of the actors are often overlooked, aspects that are of crucial interest in an interpretive study. These are conditions that the actors themselves often are unaware of and that traditional researchers usually regard as irrelevant.

What do we know more about the young people in the study? Although rebellious, they have little in common with Willis' lads (Willis, 1977). They are middle-class children, two living in flats in a suburb and one in a cottage in the country-side. All three have families that are intact and they have either brothers or sisters. One of the parents immigrated many years ago. In the primary school their level of achievement was average or better than average.

The experience of the school class they have belonged to and the groups of schoolmates of whom they have been members, together with the selection of mates they bring along, seem to affect their way of dealing with the new situation. How the school authorities have succeeded in maintaining or breaking existing peer relations seems to have had great significance for how these young people have experienced the transition. The more the school as an institution has inter-vened or even interfered in the life world of the young people, the more critical the transition appears to have become at least in two aspects. First, it seems to have affected group processes towards more restructuring concerning relations and group formation. Second, it seems to have caused more problems for some individuals, resulting in the risk of marginalisation in some cases. From this one can understand the importance of the peer group for students' attitudes and perspectives to the school, the classmates and themselves.

This paper shows how the transition to the lower secondary school might be regarded as a critical incident for young people such as Fred, Tommy and Helen. How these young people and their schoolmates will cope with the remaining three years, and how will they approach their transition *from* this lower secondary school, are some of the issues on today's agenda in the research project, 'Young People Meet the Lower Secondary School' (Garpelin, 1999).

References

Andersson, Bengt-Erik & Lindblad, Sverker (1989). Skolan och ungdomarna: en bortglömd kombination i forskningen. (School and youth: a forgotten combination in research). *Locus*, 4, pp. 23-27.

Asplund, Johan (1987). *Det sociala livets elementära former*. (Elementary forms of the social life). Göteborg: Korpen.

Berteaux, Daniel (Ed.). (1981). *Biography and society*. London: Sage.

Brice Heath, Shirley (1982). Questioning at home and at school: A comparative study. In G.D. Spindler (Ed.), *Doing the ethnography of schooling*. New York: Holt Rinehart and Winston.

Bron-Wjciechovska, Agnieszka (1992). Life history som forskningsansats och undervisningsmetod. Forskares och lärares erfarenheter. (Life history as research approach and teaching method). *Spov*, 17, pp. 35-49.

Callewaert, Staf, & Nilsson, Bengt-A. (1980). *Skolklassen som socialt system -lektionsanalyser*. (The school class as a social system - analyses of lessons). Lund: Lunds bok och tidskrifts AB.

Elgqvist-Salzman, Inga, Forsslund, Annika, Sampei, Keiko, & Sjöström, Margareta (1986). *The life-history approach - A tool in establishing north-south education research cooperation?* (Arbetsrapporter från pedagogiska institutionen, 32). Umeå University, Department of Education, S-901 87 Umeå.

Erickson, Frederick (1986). Qualitative methods in research on teaching. In M.C. Wittrock (Ed.), *Handbook of Research on Teaching*. (3rd ed.). New York: Macmillan.

Erickson, Frederick, & Shultz, Jefferey (1992). Students´ experience of the curriculum. In P.W. Jackson (Ed.), *Handbook of research on curriculum: a project by the American Educational Research Organisation*. New York: Macmillan.

Erikson, Erik H. (1959). *Identity. Youth and crises*. New York: W.W. Norton.

Garpelin, Anders (1997). *Lektionen och livet. Ett möte mellan ungdomar som tillsammans bildar en skolklass.* (Lesson and life. How young people meet and form a school class). (Uppsala Studies in Education 70). Uppsala: Acta Universitatis Upsaliensis.

Garpelin, Anders (1999). *Young people meet the lower secondary school.* Paper presented at the NFPF congress in Copenhagen, March 1999. Uppsala University, Department of Teacher Training, Box 2136, S-75 002 Uppsala.

Garpelin, Anders, & Lindblad, Sverker (1993). *Att fånga ungdomarna i skolan: Erfarenheter av en förstudie.*(To catch young people in school: Experiences from a pilot study). (Arbetsrapporter från Pedagogiska institutionen, 182). Uppsala University, Department of Education, Box 2109, S-750 02 Uppsala.

Garpelin, Anders, & Lindblad, Sverker (1994). *On Students' Life Projects and Micropolitical Strategies. A Progress Report from Explorations of Swedish Comprehensive Schools.* Paper presented at the AERA meeting in New Orleans, april 1994. Uppsala University, Department of Education, Box 2109, S-750 02 Uppsala.

Garpelin, Anders, Lindblad, Sverker, & Sahlström, Fritjof (1995). Vikings and hip-hoppers in the classroom - An explorative study of cultural conflict in an educational setting. *Young. 3* (3), 38-53.

Goffman, Erving (1959). *The presentation of self in everyday life.* New York: Doubleday & Company, Inc.

Goffman, Erving (1961). *Asylums: Essays on the social situation of mental patients and other inmates.* New York: Doubleday & Company, Inc.

Goffman, Erving (1963). *Stigma: notes on the management of spoiled identity.* Prentice-Hall.

Goffman, Erving (1967). *Interaction ritual: Essays on face-to-face behavior.* New York: Doubleday Anchor.

Karlsson, Gunnar (1993). *Psychological qualitative research from a phenomenological perspective.* Stockholm: Almqvist & Wiksell.

Jonsson, Gustav (1967). *Delinquent boys, their parents and grandparents.* Acta psychiatrica Scandinavica. Supplementum ; 195. Copenhagen : Munksgaard.

Laing, Ronald D. (1971). *The politics of the family and other essays.* London: Tavistock.

Lindblad, Sverker (1992). *Longitudinella studier av mikro-politiska strategier och ungdomars skolkarriärer.* (Longitudinal studies of micropolitical strategies and school careers among youth). (Application to HSFR, plan for a research project). Uppsala University, Department of Education, Box 2109, S-750 02 Uppsala.

Lindblad, Sverker (1993). Skolkarriär och levnadsbana. Om elevers erfarenheter av ungdomsskolan och formandet av levnadsbanor. (School and life career. About students experiences from the school for youth and the forming of life careers). In R. Ericson & J. Jonsson (Ed.), *Skola och sortering.* (School and discrimination). Stockholm: Carlsons.

Mead, George H. (1934). *Mind, self and society. From a standpoint of a social behaviorist.* Chicago: University of Chicago Press.

Mehan, Hugh (1992). Understanding inequality in schools: The contribution of interpretive studies. *Sociology of Education 1992,* 65 (4), pp. 1-20.

Phelan, Patricia K., Davidson, Anne L., & Cao, Hanh T. (1991). Students´ multiple worlds: Negotiating the boundaries of family, peer, and school cultures. *Anthropology and Education Quarterly.* 22 (3), pp. 224-250.

Schutz, Alfred (1967). *The phenomenology of the social world.* New York: Northwestern University Press.

Stafseng, Ola (1990). *Ungdomsforskningen i Sverige. En vetenskaplig granskning.* (Youth research in Sweden. A scientific study). (Skolöverstyrelsen: F 90:1/Vad säger forskningen). The Swedish Board of Education, S-106 42 Stockholm.

Talbert, Joan E., McLaughlin, Milbrey W., & Rowan, Brian (1993). Understanding context effects on secondary school teaching. *Teachers Collage Record.* **95** (1), pp. 45—68.

Thomas, William.I., & Znaniecki, Florian (1918). *The Polish peasant in Europe and America.* Chicago: University of Chicago Press.

Willis, Paul (1977). *Learning to labour.* Farnborough: Saxon House.

Life in School: Constants and Contexts in Pupil Experience of Schooling and Learning in Three European Countries

Marilyn Osborn & Claire Planel

The paper reports on selected findings of a major research project (ENCOMPASS) which examines the relationship between national educational values as these are mediated by the school context, teacher beliefs, and classroom processes, and eventually translated into pupil perspectives on learning and schooling. The theoretical rationale for such resarch is presented and findings are drawn from questionnaires to 1800 pupils in England, France and Denmark, and from individual and group interviews with a smaller sample of pupils in each country. The paper draws upon a socio-cultural context in which learning occurs. Pupil perspectives on the purpose of schooling and learning and on the teaching they receive are examined and the 'constants' and 'contexts' of pupil experience in the three countries are discussed.

This paper explores the significance of the cultural context in which learning occurs by examining the perspectives of pupils in three European countries on the purposes of schooling and on themselves as learners. It reports some findings from a research project which is currently taking place in England, France and Denmark. These findings suggest that although pupils in different European countries share many common concerns, they also come to school with significantly different attitudes towards themselves as learners, towards school and towards achievement. As a result, their expectations of themselves and of their teachers are also different.

The research reported here traces the relationship between national educational values (as represented in official policy documents and policy statements) as these are translated into the school context and into pupil perspectives on learning and schooling. Using a socio-cultural theoretical perspective (Vygotsky 1978, Wertsch 1985, 1991) the aim of the paper is to explore the social reality of schooling for pupils in the three contrasting educational systems of England, France, and Denmark, and the relative significance of the factors that influence the development of a learner identity in these three national settings.

There are important theoretical reasons for a study of pupilhood in these three national contexts. The differences between the systems and the consequent differential impact on pupils may be decreasing in the context of a united Europe, the internationalisation of adolescent peer culture, and the effects of globalisation (Eide 1992, Masini 1994). The paper explores whether there are significant differences related to the national context or whether pupils' experience of schooling is becoming more similar as they try to construct their identity as learners and as adolescents, and to negotiate pathways which lead to success on the dimensions of academic achievement, peer status, and social conformity (Rudduck et al 1995, Keys and Fernandes 1993).

Continuing differences in terms of school structure, organisation, ethos, environment and learning culture in the three countries may impinge significantly on the creation of pupils' identities and on their views of themselves as learners. Gender, socio-economic status, and ethnicity are also likely to be highly significant. Current research evidence suggests that, in England it may be difficult for children to negotiate strategies which achieve a balance between academic success as a pupil, social and peer group success as an adolescent, and success in conforming to school norms for social behaviour (Abrahams 1995, Raphael Reed 1996, Woods 1990, Lacey 1970, Hargreaves 1967). However, the process of negotiation and the strategies required may be quite different in France and Denmark, mediated as they are by different national traditions, school ethos, and structures (Charlot et al 1992, Dubet et al 1996, Frønes 1995, Jensen et al 1992).

Study of policy documentation at the national level suggests that the prevailing educational traditions in each country are very different. In England there is an emphasis on differentiation and individualisation (DfEE 1997, Best 1998), in France on republicanism and universalism (OECD 1997, Osborn et al 1997, Osborn and Planel 1999, Corbett and Moon 1996) in Denmark on collaboration and consensus (Frønes 1995, Jensen et al 1992). As a result the structures put in place by schools to deal with both the cognitive and the affective aspects of children's experience are significantly different.

In Denmark there is a strong concern with the development of the 'whole child' and with the affective dimension of education. In Danish schools pastoral care is emphasised as part of the teacher's role, and there is a focus on participatory democracy and lessons in citizenship (Kryger and Reisby 1998). Children are encouraged to make decisions jointly with teachers about the direction of lessons. In addition, children often remain with the same class teacher throughout their school careers.

In England there remains a dual emphasis on both cognitive and affective concerns. While the existence of a National Curriculum and national assessment emphasise academic objectives for pupils, structures such as the pastoral care system, the inclusion in the curriculum of personal and social education, the emphasis on behavioural and moral norms and the wearing of uniform, reflect a continuing concern with the child as 'person' or 'the whole child' (Best 1998).

In contrast, in France, the main focus of the school is on the child as 'pupil' and on cognitive rather than affective concerns. Academic objectives are emphasised as the school's main area of concern. A distinctive institutional ethos and associated behavioural norms are less important and concern with pastoral care is left to outside agencies (Cousin 1998, Audiger and Motta 1998). This paper therefore considers pupil perceptions of schooling and of the teaching they receive and the main sources of influence on these perspectives. While the emphasis is on national differences and similarities the relative significance of intra-national differences such as socio-economic status and gender are also discussed.

Methods of Data Collection

The research we report on here draws particularly upon questionnaires, individual and group interviews with pupils collected in a matched sample of secondary schools in each country selected to be as representative as possible of a socio-economic mix. In England three comprehensives, one in an area of relatively high socio-economic status in the Midlands, one in a 'mixed' area in the south-west, and one in a highly disadvantaged area in London were selected. These were matched as far as possible with schools in Denmark, two in Copenhagen and one in the north of Denmark, and with three schools in France, one an area of relatively high socio-economic status in the south-west, one in a 'mixed' suburb of Paris, and a third in a highly disadvantaged suburb of Paris. In these schools all the qualitative data collection, teacher and pupil interviews and observation was carried out. However, for the questionnaire phase of the study which required a sizeable sample, since English comprehensives are considerably larger than comparable schools in France and Denmark, in order to collect comparable numbers of pupil responses we included twenty additional schools in Denmark and one in France. In both cases these were drawn from areas of 'mixed' socio-economic status.

Data collection at pupil level combined quantitative and qualitative approaches to provide for both generalisability and richness of data. Approximately 1800 thirteen and fourteen year old pupils in their second year of study completed questionnaires. Careful consideration was given to linguistic and conceptual cross-cultural differences in the construction of the questionnaires. These were extensively piloted and revised a number of times as a result. Production of both French, English and Danish questionnaires took place simultaneously with team members from all three countries present. A sub-sample of 'target' children was then selected for further detailed study over the course of the two years including individual and group interviews and classroom observation. The 'target' group included equal numbers of boys and girls who were chosen to represent a mix of high, medium, and low achievers from a range of socio-economic and ethnic backgrounds.

Each group interview included one target pupil and four friends chosen by the individual target child. Approximately six group interviews took place in each school and eighteen in each country. These were designed to elicit insights into peer group culture and the relationship of this to children's identity as learners and to school culture (Dubet et al 1996). To extend and validate the findings of the questionnaires and individual interviews the researchers fed back findings from these to the groups, based on what children in their school, their country, and in the other countries had said about their experience of schooling. Selected quotations from children in all three countries were used to stimulate group discussion and were followed up with a series of probes designed to explore meaning and to examine some of the influences on children's perspectives.

Findings

The findings presented here focus particularly on pupils' perceptions of their schooling and of their teachers, and compare and contrast both *inter* and *intra-* nationally, looking at children in the three countries and at the influence of gender and socio-economic differences *within* each country on pupil attitudes.

International Differences in Pupil Experience

Overall, many of the findings from both the questionnaires and the individual and group interviews suggest that pupils' perceptions, filtered as they are through the mediation of teachers and the particular interpretations which pupils bring to school with them, do nevertheless resonate fairly closely with the particular emphases of the goals of the national systems. The Danish emphasis on collaboration and consensus and the concern with education for citizenship and democracy as well as with the academic goals of education emerged strongly in the pupils' responses. Danish pupils were broadly the most positive towards schooling, learning and teachers. They saw school as helping them to fit into a group situation rather than emphasising the development of the individual. They did not in general feel that their teachers placed a great deal of emphasis on making them work hard. They were less likely than the other groups to want to leave school as soon as they could or to see school as getting in the way of their lives (Tables I and II).

In some respects, the English children, like those we studied previously at primary level, were still the least enthusiastic about school. They enjoyed school and lessons the least and were the most likely to want to leave school as soon as they could and to feel that school got in the way of their lives (Table I). However, there were a number of positive elements of teaching for this group who emphasised their teachers' concern with pupils expressing their own ideas and with pupils as people. Encouragingly, they also felt that they had good feedback from teachers about their work and felt that teachers made them work hard (Tables IIIa

Table I – My Feelings About School. Here are some statements of what you might think about your school. Please show how much you agree or disagree by filling in the appropriate bubble.

| | Strongly agree / agree (%) | | |
	Denmark	England	France
1. On the whole I like my teachers.	64	69	63
2. School gets in the way of my life.	21	30	31
3. I enjoy school.	67	54	56
4. I really enjoy most lessons.	63	52	54
5. I want to do well at school.	92	96	96
6. I feel as though I'm wasting my time at school.	10	7	13
7. The best part of my life is the time I spend in school.	11	17	18
8. I'd like to leave school as soon as I can.	17	23	17
9. School is the first step on the way to my career.	85	91	85
Totals	n = 610	n = 577	n = 444

Table II – My Feelings About School. Here are some statements of what you might think of school in general. Please show how much you agree or disagree by filling in the appropriate bubble.

| | Strongly agree / agree (%) | | |
	Denmark	England	France
1. School teaches you to understand other people's feelings.	33	58	42
2. An important thing about school is meeting up with friends.	66	79	86
3. School helps you to sort out your life.	65	67	58
4. School helps you to become mature.	57	76	75
5. School is boring.	36	36	27
6. Important about school is learning to co-operate.	91	84	78
7. School is all about getting jobs when you leave.	75	70	84
8. Important about school is that it helps to get qualifications.	80	95	75
9. An important thing about school is learning new things.	94	95	97
10. School makes aware of your strengths and weaknesses.	78	79	86
11. School is a place where you learn to obey rules.	45	78	80
12. School is a place where you can express your ideas.	59	73	48
13. School is a place where it is difficult to succeed.	25	20	43
Totals	n = 610	n = 577	n = 444

and IIIb). The English pupils' responses reflected the emphasis at national level on the affective dimension of education as well as the cognitive, and the stress on individualisation and differentiation. The English findings suggested that the dual concerns at national level with both the 'whole child' and the child as pupil, with both cognitive and affective concerns were equally reflected in their school experiences.

Table IIIa – Teachers. Please read the statements below about teachers and mark a bubble in each
row to show whether you think this applies to: most of your teachers / many of your teachers /
only a few of your teachers / hardly any of your teachers.

	Most / many teachers (%)		
	Denmark	England	France
I believe teachers			
1. are there to help pupils pass exams.	75	71	65
2. are there to help pupils learn.	92	92	84
3. aren't really interested in pupils as people.	33	24	57
4. make all the decisions about what happens in lessons.	71	79	72
5. give challenging work.	66	74	64
6. really want their pupils to do well.	85	79	74
7. live in a different world from their pupils.	49	35	40
8. encourage pupils to say what they think in class.	62	65	47
9. will have a laugh with pupils.	47	43	23
10. make pupils want to work hard.	49	73	39
11. are understanding about pupils' problems and worries.	54	45	34
12. give pupils a say in how they learn.	67	36	37
13. are only interested in their own subject.	46	51	51
14. will be helpful if pupils go to them with a problem.	71	64	37
Totals	n = 610	n = 577	n = 444

Table IIIb – Teachers. Please read the statements below about teachers and mark a bubble in each
row to show whether you think this applies to: most of your teachers / many of your teachers /
only a few of your teachers / hardly any of your teachers.

	Most / many teachers (%)		
	Denmark	England	France
I believe teachers			
1. make pupils feel they aren't good enough in their work.	24	25	58
2. are a good example for their pupils.	52	57	53
3. are interested in pupils' opinions.	68	61	42
4. treat all pupils equally.	50	53	48
5. are more interested in pupils who can do well.	43	48	57
6. show what they really think and feel.	30	43	29
7. are interested in building friendly relationships with pupils.	71	45	49
8. are respected by pupils.	54	52	47
9. make pupils feel they can be successful.	72	67	59
10. like and enjoy their job.	69	61	65
11. provide guidance about how you can improve your work.	72	74	58
12. trust pupils.	63	48	35
13. do not listen to pupils.	27	23	30
14. try to make pupils get on well as a group.	80	77	52
15. spend too much time with pupils who need extra help.	36	32	18
Totals	n = 610	n = 577	n = 444

In France with its emphasis on universalism and republicanism and on all children being treated equally and with its separation of academic and social/personal development goals, children nevertheless had strong concerns about teachers who do not respect pupils and who do not explain things properly (Tables IIIa and IIIb). The French secondary pupils in our sample did not show much evidence of having experienced an affective or social and personal dimension to their school experience. Neither did they feel that they were getting the guidance they needed to improve or an emphasis on hard work from teachers. There is some suggestion from these findings of a lowering of teacher expectations at secondary level and a drop in pupil motivation.

Although there was continuing evidence from these results of the influence of national context on pupil perceptions of schooling, there was also a clear suggestion of the globalisation of many concerns. All pupils shared a certain number of similar priorities for teaching and a similar concern with the economic function of education and its link to the job market.

Intra-national differences in pupil experience: gender and social inequality

Within each education system gender and socio-economic issues were mediated differently so that the impact of these on pupils' views of themselves as learners varied. There were gender differences in perceptions of schooling in all three countries, but the differences in perceptions of schooling between boys and girls were more marked in France than in the other two countries. In general, French boys were the least likely of all the groups to be positive about school.

In all three countries the girls in our sample were more positive about school and about teachers than the boys. Thus girls were less likely to see school as 'getting in the way of my life' (Table IV). However there were variations in the size of the 'gender' gap from one country to another. For example Danish pupils were positive about their teachers regardless of gender (there were no statistically significant differences between boys and girls) whereas, in both England and France, girls agreed significantly more often than boys that they liked their teachers.

Where the difference in the perspectives of boys and girls was statistically significant in all three countries, the gap was often smallest in Denmark and greatest in France, with England somewhere in the middle. Whereas in Denmark and England, both boys and girls enjoyed school equally, only 45% of French boys did so compared with 67% of French girls. French boys were also significantly more likely than girls to feel that they were wasting time at school, to feel bored by school and to disagree that 'the best part of my life is the time I spend in school'. Of the three countries England was the only one where there was no statistically

Table IV – Gender and Attitudes to School. Here are some statements of what you might think about your school. Please show how much you agree or disagree by filling in the appropriate bubble.

| | Strongly agree / agree (%) | | | | | |
| | Denmark | | England | | France | |
	Girl	Boy	Girl	Boy	Girl	Boy
1. On the whole I like my teachers.	66.9	63.6	71.3*	66.7	68.1*	59.4
2. School gets in the way of my life.	18.1*	25.3	22.0*	37.0	26.3*	35.1
3. I enjoy school.	71.3	63.6	59.4	51.8	66.8*	44.7
4. I really enjoy most lessons.	66.9	61.0	54.9	50.6	59.7	51.0
5. I want to do well at school.	94.6	92.8	98.0	97.7	97.5	97.4
6. I feel as though I'm wasting time at school.	6.5	12.4	3.3	9.3	7.3*	18.2
7. Best part of my life is time I spend in school.	7.9*	13.0	15.0	19.3	24.2*	11.0
8. I'd like to leave school as soon as I can.	13.6	18.9	21.1	24.7	14.0	20.8
9. School is first step on the way to my career.	89.3*	83.0	92.3	91.3	87.8*	83.2
10. School is boring.	31.0	42.3	34.7	38.8	18.8*	36.7
Totals	n = 280	n = 324	n = 244	n = 311	n = 233	n = 199

(* = differences within each country which are statistically significant)

significant 'gender gap' in pupil views of the future. English boys and girls were equally likely to see school as the first step on the way to their career whereas in the other two countries girls were more likely than boys to see the career uses of school.

In summary, for pupils of this age group, the much publicised 'gender' gap in England was not so striking as might have been expected, given the concern of English policy makers with boys under-achievement and lack of motivation (OFSTED 1998). In fact the most significant gender differences occurred in France where traditionally the under-motivation of boys has not been seen as an issue.

Socio-economic differences in perceptions of schooling were evident in all three countries, but were more significant in England and Denmark than in France, suggesting evidence of a 'long tail of under-motivation' of children from different social groups in these countries. In order to examine socio-economic differences in pupil perspectives, we divided pupils into three groups according to parental employment (either father's or mother's, whichever fell into the 'highest' category). The categories were: professional/managerial, white/blue collar, and unemployed. Table V indicates how pupils in each of these three categories responded to a series of statement about school and teachers. On the whole, for each country, the pattern of difference is fairly consistent, with the children of professional/managerial parents most positive about school, teachers, and learn-

Table V – *Socio-Economic Status and Attitudes to School.* Here are some statements of what you might think about your school. Please show how much you agree or disagree by filling in the appropriate bubble.

	Strongly agree / agree (%)								
	Denmark			England			France		
	P/M	W/B-C	Unem.	P/M	W/B-C	Unem.	P/M	W/B-C	Unem.
1. On the whole I like my teachers.	80.6*	58.7	62.5	71.1*	74.2	68.6	79.1*	53.8	52.9
2. School gets in the way of my life.	13.2*	23.5	29.5	28.0*	28.8	40.0	26.4	33.8	31.3
3. I enjoy school.	83.9*	61.0	65.1	52.7	54.9	54.3	60.2	53.6	70.6
4. I really enjoy most lessons.	72.3	60.1	67.2	47.6	54.6	51.4	52.6	55.3	62.5
5. I want to do well at school.	95.5	92.8	95.3	98.4	98.1	91.4	97.6	97.2	100.
6. I feel as though I'm wasting my time at school.	5.8*	9.6	15.6	2.7*	5.1	17.1	10.4	14.3	18.8
7. The best part of my life is the time I spend in school.	5.2	11.3	17.2	15.0	17.6	20.0	18.1	19.0	17.6
8. I'd like to leave school as soon as I can.	8.4	18.8	20.6	18.7	23.0	34.3	22.7	25.0	8.8
9. School is the first step on the way to my career.	85.9	86.0	85.9	93.0	92.1	91.4	87.9	83.9	94.1
Totals: n =	155	293	64	108	125	16	172	208	17

(* = differences which are statistically significant)

(P/M = Professional/Managerial; W/B-C = White Collar; Unem. = Unemployed)

ing and the children of unemployed parents the least positive. However there were some exceptions to this and it is striking that in all three countries, pupils from all social groups were equally concerned to do well at school and to use school as a step to a future career.

In England and Denmark there were more statistically significant differences between social groups. The children of unemployed parents were the most likely to see school as a waste of time. or as getting in the way of their lives. There were significant differences in enjoyment of school in Denmark with the children of professional/managerial parents far more positive than other social groups. Although, in France, this group more often liked their teachers than the children of white/blue collar or unemployed parents did, in general there were fewer significant differences in the perspectives of pupils from different social groups than was the case in the other countires.

It is possible that the French emphasis on universalism and on a clear understanding of progress through the system, aimed at bringing all children to a common level of achievement, rather than on individualisation and differentiation, may have contributed to the narrowing of the socio-economic gap.

Constant and contexts in the concerns of European Pupils

Part of the value of cross-cultural research is the extent to which it is able to identify both constants and contexts in educational experience (Broadfoot and Osborn 1988). Cross-cultural comparisons of pupil experience identify pupil responses to learning which are more universal to the situation of 'being a secondary school pupil' from those which may be more culturally specific. As the more quantitative findings in the previous section demonstrated, pupils in England, Denmark and France pupils have to engage with school contexts which relate to cultural, philosophical, political and historical differences between the three countries. Thus this section draws upon the individual and group pupil interviews in order to illuminate understanding of the relationship between social and cultural influences and cultural practices, and to explore how these might affect pupil behaviour and ultimately pupil learning. Using the pupils' own voices as far as possible, the key concerns of the pupils are considered under three headings: the teacher pupil relationship; social identity; and pupils' perception of learning.

The teacher-pupil relationship
There were notable differences between pupils in the three countries in how they perceived the teacher-pupil relationship. Pupils in France expressed a strong perception of distance between teacher and pupil. There was a strong difference in status relating to a concept of adult (and particularly teacher as the fount of all

knowledge) superiority and pupil inferiority. Adults were *'grands'* (teachers were particularly *'grands'* as their role was to form children), children and pupils were *'petits'*: *'Des êtres incomplets, encore naturels, parfois dangereux, et qu'il convient de dresser'* (Dubet 1996, p.31). French pupils were very aware of their perceived inferiority:

> 'Un prof c'est plus grand que nous, il nous apprend des trucs.' *Teachers are bigger (more important) than us, they teach us things.*

French pupils thought that teachers used their perceived superior status to maintain their distance from pupils:

> 'Les professeurs, ils méprisent les élèves. Nous on est des enfants et ils ne considèrent pas vraiment ce qu'on dit. Ils disent que ça nous concerne pas.' *Teachers look down on pupils. We're children and they don't pay much attention to what we say. They say it's got nothing to do with us.*

Pupils used terms like *'esclaves'* slaves, and *'robots'* robots, to describe their role in relation to teachers. There was also a distance between French teacher and pupil in terms of time and social class. Both high and low achieving pupils from middle class and working class backgrounds, of French and ethnic minority parentage thought that many teachers had not changed with the times and did not understand the needs of the new generation. They thought that teachers were out of touch with their lives:

> 'Un professeur qui est dans les cinquante ans, c'est plus son temps. Lui quand il était jeune, les élèves il étaient comme ça ... mais évidemment c'est plus comme ça, ça a complètement changé'. *A teacher who's in his fifties is out of step. When he was young children were like that ... but obviously it's not like that anymore* (High achieving girl from Paris)

> 'C'est pas le même environnement que quand eux ils ont grandi. Eux quand ils ont grandi on leur a toujours dit ..., mais nous on est livré à nous même, c'est dehors qu'on apprend. Il faut comprendre que nous on est jeune, on est d'une autre génération. Il faut qu'ils se renseignent sur ce qui se passe. Ils nous voient pas quand on est dehors ce qu'on subit.' *It's not the same world as when they grew up. When they were little they were always told what to do, but we bring ourselves up, we learn outside school. They have to understand that we're young and that we're from a different generation. They need to find out what's happening now. They don't see us outside school, what we endure.* (Low achieving, half Arab boy from Paris)

The distance between French teacher and pupil was traditional and institutionalised. English pupils were less conscious of the difference between teacher and pupil status. In some cases they acknowledged that there was an imbalance of power: 'Some teachers think they are higher than you', and there was some awareness of time and social distance: 'There still back in the seventies', 'They have to realise there's drink and drugs ... they don't want to believe that's going on; but it is.'

But it was not an issue which overtly pre-occupied them. Instead in most cases English pupils were more concerned with negotiating their own individual status with their teachers. Arguably, this type of individual relationship held by pupil and teacher in England is likely to have a greater impact on the pupil's academic performance. The strength of individualisation and differentation in the English context of education made the teacher pupil relationship more open to negotiation.

Danish pupils, like English pupils, referred to, but did not dwell on, the time distance between teacher and pupils. They were concerned that their teachers be relatively young and up-to-date. As one pupil expressed it 'modern teachers, fairly young teachers who have modern views on teaching and learning'. However, like English pupils, they were more concerned with their personal relationships with teachers which were independent of institutionalised norms. Relationships between teachers and pupils were again open to negotiation and negotiation itself was institutionalised.

The concèpt of a teacher as a friend was particularly difficult for French pupils to comprehend. English pupils had less difficulty with the idea but were reluctant to identify teachers as 'friends' in any real sense: 'They're just teachers' 'Not someone you would go out with at weekends' 'When you're in trouble they can't forgive you; they've got to punish you'.

Danish pupils, although held back (in this respect like English and French pupils by the concern that teachers should not be too friendly in case this led to interference with their private lives, did acknowledge in some cases that teachers could almost be friends: 'Not a real friend, but someone who knows something about you .... with whom you feel good'.

An important constant for pupils from all three countries, which prevented them from regarding reachers as real friends and confiding in them, was their concern about their teachers' personal and professional ability to keep confidences.

Another significant constant for English, French and Danish pupils was that there should be mutual respect between teachers and pupils before learning could take place. In the English context respect was not automatic for either party. Teachers could earn their pupils' respect by a combination of listening to pupils and giving them a voice. Pupils were more likely to gain respect from their teachers if they had a positive work attitude. English pupils in particular seemed to be caught by contradictory pressures: the need to negotiate a good working relationship with their teacher by earning his/her respect through their positive work orientation at the same time as the need to not be too positive towards their work for fear of losing their peers' support.

An important cultural difference in how English, Danish and French responded to their teachers and their schools' demands was in relation to the presence or absence of a sense of solidarity within the class. In the English context of classes with changing pupil composition, due to the relative use of banding, setting and streaming in the three schools, there was little evidence of classroom solidarity or even of solidarity with the school as a whole. Internal classroom social relationships were more pertinent to English pupils' sense of social identity. However there were similarities between France and Denmark in the pupils' attitude to solidarity and commonality. In the Danish cultural context of consensus and where the school practice is for pupils to remain in the same class for key subjects over many years, pupils had a strong sense of commonality in their class "because that's where you spend most of your time'. The class was a collective unit: 'The class holds us together not the school'.

In the French cultural context of universalism and republicanism and where the school practice is for pupils remain in the same class for nearly all subjects on a yearly basis, pupils seemed to use classroom solidarity as a positive strategy for mutual support:

'La classe c'est un ensemble' 'C'est à nous de les aider, nous sommes un groupe' *The class is a group. It's up to us to help them, we make up a group.*

'Il faut se tenir la main pour que ça marche ...il faut se tenir à l'écoute, il faut s'entre aider' *We've got to stand together to make things work .. you've got to be ready to listen, you've got to help each other.*

Teachers were aware of pupil solidarity: 'La classe c'est un groupe, c'est tout un groupe, ils font un bloque' *The class is a group, one group, they're one entity.* Occasionally solidarity seemed to be contrived rather than reflecting reality: 'Il n'y a pas de groupes (dans la classe), il n'y a qu'un seul groupe' *There aren't any separate groups we're all one group* which suggests that French pupils were responding to the relatively harsh learning environment of the French context by presenting a face of solidarity; in accordance with the French saying, 'L'union fait la force' *There's strength in unity.* Perhaps the strategy of solidarity and the pupils' exploitation of the institutional distance between French teacher and pupil enabled French pupils to protect themselves from entering into more individual relationships with teachers, which in the face of relatively high negative teacher assessment, might have had negative consequences on pupils' 'real' identities

Social identity

In all three countries pupils were, to a greater or lesser extent, concerned with establishing their social identity. To many pupils, particularly English pupils, social identity dominated and determined learner identity. There was some evidence to show that English pupils divided their classes into groups of three different types of pupils on the basis of their academic achievement: 'One group works really hard, another group doesn't, they mess around in class. Another group works sometimes and messes about sometimes' (English pupil). English pupils' school experience seemed to be dominated by these academic and social groups and English pupils' social identity was defined by membership of such groups. At one school where high attainment was more evident there was a gloss on working hard. 'Keeners', were described as 'not necessarily clever but very interested', 'they work hard, do extra work'. These were distinct from people who generally did good work, tried hard and conformed, and from 'people who don't bother doing their work and behave badly', who, 'had a bad attitude to work', 'often they don't do well with school work and don't try hard', and 'they can be nasty to other pupils.' In the inner London school pupils expressed an even more finely-shaded version:

> 'There's boffins - really brainy, always quiet, always answer the question, always do their work. They know what they're doing, they push hard with their work ... don't talk when they're working, never stop to enjoy themselves, put their heads down in their books even when everyone else is laughing.'

> 'Some (other) people talk and mess about in their lessons but they still do their work as well.'

> 'There's 'bad' boys - they're popular, like to joke.' 'Some people smoke, drink, bully, get on report for being late and for bad behaviour'.

Group identity in the English schools involved codes for behaviour as well as social and learning identity:

> 'Everything perfect – not just work. The right uniform – not hipsters, not thick soles or jewellery, not a polo shirt, no make-up'

> 'Top of the class, always do work, set their pencil cases our tidily, would bring a briefcase if they had the choice'

As might be expected the exact description of these groups was dependent on who was doing the describing and their relationship to this particular sub-set. Something of the flavour of the speaker's own positioning is detectable even in the short extracts above. For pupils in all three English schools the epithet of 'boffin' or 'keener' was not particularly complimentary, though not always unwelcome. For many average and low achievers it was a way of categorising 'the other' as something undesirable. Pupils like Simon in Year 7 did not want to be seen as keener: 'People think you are really good and they don't want to be with you'. Pupils in 'top sets' were often characterised by pupils in lower sets as: 'Clever and boring ... they don't have much of a social life'. They were said to be: 'Nerdish', 'sad', and 'They don't have a good time at school'. However for some pupils there might have been an element of jealousy in their attitude to high achieving pupils. As one English pupil explained: 'You can use it to tease people because you're a bit annoyed that they have done better.'

The link between social and learner identity was a strong one for English pupils. Boys were in a particularly difficult position as it was more acceptable for girls to work hard than boys: 'For boys there is an image to keep up about not working hard'. The negotiation of social identity required boys to make people laugh, mess around or confront teachers. This quality was though to be particular asset for boys who wished to make themselves attractive to girls. A boy observed: 'Girls would say they liked a hard worker but they would really like one who had a laugh'. Boys with natural charisma could afford to be 'laid back'; others had to establish their credibility by: 'having a big mouth', 'being loud', 'being hard', 'doing the opposite of what the teachers tell you', and generally establishing an anti-work reputation.

There was less evidence in France and Denmark of this division of classes into social groups although some French pupils also acknowledged the existence of friendship groupings which followed a rough division into low, average and high achievers. The French term 'intello' also matched the English 'keener' and 'boffin': 'C'est quelqu'un qui passe ses weekends à la bibliothèque' *It's someone who spends their weekends in the library*. 'C'est quelqu'un qui a tout le temps de bonnes notes, jamais de zéros, jamais au dessous de la moyennne.' *It's someone who always gets good marks, never a zero, always above the average mark*. 'Intello' also had negative connotations: 'C'est en général un terme plutôt perjoratif' *It's generally rather a pejorative term*.

Despite these similarities with English pupils there was evidence that French pupils tended to play down the importance of learner and social differentiation. They tried again to convey the idea of unity. Lower achieving pupils stressed that 'intellos' were not discriminated against by the rest of the class. Pupils claimed that anyone could be friends with 'intellos'. A boy explained, 'Ils sont avec nous' *They're with us*.

Academic performance played an even smaller role in the social identity of Danish pupils. They appeared to be more preoccupied with social behaviour: 'School is not just academic', 'You should behave well and be a good friend'. As one pupil put it: 'You are allowed to do well and be a bit of a 'keener', but you also have to be nice towards others.'

In the Danish cultural context of a philosophy of 'consensus' and a school context of small classes, small schools and classes where pupils remained together for seven years, maintaining, good social relationships and behaving well were perhaps important survival skills as well as learning skills. For Danish pupils, instead of academic achievement, it was personal interests, fashion (also important in England and France) and the degree of freedom allowed to pupils by their parents which seemed to dictate group composition.

Attitudes to Learning

Pupils in England, France and Denmark were in considerable agreement over what constituted effective teaching and learning. The first requirement was that pupils should be active: 'doing something' (English pupil), 'si on faisait que parler et copier sur le cahier personne apprendrait' *If all that happened was (the teacher) talking and us copying it down no-one would learn anything*, 'mixing the dry reading stuff with a film and the like... makes you feel more engaged' (Danish pupil). Pupils from the three countries all decried teacher monologues and copying. The second requirement for effective learning was that learning had to be interesting. 'Interesting' was defined in the three countries as a lesson which had an element of 'fun' or humour: 'Monsieur Giroud est rigolo tandis que Madame Bonnard ..... elle raconte, elle raconte... elle dicte, elle dicte' *Mr Giroud is funny whereas Mrs Bonnard goes on and on and on, she endlessly dictates.* 'C'est endormant, c'est toujours 'ha hein ha hein ha hein ha hein'. On dirait qu'ils ravagent toujours les mêmes choses, c'est sur mëme ton, toujours monotone.' *It puts you to sleep, it's always blaa blaa blaa. They always seem to go over the same things, with the same monotonous tone of voice.* 'He goes on and on ... reads it out' (English pupil).

Pupils in all three countries appreciated teachers who, 'have a laugh', 'can make a joke', liven it up'. In the event of the teacher not being able to fulfil these conditions it was pupils who provided the interest. As a French girl explained: 'Dans le cours il y a toujours quelqu'un là pour mettre de l'ambiance' *There's always someone in the lesson who'll make it interesting* and that role was generally occupied by a boy. Pupils from the three countries also thought that they learnt more when teachers brought in themes from contemporary life.

Danish pupils differed from English and French pupils in that they felt they had a considerable degree of choice in the content and organisation of their lessons and that this helped their learning. For example, Danish pupils reported having a say in the history issues they wanted like to work on, the form a biology report was to take, or whether pupils wanted to work in groups or as a class. In German a pupil reported, 'It's almost up to us to decide what to do'. Two Danish pupils summarised their degree of choice: 'To my mind we have a say in learning in this school', 'We can choose to say if we want or not... if we don't want, the teacher can't do anything.'

Effective teaching and learning in Denmark implied a certain amount of pupil choice. A Danish pupil explained: 'There is no reason for the teacher just to go on in one particular way'. French pupils differed from English and Danish pupils in their criticism of how their teachers differentiated between low ('mauvais élèves') and high achieving pupils ('bons élèves') in the same class. French pupils of all levels of achievement thought that many of their teachers neglected lower achieving pupils with negative consequences for their learning:

'Les professseurs ils s'occupent que des élèves qui travaillent, mais les élèves qui travaillent pas ils les abandonnent' (Low achieving girl in a Paris school). *Teachers only relate to hardworking pupils, they don't do anything with those that don't work*

'Les professeurs ils mettent les mauvais élèves à part. Ils n'essayent pas tous. Il y en a qui les laissent à part. J'avais une prof de français et franchement elle mettait ceux qui ne travallaient pas au fond de la classe et elle les laissait dormir, elle ne faisait pas d'efforts.' (High achieving girl from Bordeaux). T*eachers put the weak pupils to one side. They don't all try to help them. They leave them out. I had a teacher of French who quite honestly put those that didn't work at the back of the class and she let them go to sleep. She made no effort..*

This common criticism of French teachers is another example of French pupils' expression of solidarity.

Discussion

What can be learnt from the similarities and differences of the school experience of English, French and Danish pupils and their attitude to learning? In terms of pupils' own perceptions about effective learning there was striking unanimity about the definition of an 'interesting' lesson and a 'good' teacher, despite the national and institutional differences in pupils' school contexts. What is less clear is the relation between pupils' contrasting national, social and cultural responses to the school context and pupil learning. Does the French pupil response of solidarity help to motivate pupils, particularly lower achieving pupils? Does the English pupil response of complex social interactions and negotiation of group identity divert and de-focus English pupils from a learning objective? Does the Danish pupil response of downplaying academic objectives in favour of social relationship objectives have a negative effect on pupil learning? At this stage of the study it is only possible to hypothesise what might be the possible consequences of the English, French and Danish pupil responses to their school experiences.

What is clear, however is that that in spite of the many pressures towards greater homogenisation of educational systems, the national culture and educational traditions of the three European countries under study continue to lead to significant differences in the way in which pupils define their relationship to school. Overall the study emphasises the importance of understanding how pupil attitudes to teaching, learning, and schooling are situated within a wider cultural context.

References

Abrahams, J. (1995) *Divide and School: gender and class dynamics in comprehensive education* (London, Falmer Press)

Audiger, F. & Motta, D. (1998) The strange concept of affective education: a French perspective, in: Lang, P. (Ed) *Affective Education: a comparative view* (London, Cassell)

Bakhtin, M. M. (1986) *Speech Genres and Other Late Essays* (Austin, University of Texas Press)

Best (1998) The development of affective education in England, in: Lang, P. (Ed) *Affective Education: a comparative view* (London, Cassell)

Broadfoot, P. and Osborn, M (1988) What professional responsibility means to teachers: national contexts and classroom constants. British Journal of Sociology of Education, 7(3). 265-82

Bronfenbrenner, U. (1979) *The Ecology of Human Development: experiments by nature and design* (Cambridge, Mass., Harvard University Press)

Bruner, J. S. (1990) *Acts of Meaning* (Cambridge, Mass., Harvard University Press)

Charlot, B., Bautier, E. & Rochex, J-Y. (1992) *École et Savoir dans les Banlieues... et Ailleurs* (Paris, Armand Colin)

Corbett, A. & Moon, R. (Eds) (1996) *Education in France: continuity and change in the Mitterand years, 1981-1995* (London, Routledge)

Cousin, O. (1998) *L'Efficacité des Collèges: sociologie de l'effet établissement* (Paris, Presses Universitaires de France)

Dubet, F. and Martucelli, D., (1996) *A l'Ecole* Paris, Editions du Seuil

Dubet, F., Cousin, O. & Guillemet, J. P. (1996) A sociology of the lycée student, in: Corbett, A. & Moon, R. (Eds) *Education in France: continuity and change in the Mitterand years, 1981-1995* (London, Routledge)

Eide, K. (1992) The future of European education as seen from the north, *Comparative Education*, Vol. 28, No. 1, pp. 9-17

Frønes, I. (1995) *Among Peers: on the meaning of peers in the process of socialisation* (Scandinavian University Press)

Gewirtz, S., Ball, S. J. & Bowe, R. (1995) *Markets, Choice and Equity in Education* (Buckingham, Open University Press)

Great Britain: Department for Education and Employment (1997) *Excellence in Schools* (HMSO)

Hargreaves, d. (1967) *Social Relations in a Secondary School* (London, RKP)

Jensen, B., Nielsen, M. & Stenstrup, E. (1992) *The Danish Folkeskole: visions and consequences* (Copenhagen, The Danish Council for Educational Development in the Folkeskole)

Keys, W. & Fernandes, C. (1993) *What Do Students Think About School?* (Slough, National Foundation for Educational Research)

Kryger, A. & Reisby, K. (1998) The Danish class teacher: a mediator between the pastoral and the academic, in: Lang, P. (Ed) *Affective Education: a comparative view* (London, Cassell)

Lacey, C. (1970) *Hightown Grammar: the school as a social system* (Manchester, Manchester University Press)

Masini, E. (1994) The futures of cultures: an overview, in: *The Futures of Cultures* (Paris, UNESCO Publishing)

Osborn, M., Broadfoot, P. M., Planel, C., Sharpe, K. & Ward, B. (1998) Being a pupil in England and France: findings from a comparative study, in: A. M. Kazamias, with M. G. Spillane (Eds) *Education and the Structuring of the European Space* (Athens, Seirios Editions)

Osborn, M. & Planel, C. (1999) Comparing children's learning, attitude and performance in French and English primary schools, in: Alexander, R., Broadfoot, P. & Phillips, D. *Learning from Comparing*, Vol. 1 (Wallingford, Triangle Books)

Organisation for Economic Co-operation and Development (1996) *Reviews of National Policies for Education: France* (OECD, Paris)

Payet, J.-P. (1997) *Collèges de Banlieu Ethnographie d'un Monde Scolaire* Paris, Armand Colin

Pollard, A. With Filer, A. (1995) *The Social World of Children's Learning* (London, Cassell)

Pollard, A. & Filer, A. (1996) *The Social World of Pupil Career in Primary School* (London, Cassell)

Raphael Reed, L. (1996) Working with boys: a new research agenda, *Redland Papers no. 3* (Bristol, University of the West of England)

Richards, M. & Light, P. (1986) *Children of Social Worlds* (Cambridge, Polity)

Rudduck, J., Chaplain, R. & Wallace, G. (1995) *School Improvement: what pupils can tell us* (London, Fulton)

Vygotsky, L. S. (1978) *Mind in Society: the development of higher psychological processes* (Cambridge, Mass., Harvard University Press)

Wertsch, J. V. (1991) *Voices of the Mind: a socio-cultural approach to mediated action* (Cambridge, Mass., Harvard University Press)

Wertsch, J. V. (Ed) (1985) *Culture, Communication and Cognition: Vygotskian perspectives* (Cambridge, Cambridge University Press)

Wertsch, J. V. & Smolka, A. L. (1993) Continuing the dialogue: Vygotsky, Bakhtin and Lotman, in: Daniels, H. (Ed) *Charting the Agenda: educational activity after Vygotsky* (London, Routledge)

Whiting, B. B. & Edwards, C. P. (1988) *Children of Different Worlds* (Cambridge, Mass., Harvard University Press)

Woods, P. (1990) *The Happiest Days?* (Basingstoke, Falmer Press)

Notes

This paper is based on the ESRC funded ENCOMPASS project, Education and National Culture: a comparative study of pupil attitudes to secondary schooling. ESRC's continuing support for this work is gratefully acknowledged.

The ENCOMPASS project team who all contributed to this paper are: Birte Ravn and Thyge Winther-Jensen, University of Copenhagen; Olivier Cousin, CADIS, University of Bordeaux II; Marilyn Osborn, Patricia Broadfoot, Elizabeth McNess, Claire Planel, Pat dTriggs, University of Bristol.

Part 6
Vocational Education and Lifelong Learning

The Costs and Benefits of Lifelong Learning: The Case of the Netherlands

MARKO J. VAN LEEUWEN & BERNARD M.S. VAN PRAAG

Policies stimulating lifelong learning generate costs and benefits for individuals, firms, and the government. In order to be able to select the most cost-effective measures we have developed an economic model for lifelong learning and applied it to the Netherlands. First, the actors on the vocational education market and the most relevant types of costs and benefits related to on-the-job training are described. Next, several explanations for failures on the market of vocational education are explored. The model distinguishes between 9 economic sectors and 216 types of employees and calculates detailed costs and benefits for actors on the Dutch vocational education market and the macro-economic consequences of policy measures. The model parameters are estimated using information from a query under employers and employees in the Netherlands. The model is briefly introduced and the results of two policy scenario's are compared to a baseline projection. The scenario's describe proposed policy measures for

An international comparison shows that the Dutch education system belongs to the world's top-10 (The Economist, 1997). But, as the OECD (1996, pp.122) recognises: 'Lifelong learning presumes continuity between initial education and training, and the organised learning experiences that take place thereafter, during working life. What is sometimes overlooked is that continuity is absolutely essential throughout initial education and training.' Therefore, the Dutch government is seeking for ways to stimulate lifelong learning.

In December 1997 the Dutch government launched the National action plan 'A Lifelong Learning' as part of the National Knowledge debate (Projectteam, 1998). SEO was asked by the ministry of Education, Culture and Sciences to make a study of the economic effects of (fiscal policy measures for the stimulation of) lifelong learning.[1] The study comprises three parts: 1) a literature search after potential costs and benefits and elements determining failures on the market of vocational education and training; 2) a query among employers and employees focusing on on-the-job training and 3) construction of a calculation model for the costs and benefits of lifelong learning.

The acceptability of new policies depends not only on pedagogical, sociological and organisational aspects of learning and training, but also on the money available and the costs involved. A rightful question also in education is how scarce financial resources are most efficiently distributed; i.e. taking into account both costs and benefits. This paper describes the results of the study in which the costs and benefits of policy measures for stimulation of lifelong learning are evaluated. First of all the actors on the vocational education market are introduced and an inventory is made of potential costs and benefits. Next, the training-on-the-job market in the Netherlands in the second half of the nineties is described. In order to be able to evaluate the costs and benefits of the introduction of policy measures aimed at stimulation of lifelong learning a calculation model is developed. In the model the behavioural effects on micro-level are translated into sector, meso and macro-economic level. The calculation model is used for running a baseline projection and several policy scenario's. Two of them are described at the end of the paper in more detail.

Actors, costs and benefits

On the market of vocational education many players are active. The model focuses on training and education in the work situation and a distinction is made between three types of actors:
- employees, receiving formal or informal training, on-the-job or at specialised institutes;
- employers (firms), demanding internal and external training for their employees;
- the government, not as employer, but as moderator and stimulator.

On-the-job training involves both costs and benefits. First of all there are the direct *costs* of the training. These involve amongst others, the training fee, training materials and travelling costs. Depending on the situation these costs will be borne by the employee, the employer or the government (subsidies). Indirect costs of training are the loss of time. Training during working hours involves costs of loss of productivity and costs of absenteeism for employers. If employees follow training in spare time they face opportunity costs of leisure time and vacation. The government (not as employer) faces the possible costs of subsidies paid and tax exemptions given for the stimulation of training. Other indirect costs of training are the additional wage employers pay after (successful) training of the employee. Higher wages are costs for employers, but are at the same time a benefit for the employees, therefore the net effect on macro-level is zero. This is one of the reasons for making the distinction between the three types of actors.

On the *benefits* side employees receive higher wages, more labour satisfaction, increased status, higher job security, better employability and opportunities for extended working life. For employers training of employees increases productivity, commitment of employees to the firm, less deterioration of human capital and reduction of labour market bottlenecks. Also the government benefits from additional training. First of all the country will have a higher educated and more productive population with less unemployment (and less payment of sickness and unemployment allowances). Additional wages and productivity will increase tax receipts and social security premiums.

Failures on the market of vocational education

If additional vocational education is expected to have net positive effects an obvious question is why there is under-investment in this type of education. We start our analysis with Beckers' Human capital approach, which suggests that only general training is transferable from one job to another. Specific training can only be applied in the agency in which the skills are acquired. Therefore, under-investment in vocational education and general on-the-job training is likely. In the literature various types of market failure are described.[2] They can also serve as explanations for the, from an economic point-of-view, suboptimal allocation of resources for lifelong learning. First of all, there can be an *information problem*. It is not always exactly clear what is learned during a training and therefore what will be the return, both for the trainee (higher wage, improved employability) and the firm (improved productivity). Another prominent reason for mismatches on the market of permanent education is the poaching problem. Firms face the risk of other employers 'poaching' trained workers, or of workers bidding up wages as a consequence of acquiring a higher qualification. The, in training investing, firm risks ending-up with less than the full range of the expected returns of training. On the other hand individuals may withhold from (investing in) training if gains in qualifications and competence are not adequately recognised, or if there is *uncertainty* about the returns as was mentioned before. This last issue is especially important if individuals have little financial resources and are facing a *liquidity constraint*. Which means that if future returns of investing in training are uncertain, they are not suited to serve as collateral for this investment. In that case, borrowing on the money or capital market is either impossible or at least very expensive. The information problem, the liquidity constraint and the uncertainty result in less than optimal investment in training.[3]

Several approaches are suggested for addressing the problems that arise from the various types of market failures. They can be divided into two groups: *financing models* (single employer financing, self-financing, drawing rights, vouchers, actions and para fiscal fund) and *instruments* (fiscal instruments, training-subsidies, information, certification of diploma's, accreditation of training institutes, apprenticeship contracts, differentiation of etc.). The cost-effectiveness of a policy measure depends also on the level of aggregation and the point of view. As will be shown in section 5 a more cost-effective policy measure on a macro level can have large impact on the distribution of costs and benefits between actors. A distinction can be made of who is affected (positively of negatively) by the policy measure.

The market for training activities in the Netherlands

The Dutch Central Statistical Office (CBS) monitors vocational training activities in the Netherlands.[4] In 1993 45% of all enterprises in the private sector with five or more employees did some kind of training effort. One out of four employees in the Netherlands followed that year one or more internal or external courses, while approximately 12% underwent some training in the work situation. The total number of attended internal and external courses was 1.2 million (an increase of 5% per year since 1990), with an average duration of six days. About 60% of the man-days in training were given in working time. Dutch enterprises spent in 1993 about 3.5 billion guilders on internal and external training (including cost of lost working time, fees of training institutes, compensation to workers and other costs). This is approximately 1.7% of total labour costs (2.3% if only enterprises with courses are considered), which is on average 990 guilders for all Dutch employees (or 1.350 guilders if only enterprises with courses are considered). Per attended course the average costs where 2.820 guilders.

The information on employment, wages, taxes and on-the-job training in the Netherlands from official sources (CBS, branch organisations) has certain drawbacks. First, it dates back to 1993 and is therefore somewhat outdated. Second, the CBS data do not cover training activities in organisations with less than 5 employees, while another drawback is that it does not give any detail on the reasons for following training (or not). Finally, the aim of this study is to evaluate the effects of new policy measures, which cannot be measured and quantified by using existing information. Therefore, Intomart-SEO carried out four surveys among employers and employees in two economic branches. For each of the four surveys 175 persons were approached of which approximately 120 are interviewed; adding-up to approximately 480 interviews. Through the queries it is possible to determine the amount of training consumed, the costs of training, who pays for the training (in money and time) and the effects of (additional) training in terms of productivity, employability, job security and wage levels. Furthermore the respondents are asked to indicate the attractiveness of several (fiscal) policy measures aimed at stimulation of training. The information from the queries is used to estimate the model parameters.

The results from the queries show that in the Netherlands both the need and the willingness to participate in on-the-job training is high. Especially learning by doing, learning from colleagues and combinations of learning and working are popular. Employers and employees are not easily persuaded to invest in recurring and fresh-up courses that are considered to be most important for lifelong learning. Government policy therefore should be directed towards these types of courses. Two out of three of the training courses are external which usually have a longer duration. Employers prefer short-term courses. The group of employees already in a favourable position, the highly educated, react strongest on financial stimulation measures. Given the scarcity of resources attention should be given to policy measures aiming more specifically at lower educated groups.

The direct costs of on-the-job training are almost completely borne by the firms. Fiscal stimulation measures are most effective if directed towards them. A sector training tax is strongly rejected by employers, this observation is in line with the under participation of firms in using existing schooling funds in the construction sector. The driving force behind training is for employers increasing the skills of their employees. Increasing employability is the key factor behind training for employees. They want training to increase job security, increase job mobility and to keep their skills up-to-date.

Women appreciate training better than men, while employers choose men above women when training is offered. Employers also prefer to train full-time staff above part-timers. Furthermore, participation in training activities is sector specific and is higher in bigger firms and higher for higher educated employees. Finally, older workers (age: 45+) and workers staying longer with the same firm are trained significantly less than younger workers (15-44) and new employees; again these factors are strongly correlated. In order to increase the employability of women, part-timers and senior staff, special attention to those groups is recommended.

Conjoint Analysis

With new policy measures it is impossible to measure the effects directly. In order to discover the preferences of employers and employees concerning fiscal stimulation measures of on-the-job training we use 'conjoint analysis'.[5] In this method respondents are shown several training profiles ('vignettes'), with each profile consisting of a set of characteristics or attributes of a certain type of training within a specific setting. The attributes are chosen carefully, each of them representing a dimension which is important to the decision making process of the respondent.

The dimensions or attributes of the vignettes are: characteristics of the training (type, time, duration, and price/costs), the fiscal measure considered and a set of remarks concerning the results of training and other circumstances.[6] A typical example of an 'employee vignette' in the construction sector is the offer of a special external practise training for one week during working hours. The costs of the training (f20.000) are fully paid by the employer who receives a subsidy for the costs of absenteeism of the employee during the training. The effect of the training will be that the employees' employability increases. A further remark is that the employee signs a special training contract, by which he promises not to leave the employer within the next three years after the training is completed. By varying the attributes a large number of different profiles or vignettes are created. The respondents are asked to score each of the vignettes selected for them on a ten point scale, based on 1) the attractiveness of the vignette, and 2) the chance of accepting the training in given circumstances. The scores are analysed using both Ordinary Least Squares and Ordered Probit, with the vignette attributes and other characteristics of the respondents (as taken from the rest of the query) as explanatory variables. The method makes it possible to detect and quantify the effects of new policy measures within a realistic setting. Next, the results are translated into model parameters, measuring the sensitivity of respondents (employers or employees) with respect to the attributes in the vignette.

Analysis of the vignettes shows that compulsory training measures are more effective in terms of participation rates, but at the cost of lower valuation of the measures. Which effect is strongest in the longer run is unclear. Compulsory training measures are therefore not recommended. Furthermore we see that employees who have been trained before have a more positive attitude towards future training, than employees without previous training experience. The same holds for employers that have a tradition in training their employees. Therefore, training is a positive stimulus for lifelong learning. The important policy advise here is that once the flywheel is at steam, for example generated by a government measure tackling one of the market failures, the system of learning will continue more or less automatically.

Employees prefer more generally oriented training courses, not directly linked to their current job. These types of training increase their general employability and offer opportunities for switching to other jobs in other firms sometimes even other sectors. Employers on the other hand prefer specific training for their employees that offer direct improvement of skills. These observations confirm Becker' human capital theory, which suggests that only general training is transferable and therefore preferred by employees.

In the Dutch situation employers are the main financial contributors of on-the-job training. The analyses show that the employer and the employee both try to persuade the 'other party' to invest money and time in training. From this we can conclude that, since employers usually pay for the training, fiscal measures are most effective if directed towards them. Employees react more positively on measures from the side of the employers than those directed towards themselves. The willingness for training in own time is low for both employers and employees. An effective policy measure is one that compensates the party that invests time in the training, for example an employers' compensation for forgone hours due to absenteeism of the employee. Also stimulation of more flexible training schemes and reciprocal courses are most effective.

Lifelong learning: a model for the Netherlands

For the determination of costs and benefits of policy measures aimed at stimulation of on-the-job training in the Netherlands a calculation model is developed. The base year of the model is 1996. The model focuses on the 5.7 million employees in the Netherlands and distinguishes between 216 types of employees (amongst others age, gender, education level), nine economic branches and two types of training (internal and external). Furthermore, the model distinguishes the schooling related costs and benefits, distinguished by type of actor, as described in Section 2. Inputs for the exogenous variables are taken from the query amongst employers and employees and from several statistical sources.

The schedule on the next page gives an overview of the most important factors considered in the model and the relations between them. Boxes representing behavioural relations (endogenous variables in the model) have round corners. Boxes with squared corners represent variables determined outside the model and definition equations. Three broad lines of relations can be distinguished. First, there are equations concerning employees; their personal characteristics (gender, age) and labour characteristics (sector, wage, type of contract, working hours, taxes, social security). Second, the schedule displays a block of equations on training and education (participation rates, types of training, costs of training, contributions in time and money). Finally, there are equations in the model describing the effects of training for employees (making promotion, receiving higher wage, increasing employability, etc.), for employers (changes in productivity during and after training, flexibilisation, employability) and for the government (taxes, subsidies).

Baseline projection
First of all the calculation model is used to run a baseline projection. The baseline projection is fine-tuned, to match reality in the base year as close as possible, by changing the exogenous parameters of the model. Information on the base year situation is taken from the aforementioned query and the following statistical sources: National Accounts 1996, survey of employer sponsored training in the Netherlands and the Labour Force Survey 1995 (ebb in the schedule on the next page). Table 2 shows the key indicators of economic performance (gross wage, value added, employment) and training (number of training days, training costs) per sector as calculated by the model for the base year 1996.

Schedule of the SEO Calculation Model I Lifelong Learning –Source: SEO

- unemployment and other inactivity
- total number of employees
- sector / sexe / age / position / education

- labour union participation
- sector & type of contract
- tariffs / premiums / subsidies
- cbs-data
- gross wage per sector and type of employee
- net wage bill / social security / wage taxes
- wage per hour / number of hours
- number of employees per sector, type and type of contract

- % fixed contract
- % full-time
- # employees
- ebb
- cbs-data; query

- wage increase
- change in position
- productivity increase
- participation sector & type
- situation on labour market
- query

- % employees / days per year / costs per day
- internal / external
- type of training
- query
- effectiveness of training
- personal characteristics
- government measures

- loss of leasure
- costs of absenteeism
- costs of training
- employee contribution / school fund / subsidies / fiscal policy
- employer
- employee
- school fund
- government
- %

- layoff of employees
- profit: extra employees
- competitiveness / profitability / future perspective
- sector & type of contract

- change in number of employees
- labour productivity per sector, in base year

Table 1 – Model output: key indicators of the base projection, 1996 – Source:: SEO calculations and CBS (1993, 1997)

		labour costs (model)					labour costs (CBS, 1996)				value added	
		gross wage bln. dfl.	labour tax bln. dfl.	social security employees	social security employers	total bln. dfl.	gross wage bln. dfl.	labour tax bln. dfl.	social sec bln. dfl.	total bln. dfl.	CBS, 1996 bln. dfl.	model bln. dfl.
S1	construction	12.0	3.6	1.2	2.1	14.1	11.3	–	3.5	14.8	20.3	21.2
S2	commercial services	9.7	3.1	0.9	1.5	11.2	9.5	–	1.1	10.6	23.8	25.8
S3	other construction	8.3	2.5	0.8	1.4	9.7	7.2	–	1.6	8.9	11.1	11.6
S4	other services	33.7	10.5	3.3	5.1	38.9	33.7	–	6.9	40.6	135.6	139.5
S5	agriculture	10.8	3.2	1.1	1.8	12.5	13.3	–	0.6	13.9	19.9	19.2
S6	trade and transport	54.6	15.5	5.0	8.7	63.3	70.9	–	9.4	80.3	132.1	126.1
S7	industry	49.3	14.7	4.9	8.6	58.0	56.0	–	10.3	66.3	140.4	152.9
S8	health care	24.7	6.7	2.0	3.2	27.9	26.4	–	4.7	31.1	41.1	47.2
S9	government	52.9	15.7	5.1	8.4	61.3	56.7	–	14.9	71.6	79.5	91.4
	Total	256.1	75.6	24.3	40.8	296.8	285.1	83.1	53.0	338.1	603.9	634.9

Model output		number of training days					costs of training		costs of absenteeism mln.dfl.	costs of courses born by		
		external x1000	internal x1000	total x1000	working hours	in free time x1000	per employee guilders	total mln. dfl.		total mln.dfl.	employer %	employee %
S1	construction	495	312	807	57%	863	758	176	109	67	86.1%	4.7%
S2	commercial services	885	45	929	55%	978	3,120	545	133	412	95.0%	5.0%
S3	other construction	450	264	714	54%	763	872	144	89	55	85.9%	4.7%
S4	other services	2,586	172	2,758	54%	2,904	2,163	1,345	385	960	95.0%	5.0%
S5	agriculture	668	237	905	58%	962	732	162	98	64	95.2%	4.8%
S6	trade and transport	4,617	1,276	5,893	57%	6,251	910	1,313	598	716	95.2%	4.8%
S7	industry	3,456	1,240	4,696	57%	4,993	1,115	1,177	596	582	95.2%	4.8%
S8	health care	3,597	446	4,043	56%	4,267	1,188	965	382	583	95.1%	4.9%
S9	government	4,327	625	4,952	58%	5,231	1,115	1,289	623	666	95.1%	4.9%
	Total	21,082	4,615	25,697	57%	27,213	1,814	7,117	3,012	4,105	94.8%	4.9%

The 5.7 million employees in the Netherlands in 1996 generated a total value added of just over 600 billion guilders. The baseline projection per sector, based upon model calculations, is within reasonable error ranges of the official figures by CBS. Also the total calculated labour costs of 338 billion guilders are somewhat higher than the 297 billion guilders the official records indicate. The sectors industry and trade & transport are the major course of this overestimation.

In the bottom half of Table 1 details are given of training activities in the Netherlands as calculated by the SEO model. These are the basis for the calculation of the effects of policy measures. Contrarily to the CBS data, training activities in organisations with less than 5 employees are included such that a more complete picture of training activities in the Netherlands is given. Firms in the Netherlands (including the government as an employer) pay approximately 7 billion guilders for all kinds of direct and indirect training costs, including cost of absenteeism during training (3 billion guilders).

In the query and the model simulations the costs and benefits of several proposed fiscal policy measures are evaluated. The policy measures range from refunding the costs of training borne by employees and income tax reduction for sacrificing leisure for training to refunding the costs of absenteeism or a premium for investment in the training employers. Two of them are selected and described in more detail below, together with the sensitivity as measured by OLS and Ordered Probit analysis.

The first policy scenario calculates the effects of the employee sacrificing free time (ADV) in return for a 25% refunding by the government of the total direct cost of the training. Another assumption in this scenario is that employers pay 50% of the total training costs. The policy measure is open to all types of employees in all sectors. The measured effect on the willingness to participate is 130% in the construction sector and negligible in the services sector. For the other sectors the percentage is assumed to be a combination of both extremes, based on the characteristics of the sector compared to construction and services.

In the second scenario discussed in this paper employers receive a tax credit of $f250$ for every additional trained employee. The measured effect on the willingness to participate is 9% in the construction sector and 100% in the services sector. Since employers receive compensation it is assumed that they bear the biggest share of the training costs. The prevailing type of additional training will be close to the employers' preferences, i.e. job-specific training. Again the policy measure is the same for all employers for all of their employees.

Table 2 shows the results of two scenario's in deviation from the baseline projection. From a macro-economic point of view the introduction of a 25% subsidy for direct costs of training borne by employees in return for sacrificing free time is profitable. The total net effect is 115 million guilders. Employers collect a net increase in value added (after tax) of 1.7 billion guilders at the expense of an additional 1.1 billion training costs and a 0.5 billion increase in the gross wage bill. A disadvantage of the scenario is that it generates large transfers of income between the three types of actors.

Table 2 – Net effects of policy measures on the side of employees (25% subsidy of training costs when sacrificing free time) and employers (lower profit tax of f 250 per trained employee) – Source: SEO calculations

	employees sacrifice free time in return for 25% refunding of training costs			lower profit tax for firms of f250 per trained employee		
	employers	government	employees	employers	government	employees
value added	1,725			1,953		
loss of productivity				-394		
costs of absenteeism				-296		
costs of training courses	-1,103	-225	-282	-978	-25	-33
change in gross wage bill	-474			-366		
change in net wage bill			243			189
change in labour tax proceeds		124			-81	
change in social security		107			83	
crowding out		-545	545	176		
Total net benefit	*149*	*-540*	*506*	*95*	*-24*	*156*

An even more profitable and much more balanced scenario is the scheme where employers receive a tax credit of f250 per trained employee. In this scenario 251 million guilders is generated at the expense of 'only' 24 million guilders net investment by the government. The additional costs of training and wages for employers, is more than off-set by an increase in value added and a net government transfer (crowding out payments by the government for already undertaken training). Employees pay little extra for training (33 million guilders) and receive in return additional wages of 189 million guilders. The net macro-economic result is plus 228 million guilders.

Concluding remarks

Policies stimulating lifelong learning generate costs and benefits, may vary between the groups of actors on the market for vocational education, i.e.: employees, employers (firms) and the government. For the evaluation of the effectiveness of financial and other policy measures aimed at stimulation of vocational education and on- the-job training an economic model is developed and applied to the Netherlands. The model tries to capture and quantify the full range of tangible and intangible costs and benefits on the sector, and macro level. In the model 216 different types of employees are distinguished.

Compared to a baseline projection the two scenario's show positive net macro-economic effects of proposed fiscal policy measures for stimulation of lifelong learning. Furthermore, the results indicate that the costs and benefits of those policy measures can be quite different for the parties involved in vocational training.

In order to improve the quality of the output of the scenario's further research after the model parameters is needed. This can be done by means of additional queries amongst employees and employers and updating. Furthermore the model can be applied to other countries under the condition that sufficient data are available or collected.

References

Becker, G.S. (1964), Human Capital: a theoretical and empirical analysis with special reference to education, *Cambridge University Press*, Cambridge

Beek, K.W.H. van, C.C. Koopmans and B.M.S. van Praag (1997), Shopping at the Labour Market, a Real Tale of Fiction, in: *European Economic Review* no.41, pp. 295-317

CBS (1995), Bedrijfsopleidingen 1993; particuliere sector [Employer sponsored training in the Netherlands in 1993; the private sector], *the Netherlands Central Bureau of Statistics*, Voorburg/Heerlen

Cloonan, M., A. Hearinger, B. Matarazzo, M. Murphy and M. Osborne (1999), The use of cost-benefit analysis in funding continuing education: steering the fifth wheel? *International Journal of Lifelong Education*, Vol. 18, no. 6, pp.492-504

The Economist (1997), Education and the wealth of nations, 29-3-1997

Leeuwen, M.J. van, I. Overtoom en B.M.S. van Praag (1997), De kosten-effectiviteit van een leven lang leren [the cost-effectiveness of lifelong learning], *SDU publishers*, the Hague

OECD (1996), Life-long learning for all, *OECD report*, Paris

Oosterbeek, H. (1996), Financing lifelong learning, *Mimeo, University of Amsterdam*

Projectteam 'Een Leven lang leren' (1998), Nationaal actieprogramma een leven lang leren [National action plan: a Lifelong Learning], Ministry of Education, Culture and Sciences, Zoetermeer

Notes

[1] See Van Leeuwen, Overtoom and Van Praag (1997).

[2] For a more detailed description of types of market failures see also Oosterbeek (1996) and OECD (1996).

[3] Other types of market failures, here to be mentioned but not spelled-out, are economies of scale, poor basic skills of (certain parts of) the population, external effects, the social security system

(amongst others minimum wage legislation), (too) narrow wage differentials and high unemployment rates.

[4] CBS (1995), i.e. the most recent complete survey held referring to the year 1993 in which three types of training are distinguished: courses, training in the work situation and other training activities. The survey refers to all enterprises in the private sector with 5 or more employees covering 86.000 enterprises and 3.5 million out of the total 5.9 million employees in the Netherlands.

[5] See Van Beek, Koopmans and Van Praag (1997) for details, an application and further references on this method.

[6] In the employers vignettes characteristics are added of the employee who is to take the training (age, gender, position in the firm, type of contract).

The Contribution of 'Inclusion' to Active Citizenship: Examples of Effective Practice within the French VET System

M'HAMED DIF

The crisis of unemployment and its intensification since the early 70s has generated many mixed and complex situations of exclusion: Longer school-to-work transition, increased precariousness and marginalisation of many people, especially among those who are already disadvantaged. In the context of an active citizenship based on the promotion of the individual's capacity to participate effectively in social, cultural, economic and political processes, a conceptual framework for the concept of inclusion will be proposed in the first section of this paper. Within this framework, the concept of inclusion and consequently the nature of the policy measures to be undertaken will be explored. The second section of the paper presents and assesses, in the context of the proposed conceptual framework, two examples of effective practice within the French VET system. The first example concerns the 'Programme of Active Access to Employment and Qualifications' designed for non qualified young people (16-25 years old) who are in a precarious situation and are unable to have any direct access to qualification and employment. The second example is the 'Qualification Contract' regime introduced and implemented, within the framework of the 'Alternating Vocational Training' system, in favour of young people under the age of 26 years old. Its extension to adults beyond this age is under experimentation.

Until the late sixties, inclusion policy had dealt simply with the problem of smoothening the transition from school to work, in addition to a very limited number of specific cases concerning the first professional integration of inactive and disadvantaged adults. Then, the crisis of unemployment and its intensification since the early 70s has generated many mixed and complex situations: Longer school-to-work transition, increased precariousness, marginalisation and exclusion of many people, especially among those who are already disadvantaged. To adapt the concept of inclusion to these new complex situations and help policy makers to take the necessary measures and actions, a 'Centre for Research on Qualifications: CEREQ' was created for this purpose (cf. Vérnières, 1997).

In this context, the first section of the paper proposes, after an overview of the general structure of the existing French VET system, some basic elements for a conceptual framework in an active citizenship. In the second section, two examples of effective practice within the proposed framework will be examined.

Towards a conceptual framework for inclusion within the French VET system

The first part of this section gives an outline on the general structure of the present VET system through which most of the vocational inclusion measures are introduced and implemented. In the context of more open and dynamic approach to the concept of citizenship (based on the promotion of the individual's ability to participate effectively in larger and multidimensional social production processes), a basic framework for the concept of inclusion will be presented through the last part of this first section.

Overall structure of the existing system
As a complement to the dominant general education (usually referred to as the 'normal' system), the French VET system is a combination of a variety of vocational and training sub-systems. They are traditionally grouped into two main separate systems (cf. Dif, 1998b; Terrot, 1997):
– Initial vocational education and training system (IVET);
– Continuing vocational training system (CVT).

This distinction is the result of a long traditional separation between the two spheres: education and production. Providing a bridge between the two systems was one of the main objectives of the reforms launched during the last decade. The development of alternating vocational training, and involving firms and local authorities in the system were the main elements of this reform.
     The IVET is, in its turn, made up of two main systems: The vocational education system (a traditionally dominant system) and the initial vocational training system.

Vocational education system (VES)
The VES is a combination of three school-based sub-systems: vocational education, technological education and university-level vocational and technological education:
– The first category, 'vocational education', allows pupils to pursue vocational studies leading to the following degrees:
  - a vocational competency certificate (CAP) or a vocational studies diploma (BEP) at the end of a two or three-year course.
  - a vocational higher secondary school diploma (Bac. prof.). It is a two-year degree which allows for further higher education.
– The technological education leads to:
  - a higher secondary school diploma in technology (BTn);
  - a university-level diploma in technology (DUT) or a higher technician diploma (BTS).

– The third category includes all the other university-level vocational and technological studies (under-graduate and post-graduate levels).

In fact, initial vocational education plays an important role in keeping students familiar with the new technological changes. In addition, it contributes to smoothing the transition between school and working life.

Initial vocational training (IVT)
The IVT system provides an important bridge between the initial education system as a whole and working life. It includes apprenticeship, alternating vocational training and other specific regimes.

a) Apprenticeship: It is generally carried out through a specific work contract between the employer and the apprentice. It allows the latter to follow a vocational training on the company's production site and within an apprenticeship centre. It is financed through an apprenticeship tax provided for by companies, the state and local authorities.

b) Alternating vocational training: It is a sub-system of the initial vocational training system, which was officially introduced in February 1984 to provide a real *alternation* between school-based vocational training and in-company work experience. It includes basically three kinds of alternating vocational training regimes: the orientation contract, the adaptation contract and the qualification contract.

c) Other specific regimes: This category includes all other regimes adapted to specific and complex situations of 'inclusion' through the VET system (e.g. PAQUE Programme).

The CVT system is mainly designed to deal with the vocational training of workers. It is either an employee self-directed continuing vocational training (SD-CVT) or an employer-directed continuing vocational training (ED-CVT) (cf. Dif, 1998b &1999a).

Employee self-directed continuing vocational training
It is considered as an employee's choice guided system. But its real functioning has always been dependent on the development of the financial constraint. It is generally carried out through two main regimes of paid leave for continuing vocational training:

– Leave for self-directed continuing vocational training: LSD-CVT (*Congé individuel de formation: CIF*);
– Leave for competencies evaluation: LCE (*Congé de bilan de compétences: CBC*).

a) Leave for self-directed CVT: This regime, created in 1971, allows any employee, with a working experience of two years of which one year at least was within the last firm, to ask for a vocational training leave. The duration of the leave does not generally exceed a full time working year (or 1200 hours for a part time leave) which is counted for as a working experience. If this kind of leave has the advantage of allowing the trainee to return to the company once the training is completed, it does not oblige the employer to recognise the acquired qualifications.

The vocational training leave is financed through a special fund held and run by a parity organism (called OPACIF). This fund is fed by contributions from the employers (0,20 % of wages) and the State. However, the state contribution is still, generally, limited to financing special cases of vocational training leave such as long term training leaves and the training leaves within small companies (with less than 10 employees). But, the coverage of training costs (trainee's salary, training fees, transport and lodging) varies from 60 to 90% depending on the importance of the training content and its duration.

The financing capacity of the fund is getting more and more limited due to its decreased revenues and the increased number of applicants. At present, the parity organism for vocational training (OPACIF) can take in charge only 20,000 trainees, on average, per year (i.e. 70% of applications received).

This regime originally designed in favour of full and part time workers employed according to non-fixed duration work contracts, was extended in December 1991 to include precariously employed workers: employees with fixed duration contracts and temporary workers.

b) Leave for competencies evaluation (LCE): It can be taken by any employee possessing a working experience of five years, of which one year at least with the last employer. It allows its beneficiaries to have their vocational and personal competencies evaluated and be able to restate clearly their own career projects. Its costs are taken in charge in the same way as those linked to the vocational training leave. The precariously employed workers can always benefit from this regime in the same manner as they do under the previous regime (the LSD-CVT regime).

Employer-directed continuing vocational training
It is generally carried out through the company's vocational training scheme. It includes all kinds of short term and medium term vocational training, decided and implemented by the company in favour of its employees. It is normally the result of a concerted action aiming at the promotion of internal labour flexibility. The scheme is generally financed through the firms' obligatory contributions to a vocational training fund (a minimum of about 1% of wages).

Inclusion in an active citizenship: Elements for a conceptual framework

In the context of active citizenship, based on the promotion of the individual's capacity to participate effectively in social, cultural, economic and political processes, a conceptual framework for the concept of inclusion can be proposed. As a process, it can be reduced to two basic dimensions, namely space and time:

Space dimension
It can be identified through the answers given to the following interdependent basic questions:

What? It is to identify the subject of inclusion, i.e. the individual who is in a disadvantaged situation which does not allow him or her to exercise fully his or her fundamental rights of participating effectively in an active citizenship (cf. Daune-Richard, 1997; Marshall, 1950). The scope of an active participation is determined by the economic, social, political and cultural context of the country, the level of development attained and the degree of attachment to the universally accepted principles of human rights (cf. Constant, 1998). In France, the 1998 Act (of July, the 29th) for combating exclusion establishes, as one of the Government's major actions in this direction, the guarantee of equal rights for all individuals to have an effective access to employment, shelter, health care, justice, education, training, culture, family and childhood protection. For any individual identified to be unable to have a voluntary access to at least one of these fundamental rights, he or she is considered as an excluded or disadvantaged person who needs an individualised accompaniment in his or her own inclusion/re-inclusion track. In France, this exclusion is touching an increasing number of people. About 10% of the French households are under the poverty line. Two million people live on a minimum inclusion income (RMI) and six million on a variety of social inclusion minima. Out of about three million unemployed, one million are still in a situation of a long duration unemployment (cf. Grasset-Morel & et al, 1998).

To identify empirically the nature of exclusion and hence the type of inclusion policy to be undertaken by policy makers, a set of identification criteria needs to be determined in the light of answers given to the following two intertwined questions: *Where and how?* (cf. Alfandari, 1992; Vernières, 1997):
- Where? It is to locate the lieu of inclusion of the excluded individual. Therefore the process will be an 'educational inclusion' if the lieu is the school, a 'vocational inclusion' in the case of the enterprise and a 'social inclusion' if we consider the society as whole.
- How? It is to specify the criteria according to which the individual's precariousness (and hence the inclusion policy measure to be undertaken) is empirically defined. If we limit ourselves to the case of voca-

tional inclusion in a French context, an individual with an occupation within an enterprise can be empirically classified as a precariously employed worker. This can be the case, for instance, of any individual who is irregularly employed on a temporary or a short time basis and/or receives a salary lower than the referential wage. For more precision, in this case, it is necessary to use, a set of empirically observable and measurable criteria usually referred to as 'referential indicators' such as 'the referential work contract' and/or 'the referential wage (linking the individual's qualifications and competencies to job requirements)'. The nature of these complementary indicators changes over time and space depending on the specificity of the socio-economic context and its development.

Time dimension
For how long? It is to allow for taking into consideration, within the context of this conceptual framework, the time dimension of inclusion as a process, i.e. to determine the necessary time taken by the inclusion process to reduce or to put an end to the individual's precariousness (cf. Alfandari, 1992). As a vocational inclusion process, it is expected, at least in principle, to allow its beneficiary to have ultimately a steady access to employment. Access to steady employment is observed and assessed by means of 'referential indicator packages' which are usually defined within the socio-economic and cultural context of their application. Like the rest of social inclusion measures, most of the vocational inclusion measures adopted within the existing VET system, do not guarantee this ultimate attainment. They might trigger the process by allowing the disadvantaged beneficiaries to have access to their first inclusion or re-inclusion jobs. To secure this minimum requirement, some vocational inclusion regimes (as it was the case in the PAQUE Programme) provide for individualised social accompaniment and follow-up before, during and even after their effective launch and implementation (cf. Braun, 1998).

Examples of effective practice within the French VET system

This second section of the paper presents and assesses, in the context of the proposed conceptual framework, two examples of effective practice within the French VET system:
  − The first example concerns the 'PAQUE Programme' i.e. the Programme of Active Access to Employment and Qualifications;
  − The second example is the 'Vocational Qualification Contract' regime, which was introduced and implemented within the framework of the

'Alternating Vocational Training' system as means of vocational inclusion. It is basically in favour of young people under the age of 26 years old.

Programme of active access to qualifications and employment (PAQUE)
PAQUE is a national programme of an active preparation for qualifications and employment of non qualified young people (16-25 years old) who are in precarious situation and unable to have direct access to qualifications and employment. Launched in June 1992, PAQUE programme is considered as a preparatory stage which allows a young person excluded by the selectivity of the existing initial education system to benefit from the individualised loan for vocational training (ILVT: 'CIF-jeunes') introduced within the general framework of the initial vocational training regime (IVT). The PAQUE's basic founding principles are fourfold (cf. Mathey-Pierre, 1998):
- Enhancing innovation and efficiency of pedagogical methods in addition to the development of trainers and tutors' vocational competencies;
- Diversifying the contents of the training programmes and allowing for a regular personal and vocational competency control of the trainee;
- Integrating the social and cultural dimensions in the process;
- Encouraging financially the training bodies to be directly involved in the output of the implemented programme;

PAQUE's intermediary objectives are threefold:
- The acquisition of basic knowledge (learning to read, to write, to reason logically, to communicate);
- Intensive and active learning about different occupations and their sectors (i.e. preparation for undertaking any training or job search activity);
- Social accompaniment.

As for its ultimate aims, they are considered as success indicators. Therefore, at the end of the training period, the beneficiary will be able :
- to have access to a vocational training, (through signing a vocational qualification contract or an apprenticeship contract);
- or to acquire the status of a vocational trainee;
- or to find a regular job (and have access, through the acquired basic knowledge, to further qualifications and career development).

A follow-up study, conducted on a questionnaire basis during and after its implementation stage by the Centre for Employment Studies (CEE). The questionnaire covered only the trainees taken in charge by the Vocational Training Association for Adults (AFPA). This study led to the following results and conclusions concerning the performance of the PAQUE Programme (cf. Mathey-Pierre, 1998).

Beneficiaries of the programme

The beneficiaries of the programme were essentially young people with a low level of education and qualifications: 3/4 of them are from a working class origin and do not possess any degree. In fact, a large proportion of them accumulate the following common characteristics:

– Their parents (originally foreigners) are unemployed or inactive.
– They belong to big families (with four children per family on average).
– They were confined to a special separate schooling system in their childhood.
– They have health problems.

If any of these characteristics creates on its own a prior hindrance to any social and vocational inclusion, the combination of all these factors increases further the risk of social, cultural, economical and vocational exclusions.

In order to have a more precise picture of the particularity of the beneficiaries of the programme PAQUE, the sample surveyed can be grouped into seven, more or less, homogeneous groups of young people:

Group 1: It is represented by 3,7% respondents who are mainly young men with few brothers and sisters and live in social care centres.

Group 2: A group represented by 9,6% of respondents who are generally young married women (over 21 years old) of foreign origin with one child at least. Most of these women live in their own accommodations and benefit from the social security coverage and other social allowances with the exception of those directly linked to unemployment (ASSEDIC's allowances). They are registered with the National Agency for Employment (ANPE) as unemployed women looking for employment.

Group 3: It is made up of 18,7% respondents. They are single young men (16 to 20 years old) who are either non registered with the national agency for employment or declared as unemployed but do not benefit from unemployment allowances and social security coverage. They are financially dependent on their parents but they do not live with them.

Group 4: A group represented by 12,9% respondents who are young French people of 21 years old and more. They are financially independent and have their own personal accommodations. They are declared as unemployed in search for work and receive diverse allowances, including those linked directly to unemployment. About 33% of these people, who possess preliminary vocational qualifications, have health problems which force them to stop their initial vocational education.

Group 5: 15% of the respondents representing this group are mainly single young men (originally foreigners) who benefited, for a long time, from the general education system (including apprenticeship for some of them) and hence they are more able to precise their vocational training needs. They are not declared as unemployed but they are financially dependent on their parents (of whom only the father is working; the mother is a housewife). This group of young men has, more than the other groups, social and criminal problems.

Group 6: This group is represented by 17,3% respondents who are unemployed French women with a specialised educational background. Some of these women (a younger proportion) are married with one child and highly interested in having out-door cultural activities. They belong to big families (41% have, at least, five brothers and sisters) with an unemployed father in most cases.

Group 7: This most important group (22,8% respondents) is mainly made up of inactive young single women who belong to big 'introverted' families with unemployed parents. They are financially dependent on their parents and live with them. In addition, they declare not having any interest in out-door cultural activities. They received a specialised education and have health problems (more than the other groups).

If we consider only the groups 3, 6 and 7, they represent together 59% respondents who are in the most precarious situation which hinders their social, vocational and cultural inclusion. Thus, PAQUE is the only programme which really deals with young people who are excluded by the selectivity of the existing educational and training system.

Beneficiaries' appreciation of the programme
a) Beneficiaries expectations at the registration stage:
   - 58% of the respondents were expecting a job (groups: 6 and 7);
   - 36% of the respondents wanted to have a qualification (groups: 4 and 6);
   - 21% of the respondents were interested in an income (groups: 2 and 6);
   - 18% of the respondents wanted to improve their school-based general knowledge (groups: 2 and 5).

b) Appreciation of the results obtained two to four years after the completion of the programme:
   - 63% of the beneficiaries declared that they were generally satisfied with the programme (only 27% were dissatisfied);
   - 64% of the beneficiaries have worked at least once ;
   - 31% only of the beneficiaries of the programme have gone through a vocational training.

On the whole, the programme PAQUE contributed effectively to the opening up of progression opportunities for vocational and occupational routes in favour of young people excluded by the selectivity of the existing educational and training system. In spite of this performance, the programme was abandoned in September 1994 for its supposed high costs.

Vocational qualification contract regime

The vocational qualification contract regime (VQC) is one of the three main components of the alternating vocational training system, which was created through the 1983 agreement (October the 26th) between social partners. It was officially codified by the 1984 Act (24th February) and then completed through the 1991 Act of December the 31st. The other two components are: the adaptation contract and the preparatory vocational training. The latter was replaced through the 1991 Act by the present 'orientation contract regime'.

The vocational qualification contract is a specific work contract for a duration of 6 to 24 months. It is classified as one of the vocational inclusion policy measures. It concerns young people under the age of 26 years old (16-25) who are interested in completing their initial qualifications by a further vocational training more adapted to employment requirements. At least 25% of the trainee's time is spent outside the company in a vocational training centre. The training covers general and specific vocational subjects. A follow-up tutor for each trainee is usually designed by the employer. The trainee's income during this period is calculated with reference to the minimum wage guaranteed by law or through collective bargaining actions. Its amount varies, according to age and experience, between 30% and 75% of the minimum guaranteed wage.

The training costs are taken in charge directly by the employer or indirectly through an authorised mutual insurance institution such as the parity organism fund (OPACIF). In return, the employer is exempted, for each recruitment of this kind, from the payment of employer/social security contributions. In addition, the employer receives on each new vocational qualification contract a subsidy whose amount varies between 5000 and 7000 francs, according to whether the duration of the contract is lower or higher than 18 months.

It is considered as one of the dominant and effective instruments used, within the alternating vocational training system, to bridge the existing gap between two spheres: initial school-based learning sphere and production sphere. In this context, it was assigned the following founding missions and objectives (cf. Charraud, 1995; Legoupil, 1999):

As an inclusion policy measure, the vocational qualification contract regime was assigned the mission of promoting vocational inclusion. In the context of

1984 Act, its application is exclusively limited to a specific category of active population, namely young people aged from 16 to 25 years old who left school either without any qualifications at all (i.e. without diplomas), or with qualifications which do not allow them to have access to employment.

The basic objective in this context is to equip the beneficiaries with transversal and occupational competencies acquired through an alteration between in-company and school-based training. As a mode of certification, the regime is expected to increase the scope of the certification process via the use of three modes of certification:

- Traditional dominant mode of accreditation of vocational training through:
  - National vocational diplomas such as CAP and BTS;
  - Homologated certification.
- Mode of accreditation established through collective bargaining (i.e. CC: Conventions collectives);
- Accreditation of vocational training accepted by the National Parity Commission for Employment (CPNE: Commission Paritaire Nationale pour l'emploi) such as the delivery of the Vocational Qualification Certificate (CQP: Certificat de Qualifications Professionnelles).

Its contribution

About 100,000 young people (on average) are recruited each year on a vocational qualification contract basis with a slightly decreasing role during the period 1992-1996. For instance, the number of newly concluded contracts has gone down from 117,000 in 1994 to 99,861 during 1995, then again to 96,184 in 1996. This is basically due to transfer movements in favour of apprenticeship contracts, in particular and the worsening situation of employment in general. The beneficiaries of this vocational inclusion regime are dominantly:

- Young men (54% in 1997) whose number is decreasing in favour of young women;
- Young men and women over 20 years old (64,4% in 1997);
- Young men and women with initial qualifications at levels III (a first-two-year undergraduate diploma), IV (with a vocational baccalaureate, a university-level diploma in technology: 'DUT' or a higher technician diploma: 'BTS') and V (with a vocational competency certificate: 'CAP' or a vocational studies diploma: 'BEP') representing altogether 89% in 1997;
- Young men and women who finished their schooling and are still looking for work (57,9% in 1997).

The employers involved in the implementation of this regime are basically small and medium firms representing, in 1997, 91,3% of the whole number of companies involved. They are dominantly active within the tertiary sector (73,4% in 1997) (cf. the statistics of the Direction de l'Animation de la Recherche, des Etudes et des Statistiques: DARES).

The main present limitations of the regime as a vocational inclusion instrument are threefold:

- First, vocational qualification contract is basically a discriminatory regime in terms of age. Its timid extension by the Anti-Exclusion Act of July 1998, covers only a specific category of disadvantaged people beyond the age of 25 years old. During its experimental stage ending on the 31st of December 2000, the beneficiaries have to be exclusively unqualified people living a situation of long duration unemployment (cf. Legoupil, 1999). The number of people who are in need for, at least, one chance of vocational inclusion or re-inclusion has been exponentially increasing over the last two decades. This is mainly due to the worsening situation of unemployment and the lengthening period of initial education and training.
- Secondly, this regime is becoming more and more of an additional means for certification in favour of young people who already possess high initial qualifications, especially during the 1990s.
- Thirdly, as a specific work contract, the vocational qualification contract is, in fact, a substitute for a normal recruitment which would have been undertaken anyway by the employer. In this sense, it has the disadvantage of encouraging and subsidising the development of precarious employment.

The contribution of the VQC regime to vocational inclusion should be tested in terms of stock criteria rather than flow criteria, i.e. to test the final stage in the process of an effective transformation of a temporary and precarious employment to a steady one.

Conclusion

It is clear from the above analysis that the effectiveness of anti-exclusion measures introduced and implemented through the VET system is highly dependent on two basic sets of factors:

- Factors linked to the real content given, institutionally and in practice, to the notion of citizenship and to the related concept of inclusion;
- Factors related to the structural nature and functioning of the VET system itself as means for social inclusion in general and vocational inclusion in particular.

Citizenship is an ever changing notion over time and space. Its real content is historically determined by 'cultural trend-setters' under the majority rule for a democratic society (Dif, 1998b). This implies that there are always minorities who are forced, directly or indirectly, to accept integration (which may not be possible for real socio-economic and cultural barriers) or marginalisation and exclusion. Therefore, a notion of active citizenship, highly attached to democracy and universality, needs to go beyond this reality and have a larger content which guarantees for all individuals, within the society, an effective and voluntary participation in all 'social production' processes (cf. Constant, 1998). In this case, inclusion is a 'collective action' which allows disadvantaged individuals to have effectively the means of their voluntary active participation in theses processes. Due to the complexity of the exclusion phenomenon, any particular vocational inclusion measures, for instance, may need to be accompanied with other complementary social inclusion actions before, during and even after the implementation process.

As for the VET system, it is still characterised by the existence of structural and functioning factors which may hinder it to play its role as means of social inclusion in general and vocational inclusion in particular. These factors are mainly:

- A high degree of segmentation produced by the proliferation of many ad hoc and experimental regimes, especially those introduced and implemented within the alternating and continuing vocational training systems. It has contributed on one hand, to the dispersion of efforts and means and on the other, to an increased lack of stability over time in the whole functioning and performance evaluation of these regimes.
- Insufficient integration in terms of a learning path-fluidity and complementarity between and within different components of the existing educational and training system as a whole. For instance, the exclusion leakage produced, at present, within the initial education system is mainly due to two types of rigidities (cf. M. DIF, 1999a):
  - A growing gap between a dominant 'normal' general education and less prestigious vocational education considered as means of 'rescuing' pupils with educational problems.
  - A relatively high rate of selectivity, especially within the first component of the system: initial general education system. Moreover, access to certain curricula traditionally delivered by some prestigious institutions is still limited to the elite with socially and economically advantaged background.
- Lack of social accompaniment and performance follow-up: Most of vocational training regimes (with the exception of the explicit case of the PAQUE Programme) do not take into consideration the complexity of the exclusion phenomenon. They are generally punctual measures without any social inclusion accompaniments and real implementation

follow-up. Moreover, they are, in most cases, characterised by their discriminatory nature in terms of age and established working status (cf. Dif, 1998a , 1999a and 1999b).

References

Abdollahzadeh, A. (1998): *L'assise socio-économique et politique de la problématique de l'insertion,* In Actualité de la Formation Permanente (Dossier: *Insertion sociale et professionnelle*), janvier - février, pp.33-38.

Alfandari, E. (1993): *Conceptions de l'insertion,* In Isabelle Daugareilh et Jean-Pierre Laborde (Ed.): *Insertion et solitude,* Editions de la MSHA, pp.215-224.

Braun, F., (1998): *Sphère de l'insertion: jeu d'acteurs en quête de professionnalisme,* In Actualité de la Formation Permanente (*Dossier: Insertion sociale et professionnelle*), janvier - février, pp.66-73.

Charraud, A.-M., (1995): *La reconnaissance de la qualification: contrats de qualification et évolution des règles,* in Formation Emploi, N° 52, octobre / décembre, pp.113-130.

Constant, F. (1998): *La citoyenneté,* Montchrestien, Paris.

Dailly, J., (1998): *Les professionnelles de l'insertion et le monde du travail,* In Actualité de la Formation Permanente (*Dossier: Insertion sociale et professionnelle*), janvier - février, pp.39-45.

Daune-Richard, A.-M., (1997): *Travail et citoyenneté: un enjeu sexué hier et aujourd'hui,* In Paul Bouffartigue et Henri Eckert (Ed.): *Le travail à l'épreuve du salariat: à propos de la fin du travail,* L'Harmattan, Paris, pp.93-108.

Dif, M. (1998a): *Flexibilité du travail et ses implications pour l'emploi: réflexions sur les modèles émergents,* In Economies et Sociétés, Economie du travail, Série A.B., N° 20, pp. 231-246.

Dif, M. (1998b): *On the development of lifelong learning concept in a French context,* Paper presented at the 2nd Workshop on LIFEQUAL Project, Strasbourg (France), 15-16 October 1998.

Dif, M. (1999a) : *On the performance of self-directed learning within the French continuing vocational training system,* Paper presented at the European Conference on: "Lifelong Learning-Inside and Outside Schools", 25-27 February 1999, University of Bremen (Germany).

Dif, M. (1999b): *Role of accrediting work-based prior learning within the French VET system,* a paper presented at TSER FORUM NETWORK on "Identities in VET", Vienna (Austria), 24-27 June 1999.

Grasset-Morel, V., et al, (1998): *Loi de lutte contre les exclusions: Le choix de l'emploi,* In Inffo Flash, N° spécial, octobre, pp.1-12.

Legoupil, N., (1999): *Contrat de qualification: extension aux 26 ans et plus,* In Inffo Flash, N° 514, février, pp.1-4.

Marshall, T.H., (1950): *Citizenship and social class,* Cambridge University Press, Cambridge.

Mathey-Pierre, C. (1997): *Les jeunes gens du programme PAQUE,* In La Lettre, N° 49, octobre, Centre d'Etudes de l'Emploi (CEE).

Terrot, N. (1997): *Histoire de l'éducation des adultes en France,* L'Harmattan, Paris.

Vernieres, M. (1997): *la notion d'insertion professionnelles,* in Michel Vernières (Ed.): L'insertion professionnelle: analyses et débats, Economica, Paris, pp. 9-22.

Author's Biographical Notes

Editors

Christopher Day is Professor of Education and co-director of the Centre for Teacher and School Development at the University of Nottingham. He is Convenor of the Continuing Professional Development and Leadership Network of the European Educational Research Association, Editor of 'Teachers and Teaching: Theory and Practice', and his latest books include 'Developing Teachers: The Challenges of Lifelong Learning' (Falmer Press 1999); 'The Life and Work of Teachers' (Co-editor, Falmer Press 2000); and 'Leading Schools in Times of Change' (Co-author, Open University Press, 2000).

Dolf van Veen is director of the National Centre on Education and Youth Care, NIZW, The Netherlands and special professor at the University of Nottingham. He is convenor of the Research Network on Urban Education and Children & Youth at Risk of the European Educational Research Association.

Part 1

Vivienne Collison taught primary- and secondary-level students in Canada for 20 years before moving to tertiary-level education. She currently teaches at Michigan State University in the USA. Her research focuses on professional development, particularly the personal qualities, policies, and environments that help educators learn and improve their practices. *Maureen Killeavy* is Acting Head of the Education Department at University College Dublin. She works in the areas of professional development, educational research, IT, group dynamics, instructional design, communication studies and learning difficulties. She has taught in primary, secondary, and tertiary education. *H. Joan Stephenson*, former Head of the Department of Education at De Montfort University, UK, now works in the field of International Education for the same institution. During her 35 years in education, she has taught all levels and has researched and published in such areas as teacher education, mentoring, and values education.

Maria C. Cardona, PhD, is a professor of Diagnosis and Research Methods in Education in the School of Education at the University of Alicante, Spain. Her primary research interests focus on the identification of effective instructional strategies and practices for students with mild and moderate disabilities in inclusive classrooms.

Anne Chowne studied Primary Education at Bath College of Higher Education and taught in an inner city school in London. She joined the Institute of Education, University of London as a lecturer of Primary Education in 1998. Anne is currently researching Early Years Curriculum Policy in Finland and England with colleague Viv Moriarty.

Ton Mooij is a scientific manager and researcher in the ITS of the University of Nijmegen (The Netherlands). He focuses on multilevel improvement and research of education by combining social, didactic, organisational, and ICT-changes or interventions. The developmental processes and their effects on pupils, teachers, and schools, are the main objects of study. The longitudinal projects are usually carried out in co-operation with teachers from kindergarten up and to including university.

Pirjo Linnakylä is Professor of Educational Research at the University of Jysväskylä, Finland. She co-ordinates in the Institute for Educational Research the project called CATO, Collaboration and Authenticity in Technologically Enriched and Virtual Learning Contexts. The project belongs tot the Information Research Programme supported by the Scientific Academy of Finland. *Marja Kankaanranta* is a researcher in the University of Jyväskylä, at the Institute for Educational Research, Finland. Currently she works in the research project Collaboration and Authenticity in Technologically Enriched and Virtual Learning Contexts. Her main interest areas are authentic assessment and the use of ICT in early childhood education. *Maarit Arvaja* is a research student in the University of Jyväskylä, at the Institute for Educational Research, Finland. She takes part in the research project Collaboration and Authenticity in Technologically Enriched and Virtual Learning Contexts. The main theme of her doctoral work is social processes of collaborative learning.

Bernhard Ertl obtained his Master of Computer Science with emphasis on education 1998 at the Ludwig-Maximilians- University in Munich. Since then he is working at the Faculty for Psychology and Education of this university. His special research focus is net-based communication and online-courses. *Dr. Lai-Chong Law* obtained her Bachelor Degree of Social Sciences and Master Degree in Educational Psychology at the University of Hong Kong. With the scholarship awarded by the German Academic Exchange Service (DAAD), she accomplished her Doctoral Degree in Psychology at the University of Munich (Germany) with summa cum laude. *Heinz Mandl*, Professor, Dr. phil., Dipl.-Psych.University of Munich, Faculty for Psychology and Education Ph.D., Psychology, Education, Sociology (University of Munich), Doctor's Degree of Philosophy (Dr. phil.) (University of Munich), since 1990 Professor for Educational Research and Educational Psychology at the University of Munich, 1995-2000 Dean of the Faculty for Psychology and Education at the University of Munich, Member of the American Educational Research Association, Fellow of the American Psychological Association. Research: Designing Multimedia Learning Environments for Self-regulated and co-operative Learning; Tele-Learning; Tele-Tutoring; Knowledge Transfer; Knowledge Management; Adult Learning.

Part 2

Jacqueline Beckers is a doctor in educational sciences and professor at Liège university. She is responsible for several courses for future secondary school teachers and also for future teacher educators. Her main research interests are focused on teachers' education, teachers' professional insertion, didactics and educational system analysis. In most of them, the accent is laid on partnership and reflective approach. Germain Simons is 'premier assistant' in didactics of Germanic languages at the University of Liège. He wrote his Ph.D. Dissertation on David Kolb's experiential learning theory and its relevance to the didactics of foreign languages. Simons is co-responsible for the training of future secondary school language teachers. Besides his dissertation research on learning and teaching styles, he is particularly interested in the analysis of learning and communication strategies in foreign language learning.

Hannele Niemi, PhD, is Professor of Education, Head of the Department of Education and Vice-Dean at the University of Helsinki. She has many memberships in scientific councils, e.g. the European Science Foundation, Academy of Finland. She has been a Chair or researcher in many national and international evaluation projects for development of teacher education and an author of many publications on teachers' professional development.

Dr. María A. Martínez is Director of the Department of *Didáctica General y Didácticas Específicas* in the Faculty of Education, of the University of Alicante (Spain), Director of the PhD course in Education, and different masters and specialists courses in professional development. She has published and researched extensively on prospective and continuing professional development. She is involved in several networks and projects with European and South-American researchers. *Dr. Narcís Sauleda* is Professor of Science Education in the Faculty of Education, at the University of Alicante. He has been deeply involved in different responsibilities at the University as Director of the School of Education and of the Department of Education. He has been member of the *Consejo Interuniversitario* and of the *Consejo Escolar* in the Valencian Autonomous Community, etc. He has published numerous articles on teachers' science education and professional development.

Torlaug L. Hoel, Dr.art., professor in linguistics at the Programme for Teacher Education, Norwegian University of Science and Technology, Trondheim, Norway. Fields of research: writing in schools and at universities, cooperative writing, classroom research, teacher education (especially tuition via e-mail). The theoretical basis for my approach to research, teaching, and learning is mainly related to the tradition of Vygotsky and Bachtin. *Sigrun Gudmundsdottir* got her PhD from Stanford University in 1987. Since then she has conducted research on classrooms, teacher education and teacher biography. Her recent publications include 'Narrative research on school practice' for the Fourth handbook for research on teaching, edited by Virginia Richardson (forthcoming), 'The five Klafki questions as a conceptual framework for research on teaching,' in S. Hopmann, K. Riquerts and I. Westbury (eds.), The German didactic tradition: Teaching as reflective practice. New York: Earlbaum.

Part 3

Francesca Gobbo is Associate Professor of Education at the University of Padua where she also teaches Intercultural Education and Cultural Anthropology. Her field of study is anthropology of education and intercultural education. Her ethnographic research is in the area of minority children's enculturation and schooling. She also co-ordinates ethnographic research on the integration of immigrant and minority children in Italian schools.

José Manuel Resende is preparing his PhD in Sociology. He is Lecturer of Sociology at the New University of Lisbon and author of several articles in journals and books. He has been a member of the board of the Portuguese Sociological Association. *Maria Manuel Vieira* received her PhD in Sociology in 1998. She is Professor of Sociology of Education at the University of Lisbon and author of several articles in journals and books. She has been vice-president of the Portuguese Sociological Association.

Dr. Palmira Juceviciene, professor of Education at Kaunas University of Technology, Lithuania; director of the Institute of Educational Studies, Vice-chair of the National board of Education; expert-member of Lithuanian Science Academy. President of Lithuanian Educational Research Association. Research interests: learning environments, higher education, educational management, comparative education, organisational behaviour. Published 16 books and more than 110 articles. Supervised 14 doctoral dissertations . Awarded by UNESCO Comenius diploma in 1998.

Part 4

Joe Harkin has carried out extensive research into patterns of communication between teachers and learners in post-compulsory education. He is committed to the practice of education *as* democracy and to fostering a balance between the roles of teachers and students in learning.

Reijo Laukkanen, Ph.D., is Counsellor in the Permanent Delegation of Finland to the OECD in Paris. His work covers various policy areas: education, science and technology policies, labour, employment and social affairs, information and communication policies and public management. Since 1974 he has worked in the central educational administration in Finland, being at the moment on leave of absence from the Finnish National Board of Education. His main area of interest in is in comparative research of public policies, especially education and science policies.

Zdenko Kodelja, Ph. D, is a full-time researcher and Head of the Centre for Philosophy of Education at the Educational Research Institute, Ljubljana, Slovenia. Previous publications include two books and many articles on philosophy of education as well as a broad range of educational issues.

Luis E. Vila is Doctor in Economics, University of Valencia. Visiting scholar to CERAS, Stanford University, in 1996. Research focused on the socio-economic effects of educational investment: rates of return, labour market effects, non-monetary outcomes. Teaches undergraduate and graduate courses on the Economics of Education at the University of Valencia

Part 5

Anders Garpelin, Ph.D in Education at Uppsala University, Sweden. After his thesis 'Lesson and life' (1997), he has formed a new research project, 'Young people meet the lower secondary school' (1999). Current position as researcher and lecturer at the department of Teacher Education at Uppsala University.

Marilyn Osborn, BSc (Soc), MPhil (London), PhD (Bristol) is Reader in Education and Co-Director of the Centre for Comparative and International Studies in Education, Graduate School of Education, University of Bristol. She researches and publishes in the field of teachers' work and professional identity, comparative education and pupil experience of learning. Currently she is directing an ESRC funded project on pupil perspectives of learning and schooling in England, France and Denmark. *Claire Planel* is a Research Fellow at the Graduate School of Education at the University of Bristol. She has a bilingual and bicultural English French background with an academic background in anthropology and linguistics. Research interests and publications have centred on the importance of understanding the role of culture in pupil learning.

Part 6

Marko van Leeuwen is an Economist from the University of Amsterdam (1986). He is deputy director of *SEO, Amsterdam Economics*, and responsible for project acquisition, supervision, finance, quality management and carrying out of contract research projects in the fields of labour & knowledge, economic modelling and scenario planning. *Prof. Dr. B.M.S. van Praag* studied econometrics at the University of Amsterdam. He taught at the University of Rotterdam, Leiden, Amsterdam and

Brussels and became managing director of the Foundation for Economic Research. In 2000 he was appointed as a University Professor at the University of Amsterdam. From 1988-1992 he was a member of the (Dutch) Scientific Council for Government Policy, a prominent advisory body for the Dutch government on long term policy issues.

Dr. M'hamed Dif is an Associate Senior Researcher at BETA/Cra-Céreq Alsace (ULP-Strasbourg I) working on various multidisciplinary regional, national and European research programmes. He also worked outside Europe for 12 years as a Senior Lecturer & Researcher, Project Manager and Consultant. He published 25 papers in various related disciplines. His main research areas are: 'Flexibility, mobility and identities in VET and labour market'; 'Key qualifications and work related learning'; 'Effective practice for lifelong learning, employability and inclusion'.